GIG CYMRU NHS WALES

Bwrdd Iechyd Prifysgol
Betsi Cadwaladr
University Health Board

The NEWT Guidelines

for administration of medication to patients with
enteral feeding tubes or swallowing difficulties

WITHDRAWN

Third edition – February 2015

Editor – J. Smyth, BSc (Hons), DipClinPharm

Wrexham Maelor Hospital Pharmacy Department

Betsi Cadwaladr University Health Board
(Eastern Division)
(Previously North East Wales NHS Trust)

Editorial credits

Protocol for Administration of Medication via Enteral Feeding Tubes

1st edition, February 2000	- Brenda Murphy, MRPharmS.
2nd edition, April 2002	- Jen Smyth, MRPharmS.
3rd edition (internal only), May 2003	- Jen Smyth, MRPharmS.
4th edition, January 2004	- Jen Smyth, MRPharmS.

The NEWT Guidelines for administration of medication to patients with enteral feeding tubes or swallowing difficulties

1st edition, January 2006	- Jen Smyth, MRPharmS.
2nd edition, May 2010	- Jen Smyth, MRPharmS.
2nd (updated) edition, April 2012	- Jen Smyth, MRPharmS.
3rd edition, February 2015	- Jen Smyth, Senior Pharmacist

The information in this book is intended as a guide to administration of medication to patients with swallowing problems. Such administration is usually outside the product licence.

Betsi Cadwaladr University Local Health Board (East) does not authorise or take responsibility for any such administration, which should only be done with prescriber agreement, and a full understanding of the legal implications of medication administration outside the product licence.

Published by Betsi Cadwaladr University Local Health Board (East), Pharmacy Department, Wrexham Maelor Hospital, Wrexham, North Wales, LL13 7TD.
ISBN 978-0-9552515-3-5

Every reasonable attempt has been made to ensure that the information in this guide is accurate and up to date at the time of printing.

Acknowledgments

This guide is a compilation of theoretical, practical, and anecdotal information from a variety of sources. Many thanks to everyone who has contributed, particularly those people who have provided practical information to supplement previously theoretical guides. I would particularly like to mention the following sources, which have made significant contributions to this and previous editions.

Whipps Cross Hospital's Tube Feeding Drug Administration Guide.[40]

Derriford Hospital Pharmacy enteral feeding guide.[41]

Queen Victoria Hospital's Drug Adminstration via Enteral Feeding Tubes guide, March 2001.[94]

Southern General Hospital, South Glasgow University Hospitals NHS Trust's A to Z guide to administration of drugs via nasogastric/PEG tube. Updated June 2001.[95]

County Durham and Darlington Acute Hospitals NHS Trust's Guidelines for the administration of Drugs through Enteral Feeding Tubes, 2nd edition. July 2003.[104]

Stockport NHS Trust's Drugs via Enteral Feeding Tubes Guide (draft).[105]

Gloucestershire Hospitals NHS Foundation Trust's Guide to administration of medicines to patients with swallowing difficulties or feeding tubes (NG/PEG). Nov. 2004.[132]

Poole Hospital NHS Trust Pharmacy's Drug Administration Guidelines. July 2002.[133]

Calderdale and Huddersfield NHS Trust's Medication and Enteral Feeding. Feb. 2004.[135]

Mid Essex Hospitals Services NHS Trust's The Administration of medication via a Percutaneous Endoscopic Gastrostomy (PEG) tube. March 2002.[138]

I am also very grateful for the support of Jane Baker and the staff of the John Spalding Library, the work of Mark Oldcorne, Quality Assurance Pharmacist, and the help of colleagues in the Wrexham Maelor Hospital Pharmacy Department with compiling this document.

Jen Smyth, Editor.

New features in this edition

Welcome to the 3rd edition of 'The NEWT Guidelines for administration of medication to patients with enteral feeding tubes or swallowing difficulties.' (previously the 'Protocol for Administration of Medication via Enteral Feeding Tubes.').

This book is the result of continued work by the staff of the Pharmacy Department of Wrexham Maelor Hospital, Betsi Cadwaladr University Local Health Board, and the suggestions of the many users of the guidelines. It conforms to the same general layout as previous editions, but has some changes which should make it easier to use.

About the 3rd edition:-

New and updated monographs
Nearly 250 monographs have been updated in the 3rd edition.

Order of recommendations
There has been a major review of the order of recommendations given in each monograph. A summary of the detail behind these recommendations is given in the new section *3.8 Choosing an appropriate method of administration.*

Swallowing difficulties patients
A large number of monographs which used to contain combined advice for enteral feeding tubes patients and swallowing difficulties patients together have been divided to indicate more clearly how each patient group should be managed.

Feed guidance
A major review of the evidence behind the feed guidance has been undertaken, in order to reduce disparity between monographs and ensure the best evidence available is followed.

About the 2nd (updated) edition:-

After the publication of the May 2010 2nd edition the launch of The NEWT Guidelines Website led to a large number of minor updates and amendments as well as the usual ongoing information updates. All these amendments were included in the updated 2nd edition, which contained two hundred and seventy changes including seven new drug monographs, three new suspension formulae, further information on unlicensed liquid "specials", ethical guidance for pharmacists, and minor amendments regarding availability, formulation choice and alteration of layout.

About the 2nd edition:-

New monographs
The 2nd edition contained more than ninety new drug monographs.

Updated monographs
Over two hundred and thirty of the monographs were updated with further information since the publication of the first edition.

Feed guidance
The 2nd edition included new summary sections in the feed guidance, improving the clarity of the information for easy use by carers.

Formulary
The 2nd edition included a reference section containing formulae for the preparation of oral liquids.

Cytotoxics
The 2nd edition listed basic information on administration of cytotoxics in the main monograph section, with detailed information for Pharmacists in an appendix.

The NEWT Guidelines Website

Launched in August 2011, The NEWT Guidelines Website started out as an electronic version of The NEWT Guidelines book. It has since developed with the needs of Medicines Information services and Medicines Management teams in mind.

The website has regular content updates and a unique prescribing-guidance section designed to help professionals making prescribing decisions for patients with enteral feeding tubes or swallowing difficulties to choose the most appropriate medication in each medicine class for the patient. With the support of colleagues and feedback from users, the website is continually developing to meet the needs of its users.

> *"I find the information in NEWT guidelines invaluable – especially for advising GPs with patients with swallowing difficulties."*
>
> A Prescribing Support Pharmacist

> *"The fact that a reference source is available for this sort of thing is brilliant."*
>
> A Medicines Management Pharmacist

Visit www.newtguidelines.com to see the free-to-access visitors section.

Have <u>you</u> seen The NEWT Guidelines Website yet?

www.newtguidelines.com

Monograph Layout

Each drug monograph should be read in conjunction with the notes on administration (section 3). The monographs are laid out as follows:-

Presentation

The available formulation presentations for each drug are listed at the start of each monograph. The presence of the formulations here does not indicate that they are suitable for administration to patients with enteral feeding tubes or swallowing difficulties, but is merely a guide to what is available.

Some formulations may be unlicensed 'specials' available only at some centres, and sometimes having to be ordered in on a named patient basis.

Administration – enteral tubes / swallowing difficulties

Some monographs have a combined administration section, when the guidance for patients with enteral feeding tubes can equally be applied to patients with swallowing difficulties.

Administration – enteral tubes

Some monographs have a separate section with specific guidance on how to administer via enteral feeding tubes.

Administration – swallowing difficulties

Some monographs have a separate section with specific guidance on how to administer to patients with swallowing difficulties.

Administration – NG / PEG tubes / swallowing difficulties

Where method of administration differs depending on whether the drug is delivered to the stomach or the jejunum, separate instructions are given.

Administration – NJ / PEJ / PEGJ tubes

Where method of administration differs depending on whether the drug is delivered to the stomach or the jejunum, separate instructions are given.

Clinical guidance

This important section lists any clinical problems which may commonly occur when medications are administered via enteral feeding tubes, or formulations are altered for patients with swallowing difficulties. It also indicates any monitoring which may be required (in addition, or more frequently, than would usually be the case).

Feed guidance

This section lists any known interactions with feeds (other than standard before / after food guidance which is commonly given with the listed medication), and any feeding breaks which may be advised when a patient is receiving the monograph medication.

Abbreviations

AUC – area under the curve

CR – controlled-release

CHMP – Committee for Medicinal Products for Human Use

e/c – enteric-coated

GPhC – General Pharmaceutical Council

GTN – glyceryl trinitrate

mcg – micrograms

mg – milligrams

MHRA – Medicines and Healthcare products Regulatory Agency

mL – millilitres

MR – modified-release

NG – nasogastric enteral feeding tube

NJ – nasojejunal enteral feeding tube

NSAID – non-steroidal anti-inflammatory drug

PEG – percutaneous endoscopic gastrostomy enteral tube

PEGJ – percutaneous endoscopic gastro-jejunostomy enteral tube

PEJ – percutaneous jejunostomy enteral tube

Contents

1. Legality, ethics and safety

1.1 Legal and ethical aspects of administering medication via enteral feeding tubes and altering formulations

Drug administration via enteral feeding tubes is almost always an unlicensed method of administration, therefore in all cases where a patient with an enteral feeding tube fitted requires oral medication, alternative (licensed) routes of administration should be sought. Medication designed and given via a licensed route of administration will produce a more predictable response than oral medicines given via an enteral feeding tube.[1]

The alteration of medication formulations (e.g. crushing tablets, opening capsules) to aid administration to patients with swallowing difficulties is also usually an unlicensed activity, with the same legal implications as medication administration via enteral feeding tubes.

When drug administration via enteral feeding tubes is necessary, the prescriber takes responsibility for the off-licence use of the drug concerned. According to the Medicines Act 1968, only a medical or dental practitioner can authorise the use of unlicensed medicines.[135] However the person administering the medication may still share some responsibility, even if they have written authority from the prescriber. Giving medicines via alternate routes (e.g. via enteral feeding tubes) or by alternate methods (e.g. crushing tablets) contrary to the directions of a prescriber is a breach of the Medicines Act 1968, and could result in a finding of professional misconduct.

Patient response to drugs administered via unlicensed routes can be unpredictable. Drugs may have a greater or lesser therapeutic effect than when given by the oral route. The onset and duration of effect may be affected. Side effects, particularly those involving the gastrointestinal system, are likely to be exacerbated. The side effects of drugs which have been given by an unlicensed route are also the responsibility of the prescriber.

If putting medication down an enteral feeding tube is unavoidable then it is sensible to keep drug therapy to a minimum. If problems do arise, please contact your Pharmacist who is in an ideal position to advise on the formulation, timing, and route of administration of drugs.

These guidelines are intended only as a guide to administration, and are **not** an authority for unlicensed administration of medication. The information contained in this guide is mostly anecdotal, as there is very little information on drug administration outside product licence.

Drugs should only be put down a feeding tube as a last resort because of the implications for drug therapy and nutritional status.

Consent

Every adult of sound mind who is able to give consent, must consent to the administration of medication. Attempting to disguise medication ('covert administration') in such cases is a trespass against the person.[115] When a person is unable to give consent, such as when they are unconscious, or suffering from an impairment of mental functioning which leaves them unable to make informed decisions about their care, the law allows medicines to be given in the absence of consent, in the best interests of the patient. In England and Wales, relatives have no legal right to consent on behalf of incapable adults.[115]

"Special" liquids

A "special" liquid may be any one of the following:-
- a medicine manufactured by a company holding a Manufacturer's Specials Licence, with end-product analytical testing
- a bespoke medicine manufactured by a company holding a Manufacturer's Specials Licence, without end-product testing
- an extemporaneously-prepared medicine made under the supervision of a pharmacist[558]

There is no formal assessment of product safety or efficacy for these medicines. All "specials" are therefore unlicensed.[563]

Ethical considerations for pharmacists

The GPhC standards of conduct, ethics and performance for pharmacists places certain responsibilities on professionals providing medication to patients[565]:-

1. Make patients your first concern.
  1.1. Make sure the services you provide are safe and of acceptable quality.
  1.6. Do your best to provide medicines and other professional services safely and when patients need them.

2. Use your professional judgement in the interests of patients and the public.

The interim GPhC standards for pharmacy owners and superintendent pharmacists of retail pharmacy businesses require that pharmacists[565]:-

4.6. Make sure systems are in place to ensure that the supplier and the quality of any medicines, devices and pharmaceutical ingredients obtained are reputable.

4.11. Ensure products with a marketing authorisation are supplied where such products exist in a suitable form and are available, in preference to unlicensed products or food supplements, except where an exemption has been authorised.

A guidance note from the Medicines and Healthcare products Regulatory Agency indicates that supply of a special is justified only when there is no available licensed medicine which fully meets the patient's clinical needs.[563]

To meet these standards, pharmacists have a responsibility to ensure that[563]:-

- Patients receive medication that is safe, appropriate for their condition and circumstances, and of acceptable quality in a timely fashion
- A special is only supplied when there is no available licensed medicine which fully meets the patient's clinical needs
- Any special supplied is of appropriate quality and clinically appropriate for the patient

When no appropriate licensed medicine is available, options to consider include[563]:-

- Importation of a product licensed in Europe, USA, Canada, Australia, or in another MHRA recognised authority
- Purchase of a special from an external manufacturer with a Manufacturer's specials Licence
- Prescription and supply of an alternative licensed presentation
- Extemporaneously dispensing – this would include crushing tablets

When making the choice, the pharmacist should consider the patient's clinical need, which option minimises the risk to the patient and the urgency with which the supply must be made.

1.2 Safety warnings

The use of enteral feeding tubes to administer food and medication to patients is a complex process. A National Patient Safety Agency (NPSA) alert[597] reported 21 deaths and 79 cases of harm due to misplaced enteral feeding tubes. A 2007 NPSA safety alert[596] warned against the use of intravenous syringes for the preparation and administration of enteral medication; a process which had caused 33 adverse incidents over a 17 month period. The accidental intravenous administration of medicines intended for oral / enteral use (e.g. phenytoin syrup) has been responsible for causing patient harm, including death in some cases.[230]

Below are some of the national recommendations which have been made regarding the use of enteral feeding tubes – please note that the recommendations have been summarised.

National Nurses Nutrition Group: Guidelines for confirming correct positioning of nasogastric feeding tubes, June 2004[595]

Regarding tube position testing:-
- Correct tube positioning should be confirmed following initial placement, and before each use.
- Radiography should not be used for daily confirmation of tube position due to increased exposure to radiation, cost implications, loss of feeding time and impracticality.
- Placing the proximal end of the tube under water and observing for air bubbles is unreliable and should not be used.

NPSA Patient Safety Alert 05: Reducing the harm caused by misplaced nasogastric feeding tubes, February 2005[120]

Regarding tube position testing:-
- Measuring the pH of aspirate using pH indicator strips / paper is recommended.
- DO NOT use the 'whoosh' test.
- DO NOT use blue litmus paper.
- DO NOT interpret absence of respiratory distress as an indicator of correct positioning.

NPSA Patient Safety Alert 19: Promoting safer measurement and administration of liquid medicines via oral and other enteral routes, March 2007[596]

Regarding oral / enteral syringes:-
- Only use labelled oral / enteral syringes that cannot be connected to intravenous catheters or ports to measure and administer oral liquid medicines.
- DO NOT use intravenous syringes to measure and administer oral liquid medicines.

Regarding enteral feeding systems:-
- Enteral feeding systems should not contain ports that can be connected to intravenous syringes or that have end connectors that can be connected to intravenous or other parenteral lines.
- Enteral feeding systems should be labelled to indicate the route of administration.

NPSA Patient Safety Alert NPSA/2011/PSA002: Reducing the harm caused by misplaced nasogastric feeding tubes in adults, children and infants, March 2011[597]

- Placement of a feeding tube should be delayed if there is not sufficient support available to accurately confirm tube placement (e.g. at night), unless clinically urgent.
- Nasogastric tubes used for the purpose of feeding should be radio-opaque throughout their length and have externally visible length markings.
- pH indicator paper must be CE marked and intended by the manufacturer to test human gastric aspirate.
- Nasogastric tubes must not be flushed, nor any liquid / feed introduced through the tube following initial placement, until the tube tip is confirmed, by pH testing or x-ray, to be in the stomach.
- **pH testing is <u>the first line test method</u>, with pH between 1 and 5.5 as the safe range. Each test and test result should be documented on a chart kept at the patient's bedside.**
- **X-ray should be used only as a second line test when no aspirate can be obtained or pH indicator paper has failed to confirm the position of the nasogastric tube.**

9

- Documentation of the tube placement checking process should include confirmation that any x-ray viewed was the most current x-ray for the correct patient, and how placement was interpreted. Any tubes identified to be in the lung must be removed immediately.
- A full multidisciplinary supported risk assessment must be made before a patient with a nasogastric tube is discharged from acute care to the community.

2. Practical aspects of medication administration via enteral feeding tubes

2.1 Practical points

Tube types[137]

Nasogastric (NG) – inserted into the stomach via the nose.
Nasojejunal (NJ) – inserted into the jejunum via the nose. These tubes may also have a gastric port.
Percutaneous endoscopic gastrostomy (PEG) – inserted into the stomach via the abdominal wall.
Percutaneous endoscopic jejunostomy (PEJ) – inserted into the jejunum via the abdominal wall.
Percutaneous endoscopic gastro-jejunostomy (PEGJ) – inserted into the jejunum via the abdominal wall and through the stomach.

Nasogastric and nasojejunal tubes are long fine-bore tubes with a large surface area for potential drug absorption and may block easily due to their small bore. Percutaneous endoscopic gastrostomy, and jejunostomy tubes are short tubes with a wider bore.

When administering medicines via a tube that ends in the jejunum, sterile water should be used because the acid barrier in the stomach is by-passed. Drug absorption may be unpredictable if the tube extends beyond the drug's main site of absorption (e.g. cefalexin, ketoconazole).[137] There is a higher risk of diarrhoea with sorbitol-containing liquids and hypertonic solutions when administered directly into the jejunum as the buffering effect of the gastric contents is lost.[26,155,245]

The material from which the tube is made can have an effect on the frequency of tube occlusion. Polyurethane tubes have been found to be less likely than silicone tubes to cause clotting of the enteral feed solution.[442]

Tube size

Enteral tube sizes are usually expressed in French size. The internal and external diameters may be printed on the original packaging, but sometimes only French size is listed. The table below gives approximate inner diameters of enteral feeding tubes – these may differ slightly between manufacturers.[422,446]

French size	Inner diameter (mm)
5	1.10
6	1.37
8	1.96
10	2.54
12	2.67

Tube position

Tube tips can easily become dislodged by movement. Tube tip position should be tested using pH indicator paper, or according to local guidelines. Blue litmus paper is no longer considered to be appropriate for use, as it may not distinguish between bronichial and gastric placement.[118]

Tube tip position is most accurately checked by radiography, but in order to minimise exposure to radiation and to reduce handling of the patient, pH testing is the preferred method for most patients (excepting neonates). pH indicator strips should have 0.5 gradations and a range including 1-6. It is particularly important to be able to distinguish at the pH 5-6 range.[120]

Tube tip position should be checked: - [120]
- following initial insertion
- before administering each feed
- before giving medication
- at least once daily during continuous feeding
- following episodes of coughing, vomiting, or retching
- following evidence of tube displacement (e.g. more tube visible, loose tape)

pH testing results[120]

pH 5.5 or below – Commence feeding (there have been no reported cases of pulmonary aspirates below this figure).

pH above 6 – Do not feed. Wait 1 hour and try again (to allow feed to leave the stomach, and gastric acid levels to rise).

Patients on antacids, H_2 antagonists, or proton pump inhibitors may have gastric aspirates with pH of 6 or above. Seek advice and alternative methods of checking tube tip position in these patients if aspirate pH is high.[120]

General handling of enteral feeding tubes

Carers should wear gloves when handling enteral feeding tubes and preparing medicines for administration (e.g. when crushing tablets).

A 50mL oral, enteral, or catheter-tipped syringe should be used for administration of medication.[112] Intravenous syringes should NOT be used due to the risk of accidental parenteral administration. The use of intravenous syringes has led to fatalities when medications for enteral use have been accidentally given intravenously.

Catheter-tipped syringes should not be used for measuring liquid medicines due to the large dead-space volume in the catheter tip. This can be up to 2mL in some cases, which can lead to doses in excess of those intended being administered to the patient. If it is necessary to use a catheter-tipped syringe to measure a liquid, a different syringe should be used to flush the enteral tube, so that the medication in the dead-space is not administered (this amount will be in excess of the dose volume desired). However, if a catheter-tipped syringe is used to administer a dispersed tablet, the **same** syringe should be used to flush the enteral tube, in order to ensure that the medication in the dead-space, which is part of the intended dose, is administered to the patient.

Luer-tipped and oral syringes have smaller dead-space volumes, and the problem is not as significant with these syringe types. However when the dose volume of a liquid medicine is very small (e.g. with digoxin, which is 50mcg/mL, or when dosing neonates) the dead-space volume (around 0.4mL in a syringe used in Wrexham Maelor Hospital) may be significant, and the same precautions as described above should be taken.

Coloured enteral syringes are available in some centres. These may not be sterile, and may be re-used for the same patient. They should be clearly labelled with the patient details, washed in hot soapy water immediately after each use, and allowed to dry in air.

Immunocompromised patients and patients with enteral feeding tubes terminating in the jejunum may require the use of sterile equipment to reduce infection risk.

All equipment used for administering medicines must be cleaned in between each use to prevent cross-contamination of medicines. Particular care should be taken when handling drugs to which patients frequently suffer allergies, e.g. the penicillins.

Flushing enteral feeding tubes

Tube flushing should be done using a push-pause technique to create turbulence within the tube which helps to dislodge particles. Enteral feeding tubes should be flushed with 30mL of distilled water after the feed is stopped and before any medications are given, then with 10mL of distilled water between medications to prevent drug-drug interactions. When all the medications have been administered, flush the tube with at least 30mL of distilled water again before restarting the feed. This procedure reduces the risk of tube blockage and helps with the delivery of the drug to the stomach.[1] If the patient is fluid-restricted, consult your Pharmacist or the Doctor.

Medications can react with the ions in tap water, therefore distilled water should be used for drug administration and enteral tube flushing unless otherwise directed. A separate bottle should be used for each patient, and discarded at the end of 24 hours.

Enteral feed interactions with gastric acid have been associated with coagulation of the feed and tube occlusion. For this reason, it is recommended that if gastric contents are to be aspirated from an enteral feeding tube through which feed has previously been delivered, the tube should be flushed before and after aspiration.[214] Some authors also recommend flushing the enteral feeding tube at the end of each period of feeding, as retrograde migration of gastric juices can occur, which may cause coagulation of any feed remaining in the tube.[214]

Drug absorption via enteral feeding tubes

There are two main consequences for drug absorption via the stomach when an enteral feeding tube is in place.[1]

1. The delivery of drugs directly into the stomach bypasses the normal enteral route where saliva may assist degradation of the drug.
2. The residence time in the stomach is reduced. Absorption of drug will be impaired if prolonged contact with the acid environment of the stomach is required for drug dissolution. When an enteral tube terminating in the jejunum (NJ, PEJ, PEGJ) is used the acid environment of the stomach is bypassed altogether, which can result in only partial or no absorption of the drug.

Some studies have shown that drug absorption is reduced when administered via enteral feeding tubes.[555] Concomitant patient conditions (often those which may have resulted in the need for the enteral feeding tube in the first place) such as recent surgery, or acute illness, may also account for reduced absorption.

Gastric motility and nasogastric suction

Gastric motility can inhibit absorption of medications administered via nasogastric or percutaneous gastrostomy tubes. If motility is believed to be a problem, referral to the local Nutrition team is advised.

Some drugs have been used to try and aid gastric motility through their prokinetic side effects. Metoclopramide (10mg three times a day) and erythromycin (250mg two or three times a day, preferably by the intravenous route) are the most commonly used.[90] Metoclopramide increases gastric emptying by contracting gastric smooth muscle.[2]

In patients with slow gastric emptying, it may be advisable to suspend nasogastric drainage / nasogastric suction following dosing for sufficient time to allow the dose to be absorbed.[90]

Medications should not be administered through enteral tubes on free-drainage.[137]

> When a patient who was previously on oral medication has an enteral feeding tube fitted and is likely to have medication administered via this route, contact Pharmacy for advice.

2.2 Problem solving

What do you do if giving several medications?

Do not mix drugs together during preparation, dispersal, or in the syringe. Drugs are more likely to interact with each other if mixed together directly, particularly following tablet crushing. Also if the tube becomes blocked it may be difficult to determine how much of the dose has been given.

Administer each drug separately (see flow chart, section 3.2).

What can be done if the tube becomes blocked?

Adequate tube flushing and appropriate preparation of medications should prevent tube blockage. However if blockage does occur, first aspirate to try and remove any particulate matter, then flush the tube with warm water.[4,113] Do NOT use excessive force.[112]

Other methods which have been tried include flushing the feeding tube with lemonade, sodium bicarbonate, cola or soda water. The combination of the acidity of these drinks, the effervescence due to carbonation and the flushing action may dislodge the blockage. However some sources consider the use of acidic drinks to contribute to tube blockage through protein denaturation.[119]

Another method involves adding the contents of three Pancrex V capsules and 1g of sodium bicarbonate powder to 20mL distilled water, instilling the solution into the enteral feeding tube and leaving it in the tube for twenty minutes before flushing with distilled water. Both the Pancrex V capsules and the sodium bicarbonate must be prescribed before this method is used.[155]

Are injectable drugs suitable to be used down the tube?

Some injectable drugs are suitable for oral administration and can be given via enteral feeding tubes, e.g. vancomycin, hyoscine. Injections with a high polyethylene glycol content are not suitable for enteral administration.[104] See individual drug monographs for advice.

Is it possible to add medication to the feed?

No, medication must never be added to feeds.[2] Changes in feed rate would alter drug dosage with a risk or under / over-dosing. There is a risk of microbiological contamination of the feed and there are difficulties in predicting the effect the feed will have on the physical characteristics and stability of the medication, and vice versa. Most medications are intended to be administered as discrete bolus doses, to achieve therapeutic peaks. The effect of administering medication over a prolonged period as would occur if medication was added to the feed is difficult to predict in most cases.

Some studies have investigated the effect of adding liquid medications to enteral feeds prior to administration as a way of tackling gastrointestinal intolerance due to the high osmolality of liquid dosage forms. In many cases, addition of medication results in altered pH of the feed, which may cause precipitation.[25]

Is it possible to add medication to soft food to aid swallowing?

Sometimes this may be done, but it is usually outside the product licence. When this is done, the medication should be added to the first mouthful of food so that the whole dose is given. Some medications can be added to fruit juice or other fluids for administration. See individual drug monographs for advice. Due to the potential for drug interactions, do not add drugs to grapefruit juice.

2.3 Reasons for unpredictable response

Reason One

Drugs may bind to the enteral feeding tube, resulting in reduced absorption and bioavailability of the drug.

Examples:
- Lansoprazole suspension.
- Carbamazepine suspension.
- Phenytoin suspension.

Reason Two

Nutrients in the enteral feed may increase or decrease absorption of the drug from the stomach. This will consequently affect the drug levels in the body.

- Highly protein bound drugs such as theophylline may interact with the protein content of the feed. This may result in decreased effects.
- Some drugs may be required to be taken on an empty stomach e.g. flucloxacillin, tetracyclines. Tetracyclines may bind to some components of the feed, causing a decrease in the bioavailability of the drug.
- Digoxin interacts with enteral feeds which are high in fibre such as Jevity®.

Reason Three

Diarrhoea can be a problem in post-pyloric feeding. This is partly because the jejunum lacks the reservoir effect provided by the gastric fluids in the stomach and partly because the protective action of the pylorus in the regulation of delivery of nutrients into the intestine is bypassed.[3] Many liquid medications are hyperosmolar or hypertonic, and when administered directly into the jejunum osmotic diarrhoea and nausea can occur.[6]

3. General guidance on administration of medication

3.1 Review process for patients who have had an enteral feeding tube fitted[225]

Step One

Can the current oral medication be administered by an alternative route?

Other methods of administration

Rectal	e.g. aspirin, diclofenac, and paracetamol suppositories
Parenteral	e.g. intravenous, intramuscular and subcutaneous injections
Transdermal	e.g. hyoscine, glyceryl trinitrate, and hormone replacement therapy patches
Sublingual / buccal	e.g. prochlorperazine 3mg tablets

Step Two

Can the current oral medication be changed to another medication which has a more suitable method of administration?

e.g. mefenamic acid tablets changed to diclofenac suppositories.
e.g. isosorbide mononitrate tablets changed to glyceryl trinitrate patches.

For patients who will only have enteral feeding tubes in situ for a short time, it may not be appropriate to change certain types of chronic medication, e.g. psychiatric or epileptic medication, to alternative treatments, when the difficulty in administration will only last for a short period. Consider the stability of the patient's chronic condition before making medication changes.

Step Three

If the medication cannot be changed to an alternate route or medication, does it come as a liquid or as a dispersible / soluble tablet?

When medications have to be given by enteral feeding tube, liquids / dispersible tablets are the preferred formulations. Tablets should only be crushed as a last resort.

Many sugar–free liquids contain sorbitol, an artificial sweetener, which is a laxative and at total daily doses of 7.5g and upwards can result in abdominal cramping and diarrhoea.[116,245] Sorbitol has a cumulative effect and it is therefore important to minimise the intake of sorbitol where possible. Diarrhoea in enteral tube-fed patients has been attributed to sorbitol intake in up to 48% of cases.[2] Cost implications occur when the drug is only available in paediatric preparations and large volumes will be required.

Step Four

When changing from solid to liquid dosage forms should any dose changes be made?

If changing from modified-release tablets / capsules to liquid it may to necessary to decrease the dose and increase the frequency of administration.

Some drugs have a different bioavailability when being changed from a tablet to a liquid, e.g. digoxin. Other drugs contain a different salt of the drug in the liquid and tablet form, e.g. phenytoin. See recommendations under individual drug monographs, or contact Pharmacy for advice.

Step Five

Does the feeding regimen need to be adjusted?

Many medications interact with enteral feeds. This can result in increased or decreased absorption, altered therapeutic effects and adverse effects, and sometimes blockage of the enteral feeding tube. Medications may have to be given during a feeding break, which may necessitate pausing the enteral feed (and therefore increasing the feed rate at other times to ensure that adequate nutrition is achieved). In order to reduce the number of feed breaks required, drug frequency may have to be adjusted. See recommendations under individual drug monographs.

Contact Pharmacy and the Nutrition team for advice on patient management.

3.2 Medicine administration flow chart
– enteral tubes[112]

Review medication and agree with the prescriber how it is to be given. Contact Pharmacy for advice. If any of the medication has to be given during feeding breaks, consult with the Nutrition team and Pharmacy to rearrange doses and feeding breaks to coincide.

When a dose is due:-

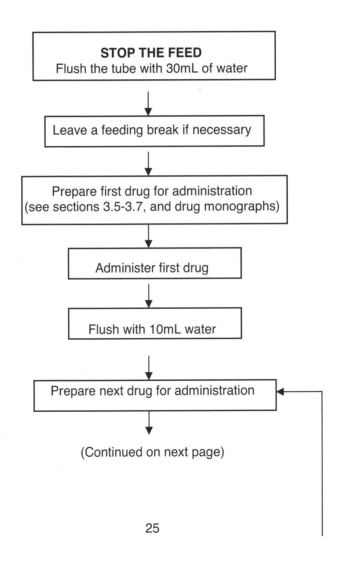

STOP THE FEED Flush the tube with 30mL of water

↓

Leave a feeding break if necessary

↓

Prepare first drug for administration (see sections 3.5-3.7, and drug monographs)

↓

Administer first drug

↓

Flush with 10mL water

↓

Prepare next drug for administration

↓

(Continued on next page)

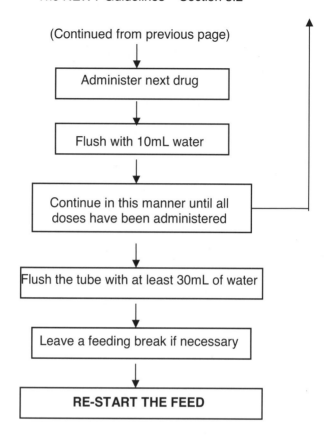

(Continued from previous page)

Administer next drug

Flush with 10mL water

Continue in this manner until all doses have been administered

Flush the tube with at least 30mL of water

Leave a feeding break if necessary

RE-START THE FEED

3.3 General guidelines for administration of medications through enteral feeding tubes

Standard tablets
Crushing should be avoided. If crushing is the only option then the tablets should be crushed well enough to prevent clogging of the tube. Care should be taken when crushing drugs which have a high incidence of allergic reactions e.g. antibiotics, chlorpromazine. It is important to ensure that the whole dose is administered.

If tablets need to be halved in order to obtain the prescribed dose, it is best to cut them using a tablet splitting device. Such devices split tablets more accurately than splitting scored tablets by hand, or cutting tablets with a knife.[558]

Sugar-coated (s/c) and film-coated (f/c) tablets
These tablets are usually coated to improve appearance or to mask unpleasant taste, and they are usually suitable for crushing.[225] However the presence of a coating may make crushing difficult and increase the probability of the drug blocking the enteral feeding tube. If these tablets are crushed it is particularly important to ensure that the coating is well broken up, and that the feeding tube is flushed well after the dose.

Dispersible and effervescent formulations
These have a low osmolality and will not cause diarrhoea. Most dispersible and effervescent formulations contain sodium, which may be a problem in sodium-restricted patients.

Enteric-coated (e/c) tablets – do not crush
The enteric coating is designed to prevent drug dissolution in the stomach and to promote absorption in the small intestine. If the tablet is crushed and passed down the enteral feeding tube, undesirable side effects may occur. These could include stomach irritation and a decrease in drug effectiveness. When crushed, the tablet will break into small chunks that bind together when moistened and subsequently clog the feeding tube.[4,212,214]

Buccal and sublingual tablets – do not crush

Drugs formulated in these dosage forms such as prochlorperazine (Buccastem®) or glyceryl trinitrate are designed not to pass through the stomach in order to avoid the first pass metabolism effects in the liver. If these tablets are passed down the enteral feeding tube, drug effect will be decreased. Buccal and sublingual tablets are suitable to be used as normal in most cases even if a patient becomes nil by mouth, provided that the patient is safe to have tablets held in their mouth, and is still producing normal quantities of saliva.[225,249]

Modified-release (MR) and controlled-release (CR) preparations (also ER, SR, LA, XL, XR, Retard, Once Weekly) – do not crush

These drugs are intended to be released gradually over time, and often have a special coating to enable this. If the tablet is crushed and passed down the enteral feeding tube, an increase in the expected peak plasma level may occur ("dose-dumping").[225] The patient will be initially exposed to significantly higher-than-normal levels which will increase the chance of side effects. Later, the drug will not last the full dosage interval, resulting in a period with little or no drug present, possibly resulting in loss of control of the patient's condition. Modified-release preparations are also unlikely to disperse completely when crushed, leading to an increased risk of tube occlusion.[214]

Cytotoxic tablets – do not crush

All staff should avoid contact with cytotoxic drugs. There is a risk of cytotoxic powder being aerosolized if cytotoxic tablets are crushed, exposing staff to hazardous materials.[225] Cytotoxics should be handled in accordance with local procedures. Contact Pharmacy for advice.

Chewable tablets – do not crush

Some of these tablets, e.g. Tegretol® Retard Chewtabs, are formulated so that they are partially absorbed in the mouth.[5] If the tablet is crushed decreased drug absorption will occur.

3.4 General guidelines for administration of medications to patients with swallowing difficulties

Liquids
Liquids are the preferred method of administering medications to patients with swallowing difficulties. Sorbitol-containing preparations can cause diarrhoea when large volumes (and therefore large sorbitol doses) are given.[245] Hyperosmolar liquids can cause nausea, bloating, and diarrhoea.[22,26] Dilution of liquids with water can reduce their osmolality and thereby reduce the rate of adverse effects.[26]

Unlicensed "special" liquids are sometimes very expensive, and it may be necessary to consider this when choosing how to administer therapy to patients, particularly when the therapy is likely to be long-term.

Standard tablets
Crushing tablets to aid administration to patients with swallowing difficulties is almost always outside the product licence. Crushed tablets are often unpalatable, and may sometimes have an anaesthetic effect on the oral mucosa, which can put the patient at risk of burns. Rinsing the mouth with water after administration of tablets may help to reduce this.

If tablets need to be halved in order to obtain the prescribed dose, it is best to cut them using a tablet splitting device. Such devices split tablets more accurately than splitting scored tablets by hand, or cutting tablets with a knife.[558]

Sugar-coated (s/c) and film-coated (f/c) tablets
These tablets are usually coated to improve appearance or to mask unpleasant taste, and they are usually suitable for crushing, although the presence of the coating may make crushing difficult.[225]

Dispersible and effervescent formulations
Dispersible and effervescent tablets can usually be administered to patients with swallowing difficulties in the normal manner. They have

a low osmolality and will not cause diarrhoea. Most dispersible and effervescent preparations contain sodium, which may be a problem in sodium-restricted patients. They should not be mixed with fluids other than water unless specifically indicated in the product information or the individual drug monograph, as this would cause administration to be outside the product licence.

Enteric-coated (e/c) tablets – do not crush
The enteric coating is designed to prevent drug dissolution in the stomach and to promote absorption in the small intestine. If the tablet is crushed undesirable side effects may occur. These could include stomach irritation and a decrease in drug effectiveness.[4,212,214]

Buccal and sublingual tablets – do not crush
Drugs formulated in these dosage forms can be used as normal in most cases even if a patient becomes nil by mouth, provided that the patient is safe to have tablets held in their mouth, and is still producing normal quantities of saliva.[225,249]

Modified-release (MR) and controlled-release (CR) preparations (also ER, SR, LA, XL, XR, Retard, Once Weekly) – do not crush
Using modified-release preparations in patients with swallowing difficulties poses the same problems as using them in patients with enteral feeding tubes. If the tablet is crushed, an increase in the expected peak plasma level may occur ("dose-dumping").[225] The patient will be initially exposed to significantly higher-than-normal levels which will increase the chance of side effects. Later, the drug will not last the full dosage interval, resulting in a period with little or no drug present, possibly resulting in loss of control of the patient's condition.[214]

A conversion to a non-modified-release preparation is necessary, usually requiring a dose decrease and a dosing frequency increase. Some modified-release capsules contain modified-release beads or granules which can be administered in water or on soft food to patients with swallowing difficulties. However there is a risk of giving excessive doses to patients if the beads / granules are crushed prior to swallowing. Therefore this method should only be used where it is the best possible option for a specific patient, and only if the patient has the ability and understanding to be able to swallow the water / soft food without chewing.

Cytotoxic tablets – do not crush
All staff should avoid contact with cytotoxic drugs. There is a risk of cytotoxic powder being aerosolized if cytotoxic tablets are crushed, exposing staff to hazardous materials.[225] Cytotoxics should be handled in accordance with local procedures. Contact Pharmacy for advice.

Chewable tablets – do not crush
Chewable tablets can be used as normal in patients with swallowing difficulties.

Capsules
Opening capsules for administration to patients with swallowing difficulties is almost always outside the product licence. The contents of capsules are often unpalatable, and they may have an anaesthetic effect on the oral mucosa, which can put the patient at risk of burns. The capsule shell may provide stability to the medication or protect if from gastric acid.

3.5 Directions for administration of tablets

IMPORTANT! – Never leave medication drawn up into a syringe unattended. Never give the syringe to someone else to administer to the patient. Accidental intravenous administration of oral / enteral medication drawn up in syringes has led to fatalities.

Dispersible / disintegrating / soluble tablets – enteral tubes
Some tablets may disperse or disintegrate in water without crushing. If this is the case the tablet should be prepared as follows:

1. Place intact tablet into the barrel of a 50mL oral or bladder-tipped syringe.
2. Replace the plunger and draw up 10-15mL of distilled water.
3. Cap the syringe and allow the tablet to dissolve.
4. Shake well and administer dose down the enteral feeding tube.
5. Flush the tube post dose with 10mL of distilled water.

Effervescent tablets – enteral tubes
These tablets will effervesce and disperse when placed in water. The resulting gases need to be allowed to escape. Prepare as follows:

1. Pour 50mL distilled water into a beaker (some tablets require greater volumes of water – see individual monographs for advice).
2. Add the tablet to the water.
3. Wait for the effervescent reaction to finish.
4. Swirl the solution and draw it all up into a 50mL oral or bladder-tipped syringe (in two aliquots if necessary).
5. Administer the dose down the enteral feeding tube.
6. Rinse the beaker with water and administer this also.
7. Flush the tube post dose with 10mL of distilled water.

Dispersible / effervescent tablets – swallowing difficulties

Put the tablet in a beaker of water (sometimes a large volume is required – see individual monographs for details), and wait for the dispersal / effervescent reaction to finish. The patient should drink the solution immediately, and the beaker should then be rinsed with water and this should be drunk also to ensure the whole dose is given.

Tablets suitable for crushing – enteral tubes

Prepare the tablet as follows:

1. Crush the tablet with a pestle and mortar, a tablet crusher, or between two metal spoons.
2. Add the powder to 15-30mL of distilled water and mix well.[214,225]
3. Draw up the solution into a 50mL oral or bladder-tipped syringe.
4. Administer the dose down the enteral feeding tube.
5. Rinse out the mortar / tablet crusher with distilled water and administer this also.
6. Flush the tube post dose with 10mL of distilled water.

Tablets suitable for crushing – swallowing difficulties

Prepare the tablet as follows:

1. Crush the tablet with a pestle and mortar, a tablet crusher, or between two metal spoons.
2. Add the powder to 15-30mL of distilled water and mix well.[214]
3. Draw up the solution into an oral or bladder-tipped syringe.
4. Administer the dose to the patient.
5. Rinse out the mortar / tablet crusher with distilled water and administer this also.

DON'T

... crush tablets in plastic containers as the drug may adhere to the plastic.

... use boiling water to dissolve tablets as it may affect bioavailability.

... leave oral medicines unattended in syringes.

... administer any medicine that you have not prepared yourself.

3.6 Directions for administration of liquids

IMPORTANT! – Never leave medication drawn up into a syringe unattended. Never give the syringe to someone else to administer to the patient. Accidental intravenous administration of oral / enteral medication drawn up in syringes has led to fatalities.

Syringes

Catheter-tipped syringes should not be used for measuring liquid medicines due to the large dead-space volume in the catheter tip. This can be up to 2mL in some cases, which can lead to doses in excess of those intended being administered to the patient. If it is necessary to use a catheter-tipped syringe to measure a liquid, a different syringe should be used to flush the enteral tube, so that the medication in the dead-space is not administered (this amount will be in excess of the dose volume desired).

Luer-tipped and oral syringes have smaller dead-space volumes, and the problem is not as significant with these syringe types. However when the dose volume of a liquid medicine is very small (e.g. with digoxin, which is 50mcg/mL, or when dosing neonates) the dead-space volume (around 0.4mL in a syringe used in Wrexham Maelor Hospital) may be significant, and the same precautions as described above should be taken.

Liquids / solutions – enteral tubes

Liquids are the preferred formulation for administration via enteral feeding tubes.[225] It is usually not necessary to dilute liquid preparations before administration (but see individual monographs for details). Liquids containing sorbitol may cause diarrhoea, therefore the highest strength product appropriate should be used in order to minimise sorbitol dosage. Sorbitol-containing liquids **should** be diluted before administration.[245]

Flush the tube post dose with 10mL of distilled water.

Syrups – enteral tubes

Syrups have viscous and hyperosmolar properties. It is best to dilute the syrup with the same volume of distilled water before administration.[4,214]

If the syrup is one of several drugs to be administered it is preferable to administer the syrup last.

Flush the tube post dose with 10mL of distilled water.

Suspensions – enteral tubes

The majority of suspensions are suitable for administration via enteral feeding tubes, however some e.g. ispaghula husk (Fybogel®) sachets for suspension, may block the tube. See individual monographs for advice.

Flush the tube post dose with 10mL of distilled water.

Liquids / solutions / syrups / suspensions – swallowing difficulties

These are the preferred formulations for administering medications to patients with swallowing difficulties.

Injections

Use of injections via the enteral route is usually an expensive method of administration, and should be done only if there is no other suitable route or formulation. Not all injections are suitable to be given via the enteral route. Some are hypertonic, and some contain ingredients which are unsuitable for enteral administration, e.g. polyethylene glycol.[137] Only do this on the advice of Pharmacy.

Powder injections should be reconstituted with water for injections. All injections should then be diluted with 30-60mL of water before administration to reduce gastrointestinal side effects.[133,137]

Flush the tube post dose with 10mL distilled water.

3.7 Directions for administration of capsules

IMPORTANT! – Never leave medication drawn up into a syringe unattended. Never give the syringe to someone else to administer to the patient. Accidental intravenous administration of oral / enteral medication drawn up in syringes has led to fatalities.

Hard gelatin capsules – enteral tubes
Prepare the capsule as follows:

1. Gently ease open the capsule to release the powder.
2. Tip the powder into a beaker – be sure to obtain all the powder.
3. Mix the powder with 15-30mL of distilled water.[214,225]
4. Draw up the solution in an oral or bladder-tipped syringe.
5. Administer the solution through the enteral feeding tube.
6. Rinse the beaker with distilled water, and administer this also.
7. Flush the tube post dose with 10mL of distilled water.

Hard gelatin capsules – swallowing difficulties
Prepare the capsule as follows:

1. Gently ease open the capsule to release the powder.
2. Tip the powder into a beaker – be sure to obtain all the powder.
3. Mix the powder with 15-30mL of distilled water.[214]
4. Draw up the solution in an oral or bladder-tipped syringe.
5. Administer the solution to the patient.
6. Rinse the beaker with distilled water, and administer this also.

Modified-release capsules – enteral tubes

Contact Pharmacy for advice. It may be necessary to change to another preparation.

See section on modified-release tablets (section 3.4). Some modified-release capsules can be opened without losing their modified-release properties (see individual monographs for advice). The beads / granules inside are themselves modified-release, and should not be crushed or chewed.

Modified-release capsules – swallowing difficulties

Contact Pharmacy for advice. It may be necessary to convert to a non-modified-release preparation. Some modified-release capsules contain modified-release beads or granules which can be administered in water or on soft food to patients with swallowing difficulties. There is a risk of giving excessive doses if the beads / granules are crushed prior to swallowing. This method should only be used where it is the best possible option for a specific patient, and only if the patient has the ability and understanding to be able to swallow the water / soft food without chewing.

Soft gelatin capsules e.g. nifedipine – enteral tubes

Method one[225]

1. Pinprick one end of the capsule.
2. Drain out the contents with a syringe.
3. Remove the needle from the syringe.*
4. Dilute if necessary (see individual monographs for advice).
5. Administer through the enteral feeding tube.
6. Flush the tube post dose with 10mL of distilled water.

Take great care when using needles to prepare doses for oral / enteral administration.

Some of the drug may adhere to the soft gelatin capsule, resulting in a smaller dose than intended being given.

Method two

1. Dissolve capsule in 15-30mL of warm (not hot) water.
2. Remove undissolved gelatin.
3. Draw up the solution in an oral or bladder-tipped syringe.
4. Administer the solution through the enteral feeding tube.
5. Flush the tube post dose with 10mL of distilled water.

Soft gelatin capsules e.g. nifedipine – swallowing difficulties

Method one

1. Pinprick one end of the capsule.
2. Drain out the contents with a syringe.
3. Remove the needle from the syringe.*
4. Dilute if necessary (see individual monographs for advice).
5. Administer to the patient.

Take great care when using needles to prepare doses for oral / enteral administration.

Some of the drug may adhere to the soft gelatin capsule, resulting in a smaller dose than intended being given.

Method two

1. Dissolve capsule in 15-30mL of warm (not hot) water.
2. Remove undissolved gelatin.
3. Draw up the solution in an oral or bladder-tipped syringe.
4. Administer the solution to the patient.

DON'T...

... microwave – this will affect the stability of the medication.

3.8 Choosing an appropriate method of administration

There are many points to be considered when choosing the most appropriate formulation and route of medication administration for patients with enteral feeding tubes or swallowing difficulties. For this reason it is recommended that such patients are reviewed by a health professional with a full understanding of the issues involved.

Some of the factors to be considered include:-

- whether the situation is short-term or long-term – alterations to medication should be kept to a minimum for management of short-term swallowing problems
- the likelihood and potential seriousness of causing a feeding tube blockage – possibly resulting in admission to hospital
- the ability to monitor the effect of medication – where the effect of medication can be monitored, the absorption (or failure to absorb) can be easily seen
- the potential seriousness of missing medication doses, and the importance of the medication during the period of the swallowing problem (particularly when the problem is short-term)

For most medicines in this guide, a variety of administration methods are offered. Where more than one method is available for a specific medicine, a suggested order of preference for the recommendations is indicated.

Not all of the options will be appropriate for all patients, therefore a full patient review is always recommended.

The reasoning behind the standard order of preference used in this guide is given below:-

(Please note that with certain drugs The NEWT Guidelines editorial board may recommend that a different order be followed to that shown below).

Enteral tubes:-

1st choice – An enteral formulation licensed for administration via enteral feeding tubes,
- licensed method of administration
- licensed product with full quality-control testing
- maintains the enteral route

2nd choice – Non-enteral administration (the same medication, or an alternative), e.g. intravenous, suppositories,
- licensed method of administration
- licensed product with full quality-control testing
- placing intravenous access solely for the administration of medication may not be appropriate due to the risks of intravenous catheterisation – infection, etc.
- consider tolerability (to patient) of alternative route
- may not be suitable for long-term swallowing problems

3rd choice – Licensed liquid formulation, dispersible tablet or effervescent tablet (the same medication, or an alternative), given via enteral feeding tube,
- unlicensed method of administration (unlicensed route)
- manufactured product with full quality-control testing
- maintains the enteral route
- reduced particle size and improved dispersion of particles compared with crushed tablets, reducing the likelihood of tube blockage

4th choice – Crush tablets / open capsules,
- unlicensed method of administration (unlicensed route)
- manufactured product with full quality-control testing
- readily available medication, reducing missed doses
- maintains the enteral route
- larger particle size compared with manufacturered liquids, increasing the possibility of tube blockage

5th choice – Pharmacy-prepared liquid product (extemporaneous),
- unlicensed method of administration (unlicensed route)
- unlicensed product
- reasonably readily available
- expensive on staff time and pharmacy resources
- relatively short product expiry
- maintains the enteral route

6th choice – "Special" liquid produced by a known specials manufacturer complying with Good Manufacturing Practice,
- unlicensed method of administration (unlicensed route)
- unlicensed product
- may take some time to obtain
- maintains the enteral route
- can be considerably more expensive than other enteral options

7th choice – Injection solution administered enterally (only certain injections are suitable for this),
- unlicensed method of administration (unlicensed route)
- manufactured product with full quality control testing
- readily available in secondary care settings
- may take longer to obtain in primary care
- can be considerably more expensive than other enteral options
- serious safety issues around using a product enterally which is intended for use parenterally (see section 1.2)

Swallowing difficulties:-

1st choice – Licensed liquid formulation, dispersible tablet or effervescent tablet (the same medication, or an alternative),
- licensed method of administration
- licensed product with full quality-control testing
- maintains the enteral route
- improved patient tolerance to the medication (acceptable route, and good palatability)

2nd choice – Non-enteral administration (the same medication, or an alternative), e.g. intravenous, suppositories,
- licensed method of administration
- licensed product with full quality-control testing
- placing intravenous access solely for the administration of medication may not be appropriate due to the risks of intravenous catheterisation – infection, etc.
- consider tolerability (to patient) of alternative route
- may not be suitable for long-term swallowing problems

3rd choice – Pharmacy-prepared liquid product (extemporaneous),
- unlicensed product
- reasonably readily available
- expensive on staff time and pharmacy resources
- relatively short product expiry
- maintains the enteral route

4th choice – "Special" liquid produced by a known specials manufacturer complying with Good Manufacturing Practice,
- unlicensed product
- may take some time to obtain
- maintains the enteral route
- can be considerably more expensive than other enteral options

5th choice – Crush tablets / open capsules,
- unlicensed method of administration
- manufactured product with full quality-control testing
- readily available medication, reducing missed doses
- maintains the enteral route
- consider palatability of medication

6th choice – Injection solution administered enterally (only certain injections are suitable for this),
- unlicensed method of administration (unlicensed route)
- manufactured product with full quality control testing
- readily available in secondary care settings
- may take longer to obtain in primary care
- can be considerably more expensive than other enteral options
- serious safety issues around using a product enterally which is intended for use parenterally (see section 1.2)

4. Drug Monographs

Abacavir

Presentation
Film-coated tablets.
Sugar-free oral solution (contains sorbitol).

Administration – enteral tubes / swallowing difficulties
Use the oral solution.[132] It contains sorbitol 340mg/mL, so a 300mg in 15mL dose contains just over 5g of sorbitol.[16] Follow the directions in section 3.6.

Abacavir and lamivudine (Kivexa®)

Presentation
Film-coated tablets.

Clinical guidance
Kivexa® tablets contain abacavir 600mg and lamivudine 300mg.[272] No information has been located on the use of Kivexa® tablets in patients with enteral feeding tubes or swallowing difficulties. Use the individual components – see individual monographs for details.

Abacavir with lamivudine and zidovudine (Trizivir®)

Presentation
Film-coated tablets.

Clinical guidance
Trizivir® tablets contain abacavir 300mg, lamivudine 150mg, and zidovudine 300mg.[272] No information has been located on the use of Trizivir® tablets in patients with enteral feeding tubes or swallowing difficulties. Use the individual components – see individual monographs for details.

Acamprosate

Presentation
Enteric-coated tablets.

Clinical guidance
The tablets are enteric-coated, and therefore should not be crushed.[226]

Acarbose

Presentation
Tablets.

Administration – NG / PEG tubes / swallowing difficulties
1st choice – Switch to insulin if appropriate.
2nd choice – The tablets can be crushed and mixed with water for administration via nasogastric tube.[140]   Follow the directions in section 3.5. See also "Clinical guidance" below.

Administration – NJ / PEJ / PEGJ tubes
1st choice – Switch to insulin if appropriate.

Acarbose is not substantially absorbed. It has its effect by inhibiting enzymes in the brush border of the small intestine.[321]   Due to this method of action it may not have its usual clinical effect if given directly into the jejunum, and this method of administration is not recommended.[140]

Clinical guidance
Due to its mechanism of action, the use of acarbose is unlikely to be appropriate in patients on continuous enteral feeding.[27]   Contact the patient's Nutrition team for advice.

Accuretic®

Presentation
Film-coated tablets.

Clinical guidance
Accuretic® tablets contain quinapril 10mg and hydrochlorothiazide 12.5mg.[272] No information has been located on the use of Accuretic® tablets in patients with enteral feeding tubes or swallowing difficulties. Switch to an alternative ACE inhibitor, e.g. lisinopril, and an alternative thiazide diuretic, e.g. bendroflumethiazide.

Acebutolol

Presentation
Capsules, film-coated tablets.

Administration – enteral tubes / swallowing difficulties
1st choice – Switch to an alternative beta-blocker which is available in a liquid form, e.g. atenolol.
2nd choice – The capsules can be opened, and the contents dispersed in water for administration.[41,105] Follow the directions in section 3.7.

Aceclofenac

Presentation
Film-coated tablets.

Administration – enteral tubes / swallowing difficulties
1st choice – Switch to an alternative drug which has a dispersible, liquid, or rectal form, e.g. diclofenac, ibuprofen.
2nd choice – The tablet can be crushed and mixed with water for administration.[41] Follow the directions in section 3.5.

Clinical guidance
For short-term use only as aceclofenac is more irritant to the gastrointestinal tract after being crushed.

Acenocoumarol (Nicoumalone)

Presentation
Tablets.

Administration – enteral tubes / swallowing difficulties
The tablets can be crushed and mixed with water for administration.[105] Follow the directions in section 3.5.

Acetazolamide

Presentation
Tablets.
Slow-release capsules.
A suspension can be made by Pharmacy in some centres (see Appendix 1).[451,573]
Injection.

Administration – enteral tubes
1st choice – Give by parenteral injection if appropriate.
2nd choice – The standard tablets disperse with a fine sediment.[7,40,41] They disperse in one to five minutes.[8,154] Follow the directions in section 3.5. Rinse equipment well to ensure the whole dose is given.
3rd choice – A suspension can be made by Pharmacy in some centres.[38,155,451] Follow the directions in section 3.6.
4th choice – The injection can be reconstituted with water and used enterally.[40,104,138,152] Follow the directions in section 3.6.

The slow-release capsules are generally not considered suitable for use, although in some centres they have been opened and the contents flushed down enteral feeding tubes.[133] Contact Pharmacy for advice.

(monograph continues on next page)

Administration – swallowing difficulties

1st choice – Give by parenteral injection if appropriate.

2nd choice – A suspension can be made by Pharmacy in some centres.[38,155,451]

3rd choice – The standard tablets disperse with a fine sediment.[7,40,41] They disperse in one to five minutes.[8,154] Follow the directions in section 3.5. Rinse equipment well to ensure the whole dose is given.

4th choice – The injection can be reconstituted with water and used enterally.[40,104,138,152] Follow the directions in section 3.6.

The slow-release capsules are generally not considered suitable for use. Contact Pharmacy for advice.

Acetylcysteine

Presentation
Effervescent tablets (unlicensed in UK).
Injection.

Administration – enteral tubes / swallowing difficulties

1st choice – Use the effervescent tablets. Follow the directions in section 3.5.

2nd choice – The injection can be diluted 1:4 in orange juice for enteral administration.[237] It has a bitter taste.[40,152] Orange or blackcurrant syrup can also be used to dilute the injection solution.[152]

Feed guidance
Enteral feeds should be stopped prior to enteral administration of acetylcysteine, and restarted afterwards.[6]

Aciclovir

Presentation
Tablets.
Dispersible tablets.
Suspension (contains sorbitol).
Intravenous infusion.

Administration – enteral tubes
1st choice – Give by intravenous infusion.
2nd choice – Use the suspension or the dispersible tablets.[104] The dispersible tablets should be dispersed in at least 50mL of water prior to administration.[238] The suspension contains sorbitol.[239,240] Follow the directions in sections 3.5 and 3.6.

Administration – swallowing difficulties
1st choice – Use the suspension or the dispersible tablets.[104] The dispersible tablets should be dispersed in at least 50mL of water prior to administration.[238] The suspension contains sorbitol.[239,240]
2nd choice – Give by intravenous infusion.

Clinical guidance
Aciclovir is absorbed in the upper gastrointestinal tract, therefore there may be a risk of reduced absorption when the drug is given through an enteral feeding tube terminating in the jejunum.[395] Consider using doses at the higher end of the dosage range, and monitor the patient for clinical effect.

Acipimox

Presentation
Capsules.

Clinical guidance
Administration via enteral feeding tube not recommended. Consider changing to an alternative treatment if swallowing problems are likely to be long-term.[140]

Acitretin

Presentation
Capsules.

Administration – enteral tubes
The capsule contents are poorly soluble, and are therefore not suitable to be used via enteral feeding tubes as they may cause blockage.[105]

Administration – swallowing difficulties
<u>Caution – teratogenic.</u> Women of childbearing potential must not engage in any activity (i.e. capsule opening) where exposure to this drug may occur.[162]

For patients with swallowing difficulties, the capsules can be opened and their contents sprinkled onto soft food.[105]   Acitretin is light sensitive, and this should be borne in mind if the capsules are opened.[253]

Albendazole

Presentation
Tablets (named patient supply).
Suspension (named patient supply).

Administration – enteral tubes
No information about the use of this medication via enteral feeding tubes has been located.

Administration – swallowing difficulties
Use the suspension (if available). Some sources advise against crushing the tablets.[41]   However this has been done when necessary.[152] Contact Pharmacy for advice.

Alendronic acid

Presentation
Tablets.
Oral solution.[579]
Oral solution (special).[582]

Clinical guidance – enteral tubes
There is a form of zoledronic acid licensed for once-yearly intravenous administration.[544] This is probably the most appropriate form of bisphosphonate for most patients with swallowing problems – contact Pharmacy for advice.

The tablets are not considered suitable for crushing due to the risk of oesophageal damage, although this has been done in some centres and the drug is reported to be soluble.[50,155] (NB The presence of a nasogastric / jejunal tube compromises the cardiac sphincter and increases the risk of oesophageal damage). Administration also requires the patient to be able to sit or stand upright for a period of at least 30 minutes following dosing.

A very small study (five patients) of patients receiving alendronic acid via percutaneous feeding tube found administration to be generally well-tolerated.[246] If swallowing problems are likely to be long-term, and bisphosphonate therapy is considered essential, administration of alendronic acid might be possible, but should only be carried out in the clear understanding of the risks involved.

Review whether the medication is still needed. If alendronic acid is given, the enteral feed should be withheld for two hours before and two hours after each dose.[225,272,624]

Alendronic acid may cause irritation if the drug powder comes into contact with the eyes, skin, mucous membranes or if it is accidentally inhaled.[558] If the tablets are to be dispersed for administration, this would be best done by placing the tablet in the barrel of an oral or bladder-tipped syringe, and then drawing up water and allowing the tablet to disperse.

No information on administering the oral solution via enteral feeding tubes has been located.

(monograph continues on next page)

Administration – swallowing difficulties
Use the oral solution. Alternatively consider using once-yearly zoledronic acid.

Alfacalcidol

Presentation
Capsules.
Oral drops.
Injection.

Administration – enteral tubes
Recommended method - give by parenteral injection.
The oral drops are unstable and not suitable for dilution. They may adsorb onto plastic and therefore should not be given via enteral feeding tubes. Anecdotally the drops have been administered via enteral feeding tubes with effect, but this is not recommended.

Administration – swallowing difficulties
The drops can be administered on a spoon for patients with swallowing difficulties.[128] They are light sensitive.[133] Some sources state that alfacalcidol drops can be mixed with milk prior to administration, however the manufacturers do not recommend this, as studies have suggested that the dose is not reproducible when given in this manner.[128,152]

Alfuzosin

Presentation
Film-coated tablets.
Modified-release tablets.

Administration – enteral tubes / swallowing difficulties
The standard (film-coated) tablets can be crushed and dispersed in water for administration.[42] Follow the directions in section 3.5.

The modified-release tablets should not be crushed. Convert patients to standard-release tablets. Due to the risk of hypotension it may be advisable not to make a direct conversion to standard-release tablets, but to start at 2.5mg three times a day (twice a day in elderly patients) and increase as tolerated.[429]

Clinical guidance
Monitor blood pressure.

Alimemazine (Trimeprazine)

Presentation
Film-coated tablets.
Syrup (contains alcohol[545]).

Administration – enteral tubes
1st choice – Consider switching to chlorphenamine injection.
2nd choice – Use the syrup.[104] Follow the directions in section 3.6.
3rd choice – The tablets can be crushed and mixed with water for administration. The blue film-coating can be washed off the tablets to make them more easy to crush.[152] Without crushing they disperse in one to two minutes.[8] Follow the directions in section 3.5.

Administration – swallowing difficulties
1st choice – Use the syrup.[104]
2nd choice – Consider switching to chlorphenamine injection.
3rd choice – The tablets can be crushed and mixed with water for administration. The blue film-coating can be washed off the tablets to make them more easy to crush.[152] Without crushing they disperse in one to two minutes.[8] Follow the directions in section 3.5.

Allopurinol

Presentation
Tablets.
Sugar-free oral suspension (special).[582]
A suspension can be made by Pharmacy in some centres (see Appendix 1).[451,573]

Administration – enteral tubes
1st choice – Rasburicase infusion may be an appropriate alternative in some patients – contact Pharmacy for advice.
2nd choice – The tablets can be crushed and mixed with water for administration.[8,40] The 100mg tablets will disperse within one minute without crushing.[8,154] The 300mg tablets take longer to disperse and so should be crushed before dispersing in water.[8,154] They should be crushed well as the drug is not very soluble.[253] Follow the directions in section 3.5. Give immediately.[155]
3rd choice – A suspension can be made by Pharmacy in some centres. Follow the directions in section 3.6.
4th choice – Use the oral suspension (if available). Follow the directions in section 3.6.

Administration – swallowing difficulties
1st choice – Rasburicase infusion may be an appropriate alternative in some patients – contact Pharmacy for advice.
2nd choice – A suspension can be made by Pharmacy in some centres.
3rd choice – Use the oral suspension (if available).
4th choice – The tablets can be crushed and mixed with water for administration.[8,40] The 100mg tablets will disperse within one minute without crushing.[8,154] The 300mg tablets take longer to disperse and so should be crushed before dispersing in water.[8,154] They should be crushed well as the drug is not very soluble.[253] Follow the directions in section 3.5. Give immediately.[155]

Feed guidance
Allopurinol should be given after feed.[35]

Alprazolam

Presentation
Tablets.
A suspension can be made by Pharmacy in some centres (see Appendix 1).[452]

Administration – enteral tubes
The tablets can be dispersed in water for administration.[8] They will disperse in less than a minute.[8] Follow the directions in section 3.5.

No information on administering the suspension via enteral feeding tubes has been located.

Administration – swallowing difficulties
1st choice – Use the suspension (if available).
2nd choice – The tablets can be dispersed in water for administration.[8] They will disperse in less than a minute.[8] Follow the directions in section 3.5.

Aluminium hydroxide

Presentation
Tablets, capsules.
Oral suspension (no longer available in the UK).

Administration – enteral tubes
Not recommended for administration via enteral feeding tubes as it may interact with enteral feeds to form protein complexes which may block enteral feeding tubes or cause oesophageal plugs.[11,32,104]

Administration – swallowing difficulties
Use the suspension (if available).

Clinical guidance
Aluminium hydroxide can decrease gastric emptying.[2]

Alverine citrate

Presentation
Capsules.

Administration – enteral tubes / swallowing difficulties
1st choice – Consider switching to mebeverine, which is available as a liquid.
2nd choice – The capsules can be opened, and the contents dispersed in water for administration.[105] Follow the directions in section 3.7. The capsule contents have an anaesthetic effect which when given orally may cause numbing of the lips and tongue.[105]

Amantadine

Presentation
Capsules.
Syrup.

Administration – enteral tubes / swallowing difficulties
1st choice – Use the syrup (contains sorbitol[104]).[41,104] Follow the directions in section 3.6.
2nd choice – The capsules can be opened and the contents mixed with water for administration to patients with enteral tubes or swallowing difficulties.[332] The drug is very soluble.[253]

Amiloride

Presentation
Tablets.
Oral solution.

Administration – enteral tubes / swallowing difficulties
1st choice – Use the oral solution.[104] Follow the directions in section 3.6.
2nd choice – The tablets can be crushed and dispersed in water for administration.[8,94] Follow the directions in section 3.5.

Different brands of amiloride tablets may disperse in water at notably different rates.[8]

Amiloride and cyclopenthiazide (Navispare®)

Presentation
Film-coated tablets.

Clinical guidance
Navispare® tablets contain amiloride 2.5mg and cyclopenthiazide 250micrograms.[272] Use the separate components – see individual monographs for details.

Aminophylline

Presentation
Tablets.
Modified-release tablets.
Injection.

Clinical guidance
Consider changing to equivalent does of theophylline liquid (but this may be difficult to get hold of). Seek advice from Pharmacy.

There are anecdotal reports of using aminophylline injection enterally.[259,260] As doses given this way are not modified-release, the total daily dose should be split into three or four divided doses.

Feed guidance
Some sources recommend a feed break when aminophylline is to be given via an enteral feeding tube. However anecdotal experience is that levels usually remain stable without administering in a feeding break.[261,262,263] Consider monitoring levels if control appears to be a problem.

Additional notes
Aminophylline appears to be absorbed when administered directly into the jejunum.[6]

(monograph continues on next page)

Aminophylline is a salt of theophylline. Switching between the two requires a dosage change. However, as most forms of aminophylline and theophylline are modified-release, it is necessary to first calculate the total daily dose, then convert to the other drug, and then calculate an appropriate dose and frequency of the new therapy, depending on what brand is to be used. Contact Pharmacy for advice.

250mg oral aminophylline   equivalent to   200mg oral theophylline[176]

Amiodarone

Presentation
Tablets.
Oral solution (special).[582]
A suspension can be made by Pharmacy in some centres (see Appendix 1).[512,520,527,573]
Concentrate for infusion.

Administration – enteral tubes
1st choice – Give by infusion if appropriate.
2nd choice – The tablets can be crushed and mixed with water for administration.[8,42,152] Without crushing they disperse in around five minutes.[154] Follow the directions in section 3.5. Give immediately.[7]
3rd choice – A suspension can be made by Pharmacy in some centres.[155,512,520,527] Follow the directions in section 3.6.
4th choice – Use the oral solution (if available). Follow the directions in section 3.6.

Administration – swallowing difficulties
1st choice – Give by infusion if appropriate.
2nd choice – A suspension can be made by Pharmacy in some centres.[155,512,520]
3rd choice – Use the oral solution (if available).
4th choice – The tablets can be crushed and mixed with water for administration.[42,152] Without crushing they disperse in around five minutes.[154] Follow the directions in section 3.5. Give immediately.[7] The crushed tablets have a bitter taste.[105] They can be mixed with fruit juice if desired.[132]

(monograph continues on next page)

Different brands of amiodarone tablets may disperse in water at notably different rates.[8]

Amiodarone injection is not suitable for enteral administration as it contains Tween 80, which is irritant.[152]

Clinical guidance
There have been reports of reduced serum amiodarone levels when the drug is given via nasogastric tube.[394]   Patients receiving amiodarone via enteral feeding tube should be monitored closely.

Amiodarone is absorbed better from the duodenum and jejunum than from other areas of the gastrointestinal tract.[413]   Patients receiving amiodarone through enteral tubes terminating in the jejunum should therefore be monitored closely in case of insufficient absorption if the tube tip is positioned beyond the main site of absorption.

Amisulpride

Presentation
Tablets.
Solution.
Oral solution (special).[580,582]

Administration – enteral tubes / swallowing difficulties
Use the solution.[132]   Follow the directions in section 3.6.

Amitriptyline

Presentation
Film-coated tablets.
Oral solution.
Oral solution (special).[542,582,658]

Administration – enteral tubes / swallowing difficulties
1st choice – Use the oral solution.[104] Absorption may be decreased by high-fibre feeds.[41] Follow the directions in section 3.6.
2nd choice – The tablets can be crushed and dispersed in water.[105,225] They should be crushed well as the film-coating may block enteral feeding tubes if it is not broken up properly. Follow the directions in section 3.5.

There is a case report of amitriptyline being administered buccally by the tablet being crushed to powder, and the patient holding the powder in their mouth until it dissolved.[278] This method resulted in therapeutic levels and successful treatment in that case, and may occasionally be an appropriate method of administration. Contact Pharmacy for advice.

Crushed amitriptyline tablets have a bitter taste.[278]

Clinical guidance
Tricyclic antidepressants can decrease gastric emptying.[2]

Amlodipine

Presentation
Tablets.
Oral solution (special).[542,582]
A suspension can be made by Pharmacy in some centres (see Appendix 1).[453]

Administration – enteral tubes
Most tablet brands will disperse in water easily.[7,37,152] They disperse in one to five minutes.[154] Follow the directions in section 3.5. Give immediately as the drug is light sensitive.[104]

(monograph continues on next page)

No information has been located on administering the solution or the suspension via enteral feeding tubes.

Administration – swallowing difficulties
1st choice – A suspension can be made by Pharmacy in some centres.
2nd choice – Use the oral solution (if available).
3rd choice – Most tablet brands will disperse in water easily.[7,37,152] They disperse in one to five minutes.[154] Follow the directions in section 3.5. Give immediately as the drug is light sensitive.[104]

Amlodipine and valsartan (Exforge®)

Presentation
Film-coated tablets.

Clinical guidance
Exforge® tablets contain amlodipine and valsartan at various dosages.[272] Use the separate components – see individual monographs for details.

Amoxapine

Presentation
Tablets (no longer available in the UK).

Administration – enteral tubes / swallowing difficulties
The tablets can be dispersed in water for administration.[8,104] They disperse in less than a minute.[8] Follow the directions in section 3.5.

Amoxicillin (Amoxycillin)

Presentation
Capsules.
Sugar-free syrup, suspension, sugar-free suspension (some contain sorbitol), sachets.
Injection.

Administration – NG / PEG tubes
1st choice – Give by parenteral injection if appropriate.
2nd choice – Use the syrup or the suspension.[104] The suspension is quite viscous and should be diluted with an equal volume of water before administration. Follow the directions in section 3.6.

Administration – NJ / PEJ / PEGJ tubes
1st choice – Give by parenteral injection if appropriate.
2nd choice – Administer the injection, reconstituted with sterile water, via the enteral tube, as the suspension has a high osmolality which may lead to an osmotic diarrhoea.[6,26,104] It is likely that amoxicillin has a similar absorption following administration directly into the jejunum as it does following oral administration.[6]

Administration – swallowing difficulties
1st choice – Use the syrup or the suspension.[104]
2nd choice – Give by parenteral injection if appropriate.

Clinical guidance
Amoxicillin is absorbed in the duodenum and upper jejunum.[176]

Amphotericin

Presentation
Tablets.
Suspension (no longer available in the UK).
Lozenges.
Intravenous infusion.

Administration – enteral tubes / swallowing difficulties
The different formulations of amphotericin are licensed for different indications, and are not interchangeable. Use intravenous preparations where indicated. For intestinal candidiasis, use the suspension.[40] Follow the directions in section 3.6. When the lozenges are indicated, consider using nystatin suspension or fluconazole. Contact Pharmacy for advice.

Ampicillin

Presentation
Capsules.
Oral suspension.
Injection (no longer available in the UK).

Clinical guidance
Enteral ampicillin is poorly absorbed compared with enteral amoxicillin, so amoxicillin is the preferred antibiotic for enteral administration.[6]

Amprenavir

Presentation
Capsules (discontinued).
Oral solution (discontinued).

Administration – enteral tubes / swallowing difficulties
Use the oral solution. Follow the directions in section 3.6.

(monograph continues on next page)

Clinical guidance

Amprenavir capsules and oral solution are not interchangeable on a milligram per milligram basis, as amprenavir oral solution has a lower bioavailability.[241] For patients moving from one formulation to the other, contact Pharmacy for advice.

Anastrozole

Presentation

Film-coated tablets.

Administration – enteral tubes / swallowing difficulties

<u>Caution – risk to pregnancy.</u> Women who are pregnant should not crush or handle crushed tablets.[293] It may be advisable to use a closed system to administer anastrozole.

The tablets can be crushed and mixed with water for administration.[46] The drug is moderately soluble in water.[321] Follow the directions in section 3.5.

Antacids

Clinical guidance

Aluminium containing antacids may interact with feeds and form a plug.[135] Contact Pharmacy for advice on suitable alternatives.

Apixaban

Presentation

Film-coated tablets.

Administration – enteral tubes / swallowing difficulties

The tablets can be crushed and dispersed in glucose 5% for administration.[649,650] Take care to ensure the whole dose is administered, and for patients with enteral feeding tubes, flush well after each dose.

Aprepitant

Presentation
Capsules.

Administration – enteral tubes
No information about the use of this medication via enteral feeding tubes has been located.

Administration – swallowing difficulties
The manufacturer states that the beads should be stable if removed from the capsule and placed in water or on food for immediate oral administration, however they cannot recommend this. If the capsules are opened, this should only be done at the time of administration, and not in advance.[531]

Aprepitant is absorbed in the small intestine, and administration via any method which does not include passage through this site, or which reduces passage through this site, may reduce absorption.[531]

A method to prepare an oral liquid of aprepitant has been described.[532]

Arginine

Presentation
Tablets (special).
Solution.
Oral liquid (special).[582]
Powder (special).
Injection (special).

Administration – enteral tubes
No information about the use of this medication via enteral feeding tubes has been located.

Administration – swallowing difficulties
Use either the solution or the powder. They may be mixed with milk or fruit juice to improve palatability.[152] The 10% injection has been used orally.[152,160]

(monograph continues on next page)

A method of extemporaneously preparing an oral liquid with an expiry of 7 days has been described.[573]

Arthrotec®

Presentation
Tablets.

Clinical guidance
The tablets are formed of a core of diclofenac surrounded by a mantle of misoprostol. They are not suitable for crushing.[51] Consider changing treatment to rectal or dispersible diclofenac, with an acid suppressant, e.g. ranitidine or lansoprazole. See individual monographs for details.

Asasantin®

See entry under "Dipyridamole and aspirin".

Ascorbic acid

Presentation
Tablets.
Effervescent tablets.
Injection.

Administration – enteral tubes / swallowing difficulties
Use the effervescent tablets if possible.[94,104] Where lower doses are necessary, the effervescent tablets can be halved / quartered and dispersed in water, or the standard tablets can be crushed and mixed with water for administration.[8,104] Follow the directions in section 3.5.

Aspirin

Presentation
Tablets.
Enteric-coated tablets.
Dispersible tablets.
Suppositories (may not be available).

Administration – enteral tubes
1st choice – Use the suppositories (if available).
2nd choice – Use the dispersible tablets.[104] Give with food.[35] Follow the directions in section 3.5.

Do not crush enteric-coated tablets.[4]

A single case report of aspirin administration directly into the jejunum showed absorption comparable to oral administration.[6]

Administration – swallowing difficulties
1st choice – Use the dispersible tablets.[104] Give with food.[35]
2nd choice – Use the suppositories (if available).

Do not crush enteric-coated tablets.[4]

Atazanavir

Presentation
Capsules.

Administration – enteral tubes
The capsules can be opened and the contents dispersed in water for administration.[132] Follow the directions in section 3.7.

Administration – swallowing difficulties
The capsules can be opened and the contents dispersed in water or mixed with soft food.[132] Follow the directions in section 3.7.

Atenolol

Presentation
Tablets, film-coated tablets.
Syrup (contains sorbitol).
Injection.

Administration – enteral tubes
1st choice – Give by parenteral injection if appropriate.
2nd choice – Use the syrup and protect from light.[40,88] Follow the directions in section 3.6.
3rd choice – The tablets can be crushed and mixed with water for administration.[8,133] Follow the directions in section 3.5. Crush the tablets well to break up the film-coating in order to prevent tube blockage.

Atenolol is absorbed in the jejunum and so should have a good clinical effect following jejunal administration.[6,399] Some sources recommend that only the crushed tablets should be used for patients with enteral feeding tubes terminating in the jejunum.[6,155]

Administration – swallowing difficulties
1st choice – Use the syrup and protect from light.[40,88]
2nd choice – Give by parenteral injection if appropriate.
3rd choice – The tablets can be crushed and mixed with water for administration.[8,133] Follow the directions in section 3.5.

Feed guidance
Enteral absorption of atenolol can be increased by concomitant food or milk.[2]

Atenolol and co-amilozide (Kalten®)

Presentation
Capsules.

Clinical guidance
Kalten® capsules contain atenolol 50mg and co-amilozide 2.5mg/25mg.[272] Use the separate components – see individual monographs for details.

Atenolol and nifedipine (Beta-Adalat®, Tenif®)

Presentation
Capsules.

Clinical guidance
Beta-Adalat® and Tenif® capsules contain atenolol 50mg and nifedipine 20mg as a modified-release preparation.[272] Use the separate components – atenolol and an appropriate formulation of nifedipine. This will require splitting the dose and giving it several times a day. See individual monographs for details. Contact Pharmacy for advice if necessary.

Atorvastatin

Presentation
Film-coated tablets.
Oral solution (special).[582]

Administration – enteral tubes
The tablets can be crushed and mixed with water for administration.[37] Follow the directions in section 3.5. Atorvastatin tablets are not very soluble and a residue may be left, with the potential to block the enteral feeding tube.[294] Flush well after dosing.[37,104]

Give immediately as the drug is light sensitive.[321]

No information on administering the oral solution via enteral feeding tubes has been located.

Administration – swallowing difficulties
1st choice – Use the oral solution (if available).
2nd choice – The tablets can be crushed and mixed with water for administration.[37] Follow the directions in section 3.5. Atorvastatin tablets are not very soluble and a residue may be left, so take care to ensure the complete dose is administered.[294]

Give immediately as the drug is light sensitive.[321]

Atripla®

Presentation
Film-coated tablets.

Clinical guidance
Atripla® tablets contain efavirenz 600mg, emtricitabine 200mg, and tenofovir 245mg.[272] No information has been located on the use of Atripla® tablets in patients with enteral feeding tubes or swallowing difficulties. Use the individual components. See individual monographs for details.

Atropine sulphate

Presentation
Tablets.
Liquid (special).
Injection.

Administration – enteral tubes
1st choice – The tablets may be crushed and mixed with water for administration.[8,138] Follow the directions in section 3.5.
2nd choice – Use the liquid.[138] Follow the directions in section 3.6.
3rd choice – The injection has been given enterally.[152] Follow the directions in section 3.6.

Administration – swallowing difficulties
1st choice – Use the liquid (if available).[138]
2nd choice – The tablets may be crushed and mixed with water for administration.[8,138] Follow the directions in section 3.5.
3rd choice – The injection has been given enterally.[152] Follow the directions in section 3.6.

Clinical guidance
Atropine can decrease gastric emptying.[2]

Auranofin

Presentation
Film-coated tablets (may not be available in the UK).

Administration – enteral tubes / swallowing difficulties
<u>Caution – teratogenic.</u> Pregnant women should not handled crushed or dispersed tablets.[280]

In some situations it may be appropriate for patients to be converted to sodium aurothiomalate injections. Seek specialist advice.

The tablets (if available) can be dispersed in water for administration.[8] They disperse in less than a minute.[8] Follow the directions in section 3.5.

Feed guidance
Take with or after food.[429]

Avandamet®

Presentation
Film-coated tablets (no longer licensed in the UK).

Clinical guidance
Avandamet® tablets contain rosiglitazone and metformin in various dosages. No information has been located about administering the tablets to patients with enteral tubes or swallowing difficulties. Use the separate components – see individual monographs for details.

Azathioprine

Presentation
Tablets, film-coated tablets.
Oral suspension (special).[346,542,582]
A suspension can be made by Pharmacy in some centres (see Appendix 1).[451,512,573]
Injection.

Administration – enteral tubes / swallowing difficulties
Caution – cytotoxic. Contact Pharmacy for advice before giving.
1st choice – Give by parenteral injection if appropriate.
2nd choice – A suspension can be made by Pharmacy in some centres.[155,451] Follow the directions in section 3.6. Carers handling the suspension should wear gloves in case of contact with the medication.
3rd choice – Use the special oral suspension (if available). Follow the directions in section 3.6. Carers handling the suspension should wear gloves in case of contact with the medication.
4th choice – Contact Pharmacy for further advice on how to give (Pharmacists – see Appendix 2).

The tablet has a film-coating which protects carers from the cytotoxic medication inside.[295,346]

Azathioprine is absorbed in the upper gastrointestinal tract. No absorption problems are expected if the medication is delivered directly into the jejunum.[346]

Azithromycin

Presentation
Capsules.
Suspension.
Extended-release suspension (not available in the UK).

Administration – enteral tubes / swallowing difficulties
Use the standard suspension.[105] Follow the directions in section 3.6.

(monograph continues on next page)

Feed guidance

Azithromycin suspension can be taken with or without food, however the peak concentration may be increased when it is taken with food.[383,384,385]

Summary:- (suspension)	No need to stop feed

Azithromycin capsules should be taken on an empty stomach as their bioavailability is reduced by the presence of food in the gastrointestinal tract.[383,388] Food should be withheld for two hours before and one hour after each dose.[176,225,383,384,385,624]

Summary:- (capsules)	Stop feed 2 hours before dose
	Restart feed 1 hour after dose

The extended-release suspension (not available in the UK) should be taken on an empty stomach. Food should be withheld for two hours before and one hour after each dose.[225,383]

Summary:- (ER suspension)	Stop feed 2 hours before dose
	Restart feed 1 hour after dose

There is no information on where in the gastrointestinal tract azithromycin is absorbed.[414]

Withholding enteral feeds can compromise nutrition and interfere with blood glucose management. If the patient does not have a break in their feeding regimen during which azithromycin can be given, the Nutrition Team should be contacted to advise on management.

Baclofen

Presentation
Liquid (contains sorbitol).
Tablets.
Intrathecal injection.

Administration – enteral tubes / swallowing difficulties
1st choice – Use the liquid. Follow the directions in section 3.6. The liquid may be difficult to use via fine-bore tubes as it is quite thick.[132] It can be diluted with water to aid administration.[289,290]
2nd choice – Some brands of the tablets will disperse in water.[8,38,39,225,372] Follow the directions in section 3.5.

Clinical guidance
At higher doses the sorbitol content of the liquid may cause diarrhoea. In such cases, use the dispersed tablets instead.

Balsalazide

Presentation
Capsules.

Administration – enteral tubes / swallowing difficulties
The capsules can be opened, and the contents dispersed in water for administration.[104] The manufacturer advises against this, however, as the contents of the capsules will stain badly.[105] Use an alternative treatment (e.g. sulfasalazine) if possible. If this is not possible, use the capsules, and take care. Carers should consider wearing gloves and protective clothing. Follow the directions in section 3.7.

Beclometasone

Presentation
Modified-release tablets.
Inhalers.
Nasal spray.

Clinical guidance
Clipper® tablets are modified-release tablets indicated for ulcerative colitis. They should not be chewed or crushed. They are designed to release the medication in the small intestine and upper colon, where it has a topical effect.[570] Crushing the medication would therefore prevent it from reaching its intended site of action. Consider alternative treatments, such as rectal prednisolone for localised disease, intravenous steroids for short-term management, or soluble prednisolone. Contact Pharmacy for advice.

Nasal and inhaled beclometasone can usually be used as normal in patients with swallowing problems.

Bendroflumethiazide (Bendrofluazide)

Presentation
Tablets.
Oral suspension (special).[542,582,658]
A suspension can be made by Pharmacy in some centres.[573]

Administration – enteral tubes
1st choice – The tablets will disperse readily in water.[8,38,39,40,41,152] They disperse in one to five minutes.[8,154] Follow the directions in section 3.5.
2nd choice – A suspension can be made by Pharmacy in some centres.[155,573] Follow the directions in section 3.6.
3rd choice – Use the oral suspension (if available). Follow the directions in section 3.6.

(monograph continues on next page)

Administration – swallowing difficulties

1st choice – A suspension can be made by Pharmacy in some centres.[155,573]

2nd choice – Use the oral suspension (if available).

3rd choice – The tablets will disperse readily in water.[8,38,39,40,41,152] They disperse in one to five minutes.[8,154] Follow the directions in section 3.5.

Bendoflumethiazide and potassium (Centyl K®, Neo-NaClex-K®)

Presentation
Centyl K® sugar-coated tablets (no longer available in the UK).
Neo-NaClex-K film-coated tablets.

Clinical guidance
Centyl K® tablets contain bendroflumethiazide 2.5mg and potassium 7.7mmol in a modified-release preparation.[272] Neo-NaClex-K® tablets contain bendroflumethiazide 2.5mg and potassium 8.4mmol in a modified-release preparation.[272] Use the separate components – bendroflumethiazide and an appropriate standard-release formulation of potassium. See individual monographs for details. Contact Pharmacy for advice if necessary.

Benperidol

Presentation
Tablets.
A suspension can be made by Pharmacy in some centres.

Administration – enteral tubes / swallowing difficulties
A suspension can be made by Pharmacy in some centres.[138] Follow the directions in section 3.6.

Benzatropine (Benztropine)

Presentation
Tablets (no longer available in the UK).
Injection.

Administration – enteral tubes / swallowing difficulties
1st choice – Give by parenteral injection if appropriate.
2nd choice – The tablets can be crushed and mixed with water for administration.[8,41] Follow the directions in section 3.5.
3rd choice – The injection has also been administered enterally, however the manufacturers cannot recommend this.[104] Follow the directions in section 3.6.

Beta-Adalat®

Presentation
Capsules.

Clinical guidance
Beta-Adalat® capsules contain atenolol 50mg and nifedipine 20mg as a modified-release preparation.[272] Use the separate components – atenolol and an appropriate formulation of nifedipine. This will require splitting the dose and giving it several times a day. See individual monographs for details. Contact Pharmacy for advice if necessary.

Betahistine

Presentation
Tablets.

Administration – enteral tubes / swallowing difficulties
The tablets can be crushed and mixed with water for administration.[41] The drug is very soluble.[253] Follow the directions in section 3.5.

Betaine

Presentation
Tablets (special).
Powder.
Powder for oral solution (special).

Administration – enteral tubes
No information about the use of this medication via enteral feeding tubes has been located.

Administration – swallowing difficulties
Use the powder for oral solution (if available).[152] The powder should be mixed with water, juice, milk, formula or food until completely dissolved.[571]

Clinical guidance
Monitor plasma total homocysteine levels.[571]

Betamethasone

Presentation
Tablets.
Soluble tablets.
Injection.

Administration – enteral tubes / swallowing difficulties
Use the soluble tablets.[41] Follow the directions in section 3.5.

Bethanechol

Presentation
Tablets.
A suspension can be made by Pharmacy in some centres (see Appendix 1).[454]

Administration – enteral tubes
The tablets can be crushed and mixed with water for administration.[8,105] Follow the directions in section 3.5.

(monograph continues on next page)

No information about administering the suspension via enteral feeding tubes has been located.

Administration – swallowing difficulties
1st choice – Use the suspension (if available).[454]
2nd choice – The tablets can be crushed and mixed with water for administration.[8,105] Follow the directions in section 3.5.

Feed guidance
Bethanechol should be taken on an empty stomach.[136,624] Enteral feeds should be withheld for half an hour before and half an hour after each dose.[225]

Summary:-	Stop feed 30 minutes before dose
	Restart feed 30 minutes after dose

Withholding enteral feeds can compromise nutrition and interfere with blood glucose management. If the patient does not have a break in their feeding regimen during which bethanechol can be given, the Nutrition Team should be contacted to advise on management.

Bexarotene

Presentation
Capsule.

Clinical guidance
The contents of the gel-filled capsules are irritant. They should not be opened or chewed.[296]

Bezafibrate

Presentation
Tablets.
Film-coated tablets.
Modified-release tablets.

Administration – enteral tubes / swallowing difficulties
The 200mg (standard) tablet will disperse in water over 1-2 minutes, or can be crushed.[8,52,154] Follow the directions in section 3.5. If giving via enteral feeding tube, flush well after each dose. Bezalip® tablets are film-coated, and the coating may not disperse well in water, risking enteral tube blockage. When using Bezalip® tablets, ensure that the tablet is crushed well and the coating broken up before dispersing in water.

Do not crush the modified-release tablets.[52] Consider switching patients from the modified-release tablets to the standard tablets.

Bicalutamide

Presentation
Tablets.
Oral suspension (special).[542]

Administration – enteral tubes
Caution – Bicalutamide is an anti-androgen. Pregnant women should not handle crushed or dispersed tablets. Carers should wear protective clothing to minimise contact with crushed/dispersed tablets.
The tablets are very insoluble but can be crushed finely and mixed with water for administration.[46] Follow the directions in section 3.5.

No information on administering the suspension via enteral feeding tubes has been located.

(monograph continues on next page)

Administration – swallowing difficulties
<u>Caution</u> – Bicalutamide is an anti-androgen. Pregnant women should not handle crushed or dispersed tablets. Carers should wear protective clothing to minimise contact with crushed/dispersed tablets.
1st choice – Use the oral suspension (if available).
2nd choice – The tablets are very insoluble but can be crushed finely and mixed with water for administration.[46]

Biotin

Presentation
Tablets (named patient).
Injection (named patient).

Administration – enteral tubes
No information about the use of this medication via enteral feeding tubes has been located.

Administration – swallowing difficulties
The tablets may be crushed and mixed with a drink.[152]

Bisacodyl

Presentation
Enteric-coated tablets.
Suppositories.

Administration – enteral tubes / swallowing difficulties
Use the suppositories.

The tablet has an enteric coating, and is designed to release the drug in the colon where it has its effect.[291] Do not crush as it has an irritant effect on the stomach.[4,41,249]

Bisoprolol

Presentation
Tablets, film-coated tablets.
Oral solution (special).[542,582]

Administration – enteral tubes
1st choice – For short-term use consider using an alternative beta-blocker available as a parenteral formulation, e.g. metoprolol, labetalol, atenolol.
2nd choice – Change to atenolol, which has a syrup formulation. See atenolol monograph and follow the directions in section 3.6.
3rd choice – The tablets can be crushed finely and mixed with water for administration. The lower strength tablets will disperse in one to five minutes without crushing.[154] The higher strength tablets should be crushed before mixing with water.[154] Different brands may disperse at different rates.[358] Follow the directions in section 3.5. Flush well after each dose.[95]

Administration – swallowing difficulties
1st choice – Change to atenolol, which has a syrup formulation.
2nd choice – For short-term use consider using an alternative beta-blocker available as a parenteral formulation, e.g. metoprolol, labetalol, atenolol.
3rd choice – Use the oral solution (if available).
4th choice – The tablets can be crushed finely and mixed with water for administration. The lower strength tablets will disperse in one to five minutes without crushing.[154] The higher strength tablets should be crushed before mixing with water.[154] Different brands may disperse at different rates.[358] Follow the directions in section 3.5.

Additional notes
The Patient Information Leaflet of Cardicor® bisoprolol tablets states that the tablets should not be crushed. However the manufacturers confirm that there is no pharmaceutical reason why the tablets cannot be crushed, and they are aware that it is common (unlicensed) practice to do so.[348]

Bromazepam

Presentation
Tablets (not licensed in the UK).

Administration – enteral tubes / swallowing difficulties
The tablets will disperse in water for administration.[8] They disperse in less than a minute.[8] Follow the directions in section 3.5.

Bromocriptine

Presentation
Tablets, capsules.

Administration – enteral tubes / swallowing difficulties
The tablets can be dispersed in water for administration.[8,95] They disperse in one to five minutes.[154] Follow the directions in section 3.5. The drug must be protected from light, so give immediately, and flush well with water.[41]

Brompheniramine

Presentation
Syrup.

Administration – enteral tubes / swallowing difficulties
Use the syrup.[41] Follow the directions in section 3.6.

The liquid is not compatible with feeds, so flush well before and after each dose.[41]

Budesonide

Presentation
Capsules.
Granules.
Modified-release capsules.
Enema.

Administration – enteral tubes
The capsules can be opened, and the granular contents dispersed in fruit juice for administration.[105] Follow the directions in section 3.7.

The modified-release capsules are formulated for release in the ileum,[321] and they should not be opened for use via feeding tubes. The enema is for rectal use only and may not be suitable for most patients.

Administration – swallowing difficulties
1st choice – Use the granules, which should be placed on the tongue and then washed down with water without chewing.[588] This method may not be appropriate for patients with limited understanding or impaired ability to follow instructions.
2nd choice – For patients with swallowing difficulties, Entocort® CR capsules have been opened and the pellets mixed with orange juice for administration. The pellets should not be crushed, therefore this method may not be appropriate for patients with limited understanding or impaired ability to follow instructions.[132,138,152]

Feed guidance
Budesonide capsules and granules should be taken on an empty stomach.[624] Enteral feeds should be withheld for half an hour before and half an hour after each dose.[225]

Summary:-	Stop feed 30 minutes before dose
	Restart feed 30 minutes after dose

Withholding enteral feeds can compromise nutrition and interfere with blood glucose management. If the patient does not have a break in their feeding regimen during which budesonide can be given, the Nutrition Team should be contacted to advise on management.

Bumetanide

Presentation
Sugar-free liquid (contains sorbitol).
Tablets.
Injection.

Administration – enteral tubes
1st choice – Give by parenteral injection if appropriate.
2nd choice – Use the liquid. Follow the directions in section 3.6.
3rd choice – The tablets can be crushed and mixed with water for administration.[38,39,154] Follow the directions in section 3.5.

Administration – swallowing difficulties
1st choice – Use the liquid.
2nd choice – Give by parenteral injection if appropriate.
3rd choice – The tablets can be crushed and mixed with water for administration.[38,39,154] Follow the directions in section 3.5.

Bumetanide and amiloride (Burinex A®)

Presentation
Tablets (no longer available in the UK).

Clinical guidance
Burinex A® tablets contain amiloride 5mg and bumetanide 1mg.[272]
Use the separate components – see individual monographs for details.

Buprenorphine

Presentation
Sublingual tablets.
Transdermal patches.
Injection.

Administration – enteral tubes / swallowing difficulties
Use the patches or give by parenteral injection if appropriate. If the patient is safe to use the sublingual tablets and has a sufficiently moist mouth, these may continue to be used sublingually.

The sublingual tablets are not suitable to be administered via enteral feeding tube as the drug undergoes extensive first pass metabolism.[141]

Burinex A®

Presentation
Tablets (no longer available in the UK).

Clinical guidance
Burinex A® tablets contain amiloride 5mg and bumetanide 1mg.[272] Use the separate components – see individual monographs for details.

Buspirone

Presentation
Tablets.

Administration – enteral tubes / swallowing difficulties
The tablets can be crushed and dispersed in water for administration.[41] Without crushing they disperse in around five minutes.[154] Follow the directions in section 3.5.

Feed guidance
Buspirone plasma concentration may be increased by enteral feeding. The doses should be given at the same time each day in relation to feeding.[155]

Busulfan (Busulphan)

Presentation
Film-coated tablets.
A suspension can be made by Pharmacy in some centres.
Concentrate for infusion.

Administration – enteral tubes / swallowing difficulties
<u>Caution – cytotoxic.</u> The film-coating on the tablets protects carers from coming into contact with the cytotoxic drug.[297] The tablets should therefore not be crushed or divided. Contact Pharmacy for advice before giving.

A suspension can be made by Pharmacy in some centres.[138,455] Follow the directions in section 3.6.

Cabergoline

Presentation
Tablets.

Administration – enteral tubes / swallowing difficulties
The tablets can be crushed and mixed with water for administration.[105] Follow the directions in section 3.5.

Caffeine

Presentation
Sugar-free oral solution (unlicensed special).
Injection.

Administration – enteral tubes / swallowing difficulties
1st choice – Give by intravenous injection / infusion if appropriate.
2nd choice – Use the oral solution (if available). Follow the directions in section 3.6.

Calcium preparations

See:- Calcium and Vitamin D
       Calcium carbonate
       Calcium folinate
       Calcium glubionate and lactobionate
       Calcium gluconate
       Calcium resonium

Clinical guidance

Calcium salts are absorbed in the duodenum and proximal jejunum, and to a lesser extent in the distal segments of the small intestine. Absorption may therefore be reduced if they are administered into the jejunum.[176]

Calcium and Vitamin D

Presentation

Various.

Administration – enteral tubes

Contact Pharmacy for advice on equivalent doses. Consider using Cacit® D3 sachets.[132]

Administration – swallowing difficulties

1st choice – Use effervescent or liquid preparations.

2nd choice – Calcichew D3® and Calcichew D3® Forte will not disperse easily but will crush for administration to patients with swallowing problems who are not able to chew the tablets themselves.[358]

Calcium carbonate

Presentation
1.25g (500mg [12.6mmol] calcium) chewable tablets (Calcichew®).
1.25g (500mg [12.6mmol] calcium) effervescent tablets (Cacit®).
Oral solution (special).[582]
A suspension can be made by Pharmacy in some centres (see Appendix 1).[512]

Administration – enteral tubes
Use the effervescent tablets. Follow the directions in section 3.5.

No information about administering the suspension via enteral feeding tubes has been located. The chewable tablets should not be used.[94]

Administration – swallowing difficulties
1st choice – Use the effervescent tablets.
2nd choice – If the patient can safely chew, use the chewable tablets.
3rd choice – Use the suspension (if available).

Calcium folinate

Presentation
Tablets.
Injection.

Administration – enteral tubes / swallowing difficulties
1st choice – Give by parenteral injection if appropriate.
2nd choice – The tablets can be dispersed in water for administration.[40] They disperse immediately.[154] Follow the directions in section 3.5.
3rd choice – The injection can be given enterally.[152] Follow the directions in section 3.6.

Calcium glubionate and lactobionate

Presentation
108.3mg [2.7mmol] in 5mL syrup (Calcium-Sandoz).

Administration – enteral tubes / swallowing difficulties
Use the syrup.[104] Follow the directions in section 3.6.

Calcium gluconate

Presentation
600mg (53.4mg [1.35mmol] calcium) tablets (may not be available in the UK).
1g (89mg [2.25mmol] calcium) effervescent tablets.
Injection.

Administration – enteral tubes / swallowing difficulties
Use the effervescent tablets.[40,41] Follow the directions in section 3.5.

Feed guidance
Give enteral doses during a feeding break (hold enteral feeds for one hour before and one hour after dose).[41]

Summary:-	Stop feed 1 hour before dose
	Restart feed 1 hour after dose

Withholding enteral feeds can compromise nutrition and interfere with blood glucose management. If the patient does not have a break in their feeding regimen during which calcium gluconate can be given, the Nutrition Team should be contacted to advise on management.

Calcium resonium

Presentation
Powder for oral administration.
Enemas.

Administration – enteral tubes / swallowing difficulties
Use the enemas rectally.[105]

The powder for oral administration should not be given via enteral feeding tubes due to the risk of tube blockage.[105]

Candesartan

Presentation
Tablets.
Sugar-free oral suspension (unlicensed special).[585]

Administration – enteral tubes
The tablets can be crushed and mixed with water for administration.[53] Without crushing they disperse in around five minutes.[154] Follow the directions in section 3.5. No information has been located on whether candesartan is likely to block enteral feeding tubes.[53]

No information on administering the suspension via enteral feeding tubes has been located.

Administration – swallowing difficulties
1st choice – Use the suspension (if available).
2nd choice – The tablets can be crushed and mixed with water for administration.[53] Without crushing they disperse in around five minutes.[154] Follow the directions in section 3.5.

Capecitabine

Presentation
Film-coated tablets.

Administration – enteral tubes / swallowing difficulties
The tablets can be dispersed in lukewarm (not hot) water (50mL for each 500mg tablet[611]). They will disperse in 15 minutes. Follow the directions in section 3.5. The tablets have a bitter taste which can be masked with raspberry or blackcurrant juice if desired for patients with swallowing difficulties. Do not use citric juices.[275,611]

Feed guidance
Capecitabine should be taken after food.[276]

Capozide®

Clinical guidance
Capozide® tablets contain captopril and hydrochlorothiazide in various dosages.[272] Use captopril as a separate component, and an appropriate alternative thiazide diuretic, e.g. bendroflumethiazide. See individual monographs for details.

Captopril

Presentation
Tablets.
Liquid (special).[150,542,582]
A suspension can be made by Pharmacy in some centres (see Appendix 1).[456,457,573]

Administration – enteral tubes
1st choice – The tablets will disperse in water in one to five minutes.[7,8,39,40,152,154] Follow the directions in section 3.5. A fine powder sediment may be left, so flush well after each dose.[104]
2nd choice – A suspension can be made by Pharmacy in some centres.[155,456,457,458] Follow the directions in section 3.6.

(monograph continues on next page)

Administration – swallowing difficulties
1st choice – A suspension can be made by Pharmacy in some centres.[155,456,457,458]
2nd choice – The tablets will disperse in water in one to five minutes.[7,8,39,40,152,154] Follow the directions in section 3.5.

Clinical guidance
Captopril tablets have been given sublingually. To use this route, the dose should be halved and given twice as frequently, i.e. 25mg twice daily becomes 12.5mg four times daily.[105] Monitor blood pressure.

Captopril is absorbed in the proximal small intestine.[350] Monitor blood pressure if administering into the jejunum in case of poor absorption.

Feed guidance
Absorption of captopril can be decreased by concomitant food or milk.[2] If clinical effect is insufficient, consider withholding enteral feeds for half an hour before and half an hour after each dose.[225]

Captopril and hydrochlorothiazide (Co-zidocapt)

Presentation
Tablets.

Clinical guidance
Co-zidocapt tablets contain captopril and hydrochlorothiazide in various dosages.[272] Use captopril as a separate component, and an appropriate alternative thiazide diuretic, e.g. bendroflumethiazide. See individual monographs for details.

Carace Plus®

Presentation
Tablets.

Clinical guidance
Carace Plus® tablets contain lisinopril and hydrochlorothiazide in various dosages.[272] Use lisinopril as a separate component, and an appropriate thiazide diuretic, e.g. bendroflumethiazide. See individual monographs for details.

Carbamazepine

Presentation
Tablets.
Chewtabs.
Liquid (contains sorbitol).
Suppositories.
Modified-release tablets.

Administration – enteral tubes
1st choice – Use the suppositories if possible. They are licensed for a maximum of seven days (see "Clinical guidance", below), at a maximum dose of 1g/day.[35]
2nd choice – Use the liquid (contains sorbitol[104]), and dilute with an equal volume of water before administration to prevent adsorption to the feeding tube.[10,104,564] Follow the directions in section 3.6.

Administration – swallowing difficulties
Use the suppositories or the liquid (contains sorbitol[104]).

Clinical guidance
If changing from Retard formulations to the liquid preparation, give the same total daily dose but increase the frequency of administration. Consider monitoring drug levels when doses have been changed or if there is concern about under / over-dosing.

(monograph continues on next page)

Carbamazepine MR tablet 400mg twice a day	equivalent to	Carbamazepine liquid 200mg four times a day
100mg tablet / liquid	equivalent to	125mg suppository[90]

Carbamazepine is adsorbed onto PVC feeding tubes.[4,26,564] However it has been shown that when the suspension is diluted with an equal volume of water, loss is negligible.[10]

The suppositories have a maximum licensed duration of treatment of seven days. The reason for this is that clinical trials were only carried out for this length of time. The manufacturers warn that there may be a risk of rectal irritation if the suppositories are used for longer than seven days.[288]

The suppositories have a maximum licensed dose of 1g/day. The reason for this is that dose absorption from rectal doses higher than 300mg is not consistent. It should usually be possible to obtain therapeutic levels within the licensed dosage range.[288]

Changing formulations / product manufacturer
The MHRA has issued guidance recommending that patients on carbamazepine (when used for seizures) are maintained on a specific manufacturer's product, due to variability in product characteristics which may lead to a loss of seizure control when switching between brands / manufacturers.[651] When managing patients with enteral tubes or swallowing difficulties it may not be possible to maintain the patient on their previous preparation due to the need to change to an appropriate formulation. However all product switches should be carried out with care and close monitoring, and where possible patients should be maintained from then onwards on a single manufacturer's product.

Feed guidance
Carbamazepine is slowly and irregularly absorbed from the gastrointestinal tract.[9] Care must be taken to administer carbamazepine at the same time and in the same manner each day so that variations in the extent of drug absorption are minimised.

(monograph continues on next page)

Some authors have raised questions about the possibility of an interaction between carbamazepine and enteral feeds, however other studies have suggested that this isn't the case.[26,104,244] A small study of the pharmacokinetics of nasogastric carbamazepine with concomitant enteral feeding showed that the absorption of carbamazepine was generally slower than when the drug was given orally in the fasting state.[327] The authors postulate that the reduced rate of absorption may be beneficial where patients experience unwanted side effects.[327]

The possibility of enteral feed interactions should be considered in any patient who fails to achieve satisfactory carbamazepine levels. An alteration in carbamazepine handling should be considered in any patient who commences or discontinues enteral feeds, and drug level monitoring should be carried out if appropriate.

Carbamylglutamate

Presentation
Dispersible tablets.

Administration – enteral tubes / swallowing difficulties
Use the dispersible tablets.[152] Follow the directions in section 3.5.

Carbimazole

Presentation
Tablets.
Suspension (special[150,155]).

Administration – enteral tubes / swallowing difficulties
The tablets can be crushed and dispersed in water for administration.[95] Follow the directions in section 3.5.

Carbocisteine

Presentation
Capsules.
Liquid.

Administration – enteral tubes / swallowing difficulties
Use the liquid.[41] Follow the directions in section 3.6.

Carvedilol

Presentation
Tablets.

Administration – enteral tubes / swallowing difficulties
The tablets can be dispersed to form a suspension in water.[52] They disperse in one to five minutes.[154] Follow the directions in section 3.5. Use immediately.[52]

Clinical guidance
Monitor blood pressure.[558]

Feed guidance
Giving carvedilol with food may help to decrease the risk of orthostatic hypotension by reducing the rate at which the medication is absorbed.[176]

Cefadroxil

Presentation
Capsules.
Suspension.

Administration – enteral tubes / swallowing difficulties
Use the suspension.[94] Follow the directions in section 3.6.

Cefalexin (Cephalexin)

Presentation
Tablets, capsules.
Suspension, syrup.

Administration – enteral tubes / swallowing difficulties
Use the suspension, which should be diluted before administration.[104] Follow the directions in section 3.6.

Clinical guidance
There may be reduced absorption when administered directly into the jejunum, as the primary site of cefalexin absorption is the duodenum.[6,104,137] Use doses at the higher end of the dose range.

Cefalexin absorption is slightly reduced when it is taken with food, but this is unlikely to be clinically significant.[292] Monitor for effect. The suspension is hyperosmolar, and may cause diarrhoea when administered into the jejunum.[26,155]

Cefixime

Presentation
Film-coated tablets.
Suspension.

Administration – enteral tubes / swallowing difficulties
Use the suspension.[41] Follow the directions in section 3.6. Further dilution of the suspension is not recommended.[298]

Cefpodoxime

Presentation
Film-coated tablets (no longer available in the UK).
Suspension (no longer available in the UK).

Administration – enteral tubes / swallowing difficulties
Use the suspension (if available).[79] Follow the directions in section 3.6.

Cefradine (Cephradine)

Presentation
Capsules.
Suspension.
Injection.

Administration – enteral tubes
1st choice – Give by parenteral injection if appropriate.
2nd choice – Use the suspension.[41] Follow the directions in section 3.6.

Administration – swallowing difficulties
1st choice – Use the suspension.[41]
2nd choice – Give by parenteral injection if appropriate.

Cefuroxime

Presentation
Film-coated tablets.
Suspension.
Injection.

Administration – NG / PEG tubes
1st choice – Give by parenteral injection if appropriate.
2nd choice – For patients with enteral tubes terminating in the stomach, use the suspension.[41] Follow the directions in section 3.6. The suspension may be too viscous to administer via fine-bore tubes, in which case use the 3rd choice method below.
3rd choice – For patients with enteral tubes terminating in the stomach, the tablets can be dispersed in water.[8,138] Follow the directions in section 3.5.

Administration – NJ / PEJ / PEGJ tubes
Cefuroxime is not suitable to be administered via enteral feeding tubes terminating in the jejunum as absorption is reduced.[155]

Give by parenteral injection if appropriate.

(monograph continues on next page)

Administration – swallowing difficulties
1st choice – Use the suspension.
2nd choice – Give by parenteral injection if appropriate.

Cefuroxime tastes unpleasant, and therefore crushing the tablets to administer to patients with swallowing difficulties is not recommended.[558,560]

Celecoxib

Presentation
Capsules.

Administration – enteral tubes
Consider switching to an alternative therapy available via a non-enteral route, e.g. rectal diclofenac, or as a liquid, e.g. ibuprofen. It may be advisable to provide gastic protection, e.g. ranitidine, if moving to a non-selective NSAID.

Administration – swallowing difficulties
The capsules have been opened and the contents added to cold or room-temperature apple sauce for administration to patients with swallowing difficulties.[355]

Celiprolol

Presentation
Tablets.

Administration – enteral tubes / swallowing difficulties
1st choice – For long-term use, consider switching to an alternative beta-blocker available as a liquid, e.g. atenolol.
2nd choice – The tablets can be dispersed in water for administration.[55] They disperse in one to five minutes.[8,154] Follow the directions in section 3.5. Some brands of tablet are film-coated, so crush finely if giving via enteral feeding tube to prevent the coating blocking the tube.[55]

(monograph continues on next page)

Feed guidance
Celiprolol should be taken on an empty stomach.[624] Enteral feeds should be withheld for half an hour before and half an hour after each dose.[225]

Summary:-	Stop feed 30 minutes before dose
	Restart feed 30 minutes after dose

Withholding enteral feeds can compromise nutrition and interfere with blood glucose management. If the patient does not have a break in their feeding regimen during which celiprolol can be given, the Nutrition Team should be contacted to advise on management.

Centyl K®

Presentation
Sugar-coated tablets (no longer available in the UK).

Clinical guidance
Centyl K® tablets contain bendroflumethiazide 2.5mg and potassium 7.7mmol in a modified-release preparation.[272] Use the separate components – bendroflumethiazide and an appropriate standard-release formulation of potassium. See individual monographs for details. Contact Pharmacy for advice if necessary.

Cetirizine

Presentation
Tablets.
Oral solution.

Administration – enteral tubes / swallowing difficulties
Use the oral solution.[94,104] Follow the directions in section 3.6.

The manufacturers have no information on crushing the tablets.[357]

Chenodeoxycholic acid

Presentation
Capsules (named patient).

Administration – enteral tubes
No information about the use of this medication via enteral feeding tubes has been located.

Administration – swallowing difficulties
A suspension can be prepared by adding the contents of one 250mg capsule to 25mL of sodium bicarbonate solution 8.4% (1mmol/mL). This should be used immediately.[152]

Chloral hydrate

Presentation
Tablets (cloral betaine).
Elixir.
Oral syrup (special).[542,582]

Administration – enteral tubes
Use the elixir.[41,104] It is light sensitive, so give immediately.[41] Follow the directions in section 3.6.

Administration – swallowing difficulties
1st choice – Use the elixir.[41,104] It is light sensitive, so give immediately.[41]
2nd choice – Use the oral syrup (if available).

Liquid dosage	=	15-45mL with water or milk at bedtime.[106]

Chlorambucil

Presentation
Film-coated tablets.
A suspension can be made by Pharmacy in some centres.

Administration – enteral tubes / swallowing difficulties
<u>Caution – cytotoxic.</u> Contact Pharmacy for advice before giving.
A suspension can be made by Pharmacy in some centres.[138] Follow the directions in section 3.6.

Chloramphenicol

Presentation
Capsules.
Injection.

Administration – enteral tubes / swallowing difficulties
1st choice – Give by parenteral injection if possible.
2nd choice – Open the capsules and mix the contents with water.[133]
Follow the directions in section 3.7.

Chlordiazepoxide

Presentation
Tablets, capsules.

Administration – enteral tubes / swallowing difficulties
1st choice – Use an alternative agent available for administration by a non-enteral route if possible (e.g. diazepam).
2nd choice – Open the capsules and mix the contents with water.[104]
Follow the directions in section 3.7.

The tablets have been crushed in some centres,[132] but this is not recommended.

Chloroquine

Presentation
250mg chloroquine phosphate (155mg chloroquine base) tablets.
200mg chloroquine sulphate (150mg chloroquine base) film-coated tablets.
68mg/5mL chloroquine sulphate (50mg/5mL chloroquine base) syrup.
54.5mg/mL chloroquine sulphate (40mg/mL chloroquine base) injection (no longer available in the UK).

Administration – enteral tubes / swallowing difficulties
1st choice – Use the syrup.[41] Follow the directions in section 3.6.
2nd choice – The tablets can be crushed and dispersed in water for administration,[105,152] although the drug has a very bitter taste.[79] They should be crushed well to ensure that the film-coating is broken up. Without crushing they will disperse in one to five minutes (different brands may vary).[8,154] Follow the directions in section 3.5. Protect from light.[41]

The liquid should not be given at the same time as antacids.[79]

Feed guidance
The gastrointestinal adverse effects of chloroquine may be reduced by taking it with food.[176]

Chlorothiazide

Presentation
Tablets.
Suspension.
Oral solution (special).[582,659]

Administration – enteral tubes
1st choice – Use the suspension. Follow the directions in section 3.6.
2nd choice – The tablets will disperse in water for administration.[7,8,40] They disperse in less than a minute.[8] Follow the directions in section 3.5.
3rd choice – Use the special oral solution (if available). Follow the directions in section 3.6.

(monograph continues on next page)

Administration – swallowing difficulties
1st choice – Use the suspension.
2nd choice – Use the special oral solution (if available).
3rd choice – The tablets will disperse in water for administration.[7,8,40]
They disperse in less than a minute.[8] Follow the directions in section 3.5.

Chlorphenamine (Chlorpheniramine)

Presentation
Tablets.
Syrup, oral solution.
Injection.

Administration – enteral tubes
1st choice – Give by parenteral injection if appropriate.
2nd choice – Use the syrup.[40,94,104] Protect from light.[41] Follow the directions in section 3.6.
3rd choice – The injection can be given enterally.[40,164] Follow the directions in section 3.6.

Administration – swallowing difficulties
1st choice – Use the syrup.[40,94,104] Protect from light.[41]
2nd choice – Give by parenteral injection if appropriate.
3rd choice – The injection can be given enterally.[40,164] Follow the directions in section 3.6.

Chlorpromazine

Presentation
Coated tablets.
Oral solution, suspension (some contain sorbitol).
Syrup, oral solution (special).[542]
Injection.
Suppositories (unlicensed).

Administration – enteral tubes
1st choice – Use the suppositories if possible. A dose adjustment is necessary (see below).
2nd choice – Use the oral solution.[94,104] Follow the directions in section 3.6.

Administration – swallowing difficulties
1st choice – Use the oral solution.[94,104]
2nd choice – Use the suppositories if possible. A dose adjustment is necessary (see below).

Carers should avoid direct contact with chlorpromazine as contact sensitisation may occur,[132,152,213] therefore the tablets should not be crushed.

100mg (base) suppository = 40-50mg (hydrochloride) tablet.[136]

Feed guidance
Chlorpromazine has been reported as being incompatible with some enteral feeds, so ensure enteral feeding tubes are flushed well before and after each dose.[222]

Chlortalidone (Chlorthalidone)

Presentation
Tablets.

Administration – enteral tubes / swallowing difficulties
The tablets will disperse in water.[7,8,40] They disperse in less than two minutes.[8,154] Follow the directions in section 3.5. A fine powder sediment may be left, so if giving via enteral feeding tube, flush the tube well with water after administration.[104]

Ciclosporin (Cyclosporin)

Presentation
Capsules.
Oral solution.
Concentrate for infusion.

Administration – enteral tubes
1st choice – Give by intravenous infusion if appropriate.
2nd choice – Administer ciclosporin oral solution.[189,190] Do not flush with water after administering the ciclosporin solution but use the same volume of orange juice instead.

Administration – swallowing difficulties
Administer ciclosporin oral solution. The solution should be diluted before use, either with water, or with orange or apple juice to improve taste.[104,235] Do NOT use grapefruit juice.[549]

Clinical guidance
Due to the oily component of the ciclosporin solution, adherence to enteral feeding tubes may occur and subtherapeutic doses are likely. Monitor drug levels closely.

Grapefruit juice can interact with ciclosporin, increasing ciclosporin levels.[549]

Dose equivalence depends on which brand of ciclosporin was used previously. Contact Pharmacy for advice. Neoral® soft gelatin capsules and Neoral® oral solution are bioequivalent.[509]

(monograph continues on next page)

150mg Neoral® capsule = 50mg Sandimmun® IV concentrate.[430]

When giving via enteral feeding tube, leave a time gap of one hour before administering the next drug down the tube.

Cilazapril

Presentation
Film-coated tablets.

Administration – enteral tubes / swallowing difficulties
The tablets can be crushed and mixed with water for administration.[105] Follow the directions in section 3.5.

Cimetidine

Presentation
Tablets.
Syrup, oral solution.
Injection (no longer available in the UK).

Administration – enteral tubes
1st choice – Consider giving by parenteral injection (if available).
2nd choice – Use the syrup, diluted with an equal amount of water before administration.[133] Follow the directions in section 3.6.
3rd choice – The injection is suitable to be given enterally.[6,40] Follow the directions in section 3.6.

There may be reduced absorption when cimetidine is administered directly into the jejunum.[6,104]

Administration – swallowing difficulties
1st choice – Use the syrup.
2nd choice – Consider giving by parenteral injection (if available).
3rd choice – The injection is suitable to be given enterally.[6,40] Follow the directions in section 3.6.

(monograph continues on next page)

Feed guidance
Cimetidine syrup is incompatible with feeds so allow an enteral feeding gap of one hour before and one hour after each dose.[41]

Summary:-	Stop feed 1 hour before dose
	Restart feed 1 hour after dose

Withholding enteral feeds can compromise nutrition and interfere with blood glucose management. If the patient does not have a break in their feeding regimen during which cimetidine can be given, the Nutrition Team should be contacted to advise on management.

Cinnarizine

Presentation
Tablets, capsules.

Administration – enteral tubes / swallowing difficulties
The tablets can be dispersed in water for administration.[41,95] They disperse within one minute.[154] Follow the directions in section 3.5. The capsules have been opened in some centres.[133] Follow the directions in section 3.7.

Ciprofibrate

Presentation
Tablets.

Administration – enteral tubes / swallowing difficulties
The tablets can be crushed and mixed with water for administration.[104,105] Follow the directions in section 3.5.

Ciprofloxacin

Presentation
Tablets.
Intravenous infusion.
Suspension.

Administration – NG / PEG tubes
1st choice – Give by parenteral infusion.
2nd choice – The tablets will disperse in deionised water.[7,40,43] The 250mg tablets disperse in one to five minutes.[154] The 500mg tablets disperse in around five minutes.[154] The 750mg tablets should be crushed and then dispersed in deionised water.[281] Follow the directions in section 3.5. Flush the enteral tube after each dose with 65mL deionised water.

Do not use the suspension, as it is very thick and may block the enteral tube.[43]

Administration – NJ / PEJ / PEGJ tubes
1st choice – Give by parenteral infusion.
2nd choice – The tablets will disperse in deionised water.[7,40,43] The 250mg tablets disperse in one to five minutes.[154] The 500mg tablets disperse in around five minutes.[154] The 750mg tablets should be crushed and then dispersed in deionised water.[281] Follow the directions in section 3.5. Flush the enteral tube after each dose with 65mL deionised water.

Ciprofloxacin is believed to be absorbed in the duodenum[15] and not in the jejunum, therefore higher doses should be used if administered through an enteral tube terminating in the jejunum.[6] Some sources suggest that the reduction in absorption is so pronounced (particularly in the presence of enteral feeds) that an alternative route or alternative drug should be used.[193] Contact Pharmacy for advice.

Do not use the suspension, as it is very thick and may block the enteral tube.[43]

(monograph continues on next page)

Administration – swallowing difficulties

Always use the suspension for patients with swallowing difficulties as the crushed tablets have an extremely unpleasant taste.[43,560]

Clinical guidance

Use doses at the higher end of the normal range in order to compensate for lower absorption.[87,94,281]

Tap water is not suitable to use for dilution and flushing, as minerals in the tap water may bind with ciprofloxacin and decrease the amount of drug absorbed.[36,631]

Feed guidance

Ciprofloxacin interacts with enteral feeds to produce insoluble chelates,[11,193,225] and the absorption of the drug is significantly reduced. This may be particularly significant when it is administered directly into the jejunum.[155] A feeding break of two hours before and two hours after the administration of ciprofloxacin via any type of enteral feeding tube is recommended.[13,631] It has been shown that the absorption is reduced by 28% when administered with Ensure®[11] and by 33% when administered with Osmolite®.[14] Some studies have shown AUC reductions of up to 67% when ciprofloxacin is given with concomitant enteral feeds.[193]

Summary:-	Stop feed 2 hours before dose
	Restart feed 2 hours after dose

Withholding enteral feeds can compromise nutrition and interfere with blood glucose management. If the patient does not have a break in their feeding regimen during which ciprofloxacin can be given, the Nutrition Team should be contacted to advise on management.

Citalopram

Presentation
Tablets.
Oral drops.

Administration – enteral tubes / swallowing difficulties
1st choice – Use the drops. The bottle should be inverted, and the drops will flow automatically – do not shake the bottle. The required number of drops should be mixed with water, orange juice, or apple juice before administration.[123]

8mg (4 drops) of the oral drops	equivalent to	10mg tablet.[93]

2nd choice – The tablets have been crushed and dispersed in water if the drops are unavailable, but they may taste unpleasant.[132] Follow the directions in section 3.5. If giving via enteral feeding tube, flush well following administration.[155]

Clinical guidance
Citalopram is absorbed from the small intestine. Although the exact site of absorption is unknown, the drug is probably mostly absorbed from the ileum,[416] and it is therefore not anticipated that there will be any absorption problems if the drug is given via an enteral tube terminating in the jejunum.

Clarithromycin

Presentation
Tablets.
Modified-release tablets.
Granules.
Suspension.
Intravenous infusion.

Administration – enteral tubes
1st choice – Give by intravenous infusion if possible.
2nd choice – The suspension is viscous and may block the tube. If the suspension has to be used, dilute the dose with the same volume of water immediately prior to administration.[56,191] Follow the directions in section 3.6.

Do not dilute the suspension beyond manufacturer's recommendations until the point of administration, as dilution of the preservative will occur, affecting the expiry of the product.[56]

Administration – swallowing difficulties
Give by intravenous infusion, or use the suspension or the granules.

Clinical guidance
Clarithromycin has been shown to be reasonably well absorbed following administration of the suspension through a nasogastric tube.[299] Clarithromycin is absorbed throughout the whole gastrointestinal tract.[415]

Convert patients on the modified-release tablets to the standard-release by dividing the dose and giving twice daily.

Clindamycin

Presentation
Capsules.
Suspension (unlicensed).
Injection.

Administration – enteral tubes
1st choice – Give by parenteral injection if appropriate.
2nd choice – The capsules can be opened and the contents dispersed in water.[57] Give immediately. Follow the directions in section 3.7.
3rd choice – Use the suspension (if available).[138] Follow the directions in section 3.6.

Administration – swallowing difficulties
Use the suspension (if available). The capsule contents taste extremely unpleasant and may be unpalatable for oral administration in patients with swallowing difficulties.[57] The capsule contents have been mixed with grape juice or maple syrup.[132]

Clobazam

Presentation
Tablets.
Oral suspension.[610]
Oral solution (special).[542,582]
A suspension can be made by Pharmacy in some centres.[573]

Administration – enteral tubes
The tablets can be dispersed in water for administration.[105] They disperse in one to five minutes.[8,154] Take care to ensure that the whole dose is administered.[563] Follow the directions in section 3.5. Flush well.

No information on administering the oral suspension or the solution via enteral feeding tubes has been located.

(monograph continues on next page)

Administration – swallowing difficulties

1st choice – Use the oral suspension.

2nd choice – Use the (special) oral solution (if available).

3rd choice – A suspension can be made by Pharmacy in some centres.

4th choice – The tablets can be dispersed in water for administration.[105] They disperse in one to five minutes.[8,154] Take care to ensure that the whole dose is administered.[563] Follow the directions in section 3.5. The crushed / dispersed tablets taste unpleasant.[132]

A method of extemporaneously preparing an oral liquid with an expiry of 14 days has been described.[573]

Clinical guidance

Clobazam is very hard to suspend, and there has been a case report of fitting following the switching of a patient from the tablet formulation to an extemporaneous liquid product.[563] For this reason, it is advised that care is taken to ensure that the whole dose is administered.

Changing formulations / product manufacturer

The MHRA has issued guidance recommending that (where possible) patients on clobazam (when used for seizures) are maintained on a specific manufacturer's product, due to variability in product characteristics which may lead to a loss of seizure control when switching between brands / manufacturers.[651] When managing patients with enteral tubes or swallowing difficulties it may not be possible to maintain the patient on their previous preparation due to the need to change to an appropriate formulation. However all product switches should be carried out with care and close monitoring, and where possible patients should be maintained from then onwards on a single manufacturer's product.

Clomethiazole (Chlormethiazole)

Presentation
Capsules.
Syrup (may not be available in the UK).
Liquid (special).[535]

Administration – enteral tubes
The syrup interacts with enteral feeding tubes, and should not be used for patients with enteral tubes in situ.[41] Contact Pharmacy for advice on alternative medications.

Administration – swallowing difficulties
Use the syrup (if available) or the liquid.

1 capsule	equivalent to	5mL syrup[431]

Clomipramine

Presentation
Capsules.
Modified-release tablets.
Liquid.

Administration – enteral tubes / swallowing difficulties
1st choice – Use the liquid.[104] Follow the directions in section 3.6.
2nd choice – The capsules can be opened, and the contents dispersed in water for administration.[104] Follow the directions in section 3.7.

Do not crush the modified-release tablets. They are not suitable for enteral tube administration. Contact Pharmacy for advice.

Clinical guidance
Tricyclic antidepressants can decrease gastric emptying.[2]

75mg daily MR tablet	equivalent to	75mg/day capsules/liquid[431]
Capsules/liquid may need to be given in divided doses		

Clonazepam

Presentation
Tablets.
Oral drops (unlicensed).
Oral solution.[583]
Oral solution (special).[582]
A suspension can be made by Pharmacy in some centres (see Appendix 1).[451,573]
Injection (no longer available in the UK).

Administration – enteral tubes
1st choice – The tablets can be dispersed in at least 30mL of water for administration[7,40,94,104,225] (the large volume is necessary to prevent binding to the enteral tube[132]). They disperse in less than two minutes.[8,154] Follow the directions in section 3.5.
2nd choice – A suspension can be made by Pharmacy in some centres.[356,451] Follow the directions in section 3.6.
3rd choice – The injection (if available) can be given enterally after dilution with 1mL Water for Injections.[40,152] Follow the directions in section 3.6.

Administration – swallowing difficulties
1st choice – Use the oral solution. See additional information below.
2nd choice – A suspension can be made by Pharmacy in some centres.
3rd choice – Use the oral drops or the special oral solution. See additional information below.

Do not mix the drops or the solution with water or any other diluent as this may cause the drug to precipitate out.[105]

(monograph continues on next page)

Clinical guidance
Changing formulations / product manufacturer
The MHRA has issued guidance recommending that (where possible) patients on clonazepam (when used for seizures) are maintained on a specific manufacturer's product, due to variability in product characteristics which may lead to a loss of seizure control when switching between brands / manufacturers.[651] When managing patients with enteral tubes or swallowing difficulties it may not be possible to maintain the patient on their previous preparation due to the need to change to an appropriate formulation. However all product switches should be carried out with care and close monitoring, and where possible patients should be maintained from then onwards on a single manufacturer's product.

Clonidine

Presentation
Tablets.
A suspension can be made by Pharmacy in some centres (see Appendix 1).[459,573]
Transdermal plasters (unlicensed).
Injection.

Administration – enteral tubes
1st choice – The tablets have been crushed in some centres[8,132,152,225], although there is little information available on this. Follow the directions in section 3.5.
2nd choice – A suspension can be made by Pharmacy in some centres.[459] Follow the directions in section 3.6.
3rd choice – The injection can be administered via enteral feeding tubes, either neat, or diluted with water prior to administration.[100,130] The manufacturers have data to suggest that when prepared aseptically, the injection diluted with water is stable for 7 days.[130]

(monograph continues on next page)

Administration – swallowing difficulties

1st choice – A suspension can be made by Pharmacy in some centres.[459]

2nd choice – The tablets have been crushed in some centres[8,132,152,225], although there is little information available on this. Follow the directions in section 3.5.

3rd choice – The injection can be administered orally.[100] It can either be given neat, or diluted with water prior to administration.[130] The manufacturers have data to suggest that when prepared aseptically, the injection diluted with water is stable for 7 days. The injection is tasteless, but if desired it can be mixed with fruit juice for oral administration.[130]

The transdermal plasters are indicated for the management of hypertension. However onset of action takes 2-3 days, and so these are probably only suitable when the period for which the patient needs them can be planned for, or is prolonged.[96]

Clopidogrel

Presentation
Tablets.
Oral solution (special).[542]
A suspension can be made by Pharmacy in some centres (see Appendix 1).[537]

Administration – enteral tubes
The tablets can be crushed and dispersed in water for administration.[42] Most brands disperse in one to five minutes without crushing, however some take longer.[154] Follow the directions in section 3.5.

No information about using the solution or the suspension via enteral feeding tubes has been located.

(monograph continues on next page)

Administration – swallowing difficulties

1st choice – A suspension can be made by Pharmacy in some centres.

2nd choice – Use the oral solution (if available).

3rd choice – The tablets can be crushed and dispersed in water for administration.[42] Most brands disperse in one to five minutes without crushing, however some take longer.[154] Follow the directions in section 3.5.

Clozapine

Presentation

Tablets.

Suspension (contains sorbitol).

A suspension can be made by Pharmacy in some centres (see Appendix 1).[512,573]

Administration – enteral tubes / swallowing difficulties

1st choice – Use the licensed suspension. Shake well before use. The suspension can be diluted with water before administration if desired.[546] Follow the directions in section 3.6.

2nd choice – A suspension can be made by Pharmacy in some centres.[138,512] Follow the directions in section 3.6.

3rd choice – The tablets have been crushed and mixed with water for administration.[105] This is not recommended, however. The powder is not soluble.[132] Contact Pharmacy for advice.

Co-amilofruse

Presentation

Tablets.

Administration – enteral tubes / swallowing difficulties

1st choice – Give the components (furosemide and amiloride) separately as both are available as liquids. See individual monographs for details. Follow the directions in section 3.6.

2nd choice – The tablets can be dispersed in water for administration.[39,40] They disperse within one minute.[154] Follow the directions in section 3.5.

Co-amilozide

Presentation
Tablets.

Administration – enteral tubes / swallowing difficulties
The tablets can be crushed and dispersed in water for administration.[105] Most brands disperse immediately.[154] Follow the directions in section 3.5.

Co-amoxiclav

Presentation
Tablets.
Dispersible tablets (250/125) (discontinued).
Suspension (125/31, 250/62, 400/57).
Injection.

Administration – NG / PEG tubes
1st choice – Give by parenteral injection / infusion.
2nd choice – Use the dispersible tablets (if available). Follow the directions in section 3.5.
3rd choice – Use the suspension and dilute with an equal volume of water before administration to avoid "caking".[94,104] See "Clinical guidance" below for information on equivalent doses. Follow the directions in section 3.6.

There is insufficient clavulanic acid in 5mL of the 250/62 suspension for adult patients. Adult patients requiring co-amoxiclav suspension require at least 10mL of the 250/62 suspension per dose[591]

(monograph continues on next page)

Administration – NJ / PEJ / PEGJ tubes
Give by parenteral injection / infusion.

It is unclear exactly where co-amoxiclav is absorbed in the gastrointestinal tract, but one report states that most of the drug is absorbed in the upper small intestine, and that there is poor colonic absorption.[427] For this reason it is recommended that patients with enteral feeding tubes terminating in the jejunum should only receive co-amoxiclav parenterally. If it is considered necessary to give the antibiotic through the enteral tube, the dispersible tablets should be used (if available), and the patient should be monitored for appropriate response to the treatment.

Administration – swallowing difficulties
Give by parenteral injection / infusion, or use the suspension.

There is insufficient clavulanic acid in 5mL of the 250/62 suspension for adult patients. Adult patients requiring co-amoxiclav suspension require at least 10mL of the 250/62 suspension per dose[591]

Clinical guidance
The tablets cannot be directly converted to suspension. The proportions of the two drugs in the medication (amoxicillin and clavulanic acid) are different in the two preparations. Contact Pharmacy for advice.

| 375mg co-amoxiclav tablet | equivalent to | 10mL co-amoxiclav |
| & 250mg amoxicillin capsule | | 250/62 suspension |

CoAprovel®

Presentation
Film-coated tablets.

Clinical guidance
CoAprovel® tablets contain irbesartan and hydrochlorothiazide at various dosages.[272] Use irbesartan as a separate component and an appropriate alternative thiazide diuretic, e.g. bendroflumethiazide. See individual monographs for details.

Co-beneldopa (Madopar)

Presentation
Capsules.
Dispersible tablets.
Modified-release capsules.

Administration – enteral tubes / swallowing difficulties
Use the dispersible tablets. Follow the directions in section 3.5.

Do not open either type of the capsules (modified-release or standard).[104]

Clinical guidance
Dispersible tablets have a faster onset of action and shorter duration of action than modified-release capsules and a direct substitution cannot occur. Contact Pharmacy for advice on dosage conversion.

If changing from capsules to dispersible tablets a direct changeover is acceptable, but the patient should be monitored for any change in effect as there may be an altered bioavailability. It may be appropriate to prescribe a small "when-required" dose to cover any unexpected "on-off" effects.

Levodopa is mainly absorbed in the jejunum. Drug effect may be particularly unpredictable in patients with enteral tubes terminating in the jejunum.[155]

Feed guidance
Co-beneldopa's absorption may be enhanced by interactions with enteral feed proteins. To reduce fluctuations in effect, doses should be given at the same time each day in relation to the feed regimen.[135]

Co-careldopa (Sinemet®)

Presentation
Tablets.
Modified-release tablets.
Oral solution (special).[582]
A suspension can be made by Pharmacy in some centres (see Appendix 1).[528,573]

Administration – enteral tubes
1st choice – The standard Sinemet® tablets will disperse in water for administration down enteral feeding tubes.[8,49] Lower strengths disperse within one minute.[154] The 25/250 strength disperse in one to five minutes.[154] Follow the directions in section 3.5.
2nd choice – Convert the patient onto co-beneldopa dispersible tablets. Contact Pharmacy for advice.
3rd choice – A suspension can be made by Pharmacy in some centres.[155,528]
4th choice – Use the oral solution (if available). Follow the directions in section 3.6.

Give immediately as the drug will oxidise (degrade).[49]

Do not crush the modified-release (CR) tablets.

Administration – swallowing difficulties
1st choice – Convert the patient onto co-beneldopa dispersible tablets. Contact Pharmacy for advice.
2nd choice – A suspension can be made by Pharmacy in some centres.[155,528]
3rd choice – Use the oral solution (if available).
4th choice – The standard Sinemet® tablets will disperse in water for administration.[8,49] Lower strengths disperse within one minute.[154] The 25/250 strength disperse in one to five minutes.[154] Follow the directions in section 3.5.

Give immediately as the drug will oxidise (degrade).[49]

Do not crush the modified-release (CR) tablets.

(monograph continues on next page)

Conversion table[35]

Sinemet® (co-careldopa)	Madopar® (co-beneldopa)
Sinemet® 62.5mg tablet	Madopar® 62.5mg disp. tablet
Sinemet® 110mg tablet	Madopar® 125mg disp. tablet
Sinemet® Plus 125mg tablet	Madopar® 125mg disp. tablet
Sinemet® 275mg tablet	2 x Madopar® 125mg disp. tablet
Half Sinemet® CR 125mg tablet	Seek advice from Pharmacy
Sinemet® CR 250mg tablet	Seek advice from Pharmacy

Clinical guidance
A direct dose conversion may not be appropriate in all patients. Switching to Madopar® 62.5mg given up to four times a day as required by symptoms, then adjusted upwards according to patient requirements and toleration, may be more suitable for some patients.

Levodopa is mainly absorbed in the jejunum. Drug effect may be particularly unpredictable in patients with enteral tubes terminating in the jejunum.[155]

Feed guidance
Absorption of co-careldopa may be altered by enteral feed proteins. To reduce fluctuations in effect, doses should be given at the same time each day in relation to the feed regimen.[135]

Co-careldopa and entacapone (Stalevo®)

Presentation
Film-coated tablets.

Administration – enteral tubes
1st choice – Use the separate components (co-careldopa and entacapone) – see individual monographs for details. Consider switching to Madopar® dispersible.
2nd choice – The tablets can be crushed and mixed with water for administration.[367] Follow the directions in section 3.5.

(monograph continues on next page)

Administration – swallowing difficulties

1st choice – Use the separate components (co-careldopa and entacapone) – see individual monographs for details. Consider switching to Madopar® dispersible.

2nd choice – The tablets can be crushed and mixed with honey, jam, or orange juice for administration. They have a bitter taste.[367]

Clinical guidance

Stalevo® tablets contain co-careldopa and entacapone in various dosages.[272] The crushed tablets can stain clothing, so care should be used when handling.[367]

Co-codamol

Presentation

Tablets, capsules.
Effervescent tablets, sachets.

Administration – enteral tubes / swallowing difficulties

Use the effervescent tablets or the sachets.[94,104] Follow the directions in section 3.5.

Consider switching to paracetamol liquid / suppositories with or without codeine syrup or a parenteral opioid if the high sodium load of the effervescent tablets is a problem (sodium content approximately 13-17mmol per tablet, depending on brand[272]).

Co-danthramer

Presentation

Capsules.
Suspension.

Administration – enteral tubes / swallowing difficulties

Use the suspension.[104] Follow the directions in section 3.6.

Codeine

Presentation
Tablets.
Syrup, linctus, paediatric linctus.
A suspension can be made by Pharmacy in some centres (see Appendix 1).[460,461]
Injection.

Administration – enteral tubes / swallowing difficulties
Use the syrup or the linctus (contain alcohol).[40,94,104] Dilute with water before administration.[132] Follow the directions in section 3.6.

Co-Diovan®

Presentation
Film-coated tablets.

Clinical guidance
Co-Diovan® tablets contain valsartan and hydrochlorothiazide at various dosages.[272] Switch to valsartan or an alternative angiotensin-II receptor antagonist such as losartan, and an alternative thiazide diuretic, e.g. bendroflumethiazide. See individual monographs for details.

Co-dydramol

Presentation
Tablets.
Oral suspension (special).[542,582]

Clinical guidance – enteral tubes
Co-dydramol tablets contain paracetamol and dihydrocodeine. Consider changing therapy to co-codamol effervescent tablets. Alternatively, use the separate components – see individual monographs for details.

(monograph continues on next page)

Administration – swallowing difficulties

Use the oral suspension (if available). Alternatively, change to co-codamol effervescent tablets, or use the separate components – see individual monographs for details.

Co-fluampicil

Presentation
Capsules.
Syrup.
Injection.

Administration – enteral tubes
1st choice – Give by parenteral injection.
2nd choice – Use the syrup.[133] Follow the directions in section 3.6.

Administration – swallowing difficulties
1st choice – Use the syrup.[133]
2nd choice – Give by parenteral injection.

Feed guidance
Enteral co-fluampicil should be taken on an empty stomach.[624] Enteral feeds should be withheld for half an hour before and half an hour after each dose.[225]

Summary:-	Stop feed 30 minutes before dose
	Restart feed 30 minutes after dose

Withholding enteral feeds can compromise nutrition and interfere with blood glucose management. If the patient does not have a break in their feeding regimen during which enteral co-fluampicil can be given, the Nutrition Team should be contacted to advise on management.

Colchicine

Presentation
Tablets.

Administration – enteral tubes / swallowing difficulties
The tablets can be dispersed in water for administration.[8,104,105] They disperse within one minute.[154] Follow the directions in section 3.5.

Colestyramine (Cholestyramine)

Presentation
Sachets.

Administration – enteral tubes
Use the sachets. Follow the directions in section 3.6. Flush well after each dose.[41]

Administration – swallowing difficulties
Use the sachets. The sachets can be mixed with water, fruit juice, skimmed milk, thin soups, fruit smoothies or fruit sauces e.g. apple sauce.[547]

Clinical guidance
Colestyramine works by absorbing cholesterol-containing bile acids in the gut, which are then excreted. It affects the absorption of other medicines, so give all other medicines at least one hour before or four-six hours after a dose of colestyramine.

Co-magaldrox

Presentation
Maalox® suspension.
Mucogel® suspension.

Administration – enteral tubes
Not recommended for administration via enteral feeding tubes as it may interact with enteral feeds to form protein complexes which may block enteral feeding tubes or cause oesophageal plugs.[11,32,104] Consider alternative therapy, e.g. Gavison®.

Administration – swallowing difficulties
Use the suspension.

Clinical guidance
Aluminium hydroxide can decrease gastric emptying.[2]

Combivir®

See entry under "Zidovudine and lamivudine".

Co-phenotrope

Presentation
Tablets.

Administration – enteral tubes / swallowing difficulties
The tablets can be crushed and dispersed in water for administration.[105,152] Follow the directions in section 3.5.

Co-tenidone

Presentation
Tablets.

Administration – enteral tubes / swallowing difficulties
The tablets can be crushed and dispersed in water for administration.[58] Follow the directions in section 3.5. Use immediately.[58]

Co-triamterzide

Presentation
Tablets.

Administration – enteral tubes / swallowing difficulties
The tablets can be crushed and dispersed in water for administration.[7,94,105] Follow the directions in section 3.5.

Co-trimoxazole

Presentation
Tablets.
Suspension.
Solution for injection.

Administration – enteral tubes
Use the adult suspension (contains sorbitol) and dilute with an equal volume of water, shaking well, before administration.[40,104,133] Follow the directions in section 3.6.

Crushing co-trimoxazole tablets results in enteral feeding tube occlusion, and is not recommended.[442]

Administration – swallowing difficulties
Use the suspension (contains sorbitol).

Coversyl® Arginine Plus

Presentation
Tablets.

Clinical guidance
Coversyl® Arginine Plus tablets contain perindopril arginine 5mg and indapamide 1.25mg.[272]　The manufacturers do not believe that crushing the tablets would be a problem, but can't recommend it.[352] Switch to perindopril erbumine 4mg and either indapamide or an appropriate alternative thiazide diuretic.　See individual monographs for details.

Cozaar-Comp®

Presentation
Film-coated tablets.

Clinical guidance
Cozaar-Comp® tablets contain losartan and hydrochlorothiazide at various dosages.[272]　Use losartan as a separate component and an appropriate alternative thiazide diuretic, e.g. bendroflumethiazide. See individual monographs for details.

Co-zidocapt

Presentation
Tablets.

Clinical guidance
Co-zidocapt tablets contain captopril and hydrochlorothiazide in various dosages.[272]　Use captopril as a separate component, and an appropriate alternative thiazide diuretic, e.g. bendroflumethiazide. See individual monographs for details.

Cyclizine

Presentation
Tablets.
Oral solution (special).[582]
A suspension can be made by Pharmacy in some centres (see Appendix 1).[155,512]
Injection.

Administration – enteral tubes
1st choice – Give by parenteral injection.
2nd choice – Switch to an alternative anti-emetic which is available as a liquid or suppositories, e.g. metoclopramide, domperidone.
3rd choice – The tablets can be crushed and dispersed in water for administration.[41,95,152] Follow the directions in section 3.5. Protect from light.[41]
4th choice – A suspension can be made by Pharmacy in some centres.[155] Follow the directions in section 3.6.
5th choice – Use the oral solution (if available). Follow the directions in section 3.6.

Administration – swallowing difficulties
1st choice – Switch to an alternative anti-emetic which is available as a liquid or suppositories, e.g. metoclopramide, domperidone.
2nd choice – Give by parenteral injection.
3rd choice – A suspension can be made by Pharmacy in some centres.[155]
4th choice – Use the oral solution (if available).
5th choice – The tablets can be crushed and dispersed in water for administration.[41,95,152] Follow the directions in section 3.5. Protect from light.[41] The crushed tablets have a bitter taste.[105]

The injection has also been given enterally in some centres, however the manufacturers have no information on this, and cannot recommend it.[133,165]

Cyclopenthiazide

Presentation
Tablets.

Administration – enteral tubes / swallowing difficulties
The tablets can be crushed and mixed with water for administration.[8]
Follow the directions in section 3.5.

Cyclophosphamide

Presentation
Sugar-coated tablets.
A suspension can be made by Pharmacy in some centres.
Injection.

Administration – enteral tubes / swallowing difficulties
<u>Caution – cytotoxic.</u> Contact Pharmacy for advice before giving.
1st choice – Consider giving by parenteral injection.
2nd choice – A suspension can be made by Pharmacy in some centres.[138,139,172] Follow the directions in section 3.6.
3rd choice – Contact Pharmacy for further advice on how to give (Pharmacists – see Appendix 2).

Cyproheptadine

Presentation
Tablets.

Administration – enteral tubes / swallowing difficulties
The tablets can be crushed and mixed with water for administration.[8]
Without crushing they will disperse in two to five minutes.[8] Follow the directions in section 3.5.

Cyproterone

Presentation
Tablets.

Administration – enteral tubes / swallowing difficulties
The tablets can be dispersed in water for administration.[40,59] They disperse in one to two minutes.[154] Follow the directions in section 3.5. No information has been located on whether cyproterone is likely to block enteral tubes, or on the effect crushing the tablets may have on absorption.[59]

Dabigatran

Presentation
Capsules.

Clinical guidance
Dabigatran capsules should not be opened.[600] The capsule shell is specially formulated to release slowly at the correct point in the gastrointestinal tract. The pellets inside the shell are designed to create an acidic micro-environment to improve drug dissolution and absorption. Opening the capsules may greatly affect the oral bioavailability of the drug, with a risk of increased side effects (i.e. bleeding), therefore this should never be done.[600]

Dantrolene

Presentation
Capsules.
Oral solution (special).[582]
Injection.

Administration – enteral tubes
The capsules can be opened, and the contents dispersed in water or acidic fruit juice (e.g. orange[132]) for administration.[104,105] Follow the directions in section 3.7.

(monograph continues on next page)

No information on administering the oral solution via enteral feeding tubes has been located.

Administration – swallowing difficulties
1st choice – Use the oral solution (if available).
2nd choice – The capsules can be opened, and the contents dispersed in water or acidic fruit juice (e.g. orange[132]) for administration.[104,105] Follow the directions in section 3.7.

Clinical guidance
Use of the injection enterally is NOT recommended, as the drug may hydrolyse in the stomach. The injection formulation also contains mannitol. It is designed for its licensed indication, malignant hyperthermia, and is not a substitute for the oral preparation.[166]

Dapsone

Presentation
Tablets.
A suspension can be made by Pharmacy in some centres (see Appendix 1).[527]

Administration – enteral tubes
The tablets can be crushed and dispersed in plenty of water for administration.[8,104,152] Follow the directions in section 3.5. Protect from light.[41]

No information on giving the suspension via enteral feeding tubes has been located.

Administration – swallowing difficulties
1st choice – Use the suspension (if available).
2nd choice – The tablets can be crushed and dispersed in plenty of water for administration.[8,104,152] Follow the directions in section 3.5. Protect from light.[41]

Deferasirox

Presentation
Dispersible tablets.

Administration – enteral tubes
No information on administering deferasirox via enteral feeding tubes has been located.

Administration – swallowing difficulties
Disperse the tablets in 100-200mL of water, orange or apple juice. Re-suspend any residue left in the glass by adding more liquid and stirring.[548]

The tablets must not be chewed or swallowed whole.[548]

Clinical guidance
Desferrioxamine injection is an alternative, if it is not contra-indicated.[549] Deferiprone may also be an alternative.[549]

Feed guidance
Deferasirox should be taken at least half an hour before food.[548,624] Enteral feeds should be withheld for half an hour before and half an hour after each dose.[225]

Summary:-	Stop feed 30 minutes before dose
	Restart feed 30 minutes after dose

Withholding enteral feeds can compromise nutrition and interfere with blood glucose management. If the patient does not have a break in their feeding regimen during which deferasirox can be given, the Nutrition Team should be contacted to advise on management.

Deferiprone

Presentation
Film-coated tablets.
Oral solution.

Administration – enteral tubes
No information on administering deferiprone via enteral feeding tubes has been located.

Administration – swallowing difficulties
Use the oral solution.

Clinical guidance
Desferrioxamine injection is an alternative, if it is not contra-indicated.[549] Deferasirox may also be an alternative.[549]

Deferiprone is absorbed in the upper gastrointestinal tract.[550] It is unknown if absorption will be affected if it is administered into the jejunum.

Deflazacort

Presentation
Tablets.

Administration – enteral tubes / swallowing difficulties
The tablets can be dispersed in water for administration.[105] They disperse within one minute.[154] Follow the directions in section 3.5.

Demeclocycline

Presentation
Capsules.

Administration – enteral tubes / swallowing difficulties
A suspension can be made by Pharmacy in some centres. Follow the directions in section 3.6.

Do not open the capsules as the contents do not disperse in water, and this has led to enteral tube blockage. The capsule contents may cause severe irritation to the mucosa, so they should not be opened for administration to patients with swallowing difficulties either.[155]

Feed guidance
Demeclocycline absorption is reduced by calcium in enteral feeds. Withhold enteral feeds for two hours before and one hour after each dose.[155,225,549,572,624]

Summary:-	Stop feed 2 hours before dose
	Restart feed 1 hour after dose

Withholding enteral feeds can compromise nutrition and interfere with blood glucose management. If the patient does not have a break in their feeding regimen during which demeclocycline can be given, the Nutrition Team should be contacted to advise on management.

Desferrioxamine

Presentation
Injection.

Administration – enteral tubes / swallowing difficulties
The injection can be given orally or via nasogastric tube in 50-100mL water. It has an unpleasant taste.[152] No information has been located about the administration of desferrioxamine via other types of enteral feeding tube.

Desmopressin

Presentation
Tablets.
Sublingual tablets.
Nasal spray, intranasal solution.
Injection.

Administration – enteral tubes / swallowing difficulties
1st choice – Use the nasal route if appropriate.
2nd choice – Use the sublingual route if indicated and the patient has a sufficiently moist mouth.
3rd choice – The tablets can be crushed and mixed with water for administration.[104,105] Follow the directions in section 3.5.

Clinical guidance
Clinical studies have indicated that crushed desmopressin tablets have the same pharmacokinetic properties, and the same overall effect as whole tablets.[300]

Desmopressin is thought to be absorbed in the stomach, the duodenum, and the jejunum. There is therefore a risk of reduced absorption if desmopressin is given through a feeding tube terminating beyond the stomach. However, desmopressin is also broken down by enzymes in the stomach, and so conversely a greater amount of drug may be available for absorption if the stomach is bypassed.[340]

The manufacturer recommends switching the patient to an alternative route if appropriate, or starting therapy via the enteral feeding tube at the lowest dose possible, and titrating according to patient response.[340]

Dexamethasone

Presentation
Tablets.
Oral solution (contains sorbitol).
Oral solution (special).[542,582,658]
A suspension can be made by Pharmacy in some centres.[573]
Injection.

Administration – enteral tubes
1st choice – Give by parenteral injection if appropriate.
2nd choice – Use the oral solution. Follow the directions in section 3.6.
3rd choice – The tablets have been crushed and mixed with water for administration.[8,94,152,225] They should be crushed with care to avoid inhalation of dust by the carer.[251,558] Follow the directions in section 3.5.
4th choice – The injection has been used enterally.[40,152] Follow the directions in section 3.6.

Administration – swallowing difficulties
1st choice – Use the oral solution.
2nd choice – Give by parenteral injection if appropriate.
3rd choice – The tablets have been crushed and mixed with water for administration.[8,94,152,225] They should be crushed with care to avoid inhalation of dust by the carer.[251,558] Follow the directions in section 3.5.
4th choice – The injection has been used enterally.[40,152] Follow the directions in section 3.6.

Clinical guidance
It may be preferable to use the crushed tablets rather than the liquid for intrajejunal administration.

Dexamfetamine

Presentation
Tablets.
Oral solution (special).[542,582]

Administration – enteral tubes
No information on administering dexamfetamine via enteral feeding tubes has been located.

Administration – swallowing difficulties
Use the oral solution (if available).

Diazepam

Presentation
Tablets.
Syrup, oral solution (contain sorbitol).
Oral suspension (special).[542,582,658]
Injection solution, injection emulsion.
Rectal tubes.
Suppositories (no longer available in the UK).

Administration – enteral tubes
1st choice – Give by intravenous or rectal route.
2nd choice – Use the syrup or the oral solution, and dilute with water before administration to reduce viscosity and tube binding.[132] Follow the directions in section 3.6.

The injection has also been given enterally in some centres, however the manufacturers have no information on this, and cannot recommend it.[40,167]

Administration – swallowing difficulties
1st choice – Use the syrup or the oral solution.
2nd choice – Give by intravenous or rectal route.

The injection has also been given enterally in some centres, however the manufacturers have no information on this, and cannot recommend it.[40,167]

(monograph continues on next page)

Clinical guidance
If diazepam is administered through long PVC tubes, drug loss may occur as diazepam is significantly adsorbed onto PVC.[9,12] Diazepam may also contribute towards blockage of tubes.

Diazoxide

Presentation
Tablets.
Oral solution (special).[582]
A suspension can be made by Pharmacy in some centres (see Appendix 1).[512,573]
Injection (no longer available in the UK).

Administration – enteral tubes / swallowing difficulties
1st choice – A suspension can be made by Pharmacy in some centres.[138] Follow the directions in section 3.6.
2nd choice – Use the oral solution (if available). Follow the directions in section 3.6.

Diclofenac sodium

Presentation
Enteric-coated tablets.
Dispersible tablets.
Sugar-free oral suspension (special).
Modified-release tablets, modified-release capsules.
Suppositories.
Injection.
Topical gel.

Administration – enteral tubes
1st choice – Give by parenteral injection or use the suppositories for acute situations.
2nd choice – Use the dispersible tablets. Follow the directions in section 3.5.
3rd choice – Use the oral suspension (if available).[94,104,105] Follow the directions in section 3.6.

(monograph continues on next page)

Do not crush / open the enteric-coated or the modified-release preparations.

Administration – swallowing difficulties
1st choice – Use the dispersible tablets.
2nd choice – Give by parenteral injection or use the suppositories for acute situations.
3rd choice – Use the oral suspension (if available).[94,104,105]

Do not crush / open the enteric-coated or the modified-release preparations.

Diclofenac sodium and misoprostol (Arthrotec®)

Presentation
Tablets.

Clinical guidance
The tablets are formed of a core of diclofenac surrounded by a mantle of misoprostol. They are not suitable for crushing.[51] Consider changing treatment to rectal or dispersible diclofenac, with an acid suppressant, e.g. ranitidine or lansoprazole. See individual monographs for details.

Dicycloverine (Dicyclomine)

Presentation
Tablets.
Syrup.

Administration – enteral tubes / swallowing difficulties
1st choice – Use the syrup, which can be diluted with water immediately prior to administration to reduce viscosity.[41,268] Follow the directions in section 3.6.
2nd choice – The tablets may crushed and mixed with water for administration.[152] Follow the directions in section 3.5.

Didanosine

Presentation
Tablets, capsules.

Administration – enteral tubes / swallowing difficulties
The tablets can be crushed and dispersed in water for administration.[132,152] Follow the directions in section 3.5.

Clinical guidance
Videx® tablets contain antacids which may affect the absorption of other drugs.[272]

Feed guidance
Withhold enteral feeds for two hours before and one hour after each dose.[136,225,624]

Summary:-	Stop feed 2 hours before dose
	Restart feed 1 hour after dose

Withholding enteral feeds can compromise nutrition and interfere with blood glucose management. If the patient does not have a break in their feeding regimen during which didanosine can be given, the Nutrition Team should be contacted to advise on management.

Digitoxin

Presentation
Tablets.

Clinical guidance
No reports of administration of digitoxin via enteral feeding tubes has been located. According to the manufacturers, there shouldn't be a problem crushing the tablet and dispersing it in water in order to aid administration (although of course this is off-licence).[428]

Digoxin

Presentation
Tablets.
Elixir.
Injection.

Administration – enteral tubes
1st choice – Consider giving by parenteral injection. See "Clinical guidance" below.
2nd choice – Use the elixir.[41] Do not dilute the elixir.[551] Follow the directions in section 3.6.
3rd choice – Use crushed tablets for patients with enteral feeding tubes delivering to the jejunum if osmotic diarrhoea is a problem.[6,104] Follow the directions in section 3.5.

The injection has also been given enterally in some centres, but this is not recommended as bioavailability is unpredictable.[40]

Administration – swallowing difficulties
1st choice – Use the elixir.[41]
2nd choice – Consider giving by parenteral injection. See "Clinical guidance" below.
3rd choice – The tablets can be crushed for administration.[6,104] Follow the directions in section 3.5.

The injection has also been given enterally in some centres, but this is not recommended as bioavailability is unpredictable.[40]

Clinical guidance
Digoxin absorption is believed to occur primarily in the duodenum and the proximal jejunum.[227] Absorption may therefore be reduced if it is administered via nasojejunal tube or jejunostomy. The clinical significance of this is unclear. There have been some reports of failure to achieve therapeutic serum levels in patients with small intestine malabsorption or short bowel syndrome.[6,155,227] Monitor effect and consider checking drug levels if necessary. The elixir has a high osmolality.[26]

(monograph continues on next page)

The elixir has a different bioavailability from the tablets so dose adjustments may be necessary.[90] However this is controversial as the manufacturers of Lanoxin PG® say that no dosage adjustment is necessary when switching from tablets to elixir.[180] Contact Pharmacy for advice.

| 62.5mcg tablet | equivalent to | 42mcg injection[432] |
| 62.5mcg tablet | equivalent to | 50mcg (1mL) elixir |

Digoxin has been reported to decrease appetite.[33]

Feed guidance
Digoxin elixir has been reported to physically interact with enteral feeds. Ensure the feeding tube is flushed well before and after each dose to prevent this.[5]

The absorption of enteral digoxin is affected by high-fibre feeds such as Jevity®.[635] Allow a time gap of two hours before and one hour after administration of enteral digoxin before administering high-fibre enteral feeds.

| Summary:- (high-fibre feeds) Stop feed 2 hours before dose |
| Restart feed 1 hour after dose |

Withholding enteral feeds can compromise nutrition and interfere with blood glucose management. If the patient does not have a break in their feeding regimen during which digoxin can be given, the Nutrition Team should be contacted to advise on management.

Dihydrocodeine

Presentation
Tablets.
Suspension.
Modified-release tablets.
Injection.

Administration – enteral tubes / swallowing difficulties
Use the suspension.[41] Follow the directions in section 3.6.

(monograph continues on next page)

Do not crush the modified-release tablets.

60mg MR tablet twice daily	equivalent to	30mg syrup four times daily

Di-iodohydroxyquinoline

Presentation
Tablets (named patient).

Administration – enteral tubes
No information about the use of this medication via enteral feeding tubes has been located.

Administration – swallowing difficulties
The tablets can be crushed and mixed with apple sauce or chocolate syrup for patients with swallowing difficulties.[152]

Diloxanide

Presentation
Tablets.

Administration – enteral tubes
No information about the use of this medication via enteral feeding tubes has been located.

Administration – swallowing difficulties
The tablets can be crushed and mixed with water for administration.[152]

Diltiazem

Presentation
Modified-release tablets, modified-release capsules.
A suspension can be made by Pharmacy in some centres (see Appendix 1).[457]

Administration – enteral tubes
All tablets and capsules are labelled as modified-release, however the 60mg generic preparation is not slow-release and can be crushed.[14] Contact Pharmacy for advice if unsure. Follow the directions in section 3.5. A suspension can be made by Pharmacy in some centres.[155,457]

Patients on once or twice-daily modified-release preparations may need to be converted onto three-times-daily doses of the generic preparation. Contact Pharmacy for advice on equivalent doses.

Viazem® XL and Adizem® MR capsules have been opened for administration via wide-bore enteral feeding tubes.[132] The manufacturers of Adizem® capsules warn that narrow-bore feeding tubes are extremely likely to be blocked by capsule contents, which should not be crushed.[344]

Dilzem® SR and XL – there are anecdotal reports of Dilzem® SR and XL capsules being opened for administration via enteral feeding tubes.[336] The capsule contents should not be crushed.

Slozem® capsules have been opened for administration via enteral feeding tubes. They may block narrow-bore tubes (minimum recommended 12Fr).[348] The capsule contents should not be crushed.

Tildiem® LA capsules can be opened and the pellets removed, but the manufacturers do not recommend this, and if it is done it is important that the pellets are not crushed or chewed.[365]

(monograph continues on next page)

Administration – swallowing difficulties
The MR capsules have been opened and the contents mixed with soft food for administration. Do not crush the capsule contents.[132] This method may not be suitable for patients with limited understanding or impaired ability to follow instructions.

Alternatively, switch to amlodipine (NB amlodipine does not offer the rate-control effects of diltiazem).

Dinoprostone

Presentation
Tablets.
Injection.

Administration – enteral tubes / swallowing difficulties
The injection can be diluted with water for use enterally.[40,160,573] Follow the directions in section 3.6.

Dipyridamole

Presentation
Sugar-coated tablets.
Modified-release capsules.
Injection.
Suspension (NB different licensed indication to the capsules).
Oral suspension (special).[542,582]

Administration – enteral tubes
1st choice – Use the suspension. Follow the directions in section 3.6.
2nd choice – For patients with wide-bore tubes, open the capsules and disperse the contents in water for administration. Do not crush the granules. Flush well as there is a potential for the granules to block enteral feeding tubes.[333]
3rd choice – Use the injection enterally (this may be impractical due to the low strength of the injection and the high number of ampoules which would therefore be required).[44,152] Follow the directions in section 3.6.

(monograph continues on next page)

Administration – swallowing difficulties
1st choice – Use the suspension.

The modified-release capsule contents have been mixed with soft food, juice, or water for administration to patients with swallowing difficulties, but this is not recommended. The capsule contents should not be crushed, therefore this method may not be suitable for patients with limited understanding or impaired ability to follow instructions.[132,333]

Clinical guidance
There is a difference in indication between the modified-release preparation of dipyridamole and the standard-release tablets and liquid. National recommendations for secondary prevention of occlusive vascular events recommend the use of modified-release dipyridamole, according to the licensed indications.[334] The manufacturer encourages the use of the modified-release preparation where possible as the two products have significantly different pharmacokinetic profiles, and the modified-release preparation should have a better side effect profile.[333] However when it is not possible to use the modified-release preparation, such as when enteral tube blockage is a problem, the standard-release tablets can be used.[333]

A dosage adjustment is required when switching from modified-release capsules to suspension.

200mg MR capsule twice daily	=	100mg four times daily syrup

Feed guidance
Enteral dipyridamole should be given on an empty stomach, so withhold enteral feeds for half an hour before and half an hour after each dose.[117,225,624]

Summary:-	Stop feed 30 minutes before dose
	Restart feed 30 minutes after dose

(monograph continues on next page)

Withholding enteral feeds can compromise nutrition and interfere with blood glucose management. If the patient does not have a break in their feeding regimen during which dipyridamole can be given, the Nutrition Team should be contacted to advise on management.

Dipyridamole and aspirin (Asasantin®)

Presentation
Modified-release capsules.

Clinical guidance
The capsules are modified-release and should not be opened. They contain aspirin and dipyridamole. Patients should be converted onto the two component drugs (NB aspirin is not available in the UK in a 25mg dosage – 75mg daily would be the usual choice). See individual monographs for details.

The manufacturer has reports of the capsules being opened and the contents being administered via enteral feeding tubes. There is a risk that the capsule contents may block enteral feeding tubes. The capsules contain dipyridamole modified-release granules which should not be crushed, and an aspirin immediate-release tablet. The aspirin tablet can be crushed if necessary for administration.[333] However due to the wide availability of the component parts of Asasantin®, it should not be necessary to open Asasantin® capsules.

Disodium etidronate

Presentation
Tablets.
A suspension can be made by Pharmacy in some centres.

Administration – enteral tubes
1st choice – There is a form of zoledronic acid licensed for once-yearly intravenous administration.[544] This is probably the most appropriate form of bisphosphonate for most patients with swallowing problems – contact Pharmacy for advice.
2nd choice – The tablet can be crushed and dispersed in water for administration via enteral feeding tube.[104,105] Follow the directions in section 3.5. Flush post-dose with 50mL of distilled water.
3rd choice – A suspension can be made by Pharmacy in some centres.[155] Follow the directions in section 3.6.

Administration – swallowing difficulties
1st choice – There is a form of zoledronic acid licensed for once-yearly intravenous administration.[544] This is probably the most appropriate form of bisphosphonate for most patients with swallowing problems – contact Pharmacy for advice.
2nd choice – A suspension can be made by Pharmacy in some centres.[155]
3rd choice – The tablet can be crushed and dispersed in water for administration.[104,105] Follow the directions in section 3.5.

Feed guidance
Stop feed two hours before and two hours after administration of disodium etidronate.[624]

Summary:-	Stop feed 2 hours before dose
	Restart feed 2 hours after dose

Withholding enteral feeds can compromise nutrition and interfere with blood glucose management. If the patient does not have a break in their feeding regimen during which disodium etidronate can be given, the Nutrition Team should be contacted to advise on management.

Disopyramide

Presentation
Capsules.
Modified-release tablets.
Injection.

Administration – enteral tubes / swallowing difficulties
1st choice – The standard capsules can be opened and the contents mixed with water for administration.[87] Follow the directions in section 3.7.
2nd choice – The injection can be used enterally if necessary. It has a strong, bitter taste, and a local anaesthetic effect in the mouth, and so should be used with care if given orally to patients with swallowing difficulties.[40,97] Follow the directions in section 3.6.

The modified-release tablets should not be used. Contact Pharmacy for advice for patients maintained on modified-release tablets.

Distigmine

Presentation
Tablets (no longer available in the UK).

Administration – enteral tubes / swallowing difficulties
The tablets (if available) can be crushed and dispersed in water for administration.[8] Without crushing they disperse in two to five minutes.[8] Follow the directions in section 3.5.

Feed guidance
Distigmine should be given on an empty stomach. Withhold enteral feeds for half an hour before and half an hour after each dose.[225,429,616]

Summary:-	Stop feed 30 minutes before dose
	Restart feed 30 minutes after dose

Withholding enteral feeds can compromise nutrition and interfere with blood glucose management. If the patient does not have a break in their feeding regimen during which distigmine can be given, the Nutrition Team should be contacted to advise on management.

Diumide-K Continus®

Presentation
Film-coated tablets.

Clinical guidance
Diumide-K Continus® tablets contain furosemide 40mg and potassium 8mmol in a modified-release preparation.[272] Use the separate components – furosemide and an appropriate standard-release formulation of potassium. See individual monographs for details. Contact Pharmacy for advice if necessary.

Docusate

Presentation
Capsules.
Oral solution, paediatric oral suspension.

Administration – enteral tubes / swallowing difficulties
Use the oral solution. Follow the directions in section 3.6. Do not open the capsules.[41] Docusate has an unpleasant taste.[558,560,561]

Dolasetron

Presentation
Injection (may not be available in the UK).
A suspension can be made by Pharmacy in some centres (see Appendix 1).[462]

Administration – enteral tubes
Give by parenteral injection (if available). Alternatively, consider switching to ondansetron.

No information on administering the suspension via enteral feeding tubes has been located.

Administration – swallowing difficulties
1st choice – Give by parenteral injection (if available).
2nd choice – Consider switching to ondansetron injection.
3rd choice – Use the suspension (if available).[462]

Domperidone

Presentation
Tablets.
Sugar-free suspension.
Suppositories (no longer available in the UK).

Administration – enteral tubes
1st choice – Use the suppositories if possible (if available).
2nd choice – Use the suspension (contains sorbitol[104]) and dilute with an equal amount of water before administration.[133] Follow the directions in section 3.6.

Administration – swallowing difficulties
Use the suppositories (if available) or the suspension (contains sorbitol[104]).

Donepezil

Presentation
Film-coated tablets.
Orodispersible tablets.
Oral solution
Oral solution (unlicensed special).[589]

Administration – enteral tubes
1st choice – Use the orodispersible tablets. Follow the directions in section 3.5.
2nd choice – The film-coated tablets can be crushed and mixed with water for administration.[104,105] Follow the directions in section 3.5.[150]
3rd choice – Use the oral solution. Follow the direction in section 3.6.
4th choice – Use the unlicensed oral solution (if available). Follow the directions in section 3.6.

Administration – swallowing difficulties
1st choice – Use the orodispersible tablets or the oral solution.
2nd choice – Use the unlicensed oral solution (if available).
3rd choice – The film-coated tablets can be crushed and mixed with water for administration.[104,105] Follow the directions in section 3.5. They have a strong, bitter taste.[150]

Dosulepin (Dothiepin)

Presentation
Tablets, capsules.
Sugar-free oral solution (special).[582]

Administration – enteral tubes / swallowing difficulties
Use the oral solution.[104] Follow the directions in section 3.6.

The tablets have been crushed and the capsules have been opened, but this is not recommended as the tablets are very hard and many brands are coated,[132] and the powder has a local anaesthetic action.[105]

Clinical guidance
Tricyclic antidepressants can decrease gastric emptying.[2]

Doxazosin

Presentation
Tablets.
Modified-release tablets.
Oral solution (special).[542,582]

Administration – enteral tubes
The standard tablets disperse readily in deionised water for administration.[8,37] Most disperse within one minute.[8,154] Do not use tap water, as the chloride ions in the water will cause the drug to precipitate out.[104,105] Use deionised water for flushing enteral feeding tubes following each dose. Follow the directions in section 3.5.

The modified-release tablets are not suitable for enteral tube administration and should not be crushed. The bioavailability of the modified-release tablets is only 54-59% of the standard tablets,[301] therefore a dose adjustment and blood pressure monitoring may be necessary when switching between the two. It may be advisable, when moving from modified-release to standard-release tablets, to halve the total daily dose, and then titrate upwards as required. Contact Pharmacy for advice.

(monograph continues on next page)

No information on administering the oral solution via enteral feeding tubes has been located.

Administration – swallowing difficulties
1st choice – Use the oral solution (if available).
2nd choice – The standard tablets disperse readily in deionised water for administration.[8,37] Most disperse within one minute.[8,154] Do not use tap water, as the chloride ions in the water will cause the drug to precipitate out.[104,105]

The modified-release tablets should not be crushed. The bioavailability of the modified-release tablets is only 54-59% of the standard tablets,[301] therefore a dose adjustment and blood pressure monitoring may be necessary when switching between the two. It may be advisable, when moving from modified-release to standard-release tablets, to halve the total daily dose, and then titrate upwards as required. Contact Pharmacy for advice.

Clinical guidance
Deionised water must be used, and no other drugs / fluids should be mixed with doxazosin, as the drug will precipitate in the presence of chloride ions. Flush enteral feeding tubes well with water before and after each dose.[37]

Doxepin

Presentation
Capsules (no longer available in the UK).

Administration – enteral tubes / swallowing difficulties
The capsules can be opened, and the contents dispersed in water.[37] Follow the directions in section 3.7. The powder has a bitter taste.[105]

Clinical guidance
Tricyclic antidepressants can decrease gastric emptying.[2]

Feed guidance
Doxepin has been reported as being incompatible with some enteral feeds, so ensure enteral feeding tubes are flushed well before and after each dose.[222]

Doxycycline

Presentation
Capsules.
Dispersible tablets.

Administration – enteral tubes / swallowing difficulties
Use the dispersible tablets. Follow the directions in section 3.5.
Do not open the capsules as the contents are irritant.[94,561]

Clinical guidance
Doxycycline binds to calcium ions and may have reduced absorption when given via enteral feeding tubes. Prescribe at the higher end of the standard dosage range.[94]

Feed guidance
Absorption and serum levels of doxycycline have been shown to decrease if it is taken with milk.[572] Withhold enteral feeds for two hours before and one hour after each dose.[117,225,572]

Summary:-	Stop feed 2 hours before dose
	Restart feed 1 hour after dose

Withholding enteral feeds can compromise nutrition and interfere with blood glucose management. If the patient does not have a break in their feeding regimen during which doxycycline can be given, the Nutrition Team should be contacted to advise on management.

Duloxetine

Presentation
Capsules.

Administration – enteral tubes
No information on giving duloxetine via enteral feeding tubes has been located.

(monograph continues on next page)

Administration – swallowing difficulties

The capsules can be opened and their contents mixed with apple juice or apple sauce for administration to patients with swallowing difficulties.[368] The capsules contain enteric-coated beads which should not be chewed or crushed,[368] therefore this method may not be appropriate for patients with limited understanding or impaired ability to follow instructions. The mixture should be given immediately.[368]

Dydrogesterone

Presentation
Tablets.

Administration – enteral tubes / swallowing difficulties
The tablets can be crushed (preferably in water to reduce dust production) and mixed with water for administration.[105] Follow the directions in section 3.5.

Efavirenz

Presentation
Film-coated tablets, capsules.
Oral solution.

Administration – enteral tubes
1st choice – Use the oral solution.[132] The solution is non-aqueous, and diluting it before administration is not recommended.[350,351] Follow the directions in section 3.6.
2nd choice – The capsules can be opened and the contents mixed with at least 5mL of medium chain triglyceride oil.[350]

Administration – swallowing difficulties
Use the oral solution.[132] The solution is non-aqueous, and diluting it before administration is not recommended.[350,351]

Clinical guidance
A dose conversion is necessary when switching from tablets to solution. Contact Pharmacy for advice.

(monograph continues on next page)

| 600mg tablet | equivalent to | 720mg solution[132] |

Polyethylene glycol should not be used as a suspending vehicle because it affects the bioavailability of efavirenz.[350]

Feed guidance
Efavirenz tablets and capsules should be given on an empty stomach, so withhold enteral feeds for two hours before and one hour after each enteral dose.[624]

| Summary (tablets and capsules):- Stop feed 2 hours before dose |
| Restart feed 1 hour after dose |

Withholding enteral feeds can compromise nutrition and interfere with blood glucose management. If the patient does not have a break in their feeding regimen during which efavirenz can be given, the Nutrition Team should be contacted to advise on management.

Emtricitabine

Presentation
Capsules.
Oral solution.

Administration – enteral tubes
The capsules can be opened and the contents dispersed in water for administration.[132] Follow the directions in section 3.7.

No information on administering the oral solution via enteral feeding tubes has been located.

Administration – swallowing difficulties
1st choice – Use the oral solution.
2nd choice – The capsules can be opened and the contents dispersed in water for administration.[132] Follow the directions in section 3.7.

| **Enalapril** |

Presentation
Tablets.
Oral solution (special).[580,582]
A suspension can be made by Pharmacy in some centres (see Appendix 1).[452,512]

Administration – enteral tubes
1st choice – The tablets can be crushed and dispersed in water for administration.[40,41,152] Without crushing some brands will disperse in around five minutes.[8,154] Follow the directions in section 3.5.
2nd choice – A suspension can be made by Pharmacy in some centres.[150,452,463] Follow the directions in section 3.6.
3rd choice – Use the oral solution (if available). Follow the directions in section 3.6.

Administration – swallowing difficulties
1st choice – A suspension can be made by Pharmacy in some centres.[150,452,463]
2nd choice – Use the oral solution (if available).
3rd choice – The tablets can be crushed and dispersed in water for administration.[40,41,152] Without crushing some brands will disperse in around five minutes.[8,154] Follow the directions in section 3.5. The crushed tablets may have a bitter after-taste.[135]

| **Enalapril and hydrochlorothiazide (Innozide®)** |

Presentation
Tablets.

Clinical guidance
Innozide® tablets contain enalapril 20mg and hydrochlorothiazide 12.5mg.[272] Use enalapril as a separate component, and an appropriate thiazide diuretic, e.g. bendroflumethiazide. See individual monographs for details.

Entacapone

Presentation
Film-coated tablets.

Administration – enteral tubes
The tablets can be dispersed in water for administration.[104,105] They disperse in one to five minutes.[154] Follow the directions in section 3.5. Take care if crushing as this produces red dust which may stain.[132]

Entacapone does not fully dissolve in water, so if giving via enteral feeding tube, the tube should be flushed well after administration. The drug also stains orange, and may stain an enteral feeding tube.[105]

Administration – swallowing difficulties
The crushed tablet may be given in jam, honey, or orange juice. It has a bitter taste.[104,132]

Eprosartan

Presentation
Film-coated tablets.

Administration – enteral tubes / swallowing difficulties
The tablets can be crushed and mixed with water for administration.[138] Follow the directions in section 3.5.

Erythromycin

Presentation
Capsules.
Film-coated tablets.
Suspension (some brands contain sorbitol).
Injection.

Administration – enteral tubes
1st choice – Give by parenteral injection.
2nd choice – Use the suspension.[94,104] Follow the directions in section 3.6.

Administration – swallowing difficulties
1st choice – Use the suspension.[94,104]
2nd choice – Give by parenteral injection.

Clinical guidance
Erythromycin is absorbed mainly in the duodenum,[176] so there is a risk of reduced absorption if the drug is administered through enteral feeding tubes terminating in the jejunum. However some studies have shown erythromycin absorption to occur throughout the jejunum and ileum.[396] It is recommended that antibiotics are administered by injection, rather than via enteral feeding tube, if at all possible due to the nature of the conditions they are used to treat.

Escitalopram

Presentation
Film-coated tablets.
Oral drops.

Administration – enteral tubes
1st choice – Use the oral drops, which can be mixed with water, orange juice or apple juice to aid administration.[302]
2nd choice – The tablets can be dispersed in water for administration.[105] They disperse immediately.[154] Follow the directions in section 3.5. Flush well as the tablets are poorly soluble.[132]

(monograph continues on next page)

Administration – swallowing difficulties
1st choice – Use the oral drops, which can be mixed with water, orange juice or apple juice to aid administration.[302]
2nd choice – The tablets can be dispersed in water for administration.[105] They disperse immediately.[154] Follow the directions in section 3.5. The crushed / dispersed tablets have an unpleasant taste.[132]

Eslicarbazepine

Presentation
Tablets.

Clinical guidance
No information on administering eslicarbazepine to patients with enteral feeding tubes or swallowing difficulties has been located.

Changing formulations / product manufacturer
The MHRA has issued guidance recommending that (where possible) patients on eslicarbazepine (when used for seizures) are maintained on a specific manufacturer's product, due to variability in product characteristics which may lead to a loss of seizure control when switching between brands / manufacturers.[651] When managing patients with enteral tubes or swallowing difficulties it may not be possible to maintain the patient on their previous preparation due to the need to change to an appropriate formulation. However all product switches should be carried out with care and close monitoring, and where possible patients should be maintained from then onwards on a single manufacturer's product.

Esomeprazole

Presentation
Film-coated tablets.
Granules for oral suspension.

Administration – enteral tubes
Esomeprazole tablets and granules for oral suspension are licensed for administration via gastric tubes.[156,433] They will disperse in water for administration. The tablets contain micro-granules which are approximately 0.5mm in diameter.[236] These micro-granules will remain after the tablet disperses, and should not be crushed.[156] The granules for oral suspension contain granules approximately 0.6mm in diameter after reconstitution,[559] and these should not be crushed.[433]

Granules for oral suspension[433]

This formulation is suitable to be administered through enteral tubes of size 6 French and larger.[433]

1. Add the contents of a 10mg sachet to 15mL of water (use 30mL water for a 20mg dose, 60mL water for a 40mg dose).
2. Stir, and leave for a few minutes to thicken (NB medicines should never be left unattended).
3. Stir again, and draw the suspension into an oral or bladder-tipped syringe.
4. Attach to the enteral tube and administer.
5. Refill the syringe with the same volume of water.
6. Shake and flush any remaining contents down the enteral tube.
7. Flush the tube.[433]

(monograph continues on next page)

Tablets[156]

The tablets are only suitable for fairly wide-bore tubes. The 20mg tablets can be administered through tubes size 8 French and larger, the 40mg through 14 French and larger.[132]

It is recommended to use the 20mg tablets where possible as the micro-granules in these are smaller, and therefore less likely to cause blockage. For patients with fine-bore enteral tubes, consider switching to lansoprazole Fastabs®, which have smaller micro-granules.

1. Place the tablet in the barrel of an oral or bladder-tipped syringe.
2. Draw up 25mL water and 5mL air.
3. Shake the syringe for 2 minutes to disperse the tablet.
4. Hold the tip upright to ensure it has not clogged with particles.
5. Attach to the tube whilst keeping the tip upright.
6. Shake the syringe, point it down, and administer 5-10mL of the contents.
7. Invert the syringe and shake.
8. Point the tip down and administer another 5-10mL.
9. Repeat until empty.
10. Draw up another 25mL of water and 5mL of air, and administer to wash the sediment from syringe.[156]

It is important to follow the directions closely to avoid tube blockage.

Administration – swallowing difficulties
1st choice – Use the granules for oral suspension. The suspension thickens after preparation.[433]
2nd choice – The tablets can be dispersed in non-carbonated water for administration. They should not be dispersed in any other liquid. The pellets remaining after the tablet disperses should not be crushed.[156] Follow the directions in section 3.5.

Etamsylate (Ethamsylate)

Presentation
Tablets.

Administration – enteral tubes / swallowing difficulties
The tablets can be crushed and mixed with water for administration.[104] Follow the directions in section 3.5.

Ethambutol

Presentation
Tablets.
A suspension can be made by Pharmacy in some centres.[573]

Administration – enteral tubes
1st choice – The tablets can be crushed and mixed with water for administration.[104,105] Follow the directions in section 3.5.
2nd choice – A suspension can be made by Pharmacy in some centres.[95,573] Follow the directions in section 3.6.

Administration – swallowing difficulties
1st choice – A suspension can be made by Pharmacy in some centres.[95,573]
2nd choice – The tablets can be crushed and mixed with water for administration.[104,105] Follow the directions in section 3.5.

Ethosuximide

Presentation
Capsules.
Syrup.

Administration – enteral tubes / swallowing difficulties
Use the syrup.[41,104] Follow the directions in section 3.6. Emeside® syrup can be diluted with water immediately before administration if necessary to reduce the viscosity.[341]

Etidronate

Clinical guidance
See entry under Disodium etidronate.

Etodolac

Clinical guidance
No information on giving etodolac via enteral feeding tubes has been located. Consider changing to an alternative non-steroidal anti-inflammatory drug available via a non-oral route, e.g. diclofenac suppositories.

Etoposide

Presentation
Capsules.
A solution can be made by Pharmacy in some centres (see Appendix 1).[464]
Injection.

Administration – enteral tubes / swallowing difficulties
Caution – cytotoxic. Contact Pharmacy for advice before giving (Pharmacists – see Appendix 2).

Etoricoxib

Presentation
Film-coated tablets.

Administration – enteral tubes / swallowing difficulties
The tablets can be crushed and dispersed in water for administration.[349] Particles of the tablet coat may remain – flush well to prevent tube blockage.[358] Follow the directions in section 3.5.

Exforge®

Presentation
Film-coated tablets.

Clinical guidance
Exforge® tablets contain amlodipine and valsartan at various dosages.[272] Use the separate components – see individual monographs for details.

Ezetimibe

Presentation
Tablets.

Clinical guidance
Not suitable for administration via enteral feeding tubes as the excipients do not mix well with water.[124] There is no data on drug stability or whether the drug may interact with enteral feeding tubes.[124,347]

Famciclovir

Presentation
Tablets.

Administration – enteral tubes / swallowing difficulties
1st choice – Consider whether an alternative drug available in a wider range of formulations is appropriate, e.g. aciclovir, which is available as infusion and dispersible tablets.
2nd choice – The tablets can be crushed and mixed with water for administration.[105] Follow the directions in section 3.5.

Famotidine

Presentation
Tablets.
A suspension can be made by Pharmacy in some centres (see Appendix 1).[465]

Administration – enteral tubes
1st choice – Switch to an alternative drug available in a wider range of formulations, e.g. ranitidine, which is available as injection and effervescent tablets.
2nd choice – The tablets can be crushed and mixed with water for administration.[134] Without crushing they will disperse in two to five minutes.[8] Follow the directions in section 3.5.

No information on giving the suspension via enteral feeding tubes has been located.

Administration – swallowing difficulties
1st choice – Switch to an alternative drug available in a wider range of formulations, e.g. ranitidine, which is available as injection and effervescent tablets.
2nd choice – A suspension can be made by Pharmacy in some centres.
3rd choice – The tablets can be crushed and mixed with water for administration.[134] Without crushing they will disperse in two to five minutes.[8] Follow the directions in section 3.5.

Fefol®

Clinical guidance
See entry under 'Iron preparations'.

Felodipine

Presentation
Modified-release tablets.
Oral solution (special).[542]

Clinical guidance – enteral tubes
Felodipine tablets should not be crushed and are therefore not suitable for enteral feeding tube administration.[60] Consider amlodipine as an alternative.

No information on giving the oral solution via enteral feeding tubes has been located.

Administration – swallowing difficulties
Use the oral solution (if available). Alternatively consider amlodipine.

Fenofibrate

Presentation
Capsules.
Film-coated tablets.

Administration – enteral tubes
The capsules can be opened and the contents dispersed in water.[61] Follow the directions in section 3.7.

Administration – swallowing difficulties
The capsule contents have been administered in orange juice to patients with swallowing difficulties.[105]

No information on administering the film-coated tablet is available. Consider switching to the capsules, or to an alternative product. Contact Pharmacy for advice.

Fenoprofen

Presentation
Tablets.

Administration – enteral tubes / swallowing difficulties
The tablets can be crushed and dispersed in water for administration.[8] Without crushing they will disperse in two to five minutes.[8] Follow the directions in section 3.5.

Feed guidance
Take with or after food.[429]

Ferrograd Folic®

Clinical guidance
See entry under 'Iron preparations'.

Ferrous fumarate

Clinical guidance
See entry under 'Iron preparations'.

Ferrous gluconate

Clinical guidance
See entry under 'Iron preparations'.

Ferrous sulphate

Clinical guidance
See entry under 'Iron preparations'.

Fexofenadine

Presentation
Film-coated tablets.

Administration – enteral tubes / swallowing difficulties
1st choice – Switch to an alternative antihistamine available as a liquid, e.g. loratadine.
2nd choice – The tablets can be crushed and mixed with water for adminstration.[62] Without crushing they disperse in around five minutes.[154] Follow the directions in section 3.5.

Feed guidance
Fexofenadine should be given on an empty stomach, so withhold enteral feeds for half an hour before and half an hour after each dose.[62,225]

Summary:-	Stop feed 30 minutes before dose
	Restart feed 30 minutes after dose

Withholding enteral feeds can compromise nutrition and interfere with blood glucose management. If the patient does not have a break in their feeding regimen during which fexofenadine can be given, the Nutrition Team should be contacted to advise on management.

Fidaxomicin

Presentation
Film-coated tablets.

Administration – enteral tubes
No information on administering this medication via enteral tubes to real patients has been located. Small-scale laboratory testing appears to indicate that the tablets can be crushed and mixed with water for administration via enteral feeding tubes (see "Clinical guidance" below).[587] With so little data, this is not recommended unless there are no other options. The tablets are film-coated, so crush well to avoid tube blockage, and flush well post-dose to ensure that the entire dose is administered.

(monograph continues on next page)

Administration – swallowing difficulties

The tablets can be crushed and mixed with apple sauce for administration to patients with swallowing difficulties.[587] This method of administration is unlicensed.

Clinical guidance

The manufacturers have done stability studies which show that fidaxomicin is stable for 2 hours as a crushed tablet in water, and for 24 hours when mixed with apple sauce or Ensure® (note – it is not recommended to mix medications with large volume feeds, in case all the medication is not ingested). Small-scale laboratory tests indicate that after crushing a fidaxomicin tablet and passing it through a nasogastric tube, 96.3% of the dose could be recovered, suggesting that it might be possible to administer fidaxomicin this way with only a small loss of drug.[587] Good crushing and flushing technique should minimise such losses.

Finasteride

Presentation

Film-coated tablets.

Women who are or who may become pregnant should not handle crushed, broken, or dissolved tablets.[64]

Administration – enteral tubes / swallowing difficulties

Place the tablet in the barrel of an oral or bladder-tipped syringe. Draw water up into the syringe and allow the tablet to disperse[63] (in order to minimise carer contact with the medication). Follow the directions in section 3.5. If giving via enteral feeding tube, flush well after each dose as the drug is insoluble.[155]

Flavoxate

Presentation
Film-coated tablets.

Administration – enteral tubes
The tablets can be crushed and mixed with water for administration.[105] Follow the directions in section 3.5. Flush enteral tubes well after dosing.[105]

Administration – swallowing difficulties
The tablets can be crushed and mixed with water for administration.[105] Follow the directions in section 3.5. Flavoxate has a bitter taste when crushed.[105]

Flecainide

Presentation
Tablets.
Oral liquid (special).[580,582]
A suspension can be made by Pharmacy in some centres (see Appendix 1).[457]
Injection.

Administration – enteral tubes
1st choice – The tablets can be crushed and dispersed in deionised water for administration.[8,40,225] Some sources do not recommend this.[152] Follow the directions in section 3.5. Do not use tap water.[105]
2nd choice – A suspension can be made by Pharmacy in some centres. Follow the directions in section 3.6.
3rd choice – Use the oral liquid (if available). Follow the directions in section 3.6.
4th choice – The injection has been administered enterally, given undiluted. This should only be used in emergency situations, and the patient should be monitored for clinical / adverse effects.[40,168] Follow the directions in section 3.6.

(monograph continues on next page)

Administration – swallowing difficulties

1st choice – A suspension can be made by Pharmacy in some centres.

2nd choice – Use the oral liquid (if available).

3rd choice – The tablets can be crushed and dispersed in deionised water for administration.[8,40,225] Some sources do not recommend this.[152] Follow the directions in section 3.5. Do not use tap water.[105] The crushed tablets have a local anaesthetic effect, so should be used with care in patients with swallowing difficulties.[40]

4th choice – The injection has been administered enterally, given undiluted. This should only be used in emergency situations, and the patient should be monitored for clinical / adverse effects.[40,168] Follow the directions in section 3.6.

Clinical guidance

If giving via enteral feeding tube, always flush with deionised water, and do not mix with alkali solutions, sulphate, phosphate, or chloride ions.[95] Do NOT mix this drug with other medications prior to administration.

Flucloxacillin

Presentation

Capsules.
Suspension.
Injection.

Administration – enteral tubes

1st choice – Give by parenteral injection.

2nd choice – Use the suspension. Follow the directions in section 3.6.

Administration – swallowing difficulties

1st choice – Use the suspension.

2nd choice – Give by parenteral injection.

Clinical guidance

The suspension has a high osmolality.[6] Administer reconstituted injection via the enteral feeding tube in patients with tubes delivering directly into the jejunum if osmotic diarrhoea is a problem.[6,104,155]

(monograph continues on next page)

There is no information on where in the gastrointestinal tract flucloxacillin is absorbed.[419] It is likely that flucloxacillin has a similar absorption following administration directly into the jejunum as it does following oral administration.[6]

Feed guidance
Flucloxacillin suspension should be given on an empty stomach,[35,104] so withhold enteral feeds for two hours before and one hour after each enteral dose.[225] If this is not possible due to the frequency of administration (usually four times daily) then consider increasing the dose or using an alternative antibiotic.

Summary:-	Stop feed 2 hours before dose
	Restart feed 1 hour after dose

Withholding enteral feeds can compromise nutrition and interfere with blood glucose management. If the patient does not have a break in their feeding regimen during which enteral flucloxacillin can be given, the Nutrition Team should be contacted to advise on management.

Fluconazole

Presentation
Capsules.
Suspension.
Infusion.

Administration – enteral tubes
1st choice – Give by intravenous infusion if appropriate.
2nd choice – Use the suspension.[104,248] Follow the directions in section 3.6.
3rd choice – The capsules can be opened, and the contents mixed with water for administration.[155,200,201] Follow the directions in section 3.7.

(monograph continues on next page)

Administration – swallowing difficulties
1st choice – Use the suspension.[104,248]
2nd choice – Give by intravenous infusion if appropriate.
3rd choice – The capsules can be opened, and the contents mixed with water for administration.[155,200,201] Follow the directions in section 3.7.

Clinical guidance
Higher doses (20-25% greater) may be required when fluconazole is administered directly into the jejunum.[155,228] Studies have shown that seriously ill patients with recent gastrointestinal surgery and / or peritonitis achieve adequate absorption of fluconazole given via enteral feeding tube.[200,201,223]

Fluconazole penetrates all body fluids well. The concentration of fluconazole in the saliva four hours after dose ingestion is the same whether the drug was given as a capsule or as a suspension. Therefore it can be expected that a dose given intravenously or via an enteral feeding tube could still be expected to have a clinical effect on a fungal infection in the mouth or throat.[279]

Feed guidance
Some reports indicate that enteral fluconazole interacts with enteral feeds (particularly Jevity®).[105] Other studies have shown good bioavailability of fluconazole when given via enteral feeding tubes with concomitant feeds.[223,228]

If the feeding regimen allows, give enteral fluconazole during a feeding break. However if feeding is continuous it is not necessary to compromise feeding unless the patient is on Jevity®, in which case the risk of subtherapeutic treatment should be weighed against the benefits of feeding. If the feed is withheld, it should be stopped for one hour before and one hour after each dose of fluconazole.[105]

Flucytosine

Presentation
Tablets.
A suspension can be made by Pharmacy in some centres (see Appendix 1).[451,466,467]
Infusion.

Administration – enteral tubes
No information on giving flucytosine through enteral feeding tubes has been located.

Administration – swallowing difficulties
Use the suspension (if available).

Fludrocortisone

Presentation
Tablets.
Oral solution (special).[582]
A suspension can be made by Pharmacy in some centres (see Appendix 1).[512]

Administration – enteral tubes
1st choice – The tablets will disperse in water.[7,8,40,41,152] They disperse within one minute.[8,154] Follow the directions in section 3.5. Flush the feeding tube well after administration.[155]
2nd choice – A suspension can be made by Pharmacy in some centres.[155] Follow the directions in section 3.6.
3rd choice – Use the oral solution (if available). Follow the directions in section 3.6.

Administration – swallowing difficulties
1st choice – A suspension can be made by Pharmacy in some centres.[155]
2nd choice – Use the oral solution (if available).
3rd choice – The tablets will disperse in water.[7,8,40,41,152] They disperse within one minute.[8,154] Follow the directions in section 3.5.

Fluoxetine

Presentation
Capsules.
Liquid.

Administration – enteral tubes / swallowing difficulties
1st choice – Use the liquid (and if giving via enteral feeding tube, dilute with the same volume of distilled water). Follow the directions in section 3.6.
2nd choice – The capsules have been opened and the contents dispersed in 120mL water. The capsule contents will dissolve in about 5 minutes.[132] Follow the directions in section 3.7.

Clinical guidance
Fluoxetine has been reported to decrease appetite.[33]

Flupentixol (Flupenthixol)

Presentation
Sugar-coated tablets.
Depot injections.

Administration – enteral tubes
1st choice – Consider changing to the depot preparation.
2nd choice – The tablets can be crushed and mixed with water for administration.[105] Follow the directions in section 3.5. The tablets are poorly soluble, so flush well after dosing.

Administration – swallowing difficulties
Crushed tablets can be mixed with fruit juice for administration to patients with swallowing difficulties.[104] Give immediately after mixing with fruit juice.[104]

Fluphenazine

Presentation
Sugar-coated tablets (no longer available in the UK).

Administration – enteral tubes / swallowing difficulties
1st choice – Consider changing to the depot preparation.
2nd choice – The tablets can be crushed and dispersed in water for administration (some centres advise against this).[41,95] Follow the directions in section 3.5.

Flurbiprofen

Presentation
Tablets, sugar-coated tablets.
Modified-release capsules (no longer available in the UK).

Administration – enteral tubes / swallowing difficulties
The capsules (if available) can be opened and the modified-release microbeads administered in plenty of water. The onset of action may be faster when the drug is administered in this way. The microbeads should not be crushed, and may have the potential to block narrow-bore enteral feeding tubes.[138] Follow the directions in section 3.7.

Flutamide

Presentation
Tablets.

Administration – enteral tubes / swallowing difficulties
The tablets can be crushed and mixed with milk or fruit juice for administration.[105] Follow the directions in section 3.5.

Fluvastatin

Presentation
Capsules.
Modified-release tablets.

Administration – enteral tubes / swallowing difficulties
The capsules can be opened and the contents mixed with water for administration.[41,65] Follow the directions in section 3.7. There is no information available on whether fluvastatin is likely to block enteral feeding tubes. When giving via enteral tube, flush well after each dose.[65]

The modified-release tablet is not suitable for enteral tube administration. Contact Pharmacy for advice.

Fluvoxamine

Presentation
Tablets.
Film-coated tablets.

Administration – enteral tubes / swallowing difficulties
When swallowing problems are likely to be long-term, consider switching to an alternative therapy available as a liquid, e.g. fluoxetine.

For short-term use, the tablets can be crushed and mixed with water for administration.[105] Follow the directions in section 3.5.

Folic acid

Presentation
Tablets.
Syrup.
Oral solution.
Injection (unlicensed special).

Administration – enteral tubes / swallowing difficulties
1st choice – Use the syrup.[94,104] Follow the directions in section 3.6.
2nd choice – The tablets have been crushed and mixed with water for administration.[8,133] Follow the directions in section 3.5.

The oral solution can be diluted with water to reduce the osmolality if desired when giving into the jejunum, however this is outside the product licence.[360]

Forceval®

Presentation
Soluble tablets.
Capsules and junior capsules.

Administration – enteral tubes
1st choice – Use the soluble tablets. They can be dispersed in 50ml of water for administration.[664] Follow the directions in section 3.5.
2nd choice – Consider switching to an alternate multivitamin preparation available as a liquid. Contact Pharmacy for advice.

Administration – swallowing difficulties
1st choice – Use the soluble tablets. They should be dissolved in 125-200ml of water.[664]
2nd choice – Consider switching to an alternate multivitamin preparation available as a liquid. Contact Pharmacy for advice.

Fosinopril

Presentation
Tablets.

Administration – enteral tubes / swallowing difficulties
The tablets can be crushed and mixed with water for administration.[105] Follow the directions in section 3.5. The drug is soluble 1 in 10 in water.[321]

Furazolidone

Presentation
Tablets (named patient).
Oral suspension (named patient).

Administration – enteral tubes
No information about the use of this medication via enteral feeding tubes has been located.

Administration – swallowing difficulties
The tablets can be crushed and mixed with a spoonful of corn syrup.[152,157]

Furosemide (Frusemide)

Presentation
Tablets.
Sugar-free oral solution (some preparations contain alcohol).
Oral solution (special).[542,582,658]
Injection.

Administration – enteral tubes
1st choice – Consider giving by parenteral injection.
2nd choice – Use the oral solution, and dilute with the same volume of water before administration.[94] Follow the directions in section 3.6.

(monograph continues on next page)

Administration – swallowing difficulties
1st choice – Use the oral solution.[94]
2nd choice – Consider giving by parenteral injection.

Clinical guidance
Absorption may be reduced when administered directly into the jejunum.[6,104]

Furosemide and potassium (Diumide-K Continus®)

Presentation
Film-coated tablets.

Clinical guidance
Diumide-K Continus® tablets contain furosemide 40mg and potassium 8mmol in a modified-release preparation.[272] Use the separate components – furosemide and an appropriate standard-release formulation of potassium. See individual monographs for details. Contact Pharmacy for advice if necessary.

Furosemide and spironolactone (Lasilactone®)

Presentation
Capsules.

Clinical guidance
Lasilactone® capsules contain furosemide 20mg and spironolactone 50mg.[272] Use the separate components – see individual monographs for details.

Gabapentin

Presentation
Tablets, capsules.
Oral solution.[589]
Syrup (imported special – Pfizer[145]), oral solution (special).[582,658]
A suspension can be made by Pharmacy in some centres.[573]

Administration – enteral tubes
Open the capsule, dissolve the contents in water, and give immediately (gabapentin has limited stability in water).[37,41,152] Follow the directions in section 3.7.

No information on administering the oral solution via enteral feeding tubes has been located.

Administration – swallowing difficulties
1st choice – Use the oral solution.
2nd choice – Use the unlicensed syrup or the special oral solution (if available).
3rd choice – A suspension can be made by Pharmacy in some centres.
4th choice – The contents of the capsules can be sprinkled on food or given in fruit juice to mask their unpleasant taste. They should be given immediately as the drug is rapidly hydrolysed.[37,104]

Clinical guidance
Do not give at the same time as aluminium / magnesium antacids.[35]

Galantamine

Presentation
Film-coated tablets.
Modified-release capsules.
Solution.

Administration – enteral tubes / swallowing difficulties
1st choice – Use the solution if it is available. It should be diluted in water (or any non-alcoholic drink) before administration.[323] Follow the directions in section 3.6.
2nd choice – The tablets can be crushed and mixed with water for administration.[104] The drug is quite soluble.[322] Follow the directions in section 3.5.

Feed guidance
Galantamine should be taken with food in order to minimise cholinergic side effects.[322]

Galfer FA®

Clinical guidance
See entry under 'Iron preparations'.

Ganciclovir

Presentation
Capsules (now discontinued[354]).
A suspension can be made by Pharmacy in some centres (see Appendix 1).[468]
Infusion.

Clinical guidance
Ganciclovir is toxic. Do not open the capsule.[41] Consider switching to valganciclovir. Contact Pharmacy for advice.

Glibenclamide

Presentation
Tablets.
A suspension can be made by Pharmacy in some centres.

Administration – enteral tubes
1st choice – Consider whether switching to insulin would be appropriate.
2nd choice – The tablets can be crushed and mixed with water for administration.[8,62] Without crushing they disperse in one to five minutes.[8,154] Follow the directions in section 3.5.
3rd choice – A suspension can be made by Pharmacy in some centres.[155] Follow the directions in section 3.6.

Administration – swallowing difficulties
1st choice – Consider whether switching to insulin would be appropriate.
2nd choice – A suspension can be made by Pharmacy in some centres.[155]
3rd choice – The tablets can be crushed and mixed with water for administration.[8,62] Without crushing they disperse in one to five minutes.[8,154] Follow the directions in section 3.5.

Clinical guidance
There is a possibility of reduced absorption when administered directly into the jejunum.[155] Monitor blood glucose.[558]

Feed guidance
Give just before the start of a feed.[62]

Gliclazide

Presentation
Tablets.
Modified-release tablets.
Oral solution (special).[582,658]
A suspension can be made by Pharmacy in some centres.[573]

Administration – enteral tubes
1st choice – Consider whether switching to insulin would be appropriate.
2nd choice – Crush the tablets well (as the drug is practically insoluble[253]) and mix with water or orange juice for administration.[45,132] Follow the directions in section 3.5.
3rd choice – A suspension can be made by Pharmacy in some centres.[155] Follow the directions in section 3.6.
4th choice – Use the oral solution (if available). Follow the directions in section 3.6.

Do not crush the modified-release tablets.

Administration – swallowing difficulties
1st choice – Consider whether switching to insulin would be appropriate.
2nd choice – A suspension can be made by Pharmacy in some centres.[155]
3rd choice – Use the oral solution (if available).
4th choice – Crush the tablets well (as the drug is practically insoluble[253]) and mix with water or orange juice for administration.[45,132] Follow the directions in section 3.5.

Do not crush the modified-release tablets.

Clinical guidance
Switching from modified-release to standard tablets should be done with careful blood monitoring.[303]

30mg modified-release tablet   equivalent to   80mg standard tablet[303]

(monograph continues on next page)

It may be advisable to monitor blood glucose in any patient when altering the formulation / crushing the tablets.[558]

Feed guidance
Give just before the start of a feed.[132]

Glimepiride

Presentation
Tablets.

Clinical guidance
Do not crush the tablets as this may affect their bioavailability.[62] Consider whether switching to insulin would be appropriate. The tablets will disperse in less than five minutes,[358] but no information about giving dispersed tablets has been located.

Glipizide

Presentation
Tablets.

Administration – enteral tubes / swallowing difficulties
1st choice – Consider whether switching to insulin would be appropriate.
2nd choice – The tablets can be crushed and dispersed in water for administration.[8,66] Follow the directions in section 3.5. There is no information available on whether glipizide is likely to block enteral feeding tubes.[66]

Feed guidance
Glipizide should be given half an hour before food.[176,615] Enteral feeds should be withheld for half an hour before and half an hour after each dose.[225]

Summary:-	Stop feed 30 minutes before dose
	Restart feed 30 minutes after dose

(monograph continues on next page)

Withholding enteral feeds can compromise nutrition and interfere with blood glucose management. If the patient does not have a break in their feeding regimen during which glipizide can be given, the Nutrition Team should be contacted to advise on management.

Gliquidone

Presentation
Tablets (no longer available in the UK).

Administration – enteral tubes / swallowing difficulties
1st choice – Consider whether switching to insulin would be appropriate.
2nd choice – The tablets can be crushed and dispersed in water for administration.[138] Follow the directions in section 3.5.

Glyceryl trinitrate

Presentation
Acute use preparations.
Sublingual tablets.
Sublingual spray.
Injection.

Prophylaxis preparations.
Modified-release buccal tablets (no longer available in the UK).
Modified-release tablets (no longer available in the UK).
Transdermal patches.
Ointment.

Administration – enteral tubes / swallowing difficulties
Acute use preparations.
For patients with an unsafe swallow, use the sublingual spray.

Prophylaxis preparations.
Buccal tablets can be continued in patients who are able to use them appropriately.

(monograph continues on next page)

Do not crush the modified-release tablets.   Consider switching patients on modified-release tablets to transdermal patches. Contact Pharmacy for advice.

Clinical guidance
The sublingual and buccal tablets require moisture in the mouth for adequate absorption, and may be less effective in patients with swallowing difficulties.

Glycopyrronium

Presentation
Tablets (named patient only).[40]
Oral solution (special).[582,658]
Injection.

Administration – enteral tubes
1st choice – Consider using subcutaneous doses when required (unlicensed), or a subcutaneous infusion by syringe driver.
2nd choice – If the tablets are available, they can be crushed and mixed with water for administration.[40,152] Follow the directions in section 3.5.
3rd choice – Use the oral solution (if available). Follow the directions in section 3.6.
4th choice – The injection has been used via enteral feeding tubes.[132,152] Follow the directions in section 3.6.

Administration – swallowing difficulties
1st choice – Consider using subcutaneous doses when required (unlicensed), or a subcutaneous infusion by syringe driver.
2nd choice – Use the oral solution (if available).
3rd choice – If the tablets are available, they can be crushed and mixed with water for administration.[40,152] Follow the directions in section 3.5.
4th choice – The injection has been used orally.[132,152] Follow the directions in section 3.6.

Granisetron

Presentation
Film-coated tablets.
Liquid (no longer available in the UK).
A suspension can be made by Pharmacy in some centres (see Appendix 1).[469,470]
Patches.
Injection.

Administration – enteral tubes
1st choice – Give by parenteral injection.
2nd choice – The patches are indicated for the prevention of nausea and vomiting associated with chemotherapy (i.e. when nausea and vomiting can be predicted), and may be suitable in certain situations.[662]
3rd choice – Consider switching to ondansetron, which is available as suppositories and as a liquid.
4th choice – The tablets can be crushed and mixed with water for administration.[356] There is no data to support the clinical efficacy, stability or bioavailability of granisetron given in this way.[356] Follow the directions in section 3.5.
5th choice – Use the liquid (if available) or the suspension, and flush with 15-30mL of distilled water.[41] Follow the directions in section 3.6.

Administration – swallowing difficulties
1st choice – Consider switching to ondansetron, which is available as a liquid, as melt tablets, and as suppositories.
2nd choice – Give by parenteral injection.
3rd choice – The patches are indicated for the prevention of nausea and vomiting associated with chemotherapy (i.e. when nausea and vomiting can be predicted), and may be suitable in certain situations.[662]
4th choice – Use the liquid (if available) or the suspension.
5th choice – The tablets can be crushed and mixed with water for administration.[356] There is no data to support the clinical efficacy, stability or bioavailability of granisetron given in this way.[356] Follow the directions in section 3.5.

Griseofulvin

Presentation
Tablets.
Oral suspension (no longer available in the UK).
Spray.

Administration – enteral tubes
The drug is very insoluble,[253] and the tablets are therefore unsuitable to be crushed for administration. Consider an alternative treatment, e.g. terbinafine.

Administration – swallowing difficulties
Use the oral suspension (if available).

Haloperidol

Presentation
Tablets, capsules.
Oral liquid.
Oral solution (special).[542,582,658]
Injection, depot injection.

Administration – enteral tubes
1st choice – Give by parenteral injection if appropriate.
2nd choice – Use the liquid preparation. Follow the directions in section 3.6.
3rd choice – The capsules can be opened and the contents dispersed in water.[133] Follow the directions in section 3.7.

Administration – swallowing difficulties
1st choice – Use the liquid preparation.
2nd choice – Give by parenteral injection if appropriate.
3rd choice – The capsules can be opened and the contents dispersed in water.[133] Follow the directions in section 3.7.

Hydralazine

Presentation
Sugar-coated tablets.
Dispersible tablet (Special – may not be commonly available).
A suspension can be made by Pharmacy in some centres.
Injection.

Administration – enteral tubes
1st choice – A suspension can be made by Pharmacy in some centres.[155,452] Follow the directions in section 3.6.
2nd choice – The tablets can be crushed,[98] but are sugar-coated and are likely to block enteral feeding tubes. Follow the directions in section 3.5. Flush well after administration.
3rd choice – The injection can be made up with water for injections and administered via enteral feeding tubes.[40,98,152] Follow the directions in section 3.6.

Administration – swallowing difficulties
1st choice – A suspension can be made by Pharmacy in some centres.[155,452]
2nd choice – The tablets can be crushed.[98] Follow the directions in section 3.5.
3rd choice – The injection can be made up with water for injections and administered orally.[40,98,152] Follow the directions in section 3.6.

Clinical guidance
Crushing the tablets may alter their absorption rate (usually increased).[105] Monitor blood pressure.[87,90,95]

Hydralazine injection, when used for oral / enteral feeding tube administration, should only be made up with water for injections, as it interacts with metal ions found in other water sources.[98]

Feed guidance
Enteral hydralazine absorption may be either increased or decreased by food or in the presence of enteral feeds.[641,642,644] Enteral hydralazine should be taken at a consistent time each day with respect to meals.[642,644] If the observed effect is not as great as expected, consider withholding the feed for two hours before and one hour after each dose.[2,155,572]

Hydrocortisone

Presentation
Tablets.
Modified-release tablets.
Oral suspension (special).[580,582]
A suspension can be made by Pharmacy in some centres.[573]
Injection.

Administration – enteral tubes
1st choice – Give by parenteral injection if possible.
2nd choice – The standard-release tablets are insoluble but will disperse in water for administration.[8,63,152] They disperse within one minute.[8,154] Follow the directions in section 3.5.
3rd choice – A suspension can be made by Pharmacy in some centres.[63] Follow the directions in section 3.6.
4th choice – Use the special oral suspension (if available). Follow the directions in section 3.6.
5th choice – Efcortesol® injection may be given enterally.[152] Follow the directions in section 3.6.

Patients on modified-release tablets should be converted to other preparations more suitable for enteral tube administration. Contact Pharmacy for advice.

Administration – swallowing difficulties
1st choice – Give by parenteral injection if possible.
2nd choice – A suspension can be made by Pharmacy in some centres.[63]
3rd choice – Use the special oral suspension (if available).
4th choice – The standard-release tablets are insoluble but will disperse in water for administration.[8,63,152] They disperse within one minute.[8,154] Follow the directions in section 3.5.
5th choice – Efcortesol® injection may be given enterally.[152] Follow the directions in section 3.6.

Patients on modified-release tablets should be converted to other preparations more suitable for use in swallowing difficulties. Contact Pharmacy for advice.

(monograph continues on next page)

Clinical guidance
When switching from modified-release tablets to immediate-release preparations, use the same total daily dose, divided and given more frequently. Monitor clinical response.[624]

Hydromorphone

Presentation
Capsules.
Modified-release capsules.

Clinical guidance
Not recommended as there is a high incidence of tube blockage.[149] Consider switching to an alternative opioid available as a non-enteral preparation. Contact Pharmacy for advice.

Hydroxycarbamide (Hydroxyurea)

Presentation
Capsules.
Film-coated tablets.
A suspension can be made by Pharmacy in some centres (see Appendix 1).[471]

Administration – enteral tubes / swallowing difficulties
Caution – cytotoxic. Contact Pharmacy for advice before giving (Pharmacists – see Appendix 2).

Hydroxychloroquine

Presentation
Film-coated tablets.

Administration – enteral tubes
1st choice – The tablets can be crushed and dispersed in water for administration.[104,105,152] Follow the directions in section 3.5.
2nd choice – A liquid can be made by Pharmacy in some centres.[95] Follow the directions in section 3.6.

(monograph continues on next page)

Administration – swallowing difficulties
1st choice – A liquid can be made by Pharmacy in some centres.[95]
2nd choice – The tablets can be crushed and dispersed in water for administration.[104,105,152] Follow the directions in section 3.5.

Hydroxyzine

Presentation
Sugar-coated tablets.
Syrup (contains alcohol).

Administration – NG / PEG tubes / swallowing difficulties
Use the syrup.[94,104] Follow the directions in section 3.6.

Administration – NJ / PEJ / PEGJ tubes
Use the syrup, and dilute with water before administration to reduce the osmolality.[22,26,94,104] Follow the directions in section 3.6.

Hyoscine butylbromide

Presentation
Coated tablets.
Injection.

Administration – enteral tubes / swallowing difficulties
1st choice – Consider using parenteral injection.
2nd choice – The injection can be administered enterally.[40,44,152] Follow the directions in section 3.6.

Do not crush the tablet.

Clinical guidance
Hyoscine butylbromide has a different effect given enterally to that when given parenterally. It is not greatly absorbed following enteral administration.[321] It may therefore not be as clinically effective if given directly into the jejunum.

Hyoscine hydrobromide

Presentation
Tablets.
Solution (available as a special from Martindale, 3 day delivery).[582]
Transdermal patch (Scopoderm).
Injection.

Administration – enteral tubes / swallowing difficulties
1st choice – Consider using the patch or giving by parenteral injection.
2nd choice – The tablets may be sucked if the patient is able, and absorbed through the lining of the mouth,[103] although the level of absorption may vary, particularly in patients with little saliva.
3rd choice – The tablets can be dissolved[103] in water for administration via enteral tube, but again, absorption may vary. Follow the directions in section 3.5.
4th choice – The injection has been used enterally.[138,160] Follow the directions in section 3.6.

Clinical guidance
Hyoscine hydrobromide can decrease gastric emptying.[2]

Ibuprofen

Presentation
Sugar-coated tablets.
Syrup, effervescent sachets.
Modified-release tablets, modified-release capsules (capsules – no longer available in the UK).

Administration – enteral tubes
1st choice – Consider using an alternative non-steroidal anti-inflammatory drug available as injection or suppositories, e.g. diclofenac.
2nd choice – Use the syrup.[104] Follow the directions in section 3.6.

(monograph continues on next page)

201

Administration – swallowing difficulties
1st choice – Use the syrup.[104]
2nd choice – Consider using an alternative non-steroidal anti-inflammatory drug available as injection or suppositories, e.g. diclofenac.

Imatinib

Presentation
Film-coated tablets.

Administration – enteral tubes / swallowing difficulties
The tablets can be dispersed in water or apple juice for administration to patients who are unable to swallow them whole.[269] The manufacturer recommends using 50mL of fluid for each 100mg tablet (or 200mL for a 400mg tablet).[269]

Feed guidance
Take with or after food.[429]

Imipramine

Presentation
Coated tablets.
Syrup (may not be available), oral solution.

Administration – enteral tubes
1st choice – Use the syrup (if available),[104,105] or the oral solution. Follow the directions in section 3.6. The drug may adsorb to the tube, so flush well after dosing.
2nd choice – The tablets may be crushed and mixed with water for administration. Flush well after dosing as the coating has the potential to block enteral feeding tubes.[133] Follow the directions in section 3.5.

(monograph continues on next page)

Administration – swallowing difficulties

1st choice – Use the syrup (if available),[104,105] or the oral solution. Follow the directions in section 3.6.

2nd choice – The tablets may be crushed and mixed with water for administration.[133] Follow the directions in section 3.5.

Clinical guidance

Tricyclic antidepressants can decrease gastric emptying.[2]

Indapamide

Presentation

Coated tablets.

Modified-release tablets.

A suspension can be made by Pharmacy in some centres.

Administration – NG / PEG tubes

1st choice – For patients with tubes terminating in the stomach, the standard tablets can be dispersed in water for administration.[8,104,105] They disperse in one to five minutes.[8,154] Follow the directions in section 3.5.

2nd choice – A suspension can be made by Pharmacy in some centres.[155] Follow the directions in section 3.6.

Do not crush the modified-release tablets.

Administration – NJ / PEJ / PEGJ tubes

Administration via tubes terminating in the jejunum is not appropriate for indapamide as absorption will be greatly reduced.[155] Contact Pharmacy for advice.

Administration – swallowing difficulties

1st choice – A suspension can be made by Pharmacy in some centres.[155]

2nd choice – The standard tablets can be dispersed in water for administration.[8,104,105] They disperse in one to five minutes.[8,154] Follow the directions in section 3.5.

Do not crush the modified-release tablets.

Indometacin (Indomethacin)

Presentation
Capsules.
Sugar-free suspension.
Oral liquid (special).
A suspension can be made by Pharmacy in some centres.[573]
Suppositories.
Modified-release capsules.

Administration – enteral tubes
1st choice – Use the suppositories if possible.
2nd choice – Use the suspension. Follow the directions in section 3.6.
3rd choice – A suspension can be made by Pharmacy in some centres. Follow the directions in section 3.6.
4th choice – Use the oral liquid (if available). Follow the directions in section 3.6.

The modified-release capsules are irritant to the stomach, and should not be opened.

Do not crush the tablets.

Administration – swallowing difficulties
1st choice – Use the suspension.
2nd choice – Use the suppositories if possible.
3rd choice – A suspension can be made by Pharmacy in some centres.
4th choice – Use the oral liquid (if available).

The modified-release capsules are irritant to the stomach, and should not be opened.

Do not crush the tablets.

Indoramin

Presentation
Tablets.

Administration – enteral tubes
The tablets can be dispersed in water for administration.[67] They disperse immediately.[154] Protect from light.[138] Follow the directions in section 3.5.

Administration – swallowing difficulties
The tablets can be crushed and sprinkled onto soft food to mask the taste.[105]

Innozide®

Presentation
Tablets.

Clinical guidance
Innozide® tablets contain enalapril 20mg and hydrochlorothiazide 12.5mg.[272] Use enalapril as a separate component, and an appropriate thiazide diuretic, e.g. bendroflumethiazide. See individual monographs for details.

Inositol nicotinate

Presentation
Tablets.

Administration – enteral tubes
No information about the use of this medication via enteral feeding tubes has been located.

Administration – swallowing difficulties
The tablets will not dissolve but can be crushed and mixed with soft food for patients with swallowing difficulties.[132]

Irbesartan

Presentation
Tablets.
Oral solution (special).[582]

Administration – enteral tubes
The tablets can be crushed and dispersed in water for administration.[68] Without crushing they disperse in around five minutes.[154] Follow the directions in section 3.5. There is no information available to indicate whether irbesartan is likely to block enteral feeding tubes.[68] Flush well after each dose as the drug is practically insoluble.[155]

No information has been located about administering the oral solution via enteral feeding tubes.

Administration – swallowing difficulties
1st choice – Use the oral solution (if available).
2nd choice – The tablets can be crushed and dispersed in water for administration.[68] Without crushing they disperse in around five minutes.[154] Follow the directions in section 3.5.

Irbesartan and hydrochlorothiazide (CoAprovel®)

Presentation
Film-coated tablets.

Clinical guidance
CoAprovel® tablets contain irbesartan and hydrochlorothiazide at various dosages.[272] Use irbesartan as a separate component and an appropriate alternative thiazide diuretic, e.g. bendroflumethiazide. See individual monographs for details.

Iron preparations

Ferrous Fumarate
Tablets, 210mg (68mg iron).
Syrup, 140mg/5mL (45mg/5mL iron).
Fersaday® tablets, 322mg (100mg iron).
Galfer® capsules, 305mg (100mg iron).
Galfer® syrup, 104mg/5mL (45mg/5mL iron).

Ferrous Gluconate
Tablets, 300mg (35mg iron).

Ferrous Sulphate
Tablets, 200mg (65mg iron).
Ironorm® drops, 125mg/mL (25mg/mL iron).
Feospan® capsules, 150mg (47mg iron).
Ferrograd® tablets, 325mg (105mg iron).
Oral solution (special).[582]

Polysaccharide-Iron Complex
Niferex® elixir, 100mg/5mL iron.

Sodium Feredetate
Sytron® elixir, 190mg/5mL (27.5mg/5mL iron).

Administration – enteral tubes / swallowing difficulties
Convert to an appropriate dose of ferrous fumarate liquid. Follow the directions in section 3.6. Ferrous fumarate liquid can be diluted with water immediately prior to administration if desired to reduce the viscosity of the liquid.[338] Dilution with water may reduce side effects when ferrous fumarate liquid is given through enteral tubes terminating in the jejunum. The liquid should NOT be diluted with milk.[338]

When administering via enteral tubes terminating in the jejunum, absorption may be decreased.[155]

(monograph continues on next page)

Equivalent doses

200mg FeSO₄ tablet	equivalent to	7.2mL ferrous fumarate syrup
200mg three times daily	equivalent to	10mL twice daily

Do not crush iron tablets, as the medication is irritant.[561]

Clinical guidance
Iron absorption is greatest in the duodenum and the proximal jejunum, but does occur along the entire gastrointestinal tract. Higher doses may be needed when given through enteral tubes terminating in the jejunum.[176]

Sodium feredetate (Sytron®) is an iron chelate.[421] The chelate is broken down when it reaches the alkaline medium of the duodenum, and the iron is absorbed by the normal physiological mechanisms of the gut.[420]

Feed guidance
Some iron preparations have been reported as being incompatible with some enteral feeds, so ensure enteral feeding tubes are flushed well before and after each dose.[5,222,245]

Combination Products

Fefol® capsules, 150mg ferrous sulphate (47mg iron) and 500mcg folic acid.
Ferrograd Folic® tablets, 325mg ferrous sulphate (105mg iron) and 350mcg folic acid.
Galfer FA® capsules, 305mg ferrous fumarate (100mg iron) and 350mcg folic acid.
Pregaday® tablets, ferrous fumarate (100mg iron) and 350mcg folic acid.

Clinical guidance
Use the separate components – see individual monographs for details.

Isoniazid

Presentation
Tablets.
Oral solution (special).[582]
A suspension can be made by Pharmacy in some centres (see Appendix 1).[461]
Injection.

Administration – enteral tubes
1st choice – The tablets can be crushed and mixed with water for administration.[8,105] Follow the directions in section 3.5.
2nd choice – A suspension can be made by Pharmacy in some centres. Follow the directions in section 3.6.
3rd choice – Use the oral solution (if available).[104,461] Follow the directions in section 3.6.

Administration – swallowing difficulties
1st choice – A suspension can be made by Pharmacy in some centres.
2nd choice – Use the oral solution (if available).[104,461]
3rd choice – The tablets can be crushed and mixed with water for administration.[8,105] Follow the directions in section 3.5.

Clinical guidance
Isoniazid is well absorbed from duodenum, jejunum, and ileum.[409] Administration through enteral tubes which terminate in the jejunum is not anticipated to cause any absorption problems.

Feed guidance
Absorption of enteral isoniazid can be decreased by concomitant food or milk.[2] Give on an empty stomach.[624] Hold enteral feeds for half an hour before and half an hour after each enteral dose.[117,225]

Summary:-	Stop feed 30 minutes before dose
	Restart feed 30 minutes after dose

Withholding enteral feeds can compromise nutrition and interfere with blood glucose management. If the patient does not have a break in their feeding regimen during which isoniazid can be given, the Nutrition Team should be contacted to advise on management.

Isosorbide dinitrate

Presentation
Tablets.
Modified-release tablets.
Aerosol spray.
Injection.

Administration – enteral tubes / swallowing difficulties
1st choice – Give by parenteral injection if appropriate.
2nd choice – The standard-release tablets can be crushed and will disperse in water with a fine sediment.[7,8,40,94] Follow the directions in section 3.5.

There is a theoretical potential for explosion if isosorbide dinitrate tablets are crushed. However no reports of this occurring have been located, and the practice is carried out in many centres.

Do not crush the modified-release tablets. Contact Pharmacy for advice.

Isosorbide mononitrate

Presentation
Tablets.
Modified-release tablets, modified-release capsules.
Oral solution (special).[582]
A suspension can be made by Pharmacy in some centres.[573]

Administration – enteral tubes
1st choice – The standard-release tablets can be crushed and dispersed in water.[39,40,41] They may have an increased rate of absorption and therefore increased side effects.[104] Follow the directions in section 3.5.
2nd choice – A suspension can be made by Pharmacy in some centres.[155] Follow the directions in section 3.6.
3rd choice – Use the oral solution (if available). Follow the directions in section 3.6.

(monograph continues on next page)

Do not crush the modified-release tablets. If scored, they can be halved to make them easier for patients to swallow, but they should not be chewed.

There is a theoretical potential for explosion if isosorbide mononitrate tablets are crushed. However no reports of this occurring have been located, and the practice is carried out in many centres. The manufacturers do not believe there to be any risk.[159]

Administration – swallowing difficulties
1st choice – A suspension can be made by Pharmacy in some centres.[155]
2nd choice – Use the oral solution (if available).
3rd choice – The standard-release tablets can be crushed and dispersed in water.[39,40,41] They may have an increased rate of absorption and therefore increased side effects.[104] Follow the directions in section 3.5.

Do not crush the modified-release tablets. If scored, they can be halved to make them easier for patients to swallow, but they should not be chewed.

There is a theoretical potential for explosion if isosorbide mononitrate tablets are crushed. However no reports of this occurring have been located, and the practice is carried out in many centres. The manufacturers do not believe there to be any risk.[159]

Clinical guidance
Modified-release tablets and capsules are not suitable for enteral feeding tube administration. Contact Pharmacy for advice on adjusting doses and switching preparations. Alternatively, consider using GTN patches.

The modified-release capsules have been opened and the contents mixed with soft food for administration to patients with swallowing difficulties, but this is not recommended. Do not crush the capsule contents or pre-dissolve them before giving.[132,155]

Dispersing the tablets in water may alter their rate of absorption, and therefore their side effects.[448] Consider reducing the dose and giving doses more frequently if this occurs.

Isotretinoin

Presentation
Capsules.

Administration – enteral tubes
<u>Caution – teratogenic.</u> Special precautions are required in certain female patients during the use of this drug. Contact Pharmacy for advice.

Isotretinoin may cause irritation if the drug comes into contact with the eyes, skin or mucous membranes.[558] Carers handling the capsules should wear gloves and eye protection.

Use a needle and a 1mL oral syringe to pierce the capsule and withdraw the fluid contents (squeeze the capsule at the same time to aid withdrawal as the contents are quite viscous[274]). Flush the fluid down the enteral feeding tube with water.[138]

Give immediately as the drug is light sensitive.[274]

Be aware that serious errors have occurred due to the use of needles and syringes to handle oral medication.

Administration – swallowing difficulties
<u>Caution – teratogenic.</u> Special precautions are required in certain female patients during the use of this drug. Contact Pharmacy for advice.

Isotretinoin may cause irritation if the drug comes into contact with the eyes, skin or mucous membranes.[558] Carers handling the capsules should wear gloves and eye protection.

Cut the capsule open or pierce it with a needle, and squeeze the contents out into lukewarm milk or onto soft food such as cottage cheese, ice cream, or oatmeal. The drug has a slightly bitter taste.[274]

(monograph continues on next page)

Clinical guidance

A study of the pharmacokinetics of isotretinoin showed that there were lower peak levels and smaller area under the curve (drug exposure) when the capsules were opened than when they were swallowed whole, so doses may need to be adjusted when given by this route, and re-adjusted if the patient returns to taking whole capsules.[274]

Feed guidance

Isotretinoin should be taken with food.[274]

Ispaghula husk

Presentation

Granules, powder.

Administration – enteral tubes

Do not use as it may congeal and block the tube.

Administration – swallowing difficulties

Use the granules or the powder.

Isradipine

Presentation

Tablets.

Administration – enteral tubes / swallowing difficulties

The tablets can be crushed and dispersed in water for administration. Crush well as the drug is practically insoluble.[253] Protect from light.[138] Follow the directions in section 3.5.

Itraconazole

Presentation
Capsules.
Liquid.
A suspension can be made by Pharmacy in some centres (see Appendix 1).[472]
Concentrate for infusion.

Administration – enteral tubes
1st choice – Give by parenteral infusion if appropriate.
2nd choice – Use the liquid.[104] Follow the directions in section 3.6.
3rd choice – Use the suspension (if available). Follow the directions in section 3.6.

Use of the capsule contents has led to enteral feeding tube blockage, so this is not recommended.[138]

Administration – swallowing difficulties
1st choice – Use the liquid.[104]
2nd choice – Give by parenteral infusion if appropriate.
3rd choice – Use the suspension (if available).

Clinical guidance
The absorption of itraconazole liquid is not dependent on an acid environment.[253]

Itraconazole has a topical effect when used for oral / oesophageal candidiasis.[176] It may therefore be less effective if given via enteral feeding tube for these conditions.

Feed guidance
Itraconazole liquid should be given on an empty stomach so withhold enteral feeds for two hours before and one hour after each dose.[41,176,225,304,624]

Summary:-	Stop feed 2 hours before dose
	Restart feed 1 hour after dose

(monograph continues on next page)

Withholding enteral feeds can compromise nutrition and interfere with blood glucose management. If the patient does not have a break in their feeding regimen during which itraconazole can be given, the Nutrition Team should be contacted to advise on management.

Ivabradine

Presentation
Film-coated tablets.

Administration – enteral tubes
The tablets can be crushed and mixed with water for administration.[368,513] Follow the directions in section 3.5.

Administration – swallowing difficulties
The tablets can be crushed and mixed with yogurt or soft food for administration.[368,513]

Kaletra®

See entry under "Lopinavir and ritonavir".

Kalten®

Presentation
Capsules.

Clinical guidance
Kalten® capsules contain atenolol 50mg and co-amilozide 2.5mg/25mg.[272] Use the separate components – see individual monographs for details.

Ketamine

Presentation
Injection.
Oral solution (special).[658]

Administration – enteral tubes
No information on administering the injection or the special oral solution via enteral feeding tubes has been located. Consider giving by a parenteral route.

Administration – swallowing difficulties
1st choice – Use the oral solution (special) if available.
2nd choice – Ketamine injection is intended for intravenous or intramuscular use. However for certain indications it has been used orally, and for this the injection solution has been diluted with fruit cordial to disguise the bitter taste.[606]

Ketoconazole

Presentation
Tablets (no longer available in the UK).
A suspension can be made by Pharmacy in some centres (see Appendix 1) (ingredients no longer available in the UK).[473]

Administration – NG / PEG tubes
1st choice - The tablets (if available) can be crushed and dispersed in water for administration.[8,104,105] Follow the directions in section 3.5.
2nd choice – A suspension can be made by Pharmacy in some centres.[155,473] Follow the directions in section 3.6.

Administration – NJ / PEJ / PEGJ tubes
Administration of ketoconazole directly into the jejunum is not recommended as a low pH is required for absorption of this drug.[2,6,104]

(monograph continues on next page)

Administration – swallowing difficulties

1st choice – A suspension can be made by Pharmacy in some centres.[155,473]

2nd choice - The tablets (if available) can be crushed and dispersed in water for administration.[8,104,105] Follow the directions in section 3.5.

Clinical guidance

The administration of acid-suppressing drugs can decrease the bioavailability of ketoconazole by up to 95%.[176] It may be possible to improve the bioavailability of ketoconazole in these circumstances by giving it as an acidified solution, e.g. by giving it with 240mL of Coca Cola®.[176,305]

Wait for at least two hours after the administration of ketoconazole before giving antacids.[155,305]

Feed guidance

The manufacturer states that giving ketoconazole with food results in more consistent plasma concentrations and may increase the absorption of the drug by increasing the dissolution of the drug or delaying gastric emptying.[176] However the acid-neutralising effect of continuous enteral feeding may reduce the bioavailability of the drug, and this should be considered if treatment does not appear to be effective. In such situations, or in critical patients where early effectiveness of ketoconazole treatment is paramount, consider withholding enteral feeds for two hours before and two hours after each dose to allow the pH of the gastric contents to drop.

Withholding enteral feeds can compromise nutrition and interfere with blood glucose management. If the patient does not have a break in their feeding regimen during which ketoconazole can be given, the Nutrition Team should be contacted to advise on management.

Ketoprofen

Presentation
Capsules.
Modified-release capsules.
Suppositories.
Gel.
Injection (no longer available in the UK).

Administration – enteral tubes / swallowing difficulties
Use the intramuscular injection (if available), the gel or the suppositories where appropriate.

Clinical guidance
There is no difference in bioavailability between the capsules and the suppositories.[306] The suppositories are not licensed for continuous chronic treatment.[306] The injection is licensed for a maximum of three days treatment.[307] The gel is licensed for a maximum of seven days treatment.[308]

100mg capsule	equivalent to	100mg suppository[306]

For patients whose swallowing problems are likely to be short-term, or who only require ketoprofen for a limited period, use one of the alternative routes listed above. For patients requiring chronic therapy whose swallowing problems are long-term, switch to an alternative drug.

Ketorolac

Presentation
Film-coated tablets (no longer available in the UK).
Injection.

Administration – enteral tubes / swallowing difficulties
Give by parenteral injection if appropriate.

Clinical guidance
The tablets are film-coated and probably taste unpleasant. Crushing them is not recommended.[354]

Ketotifen

Presentation
Tablets.
Elixir.

Administration – enteral tubes / swallowing difficulties
1st choice – Use the elixir. Follow the directions in section 3.6.
2nd choice – The tablets will disperse in water for administration.[8]
They disperse in less than a minute.[8] Follow the directions in section
3.5.

Kivexa®

Presentation
Film-coated tablets.

Clinical guidance
Kivexa® tablets contain abacavir 600mg and lamivudine 300mg.[272]
No information has been located on the use of Kivexa® tablets in
patients with enteral feeding tubes or swallowing difficulties. Use the
individual components – see individual monographs for details.

Labetalol

Presentation
Tablets.
A suspension can be made by Pharmacy in some centres (see
Appendix 1).[206,474]
Injection.

Administration – enteral tubes
1st choice – Use the suspension (if available). Follow the directions
in section 3.6.
2nd choice – The injection can be given via enteral feeding
tube.[40,99,152] Follow the directions in section 3.6.

(monograph continues on next page)

Administration – swallowing difficulties
1st choice – Use the suspension (if available).
2nd choice – Mix the required dose of injection with orange juice to disguise the bitter taste.[40,99,152]

The tablets have been crushed but the powder tastes unpleasant,[105] and this is not recommended because the drug is sensitive to oxidation.[132] Methods for preparing labetalol suspension have been described.[206,474]

Lacidipine

Presentation
Tablets.

Clinical guidance
The tablets are very insoluble and film-coated, and are likely to block enteral feeding tubes.[44] They have been crushed but this is not recommended.[132] Consider changing to amlodipine.

Lacosamide

Presentation
Film-coated tablets.
Syrup (no longer available in the UK).
Infusion solution.

Administration – enteral tubes
Give by parenteral infusion. The dose of the infusion is the same as the oral dose.[435] There is only experience with using the infusion for up to five days.[575]

No reports of lacosamide being administered via enteral feeding tubes have been located.

Administration – swallowing difficulties
1st choice – Use the syrup (if available).
2nd choice – Give by parenteral infusion. The dose of the infusion is the same as the oral dose.[435] There is only experience with using the infusion for up to five days.[575]

Lactulose

Presentation
Solution.

Administration – enteral tubes
Dilute solution 1 in 3 or 1 in 4 with distilled water (i.e. dilute each 10mL with 30mL water).

Administration – swallowing difficulties
Use the solution.

Clinical guidance
Lactulose is almost completely unabsorbed in the GI tract.[1,286] It acts by local action in the colon and is therefore equally effective when given through a tube terminating in the jejunum as when given orally.[286]

Lamivudine

Presentation
Film-coated tablets.
Oral solution.

Administration – enteral tubes / swallowing difficulties
Use the oral solution.[132] Follow the directions in section 3.6.

Lamotrigine

Presentation
Tablets.
Dispersible tablets.
Oral solution (special).[542]
A suspension can be made by Pharmacy in some centres (see Appendix 1).[527]

Administration – enteral tubes
Use the dispersible tablets. Follow the directions in section 3.5.

(monograph continues on next page)

No information on administering the suspension via enteral feeding tubes has been located.

Administration – swallowing difficulties
1st choice – Use the dispersible tablets. Follow the directions in section 3.5.
2nd choice – Use the oral solution or the suspension (if available).

Clinical guidance
Changing formulations / product manufacturer
The MHRA has issued guidance recommending that (where possible) patients on lamotrigine (when used for seizures) are maintained on a specific manufacturer's product, due to variability in product characteristics which may lead to a loss of seizure control when switching between brands / manufacturers.[651] When managing patients with enteral tubes or swallowing difficulties it may not be possible to maintain the patient on their previous preparation due to the need to change to an appropriate formulation. However all product switches should be carried out with care and close monitoring, and where possible patients should be maintained from then onwards on a single manufacturer's product.

Lansoprazole

Presentation
Capsules.
FasTab®.
Suspension in sachet form (no longer available in the UK).
A suspension can be made by Pharmacy in some centres (see Appendix 1).[202]

Administration – enteral tubes
Zoton (lansoprazole) Fastabs® are now licensed for administration via nasogastric feeding tubes.[267]

Zoton (lansoprazole) Fastabs® contain micro-granules which are approximately 0.33mm in diameter. Zoton® capsules contain granules which are approximately 1.1mm diameter.[210] For this reason, the Fastabs® are probably less likely to block enteral feeding tubes, and different methods of administration have been described for the Fastabs® and the capsules.

Recommended method[210]

1. Place a Fastab® tablet in the barrel of an oral or bladder-tipped syringe, then draw up 10mL water and 5mL air.
2. Shake and allow the tablet to disperse (this will take about 30-45 seconds).
3. Dispel the air from the syringe and administer the solution via the enteral tube with repeated shaking to suspend the micro-granules. Do not crush the micro-granules as the syringe empties.
4. Draw up another 10mL water and repeat the process until all the granules have been administered.
5. Flush the tube well following administration.

(monograph continues on next page)

Alternative method[183,186,210,217]

This method is only recommended if the Fastabs® are unavailable, as the enteric-coated granules inside the capsules settle out very quickly when mixed with water, and are difficult to administer. This method is only suitable for large-bore enteral feeding tubes (14F or larger[186]) terminating in the stomach where the large diameter of the capsule granules will not cause tube blockage.

1. Empty the contents of a lansoprazole capsule into the barrel of an oral or bladder-tipped syringe, then draw up 10-20mL of weakly acidic fruit juice (e.g. apple or orange juice). Do not crush the enteric-coated granules.
2. Administer the solution via the enteral tube with repeated shaking to suspend the granules. Do not crush the granules as the syringe empties.
3. Draw up another 10mL of fruit juice and repeat the process until all the granules have been administered.
4. Flush the tube well following administration.

Alternative method 2[155,185,187,210,217]

This method is suitable for fine-bore enteral tubes where the larger diameter of the capsule granules may cause tube blockage if they are administered intact. The sodium bicarbonate releases the drug from the enteric-coated granules, and alkalinises the stomach contents to prevent degradation of the drug in the stomach. It has been suggested as the method of choice for tubes terminating in the jejunum, as mixing with sodium bicarbonate facilitates release of the drug.[186,187,245]

1. Empty the contents of a lansoprazole capsule into the barrel of an oral or bladder-tipped syringe, then draw up 10mL of 8.4% sodium bicarbonate injection, and 10mL of air.
2. Cap the syringe, and shake vigorously for about two minutes, until the drug has formed a suspension in the syringe.
3. Administer the solution via the enteral tube.
4. Draw up 10mL of water to wash out the syringe, and flush this down the tube.

(monograph continues on next page)

If the volume of sodium bicarbonate is a problem (for example in patients with an acid-base imbalance), this method has also been carried out using only 2.5mL sodium bicarbonate 8.4% and 2.5mL water for injections.[185] However it is not known if this volume of sodium bicarbonate is sufficient to alkalinise the stomach contents and prevent degradation of the drug in the stomach, therefore it should only be used if acid-base balance is critical and no other method is suitable.

Lansoprazole suspension (extemporaneously prepared)

Methods for preparing lansoprazole suspension have been described.[202]

Lansoprazole suspension (sachets – no longer available in the UK)

Lansoprazole suspension (sachets) is formulated using mannitol as the suspending agent. Made up to the manufacturer's recommendations, the suspension is too viscous for administration via enteral feeding tubes.[187] Further dilution of the suspension in order to administer it via enteral feeding tubes may result in the active drug coming out of suspension and failing to be delivered to the patient.[187,210] Lansoprazole suspension is therefore unsuitable for use except in patients with swallowing difficulties.

Administration – swallowing difficulties
The FasTab® can be placed in the mouth where it will disperse to release gastro-resistant granules which will be swallowed with the patient's saliva.[267] It can also be dispersed in water, leaving microgranules which should be swallowed without being crushed. The FasTab® can also be administered in apple juice or orange juice.[105] Alternatively, use the sachets.

Lansoprazole is NOT absorbed sublingually.[552] The gastro-resistant granules must be swallowed for the drug to be effective.

(monograph continues on next page)

Feed guidance
Lansoprazole should be given on an empty stomach, so withhold enteral feeds for half an hour before and half an hour after each dose.[117,225,624]

Summary:-	Stop feed 30 minutes before dose Restart feed 30 minutes after dose

Withholding enteral feeds can compromise nutrition and interfere with blood glucose management. If the patient does not have a break in their feeding regimen during which lansoprazole can be given, the Nutrition Team should be contacted to advise on management.

Lasilactone®

Presentation
Capsules.

Clinical guidance
Lasilactone® capsules contain furosemide 20mg and spironolactone 50mg.[272] Use the separate components – see individual monographs for details.

Leflunomide

Presentation
Tablets.

Clinical guidance
There is no information available on the use of leflunomide via enteral feeding tubes, however there is no pharmaceutical reason why the tablets shouldn't be crushed, and this has been done in some centres. If administering crushed tablets, monitor the patient for exaggerated or diminished pharmacological effects.[62,138] Follow the directions in section 3.5.

Lercanidipine

Presentation
Film-coated tablets.

Administration – enteral tubes / swallowing difficulties
The tablets can be crushed and mixed with water for administration.[69] Follow the directions in section 3.5.

Feed guidance
Lercanidipine should be taken on an empty stomach.[624] Enteral feeds should be withheld for half an hour before and half an hour after each dose.[225]

Summary:-	Stop feed 30 minutes before dose
	Restart feed 30 minutes after dose

Withholding enteral feeds can compromise nutrition and interfere with blood glucose management. If the patient does not have a break in their feeding regimen during which lercanidipine can be given, the Nutrition Team should be contacted to advise on management.

Levetiracetam

Presentation
Film-coated tablets.
Oral solution.
Concentrate for intravenous infusion.

Administration – enteral tubes
1st choice – Give by intravenous infusion at the same dose and frequency as oral.[256]
2nd choice – Use the oral solution. Follow the directions in section 3.6.
3rd choice – The tablets can be crushed and mixed with water for administration.[104,105] The active drug will dissolve but the excipients will not.[108] Follow the directions in section 3.5. Flush well post-dose.

(monograph continues on next page)

Administration – swallowing difficulties

1st choice – Use the oral solution. Follow the directions in section 3.6.

2nd choice – Give by intravenous infusion at the same dose and frequency as oral.[256]

3rd choice – The tablets can be crushed and administered.[104,105] The active drug will dissolve but the excipients will not.[108] Follow the directions in section 3.5. Crushed levetiracetam tablets taste unpleasant. They can be diluted in orange juice to taste.[108]

Levofloxacin

Presentation

Tablets.

A suspension can be made by Pharmacy in some centres (see Appendix 1).[475]

Infusion.

Administration – enteral tubes

Give by infusion.

If infusion is not appropriate, consider changing to another quinolone such as ciprofloxacin. Levofloxacin tablets will not disperse.[70] Crushing them is not recommended, although this has been done in some centres.[132]

Administration – swallowing difficulties

1st choice – Give by infusion.

2nd choice – Use the suspension (if available).

Alternatively, consider changing to another quinolone such as ciprofloxacin. Levofloxacin tablets will not disperse.[70] Crushing them is not recommended, although this has been done in some centres.[132]

(monograph continues on next page)

Clinical guidance

Quinolones have poor absorption when administered directly into the jejunum, and also interact with enteral feeds. Some sources suggest that the reduction in absorption is so pronounced (particularly in the presence of enteral feeds) that an alternative route or alternative drug should be used.[193]

Feed guidance

Enteral levofloxacin will interact with sucralfate, antacids,[35] and enteral feeds.[195] If the tablets are administered enterally, the enteral feed should be withheld for two hours before and one hour after each dose.[225] Decreased absorption due to interaction with enteral feeds may result in treatment failure.[195]

Summary:-	Stop feed 2 hours before dose
	Restart feed 1 hour after dose

Withholding enteral feeds can compromise nutrition and interfere with blood glucose management. If the patient does not have a break in their feeding regimen during which levofloxacin can be given, the Nutrition Team should be contacted to advise on management.

Levomepromazine (Methotrimeprazine)

Presentation
Tablets.
Oral solution (special).[582,658]
A suspension can be made by Pharmacy in some centres.
Injection.

Administration – enteral tubes
1st choice – Consider giving by parenteral injection.
2nd choice – The tablets can be dispersed in water for administration if necessary.[8,102] They disperse immediately.[8,154] Follow the directions in section 3.5.
3rd choice – A suspension may be available in some centres.[95,169] Follow the directions in section 3.6.
4th choice – Use the oral solution (if available). Follow the directions in section 3.6.
5th choice – The injection has also been used enterally.[104,164] Follow the directions in section 3.6.

Administration – swallowing difficulties
1st choice – Consider giving by parenteral injection.
2nd choice – A suspension may be available in some centres.[95,169]
3rd choice – Use the oral solution (if available).
4th choice – The tablets can be dispersed in water for administration if necessary.[8,102] They disperse immediately.[8,154] Follow the directions in section 3.5.
5th choice – The injection has also been used enterally.[104,164] Follow the directions in section 3.6.

Clinical guidance
Levomepromazine injection contains excipients which, when given enterally, degrade to products which theoretically may induce asthma attacks. No reports of attacks ever having been induced this way have been recorded by the manufacturers and the risk is considered to be small.[164]

Levothyroxine (Thyroxine)

Presentation
Tablets.
Oral solution (special).[542,582]
A suspension can be made by Pharmacy in some centres (see Appendix 1).[477,512,514]

Administration – enteral tubes
1st choice – For short-term swallowing problems, consider switching to parenteral liothyronine.
2nd choice – The tablets can be crushed and mixed with water for administration.[152] Follow the directions in section 3.5.
3rd choice – A suspension can be made by Pharmacy in some centres.[155,477,512,514] Dilute with the same volume of water before administering. Follow the directions in section 3.6.
4th choice – Use the oral solution (if available). Follow the directions in section 3.6.

Administration – swallowing difficulties
1st choice – For short-term swallowing problems, consider switching to parenteral liothyronine.
2nd choice – A suspension can be made by Pharmacy in some centres.[155,477,512,514] Dilute with the same volume of water before administering.
3rd choice – Use the oral solution (if available).
4th choice – The tablets can be crushed and mixed with water for administration.[152] Follow the directions in section 3.5.

Clinical guidance
Monitor thyroid function. There have been reports of treatment failure in patients receiving levothyroxine suspension, believed to be due to oxidation of the drug.[121,122] If thyroid function deteriorates, consider crushing tablets and mixing with water immediately prior to administration to reduce oxidation, or switching to liothyronine.

Feed guidance
Enteral feeds, especially soya based formulas, may increase faecal elimination of thyroxine.[87]

Linezolid

Presentation
Film-coated tablets.
Suspension.
Infusion.

Administration – enteral tubes
1st choice – Give by parenteral infusion if possible.
2nd choice – The tablets can be crushed and dispersed in water for administration.[71] Follow the directions in section 3.5.

The suspension may be too thick for administration through narrow-bore enteral feeding tubes,[132,355] although there are reports of it being successfully given through wide-bore tubes.[378]

Administration – swallowing difficulties
1st choice – Give by parenteral infusion, or use the suspension.
2nd choice – The tablets can be crushed and dispersed in water for administration.[71] Follow the directions in section 3.5.

Clinical guidance
Monitor the patient for suitable effect.[71] Linezolid is absorbed in the stomach and the small intestine. There is a risk of decreased absorption if it is administered via an enteral feeding tube terminating in the jejunum.[355]

Feed guidance
There is no need to alter the dose of linezolid when it is being given to a patient receiving continuous enteral feeds.[355]

Lisicostad®

Presentation
Tablets.

Clinical guidance
Lisicostad® tablets contain lisinopril and hydrochlorothiazide in various dosages.[272] Use lisinopril as a separate component, and an appropriate thiazide diuretic, e.g. bendroflumethiazide. See individual monographs for details.

Lisinopril

Presentation
Tablets.
Sugar-free oral solution (special).[582]
A suspension can be made by Pharmacy in some centres (see Appendix 1).[478,515]

Administration – enteral tubes
1st choice – The tablets can be dispersed in water.[8,40,46] The drug is soluble,[253] and the tablets disperse in one to five minutes.[8,154] Follow the directions in section 3.5.
2nd choice – A suspension can be made in Pharmacy in some centres.[155,478,515] Dilute this with the same volume of distilled water, and flush post dose with 15-30mL of distilled water.
3rd choice – The sugar-free oral solution (special) can be used (if available).[129] Follow the directions in section 3.6.

Administration – swallowing difficulties
1st choice – A suspension can be made in Pharmacy in some centres.[155,478,515]
2nd choice – The sugar-free oral solution (special) can be used (if available).[129]
3rd choice – The tablets can be dispersed in water.[8,40,46] The drug is soluble,[253] and the tablets disperse in one to five minutes.[8,154] Follow the directions in section 3.5.

Clinical guidance
Lisinopril oral solution is absorbed to a lesser extent than lisinopril tablets.[287] When converting patients to and from the liquid, monitor blood pressure and consider a dose alteration if necessary.

Lisinopril and hydrochlorothiazide
(Carace Plus®, Zestoretic®, Lisicostad®)

Presentation
Tablets.

Clinical guidance
Carace Plus®, Zestoretic® and Lisicostad® tablets contain lisinopril and hydrochlorothiazide in various dosages.[272] Use lisinopril as a separate component, and an appropriate thiazide diuretic, e.g. bendroflumethiazide. See individual monographs for details.

Lisuride (Lysuride)

Presentation
Tablets (no longer available in the UK).

Administration – enteral tubes / swallowing difficulties
The tablets can be crushed and mixed with water for administration.[8,41] Follow the directions in section 3.5.

Lithium

Presentation
Modified-release tablets.
Sugar-free oral liquid (some preparations contain sorbitol).

Administration – enteral tubes / swallowing difficulties
Use the equivalent dose of the liquid. Contact Pharmacy for advice on calculation of equivalent dose and monitoring of changeover. Follow the directions in section 3.6.

Clinical guidance
Lithium carbonate 200mg is approximately equivalent to lithium citrate 509mg, but different preparations of lithium vary widely in their bioavailability.[106] As most lithium tablets are modified-release, when being given as a liquid the total daily dose will need to be given in divided doses.

(monograph continues on next page)

A change in lithium preparation usually requires the same precautions as initiation of treatment. Lithium concentration is affected by sodium – an increase in serum sodium will result in increased lithium excretion, and therefore reduced lithium levels. Increases in lithium levels occur with sodium depletion / dehydration, or with a low salt diet.[33] As lithium is highly toxic when serum levels rise a little above the normal treatment range, close monitoring is needed in these situations.

There is significant absorption of lithium in the jejunum and ileum,[397] therefore administration of lithium through enteral tubes terminating in the jejunum is not anticipated to cause absorption problems, though monitoring of levels is still advised.

Lithium has been reported to decrease appetite.[33]

Feed guidance
Lithium absorption is decreased in the presence of enteral feeds. Feeds should be withheld for one hour before and two hours after each dose.[117]

Summary:-	Stop feed 1 hour before dose Restart feed 2 hours after dose

Withholding enteral feeds can compromise nutrition and interfere with blood glucose management. If the patient does not have a break in their feeding regimen during which lithium can be given, the Nutrition Team should be contacted to advise on management.

Lofepramine

Presentation
Tablets.
Suspension (some preparations contain alcohol and / or sorbitol).

Administration – enteral tubes / swallowing difficulties
Use the suspension. Follow the directions in section 3.6.

Rosemont do not recommend diluting the suspension with water before administration as this may destabilise the suspension.[360]

(monograph continues on next page)

The tablets are not suitable for crushing.[40]

Clinical guidance
Tricyclic antidepressants can decrease gastric emptying.[2]

Loperamide

Presentation
Capsule.
Liquid.

Administration – enteral tubes / swallowing difficulties
Use the liquid. Do not dilute.[26] Follow the directions in section 3.6.

Clinical guidance
Do not open the capsules as they may cause enteral tube blockage and the bioavailability of the drug may be altered.

Loperamide liquid is suitable for administration through enteral tubes terminating in the jejunum. The liquid should be given undiluted to facilitate its dose dependant effect on motility. Flushing should still occur. The osmolality of the liquid is approximately 8100mOsm/L.[576] The liquid does not contain sorbitol.[6,17]

Lopinavir and ritonavir (Kaletra®)

Presentation
Film-coated tablets.
Oral solution.

Administration – enteral tubes
No information has been located on the use of Kaletra® in patients with enteral feeding tubes.

Kaletra® tablets should not be crushed. See clinical guidance below.

(monograph continues on next page)

Administration – swallowing difficulties
Use the oral solution.

Kaletra® tablets should not be crushed. See clinical guidance below.

Clinical guidance
Kaletra® tablets contain lopinavir and ritonavir in two different dosages.[272]

Kaletra® tablets should not be crushed. Patient exposure to both drugs has been shown to be reduced by around 40% (range 5-75%) after crushing.[581,655] The reduction was highly variable between individuals, and is therefore unpredictable.

Feed guidance
The solution should be taken with or after food.[429]

Loprazolam

Presentation
Tablets.

Administration – enteral tubes / swallowing difficulties
The tablets will disperse in water for administration.[8] They disperse in one to two minutes.[8] Follow the directions in section 3.5.

Loratadine

Presentation
Tablets.
Syrup.

Administration – enteral tubes / swallowing difficulties
Use the syrup.[94,104] Follow the directions in section 3.6.

Lorazepam

Presentation
Tablets.
Oral solution (special).[542,582,658]
A suspension can be made by Pharmacy in some centres.[573]
Injection.

Administration – enteral tubes
The tablets can be crushed and mixed with water for administration.[104,105,225] Without crushing they disperse in one to five minutes.[8,154] Follow the directions in section 3.5.

The tablets may also be effective given sublingually,[105,152] but be aware that the patient must have a sufficiently moist mouth for sublingual absorption to occur.

No information on administering the oral solution via enteral feeding tubes has been located.

Administration – swallowing difficulties
1st choice – A suspension can be made by Pharmacy in some centres.
2nd choice – Use the oral solution (if available).
3rd choice – The tablets can be crushed and mixed with water for administration.[104,105,225] Without crushing they disperse in one to five minutes.[8,154] Follow the directions in section 3.5.

The tablets may also be effective given sublingually,[105,152] but be aware that the patient must have a sufficiently moist mouth for sublingual absorption to occur.

Lormetazepam

Presentation
Tablets.

Administration – enteral tubes / swallowing difficulties
The tablets can be dispersed in water for administration.[104] They disperse in one to five minutes.[154] Follow the directions in section 3.5.

Losartan

Presentation
Film-coated tablets.
Suspension.
Oral suspension (special).[542]

Administration – enteral tubes
The tablets can be crushed and mixed with water for administration.[63] Follow the directions in section 3.5.

No information about administering the suspension via enteral tubes has been located due to the product being new on the market.

Administration – swallowing difficulties
Use the suspension.

Losartan and hydrochlorothiazide (Cozaar-Comp®)

Presentation
Film-coated tablets.

Clinical guidance
Cozaar-Comp® tablets contain losartan and hydrochlorothiazide at various dosages.[272] Use losartan as a separate component and an appropriate alternative thiazide diuretic, e.g. bendroflumethiazide. See individual monographs for details.

Maalox®

See entry under "Co-magaldrox".

Magnesium glycerophosphate

Presentation
Tablets.
Oral liquid.
Oral solution (special).[580,582]
A suspension can be made by Pharmacy in some centres.[573]
Powder.

Administration – enteral tubes
1st choice – Use the oral liquid.[140] Follow the directions in section 3.6.
2nd choice – The tablets can be crushed and mixed with water for administration.[132,152] Follow the directions in section 3.5.
3rd choice – A suspension can be made by Pharmacy in some centres. Follow the directions in section 3.6.
4th choice – Use the special oral solution (if available). Follow the directions in section 3.6.

Administration – swallowing difficulties
1st choice – Use the oral liquid.[140]
2nd choice – A suspension can be made by Pharmacy in some centres.
3rd choice – Use the special oral solution (if available).
4th choice – The tablets can be crushed and mixed with water for administration.[132,152] Follow the directions in section 3.5.

Magnesium salts

Clinical guidance
Magnesium oxide, hydroxide, and trisilicate are converted to magnesium chloride by gastric acid. Without conversion they are not absorbed due to poor solubility.[321] For this reason these salts are not appropriate for administration via tubes terminating in the jejunum, and alternative magnesium salts should be used.

Mebendazole

Presentation
Chewable tablets.
Suspension.

Administration – enteral tubes / swallowing difficulties
Use the suspension.[41,104] Follow the directions in section 3.6.

Mebeverine

Presentation
Tablets.
Liquid.
Modified-release capsules.

Administration – enteral tubes / swallowing difficulties
Use the liquid.[104] Follow the directions in section 3.6. Contact Pharmacy for advice about patients on the modified-release capsules.

150mg (15mL) liquid	equivalent to	135mg tablet[106]

Clinical guidance
Mebeverine is best absorbed if taken 20 minutes before a meal.[324]

Medroxyprogesterone

Presentation
Tablets.
Depot injection.
Injection (no longer available in the UK).

Administration – enteral tubes / swallowing difficulties
The tablets can be crushed (preferably in water to reduce dust production) and mixed with water for administration.[66] Without crushing they disperse in one to five minutes.[8,154] Use immediately. Follow the directions in section 3.5. Depo-Provera® has been used orally, but little data is available on this.[66]

Mefenamic acid

Presentation
Tablets, capsules.
Suspension.

Administration – enteral tubes / swallowing difficulties
The strength of the suspension is such that most adult doses would require large volumes. It is recommended that patients are switched to an alternative drug. Contact Pharmacy for advice. However, if it is not clinically appropriate to switch, the suspension can be used.[104] Follow the directions in section 3.6.

Mefloquine

Presentation
Tablets.

Administration – enteral tubes
No information about the use of this medication via enteral feeding tubes has been located.

Administration – swallowing difficulties
The tablets can be crushed.[152]

Megestrol acetate

Presentation
Tablets.
Oral solution (special).[582]
A suspension can be made by Pharmacy in some centres.

Administration – enteral tubes
1st choice – The tablets can be dispersed in water for administration.[8,68,225] The 40mg tablets disperse immediately.[154] The 160mg tablets disperse in one to five minutes.[8,154] Follow the directions in section 3.5. No information has been located on whether megestrol acetate is likely to block enteral feeding tubes,[68] but take care as the drug is practically insoluble.[253]
2nd choice – A suspension can be made by Pharmacy in some centres.[155] Follow the directions in section 3.6.
3rd choice – Use the oral solution (if available). Follow the directions in section 3.6.

Administration – swallowing difficulties
1st choice – A suspension can be made by Pharmacy in some centres.
2nd choice – Use the oral solution (if available).
3rd choice – The tablets can be crushed and given in fruit juice or jam.[105] If the tablets are crushed this should preferably be done in water to reduce dust production.

Melatonin

Presentation
Capsules.
Modified-release tablets.
Oral solution (special).[542]

Administration – enteral tubes
The standard capsules can be opened and the contents mixed with water for administration.[105,152] Follow the directions in section 3.7.

No information on administering the oral solution via enteral feeding tubes has been located.

(monograph continues on next page)

Administration – swallowing difficulties
1st choice – Use the oral solution (if available).
2nd choice – The standard capsules can be opened and the contents mixed with water, milk, yogurt or fruit juice for administration.[105,152] Follow the directions in section 3.7.

Meloxicam

Presentation
Tablets.
Suppositories (no longer available in the UK).

Administration – enteral tubes / swallowing difficulties
1st choice – Use the suppositories (if available), or consider switching to an alternative non-steroidal anti-inflammatory drug.
2nd choice – The tablets can be crushed and dispersed in water for administration.[44,152] Follow the directions in section 3.5.

Clinical guidance
The tablets and the suppositories are bioequivalent.[333] Mobic® capsules are available in some countries (not licensed in the UK). These are also bioequivalent to the suppositories.[333]

Memantine

Presentation
Film-coated tablets.
Oral drops.

Administration – enteral tubes / swallowing difficulties
1st choice – Use the oral drops. The drops can be diluted in water to aid administration if necessary.[254]
2nd choice – The tablets can be crushed and dispersed in water for administration.[254] Crush well as they are film-coated. Follow the directions in section 3.5.

Menadiol

Presentation
Tablets.
A suspension can be made by Pharmacy in some centres.[573]

Administration – enteral tubes
The tablets can be crushed and mixed with water for administration.[104,105,152] Follow the directions in section 3.5.

No information on giving the suspension via enteral feeding tubes has been located.

See also the entry under 'Phytomenadione'.

Administration – swallowing difficulties
1st choice – Use the suspension (if available).
2nd choice – The tablets can be crushed and mixed with water for administration.[104,105,152] Follow the directions in section 3.5. The crushed tablets have also been mixed with food for patients with swallowing difficulties.[132]

See also the entry under 'Phytomenadione'.

Meprobamate

Presentation
Tablets.

Administration – enteral tubes / swallowing difficulties
The tablets can be crushed and mixed with water for administration.[138] They are poorly soluble.[138] Follow the directions in section 3.5.

Meptazinol

Presentation
Tablets.
Injection.

Administration – enteral tubes / swallowing difficulties
1st choice – Give by parenteral injection if appropriate.
2nd choice - The tablets can be crushed and mixed with water for administration.[138] Follow the directions in section 3.5.

Mercaptamine

Presentation
Capsules.
Eye drops.

Administration – enteral tubes
No information about the use of this medication via enteral feeding tubes has been located.

Administration – swallowing difficulties
The capsules can be opened and the contents sprinkled on food or mixed in a strongly flavoured drink. The capsule contents have an unpleasant taste and smell. Do not mix with acidic drinks (i.e. orange juice etc.) as the drug may precipitate out.[152]

Mercaptopurine

Presentation
Tablets.
A suspension can be made by Pharmacy in some centres (see Appendix 1).[479]

Administration – enteral tubes / swallowing difficulties
<u>Caution – cytotoxic.</u> Contact Pharmacy for advice before giving.[138,479]
A suspension can be made by Pharmacy in some centres.[138,479]
Follow the directions in section 3.6.

(monograph continues on next page)

The manufacturers recommend that mercaptopurine is handled in accordance with local guidelines for handling cytotoxic drugs.[346]

Mesalazine

Presentation
Tablets.
Granules.
Foam enema.
Suppositories.

Administration – enteral tubes
The tablets are enteric-coated and designed for release in the small intestine. Do not crush. Consider rectal route if appropriate to the location of the condition, or an alternative drug.[94]

Pentasa® tablets will disperse in water, leaving small beads which must be swallowed / administered whole (so are therefore suitable only for large-bore tubes).[105,152,337] The beads are approximately 0.7-1mm in diameter.[340]

The granules in the sachets are slightly larger than those released from the tablets (around 1mm), and so they are not suitable for administration via enteral feeding tubes.[340]

Administration – swallowing difficulties
Consider rectal route if appropriate to the location of the condition.

The granules can be used for patients with swallowing difficulties. They should not be chewed, and therefore this method may not be appropriate for patients with limited understanding or impaired ability to follow instructions.

Alternatively Pentasa® tablets will disperse in water, leaving small beads which must be swallowed whole (so therefore may not be appropriate for patients with limited understanding or impaired ability to follow instructions).[105,152,337]

Metformin

Presentation
Tablets.
Modified-release tablets.
Sugar-free oral solution.
A suspension can be made by Pharmacy in some centres.[573]
Sachets.

Administration – enteral tubes
1st choice – Consider whether switching to insulin would be appropriate.
2nd choice – Use the sachets, which should be made up in 150mL water (see also "Clinical guidance" below).[375]
3rd choice – Use the oral solution. Follow the directions in section 3.6.
4th choice – A suspension can be made by Pharmacy in some centres. Follow the directions in section 3.6.

It is recommended that the tablets are not crushed at the patient's bedside as some brands are quite hard. If the tablets are to be crushed (e.g. to make a suspension) this should be done with appropriate equipment, e.g. a mortar and pestle, and the use of protective eyewear should be considered.

Administration – swallowing difficulties
1st choice – Use the sachets, which should be made up in 150mL water (see also "Clinical guidance" below).[375]
2nd choice – Consider whether switching to insulin would be appropriate.
3rd choice – Use the oral solution.
4th choice – A suspension can be made by Pharmacy in some centres.

It is recommended that the tablets are not crushed at the patient's bedside as some brands are quite hard. If the tablets are to be crushed (e.g. to make a suspension) this should be done with appropriate equipment, e.g. a mortar and pestle, and the use of protective eyewear should be considered.

(monograph continues on next page)

Clinical guidance

Monitor blood glucose levels.

The sachets are intended to be made up in 150mL water before administration.[375] However the powder is highly soluble,[376] and there are reports of the powder being dissolved successfully in much smaller volumes.[377] It is recommended that 150mL is used unless the patient is fluid-restricted.

The primary site of absorption of metformin is the small intestine,[376] so there is a possibility of reduced absorption if it is given via enteral tubes terminating in the jejunum.

Metformin has been reported to decrease appetite.[33]

Feed guidance

Take after food.[325]

Metformin and rosiglitazone (Avandamet®)

Presentation

Film-coated tablets (no longer licensed in the UK).

Clinical guidance

Avandamet® tablets contain rosiglitazone and metformin in various dosages. No information has been located about administering the tablets to patients with enteral tubes or swallowing difficulties. Use the separate components – see individual monographs for details.

Methionine

Presentation

Tablets (no longer available in the UK), capsules (special).

Administration – enteral tubes

No information about the use of this medication via enteral feeding tubes has been located.

(monograph continues on next page)

Administration – swallowing difficulties
The capsules may be opened and the contents sprinkled onto food. The tablets should not be crushed.[152]

Methotrexate

Presentation
Tablets.
Oral solution (special).[582,584]
Injection.

Administration – enteral tubes / swallowing difficulties
<u>Caution – cytotoxic.</u> Contact Pharmacy for advice before giving.

1st choice – A 'special' suspension may be available.[132,582,584] Follow the directions in section 3.6.
2nd choice – Contact Pharmacy for further advice on how to give (Pharmacists – see Appendix 2).

Methylcellulose

Presentation
Tablets.

Administration – enteral tubes / swallowing difficulties
The tablets can be crushed and mixed with water for administration.[138] Follow the directions in section 3.5.

Methyldopa

Presentation
Tablets.
Suspension.
A suspension can be made by Pharmacy in some centres (see Appendix 1).[512]

Administration – enteral tubes
1st choice – Use the suspension, and dilute with an equal volume of water to aid administration.[132] Follow the directions in section 3.6.
2nd choice – The tablets can be crushed and mixed with water for administration.[8,133] They are film-coated and not very soluble.[357] Take care to crush the tablets well, and to flush the tube well to prevent blockage.[357] Follow the directions in section 3.5.
3rd choice – A suspension can be made by Pharmacy in some centres.[182,512] Follow the directions in section 3.6.

Administration – swallowing difficulties
1st choice – Use the suspension.[132]
2nd choice – A suspension can be made by Pharmacy in some centres.[182,512]
3rd choice – The tablets can be crushed and mixed with water for administration.[8,133] They are film-coated and not very soluble.[357] The crushed tablets have an unpleasant taste.[357] Follow the directions in section 3.5.

Feed guidance
Methyldopa interacts with Ensure®, Ensure Plus®, and Osmolite® feeds[225] – feeds should be stopped for two hours before and one hour after administration of the medicine.[105]

Summary:-	Stop feed 2 hours before dose
	Restart feed 1 hour after dose

Withholding enteral feeds can compromise nutrition and interfere with blood glucose management. If the patient does not have a break in their feeding regimen during which methyldopa can be given, the Nutrition Team should be contacted to advise on management.

Methylphenidate

Presentation
Tablets.
Modified-release tablets.

Administration – enteral tubes / swallowing difficulties
Use the standard tablets. Crush and mix with water for administration.[8,87] Follow the directions in section 3.5.

Do not crush the modified-release tablets.

Methylprednisolone

Presentation
Tablets.
Injection.
Intramuscular depot injection.

Administration – enteral tubes / swallowing difficulties
The tablets can be dispersed in water for administration.[8,105] They disperse within one minute.[8,154] Follow the directions in section 3.5.

Metoclopramide

Presentation
Tablets.
Modified-release capsules (no longer available in the UK).
Oral solution (some preparations contain sorbitol).
Injection.

Administration – NG / PEG tubes
1st choice – Give by parenteral injection if possible.
2nd choice – Use the oral solution. Follow the directions in section 3.6.
3rd choice – The tablets have been crushed and mixed with water for administration.[138,225] Follow the directions in section 3.5. Do not crush the modified-release tablets.
4th choice – The injection has been used enterally.[40,169] Follow the directions in section 3.6. *(monograph continues on next page)*

Administration – NJ / PEJ / PEGJ tubes

1st choice – Give by parenteral injection if possible.

2nd choice – Use the oral solution. Maxolon® syrup can be diluted with an equal amount of water before use.[285] Follow the directions in section 3.6.

3rd choice – The tablets have been crushed and mixed with water for administration.[138,225] Follow the directions in section 3.5. Do not crush the modified-release tablets.

4th choice – The injection has been used enterally.[40,169] Follow the directions in section 3.6.

Administration – swallowing difficulties

1st choice – Use the oral solution.

2nd choice – Give by parenteral injection if possible.

3rd choice – The tablets have been crushed and mixed with water for administration.[138,225] Follow the directions in section 3.5. Do not crush the modified-release tablets.

4th choice – The injection has been used enterally.[40,169] Follow the directions in section 3.6.

Feed guidance

Metoclopramide has been reported as being incompatible with some enteral feeds, so ensure enteral feeding tubes are flushed well before and after each dose.[222]

Metolazone

Presentation

Tablets (may be difficult to obtain).

A suspension can be made by Pharmacy in some centres (see Appendix 1).[473]

Administration – enteral tubes

The tablets can be crushed and mixed with water for administration.[104,105,152] Follow the directions in section 3.5.

No information on administering the suspension via enteral feeding tubes has been located.

(monograph continues on next page)

Administration – swallowing difficulties

1st choice – Use the suspension (if available).
2nd choice – The tablets can be crushed and mixed with water for administration.[104,105,152] Follow the directions in section 3.5.

Clinical guidance

Monitor the patient for postural hypotension due to increased bioavailability.[104] A dose reduction may be necessary.[135]

Metoprolol

Presentation

Tablets.
Modified-release tablets.
Suspension (special).[582]
A suspension can be made by Pharmacy in some centres (see Appendix 1).[206]
Injection.

Administration – enteral tubes

1st choice - Consider giving by parenteral injection, or switching to an alternative beta-blocker available as a liquid.
2nd choice – The tablets can be crushed and mixed with water for administration. They disperse very slowly.[7,40] Follow the directions in section 3.5. Do not crush / disperse the modified-release tablets.
3rd choice – A suspension can be made by Pharmacy in some centres.[206] Follow the directions in section 3.6.
4th choice – Use the suspension (if available).[138] Follow the directions in section 3.6.

The injection has been given enterally at some centres, but there is very little information on this, so it is not recommended.[40,175] Contact Pharmacy for advice.

(monograph continues on next page)

Administration – swallowing difficulties

1st choice – Consider giving by parenteral injection, or switching to an alternative beta-blocker available as a liquid.

2nd choice – A suspension can be made by Pharmacy in some centres.[206]

3rd choice – Use the suspension (if available).[138]

4th choice – The tablets can be crushed and mixed with water for administration. They disperse very slowly.[7,40] Follow the directions in section 3.5. Do not crush / disperse the modified-release tablets.

The injection has been given enterally at some centres, but there is very little information on this, so it is not recommended.[40,175] Contact Pharmacy for advice.

Clinical guidance

Metoprolol shows the same bioavailability along the whole intestine,[398,400,401,402] therefore administration through enteral tubes terminating in the jejunum is not expected to cause any absorption problems.

Metronidazole

Presentation
Tablets.
Suspension (metronidazole benzoate) (some preparations contain sorbitol).
Suppositories.
Intravenous infusion.

Administration – NG / PEG tubes
1st choice – Give by intravenous infusion or rectally as suppositories when possible.
2nd choice – Use the suspension (see "Feed guidance" below). Follow the directions in section 3.6. Rosemont do not recommend diluting their suspension with water before administration as this may destabilise the suspension.[360]
3rd choice – If the patient cannot have a feed break during which the suspension can be given, crush the tablets and mix them with water for administration.[379] The tablets should be crushed well before use as otherwise they can break into large clumps and flakes which may contribute to tube blockage.[358] Flush well. Follow the directions in section 3.5.

Administration – NJ / PEJ / PEGJ tubes
1st choice – Give by intravenous infusion or rectally as suppositories when possible.
2nd choice – Crush the tablets and mix with water for administration for patients with enteral tubes terminating in the jejunum, as stomach acids are required to breakdown metronidazole benzoate to metronidazole.[104,155,253] They should be crushed well before use as otherwise they can break into large clumps and flakes which may contribute to tube blockage.[358] Flush well. Follow the directions in section 3.5.

Administration – swallowing difficulties
1st choice – Use the suspension (see "Feed guidance" below). Rosemont do not recommend diluting their suspension with water before administration as this may destabilise the suspension.[360]
2nd choice – Give by intravenous infusion or rectally as suppositories when possible.

(monograph continues on next page)

Clinical guidance

Metronidazole is well absorbed from the small intestine[66] and therefore it should be well absorbed when a suspension prepared from the tablets is administered to the jejunum.

Suppositories are unsuitable for the initiation of treatment of serious conditions owing to their slower absorption and lower plasma levels.[19] They are suitable to be used during ongoing treatment. Contact Pharmacy for advice if uncertain.

Feed guidance

Food may affect the extent of absorption of metronidazole.[632] It certainly reduces the rate of absorption.[9,18]

When metronidazole is being used for gastric infections (i.e. for a local effect) the effect of food on its rate and extent of absorption is probably not relevant.[632] However if the infection is not in the GI tract, it may be necessary to consider withholding enteral feeds for a period to ensure good absorption.

Metronidazole suspension should be administered one hour before food to allow metronidazole benzoate suspension to be broken down to metronidazole by the gastric enzymes in the stomach. Withhold enteral feeds for two hours before and one hour after each dose when the suspension is being used.[117] If this is not possible, alternative methods of administration should be used, e.g. crushed tablets.

| Summary:- (suspension) | Stop feed 2 hours before dose |
| | Restart feed 1 hour after dose |

Withholding enteral feeds can compromise nutrition and interfere with blood glucose management. If the patient does not have a break in their feeding regimen during which metronidazole can be given, the Nutrition Team should be contacted to advise on management.

Metyrapone

Presentation
Capsules.

Administration – enteral tubes / swallowing difficulties
The capsules can be opened, and the liquid contents squeezed out and dispersed in water for administration.[105,132] Beware of under-dosing due to not all the dose being obtained from the capsule. Follow the directions in section 3.7.

Mexiletine

Presentation
Capsules (may be hard to obtain).
A suspension can be made by Pharmacy in some centres (see Appendix 1).[480]
Injection (may be hard to obtain).

Administration – enteral tubes
1st choice – The capsules can be opened, and the contents dispersed in distilled water for administration.[105] Follow the directions in section 3.7.
2nd choice – Use the suspension (if available). Follow the directions in section 3.6.
3rd choice – The injection has also been administered enterally.[40,170] Follow the directions in section 3.6.

Administration – swallowing difficulties
1st choice – Use the suspension (if available).
2nd choice – The capsules can be opened, and the contents dispersed in distilled water for administration.[105] Follow the directions in section 3.7.
3rd choice – The injection has also been administered enterally.[40,170] Follow the directions in section 3.6. It has a very unpleasant taste and a local anaesthetic action in the mouth.[170]

Feed guidance
When the injection is being given enterally to patients with swallowing difficulties, it should be given at least 30 minutes before food as it has a local anaesthetic effect.[40]

Mianserin

Presentation
Tablets.

Administration – enteral tubes / swallowing difficulties
The tablets can be dispersed in water for administration.[8,41,95] They disperse in one to five minutes.[8,154] Dispersed tablets may have a local anaesthetic effect on the mouth if given orally.[95] Follow the directions in section 3.5.

Micardis Plus®

Presentation
Tablets.

Clinical guidance
Micardis Plus® tablets contain telmisartan and hydrochlorothiazide at various dosages.[272] Use telmisartan or an alternative angiotensin-II receptor inhibitor such as losartan, and an alternative thiazide diuretic, e.g. bendroflumethiazide.

Midazolam

Presentation
Syrup.
Buccal liquid.
A suspension can be made by Pharmacy in some centres (see Appendix 1).[512,573]
Injection.

Clinical guidance
Give by parenteral injection or infusion, or by the intranasal or buccal route.

Midodrine

Presentation
Tablets.

Administration – enteral tubes / swallowing difficulties
The tablets can be crushed and mixed with water for administration.[151] Follow the directions in section 3.5.

Minocycline

Presentation
Tablets, capsules.
Modified-release capsules.

Administration – enteral tubes / swallowing difficulties
1st choice – Switch to an alternative tetracycline antibiotic available as dispersible tablets (e.g. doxycycline) if possible.
2nd choice – The tablets can be crushed and mixed with water for administration.[138] Follow the directions in section 3.5.

The modified-release capsules have been opened and the contents given via enteral feeding tubes with plenty of water, but this is not recommended due to the risk of tube blockage. Do not crush the contents of the modified-release capsules.[138]

Minoxidil

Presentation
Tablets.
Scalp application.

Administration – enteral tubes / swallowing difficulties
The tablets can be dispersed in water for administration.[40] They disperse in one to five minutes.[154] Follow the directions in section 3.5. If giving via enteral feeding tube, flush well after each dose.

Mirtazapine

Presentation
Tablets.
Orodispersible tablets.
Oral solution.

Administration – enteral tubes
1st choice – Use the oral solution. Follow the directions in section 3.6.
2nd choice – Use the orodispersible tablets. Follow the directions in section 3.5. The orodispersible tablets will disperse immediately in water.[154]
3rd choice – Crush the standard tablets well and mix with water for administration.[72] The tablet may not fully dissolve, so take care to flush the enteral tube well after administration. Follow the directions in section 3.5.

Administration – swallowing difficulties
Use the oral solution or the orodispersible tablet, as the standard tablet, when crushed, has a bitter taste and an anaesthetic effect on the mouth.[72,561] Follow the directions in sections 3.5 and 3.6.

Clinical guidance
Mirtazapine is mostly absorbed in the duodenum.[417] There is therefore a risk that if the drug is given through an enteral tube terminating in the jejunum that the drug will not be fully absorbed and the patient will not receive the prescribed dosage. Any patient requiring mirtazapine through an enteral tube terminating in the jejunum should be reviewed, and if the situation is long-term, consideration should be given to using a different treatment.

Misoprostol

Presentation
Tablets.

Administration – enteral tubes / swallowing difficulties
1st choice – Consider switching to an alternative medication which is available in a liquid or injection form, e.g. ranitidine, particularly if swallowing problems are likely to be long-term, due to the hazards of handling dispersed tablets.
2nd choice – The tablets can be dispersed in water for administration.[8,104,105,152] They disperse in less than two minutes.[8,154] This should be done immediately before administration. Follow the directions in section 3.5.

Women who are or who may become pregnant should not handle crushed, broken, or dispersed tablets.[105]

Moclobemide

Presentation
Tablets.

Administration – enteral tubes / swallowing difficulties
The tablets can be crushed and dispersed in water for administration.[95] Follow the directions in section 3.5.

Modafinil

Presentation
Tablets.

Administration – enteral tubes / swallowing difficulties
The manufacturer states that theoretically modafinil tablets can be crushed and dispersed in water for administration.[336] This should be done immediately prior to use as there is no stability data available. Follow the directions in section 3.5.

Moexipril

Presentation
Film-coated tablets.

Clinical guidance
No information has been located about the administration of moexipril to patients with enteral feeding tubes or with swallowing difficulties. Convert to an alternative ACE inhibitor, e.g. lisinopril.

Montelukast

Presentation
Chewable tablets.
Film-coated tablets.
Granules.

Administration – enteral tubes / swallowing difficulties
Use the chewable tablets, and disperse in water for administration. Follow the directions in section 3.5.

Feed guidance
Withhold enteral feeds for two hours before and one hour after administration of montelukast.[73,225,624]

Summary:-	Stop feed 2 hours before dose
	Restart feed 1 hour after dose

Withholding enteral feeds can compromise nutrition and interfere with blood glucose management. If the patient does not have a break in their feeding regimen during which montelukast can be given, the Nutrition Team should be contacted to advise on management.

Morphine

Presentation
Oral solution.
Film-coated tablets.
Modified-release tablets, modified-release capsules, modified-release sachets.
Suppositories.
Injection.

Administration – enteral tubes
Use parenteral morphine whenever possible. Consider subcutaneous syringe drivers or switching to transdermal opiate preparations (e.g. fentanyl patches) for patients with chronic pain.

Immediate-release preparations
When an immediate-release product is required, administer morphine sulphate oral solution (e.g. Oramorph®). This is the preferred enteral method of administering morphine. Follow the directions in section 3.6.

Modified-release preparations
The use of controlled-release preparations of morphine via enteral feeding tubes is not usually recommended due to the potential for accidental morphine overdose if any of the dose is left in the tube and subsequently administered to the patient with the next use of the tube. If possible, patients should be managed with regular small doses of immediate-release products, e.g. Oramorph® (see above). If pain control is insufficient, a continuous subcutaneous syringe driver should be considered.

If administration of modified-release preparations is considered essential, the following options could be considered:-

MST Continus® sachets can be given, diluted with at least 30mL of water, and flushed with 15-30mL of distilled water. Give immediately as the resulting suspension thickens.[105,137,138] The manufacturer of MST Continus® sachets warns that oral rehydration fluids can damage the modified-release properties of the suspension, and so care should be taken to flush well after each dose of MST Continus®.[344]

(monograph continues on next page)

It is important to ensure that no part of the dose remains in the feeding tube, where the administration of the next drug or feed might cause an unexpected dose of morphine to be administered to the patient.

Zomorph® capsules can be opened and the contents flushed down enteral feeding tubes with a diameter of 16Fr or larger.[47,104,326] The manufacturer recommends rinsing the tube following each dose with 30-50mL of water.[326]

Do not administer MXL® capsules through enteral feeding tubes, as the granules in the capsules are highly lipophilic and will clump together when in contact with water or saline.[20]

Administration – swallowing difficulties
Use MST Continus® sachets or the immediate-release oral solution, according to clinical need.

MXL® capsules can also be opened and the contents sprinkled onto cold soft food for patients with swallowing difficulties.[146] The contents of the capsules should not be chewed or crushed, and therefore this method may not be appropriate for patients with limited understanding or impaired ability to follow instructions.

Zomorph® capsules can be opened and the contents sprinkled on food, e.g. yogurt or jam.[47,326]

For patients with swallowing difficulties unable to receive morphine orally, the preferred alternative routes are rectal and subcutaneous. The bioavailabilty and duration of analgesia of morphine when given in the soluble, dispersible and rectal formulations are the same.[15]

Feed guidance
Enteral morphine interacts with Jevity® , Osmolite-HN® and Pulmocare® feeds – withhold the feed for two hours before and one hour after each dose.[105,224] This interaction may also occur with other feeds – take care to ensure that the feeding tube is flushed well before and after enteral morphine is given.

(monograph continues on next page)

Summary:- (above feeds)	Stop feed 2 hours before dose Restart feed 1 hour after dose

Withholding enteral feeds can compromise nutrition and interfere with blood glucose management. If the patient does not have a break in their feeding regimen during which morphine can be given, the Nutrition Team should be contacted to advise on management.

Movicol®

Presentation
Oral powder (various).

Administration – enteral tubes
The administration of Movicol® via enteral feeding tubes is not generally recommended as it could interact with concomitant feeds, medication, or the tubing itself.[367]
1st choice – Consider an alternative laxative, e.g. lactulose.
2nd choice – Movicol® has been given via enteral feeding tubes in some centres without apparent ill effect.[554] If it is decided to use Movicol® via an enteral feeding tube, monitor the patient for appropriate effects, both of the laxative, and of any other medication which the patient may be receiving enterally.

Administration – swallowing difficulties
The adult 13.8g sachets should be dissolved in 125mL of water for administration.

There are reports of Movicol® being flavoured with cordials or squashes, and less frequently with milk or tea.[536] The manufacturers specifically recommend **against** reconstitution with fizzy drinks as there is a risk of interaction between macrogols and phosphoric acid.[536]

Moxifloxacin

Presentation
Film-coated tablets.
A suspension can be made by Pharmacy in some centres (see Appendix 1).[539]

Administration – enteral tubes
The tablets can be crushed and dispersed in water for administration.[367] Follow the directions in section 3.5.

No information about administering the suspension via enteral feeding tubes has been located.

Administration – swallowing difficulties
1st choice – Use the suspension (if available).
2nd choice – The tablets can be crushed and dispersed in water for administration.[367] The crushed tablets have a bitter taste.[367] Follow the directions in section 3.5.

Moxisylyte

Presentation
Film-coated tablets.

Administration – enteral tubes / swallowing difficulties
The tablets can be crushed and dispersed in water for administration.[138] Follow the directions in section 3.5.

Moxonidine

Presentation
Tablets.

Administration – enteral tubes / swallowing difficulties
The tablets can be crushed finely and dispersed in water for administration.[74] Without crushing they disperse in around five minutes.[154] Follow the directions in section 3.5.

The tablets are poorly soluble and film-coated. They should be crushed well to minimise the risk of blocking enteral feeding tubes. The manufacturer recommends crushing one tablet and mixing it in 50mL of water, then allowing it to dissolve for 2 minutes before administering.[74]

Mucogel®

See entry under "Co-magaldrox".

Multivitamins

Presentation
Tablets.
Oral drops.

Clinical guidance
Consider whether vitamins are still required (vitamins are present in most enteral feeds). Use oral drops if necessary.

Mycophenolate mofetil

Presentation
Tablets, capsules.
Oral suspension (contains sorbitol).
A suspension can be made by Pharmacy in some centres (see Appendix 1).[481,482]
Intravenous infusion.

Administration – enteral tubes
1st choice – Use the intravenous infusion if possible, at the same dosage as oral.[126]
2nd choice – The suspension can be given via enteral feeding tubes (minimum size 8 French).[127] Follow the directions in section 3.6.
3rd choice – A suspension can be made by Pharmacy in some centres. Follow the directions in section 3.6.
4th choice – The intravenous powder for injection has been used via enteral feeding tubes. The injection should be reconstituted as usual and administered via enteral feeding tube with a dextrose 5% flush before and after administration. Care should be taken when handling the powder (teratogenic risk).[126] Contamination should be removed promptly by washing with soap and water (eyes – plain water).[152]

Mycophenolate capsules should not be opened and the tablets should not be crushed, as the powder is teratogenic, posing a risk to the carer.

Administration – swallowing difficulties
1st choice – Use the suspension.
2nd choice – Use the intravenous infusion if possible, at the same dosage as oral.[126]
3rd choice – A suspension can be made by Pharmacy in some centres.

Mycophenolate capsules should not be opened and the tablets should not be crushed, as the powder is teratogenic, posing a risk to the carer.

Nabilone

Presentation
Capsules.

Administration – enteral tubes / swallowing difficulties
The capsules can be opened, and the contents dispersed in water for administration.[104] Give immediately. Follow the directions in section 3.7.

Nabumetone

Presentation
Tablets, film-coated tablets.
Dispersible tablets.
Suspension.

Administration – enteral tubes / swallowing difficulties
Use the suspension or the dispersible tablets. Follow the directions in section 3.6. The dispersible tablets may not be suitable for fine-bore nasogastric tubes. Flush well after administration.[140]

Nabumetone standard tablets should not be crushed as they are film-coated and irritant.[357]

Clinical guidance
There can be increased bioavailability of nabumetone when it is given with milk.[321] This may also occur if it is given with enteral feeds.

Nadolol

Presentation
Tablets.
Oral solution (special).[582]

Administration – enteral tubes
1st choice – Consider switching to an alternative beta blocker available in a liquid formulation, e.g. atenolol.
2nd choice – The tablets can be crushed and dispersed in water for administration.[138] Follow the directions in section 3.5.

No information on administering the oral solution via enteral feeding tubes has been located.

Administration – swallowing difficulties
1st choice – Consider switching to an alternative beta blocker available in a liquid formulation, e.g. atenolol.
2nd choice – Use the oral solution (if available).
3rd choice – The tablets can be crushed and dispersed in water for administration.[138] Follow the directions in section 3.5.

Feed guidance
The absorption of nadolol can be increased by concomitant food or milk.[2]

Naftidrofuryl oxalate

Presentation
Capsules.

Administration – enteral tubes
The capsules can be opened and the contents dispersed in water for administration via enteral feeding tubes.[91] Follow the directions in section 3.7.

(monograph continues on next page)

Administration – swallowing difficulties

The powder is irritant and anaesthetic to the mouth and throat.[105] There is a risk of oesophageal stricture if the capsules are opened for oral use in patients with swallowing difficulties. To avoid this, the manufacturer recommends that the patient should drink 4-5 glasses of water after each dose.[91] Review the need for this medication, - it is seldom practical to administer these volumes of water.[105]

Nalidixic acid

Presentation

Tablets (no longer available in the UK).
Suspension (some preparations contain sorbitol).[583]

Administration – enteral tubes

1st choice – Switch to an alternative treatment.
2nd choice – Use the suspension.[138] Follow the directions in section 3.6.

Administration – swallowing difficulties

1st choice – Use the suspension.[138]
2nd choice – Switch to an alternative treatment.

Naproxen

Presentation
Tablets.
Enteric-coated tablets.
Suspension (discontinued).
Oral solution (special).[582]

Administration – enteral tubes
1st choice – Consider switching to an alternative non-steroidal anti-inflammatory drug available via a different route, e.g. rectal.
2nd choice – Use the suspension (if available).[104] Follow the directions in section 3.6.
3rd choice – The standard tablets can be crushed and dispersed in water for administration.[138] Follow the directions in section 3.5.
4th choice – Use the oral solution (if available). Follow the directions in section 3.6.

Do not crush the enteric-coated tablets.

Administration – swallowing difficulties
1st choice – Use the suspension (if available).[104]
2nd choice – Consider switching to an alternative non-steroidal anti-inflammatory drug available via a different route, e.g. rectal.
3rd choice – Use the oral solution (if available).
4th choice – The standard tablets can be crushed and dispersed in water for administration.[138] Follow the directions in section 3.5.

Do not crush the enteric-coated tablets.

Clinical guidance
Naproxen sodium is absorbed more rapidly than naproxen, but both are well absorbed,[176] so the difference is unlikely to be noticeable except in patients with reduced bowel length or transit time.

Naratriptan

Presentation
Film-coated tablets.
A suspension can be made by Pharmacy in some centres (see Appendix 1).[529]

Administration – enteral tubes
No information on administering naratriptan via enteral feeding tubes has been located. Consider switching to sumatriptan, which is available via alternative routes (intranasal and subcutaneous injection).

Administration – swallowing difficulties
1st choice – Consider switching to sumatriptan, which is available via alternative routes (intranasal and subcutaneous injection).
2nd choice – Use the suspension (if available).

Nateglinide

Presentation
Film-coated tablets.

Clinical guidance
No information about giving nateglinide to patients with enteral feeding tubes has been located. Consider switching to insulin or repaglinide.

Navispare®

Presentation
Film-coated tablets.

Clinical guidance
Navispare® tablets contain amiloride 2.5mg and cyclopenthiazide 250micrograms.[272] Use the separate components – see individual monographs for details.

Nebivolol

Presentation
Tablets.

Administration – enteral tubes / swallowing difficulties
1st choice – Consider changing to an alternative beta-blocker available as a liquid, e.g. atenolol.
2nd choice – The tablets can be crushed and mixed with water for administration.[367] Follow the directions in section 3.5.

Nefopam

Presentation
Film-coated tablets.
A suspension can be made by Pharmacy in some centres.
Injection (no longer available in the UK).

Administration – enteral tubes / swallowing difficulties
1st choice – Give by parenteral injection (if available) if appropriate.
2nd choice – A suspension can be made in Pharmacy in some centres.[138] Follow the directions in section 3.6.

The tablets should not be crushed, as they are film-coated to protect the patient from the local anaesthetic action of the drug. The manufacturers advise that the tablets are not to be crushed even in order to be given via an enteral feeding tube.[150]

Nelfinavir

Presentation
Film-coated tablets (no longer available in the UK).
Oral powder (not licensed in the UK).

Administration – enteral tubes / swallowing difficulties
The tablets (if available) can be crushed and dispersed in a small amount of water or milk to dissolve. This solution can be stored in the fridge for up to eight hours (NB stored solutions should be labelled appropriately).[176] Follow the directions in section 3.5.

The powder (if available) can be mixed with water, milk, formula feeds or pudding. It should not be mixed with acidic foods or juices.[176]

Feed guidance
Take with or after food.[429]

Neomycin

Presentation
Tablets.

Administration – enteral tubes / swallowing difficulties
The tablets can be crushed and mixed with water for administration.[105] Follow the directions in section 3.5.

Neo-NaClex-K®

Presentation
Film-coated tablets (no longer available in the UK).

Clinical guidance
Neo-NaClex-K® tablets contain bendroflumethiazide 2.5mg and potassium 8.4mmol in a modified-release preparation.[272] Use the separate components – bendroflumethiazide and an appropriate standard-release formulation of potassium. See individual monographs for details. Contact Pharmacy for advice if necessary.

Neostigmine

Presentation
Tablets.
Injection.

Administration – enteral tubes / swallowing difficulties
The tablets can be crushed and mixed with water for administration. They may not be suitable for narrow-bore tubes.[140] Follow the directions in section 3.5.

Nevirapine

Presentation
Tablets.
Suspension (contains sorbitol).

Administration – enteral tubes
1st choice – Use the suspension. Follow the directions in section 3.6.
2nd choice – The tablets can be crushed but produce a "slurry" when mixed with water, which may lead to difficulty ensuring the whole dose is given, and to tube blockage.[333] Flush well after each dose. Follow the directions in section 3.5.

Administration – swallowing difficulties
1st choice – Use the suspension. Follow the directions in section 3.6.
2nd choice – The tablets can be crushed and mixed with soft food.[333]

Nicardipine

Presentation
Capsules.
Suspension (special).
Modified-release capsules.

Administration – enteral tubes
1st choice – The capsules can be opened, and the contents dispersed in orange juice for administration.[105] Follow the directions in section 3.7.
2nd choice – Use the suspension (if available).[138] Follow the directions in section 3.6.

Do not open the modified-release capsules. Contact Pharmacy for advice.

Administration – swallowing difficulties
1st choice – Use the suspension (if available).[138]
2nd choice – The capsules can be opened, and the contents dispersed in orange juice for administration.[105] Follow the directions in section 3.7.

Do not open the modified-release capsules. Contact Pharmacy for advice.

Niclosamide

Presentation
Tablets (special).

Administration – enteral tubes
No information about the use of this medication via enteral feeding tubes has been located.

Administration – swallowing difficulties
The tablets can be crushed and dispersed in water or orange juice.[152]

Nicorandil

Presentation
Tablets.

Administration – enteral tubes / swallowing difficulties
The tablets can be crushed and mixed with water for administration.[62] Without crushing they disperse in around five minutes.[154] Some of the excipients in the tablets are insoluble, so take care to flush enteral tubes well after administration.[62] Follow the directions in section 3.5.

Nifedipine

Presentation
Capsules.
Modified-release tablets, modified-release capsules.
A suspension can be made by Pharmacy in some centres (see Appendix 1).[483,527]

Administration – enteral tubes / swallowing difficulties
Use of immediate-release nifedipine capsules for blood pressure control is no longer recommended due to the risk of rebound hypertension and tachycardia. Consider alternative methods of blood pressure control, e.g. switching to amlodipine.

There are a range of different manufacturers of nifedipine immediate-release capsules. The details given below are for Adalat® capsules. The internal volumes of capsules from other manufacturers are likely to differ.

Take care – Risk of profound drop in blood pressure if nifedipine is given incorrectly. Contact Pharmacy for advice.

(monograph continues on next page)

When an immediate-release product is required

1. When giving via enteral feeding tube, flush pre-dose with sodium chloride 0.9%.
2. At the patient's bedside remove the liquid from the capsule using a green needle and withdraw the contents into a syringe.[2,4] A 1mL syringe is ideal, as the contents are very viscous. A 5mg Adalat® capsule should contain 0.17mL and a 10mg capsule 0.34mL of solution.[147]
3. Administer immediately to the patient as nifedipine is light sensitive.[41] When giving via enteral feeding tube, flush the liquid down the enteral tube using sodium chloride 0.9%, not water, as nifedipine is poorly soluble in water.

Give immediately. Be aware that serious errors have occurred due to the use of needles and syringes to handle oral medication.

Alternatively the capsule can be given sublingually by the patient biting the capsule and the contents being administered sublingually. Consult with medical staff before doing this.

When a modified-release is required

Modified-release capsules (e.g. Coracten®) can be opened and the contents flushed down enteral feeding tubes for administration.[89,364] The capsule contents should not be crushed as this will destroy their modified-release properties.[364] Be sure to flush the enteral tube well after dose administration.

Adalat Retard® tablets have also been crushed and dispersed in water for enteral tube adminstration. This should not affect the modified-release properties, but small alterations in bioavailability may occur.[138]

(monograph continues on next page)

Clinical guidance

Do not crush any tablets other than Adalat Retard® as their modified-release mechanisms differ. Nifedipine is very short-acting. If a long-acting preparation is substituted with a short-acting preparation, side effects such as hypotension may occur, therefore monitor blood pressure more closely. Food may alter the rate but not the extent of absorption.

Nifedipine absorption occurs entirely within the small intestine, but complete absorption following administration via enteral tubes terminating in the jejunum cannot be guaranteed, so blood pressure should be monitored.[6]

Consider changing to a long-acting calcium antagonist such as amlodipine.

Feed guidance

Nifedipine levels can be decreased by grapefruit juice.[2]

Niferex®

Clinical guidance

See entry under 'Iron preparations'.

Nimodipine

Presentation

Tablets.
Infusion.

Administration – enteral tubes / swallowing difficulties

1st choice – Give by IV infusion if possible.
2nd choice – Crush the tablet down to a fine powder at the patients bedside, mix with water, and give immediately.[43] The tablets degrade rapidly once crushed and are light sensitive, so should be used immediately.[43] Check the patency of enteral tubes after administration as the film coating on nimodipine may block narrow-bore tubes. Follow the directions in section 3.5.

(monograph continues on next page)

Feed guidance
There is no need to withhold feeds when administering nimodipine using the UK tablet formulation.[590] Nimotop® tablets can be taken with or without food.[590]

The US capsule formulation (also with the brand name Nimotop®) is affected by the concomitant administration of food. The bioavailability and peak serum concentrations are reduced when the capsules are taken with food.[412] Feeds should be stopped for two hours before and one hour after each dose when using the capsule formulation.

The UK manufacturers have confirmed that there is a difference between the formulations, and that the bioavailability of the tablets is not affected by food.[590]

Nitrazepam

Presentation
Tablets.
Suspension.
Oral suspension (special).[542]

Administration – enteral tubes / swallowing difficulties
Use the suspension. Follow the directions in section 3.6.

Nitrofurantoin

Presentation
Tablets, capsules.
Modified-release capsules.
Suspension.

Administration – enteral tubes
1st choice – Use the suspension.[105] Follow the directions in section 3.6.
2nd choice - Macrodantin® capsules have been opened.[104] Follow the directions in section 3.7. Do not open the modified-release capsules.
3rd choice – The tablets have been crushed and mixed with water for administration.[138] Follow the directions in section 3.5.

Administration – swallowing difficulties
1st choice – Use the suspension.[105] Follow the directions in section 3.6.
2nd choice - Macrodantin® capsules have been opened.[104] Follow the directions in section 3.7. Do not open the modified-release capsules.

Do not crush the tablets – nitrofurantoin is an irritant.[561]

Feed guidance
Absorption of nitrofurantoin can be increased by concomitant food or milk.[2]

Nizatidine

Presentation
Capsules.
Injection.

Clinical guidance
Nizatidine capsules are not suitable to be used down enteral feeding tubes, as whilst the drug dissolves in water, the excipients do not and may coat and block the tube.[48] Consider changing to ranitidine if appropriate.

Norethisterone

Presentation
Tablets.

Administration – enteral tubes / swallowing difficulties
The tablets can be crushed (preferably in water to reduce the production of dust) and mixed with water for administration.[8,94] Without crushing they disperse in two to five minutes.[8] Follow the directions in section 3.5.

Norfloxacin

Presentation
Tablets.
A suspension can be made by Pharmacy in some centres (see Appendix 1).[484]

Administration – enteral tubes
The tablets can be crushed and mixed with water for administration.[105] Flush well as the drug is poorly soluble.[105] Light sensitive, so give immediately.[132] Follow the directions in section 3.5.

No information on administering the suspension via enteral feeding tubes has been located.

Administration – swallowing difficulties
1st choice – Use the suspension (if available).
2nd choice – The tablets can be crushed and mixed with water for administration.[105] The crushed tablets taste unpleasant.[105] Light sensitive, so give immediately.[132] Follow the directions in section 3.5.

Feed guidance
Withhold enteral feeds for two hours before and one hour after each dose, as absorption is decreased in the presence of food.[87,225,621,624]

Summary:-	Stop feed 2 hours before dose
	Restart feed 1 hour after dose

(monograph continues on next page)

Withholding enteral feeds can compromise nutrition and interfere with blood glucose management. If the patient does not have a break in their feeding regimen during which norfloxacin can be given, the Nutrition Team should be contacted to advise on management.

Nortriptyline

Presentation
Tablets.
Oral solution (special).[582]

Administration – enteral tubes
The tablets will disperse in water for administration.[8] They disperse in one to two minutes.[8] Follow the directions in section 3.5.

No information on administering the oral solution via enteral feeding tubes has been located.

Administration – swallowing difficulties
1st choice – Use the oral solution (if available).
2nd choice – The tablets will disperse in water for administration.[8] They disperse in one to two minutes.[8] Follow the directions in section 3.5.

Clinical guidance
Tricyclic antidepressants can decrease gastric emptying.[2]

Ofloxacin

Presentation
Tablets.
Infusion.

Administration – enteral tubes / swallowing difficulties
1st choice – Give by infusion if possible.
2nd choice – Consider changing to an alternative antibiotic available in a liquid or dispersible tablet formulation.
3rd choice – The tablets can be crushed and mixed with distilled water for administration.[105,358] Do not mix with tap water as chelation may occur with ions in the tap water (see under ciprofloxacin). Use distilled water for flushing enteral tubes post-dose.[105] Follow the directions in section 3.5.

Clinical guidance
Some sources suggest that the reduction in absorption is so pronounced when quinolones are administered directly into the jejunum (particularly in the presence of enteral feeds) that an alternative route or alternative drug should be used.[193]

Feed guidance
Withhold enteral feeds for two hours before and two hours after each enteral dose, as ofloxacin absorption is reduced in the presence of feeds.[105,622]

Summary:-	Stop feed 2 hours before dose
	Restart feed 2 hours after dose

Withholding enteral feeds can compromise nutrition and interfere with blood glucose management. If the patient does not have a break in their feeding regimen during which ofloxacin can be given, the Nutrition Team should be contacted to advise on management.

Olanzapine

Presentation
Film-coated tablets.
Orodispersible Velotab® tablets.
Oral solution (special).[582]
Injection.

Administration – enteral tubes
1st choice – Use the Velotab® and disperse in water.[35,152] Follow the directions in section 3.5.
2nd choice – Use the oral solution (if available). Follow the directions in section 3.6.

Administration – swallowing difficulties
1st choice – The Velotab® can be placed on the tongue or dispersed in water, orange juice, apple juice, milk, or coffee.
2nd choice – Use the oral solution (if available).

Olanzapine may be irritant to the skin and eyes, so take precautions to avoid contact (e.g. wear gloves).[133,213]

Olmesartan

Presentation
Film-coated tablets.
Oral solution (special).[582]

Administration – enteral tubes
No information has been located about giving olmesartan to patients with enteral feeding tubes. Consider switching to an alternative angiotensin-II receptor inhibitor, e.g. losartan.

Administration – swallowing difficulties
1st choice – Consider switching to an alternative angiotensin-II receptor inhibitor with a licensed liquid formulation, e.g. losartan.
2nd choice – Use the oral solution (if available).

Olmesartan and amlodipine (Sevikar®)

Presentation
Film-coated tablets.

Clinical guidance
Sevikar® tablets contain olmesartan and amlodipine at various dosages.[577] Due to lack of information consider switching to an alternative angiotensin-II receptor inhibitor, e.g. losartan, and amlodipine. See individual monographs for details.

Olmesartan and hydrochlorothiazide (Olmetec Plus®)

Presentation
Film-coated tablets.

Clinical guidance
Olmetec Plus® tablets contain olmesartan and hydrochlorothiazide at various dosages.[272] Due to lack of information consider switching to an alternative angiotensin-II receptor inhibitor, e.g. losartan, and an alternative thiazide diuretic, e.g. bendroflumethiazide. See individual monographs for details.

Olmetec Plus®

Presentation
Film-coated tablets.

Clinical guidance
Olmetec Plus® tablets contain olmesartan and hydrochlorothiazide at various dosages.[272] Due to lack of information consider switching to an alternative angiotensin-II receptor inhibitor, e.g. losartan, and an alternative thiazide diuretic, e.g. bendroflumethiazide. See individual monographs for details.

Olsalazine

Presentation
Tablets, capsules.

Administration – enteral tubes / swallowing difficulties
The tablets can be crushed or the capsules opened and mixed with water for administration.[104,105,152,364] Follow the directions in section 3.5 and 3.7. Some sources recommend the use of warm sterile water,[155] as the drug can precipitate out in cold water at higher concentrations.[364] A maximum of 20mg/mL is recommended,[364] i.e. a 250mg capsule should be dispersed in at least 12.5mL of water, and a 500mg tablet should be dispersed in at least 25mL.

The drug is alkaline, so acidic fluids, e.g. fruit juices, should not be used.

Clinical guidance
Inhalation of the powder can cause gastrointestinal upset, headache, joint pain, skin rash, and blood cell abnormalities.[364] Carers should take care not to inhale the powder whilst preparing and administering doses.

Omeprazole

Presentation
MUPS® tablets.
Capsules.
Oral solution (special).[582,658]
A suspension can be made by Pharmacy in some centres (see Appendix 1).[215,573]
Injection.

Administration – enteral tubes
Consider switching to lansoprazole or esomeprazole which are licensed for enteral tube administration.[156,267] Alternatively, consider giving by intravenous injection.

If neither of these options are appropriate, the methods below have been used.[35]

(monograph continues on next page)

Losec MUPS® contain granules which are approximately 0.5mm in diameter.[236] Losec® capsules contain granules which are approximately 1-1.6mm in diameter.[236] For this reason, the MUPS® are probably less likely than the capsules to block enteral feeding tubes.

Recommended method

1. Place the MUPS® tablet in the barrel of an oral syringe with 25mL of water and 5mL of air and shake to disperse it.[104,138] The granules left after dispersal should not be crushed.
2. Ensure the tip of the syringe has not been clogged.
3. Attach the syringe to the tube whilst keeping the tip upright to prevent clogging.
4. Administer the medication with repeated inversion of the syringe and shaking in order to disperse the contents.
5. When the fluid is gone from the syringe, a further 25mL of water and 5mL of air should be drawn up, and the process repeated.[138,148] Flush the tube very well after giving the dose, as this medication is prone to blocking tubes.

Alternative method[178]

1. For patients with nasogastric / gastrostomy tubes, administer 10mL of sodium bicarbonate 8.4% (this step is not necessary for feeding tubes terminating in the jejunum).
2. Add the MUPS® tablet or the contents of an omeprazole capsule to 10mL of sodium bicarbonate 8.4% and wait 10 minutes for a turbid solution to be obtained.[6] – Note, medicines should never be left unattended.
3. Administer via the enteral feeding tube, and flush immediately with plenty of water.

Some sources recommend use of the alternative method for all patients with tubes terminating in the jejunum.[155] Studies have shown that pH control is similar in patients receiving omeprazole through tubes terminating in the stomach, the duodenum, and the jejunum.[219]

(monograph continues on next page)

Omeprazole suspension

Methods for preparing omeprazole suspension with an expiry of up to 30 days have been described.[215]

Administration – swallowing difficulties
Disperse the MUPS® tablet in water, then mix this with orange / apple / pineapple juice, apple sauce, or yogurt.[153,178,277]

Ondansetron

Presentation
Film-coated tablets.
Melt tablets.
Syrup (contains sorbitol)
Suppositories.
Injection.

Administration – enteral tubes
1st choice – For acute use, consider giving by parenteral injection or using the suppositories.
2nd choice – Use the syrup.[40,104] Follow the directions in section 3.6.
3rd choice – The injection has been used enterally,[40,171,444] and this may be preferable for administration via enteral tubes terminating in the jejunum as the syrup contains sorbitol. The injection is acidic, so when giving via enteral feeding tube, flush well before and after each dose to prevent precipitation of the drug.[171] Follow the directions in section 3.6.

Administration – swallowing difficulties
1st choice – Use the syrup or the melt tablets.
2nd choice – For acute use, consider giving by parenteral injection or using the suppositories.
3rd choice – The injection has been used enterally.[40,171,444] The injection is acidic.[171] Stability tests have shown the injection to be stable in apple juice,[444] which may be preferable in patients with swallowing difficulties. Follow the directions in section 3.6.

Clinical guidance
Ondansetron bioavailability does not appear to be affected by delivery to sites beyond the stomach.[211]

Orciprenaline

Presentation
Syrup (may not be available in the UK).

Administration – enteral tubes
No information on administering orciprenaline via enteral feeding tubes has been located.

Administration – swallowing difficulties
Use the syrup (if available), which can be diluted with Syrup BP or sorbitol if necessary.[333]

Clinical guidance
Consider changing to an alternative drug available in a non-oral form, e.g. salbutamol.

Orlistat

Presentation
Capsules.

Administration – enteral tubes / swallowing difficulties
Review whether this drug is still appropriate. Contact Dieticians for advice. If necessary, the capsules can be opened, and the contents dispersed in water for administration.[105]

Orphenadrine

Presentation
Sugar-coated tablets.
Solution (some preparations contain sorbitol).

Administration – enteral tubes / swallowing difficulties
Use the solution.[104] Follow the directions in section 3.6.

Oseltamivir

Presentation
Capsules.
Suspension (may not be freely available – at the time of printing the suspension is reserved for patients who require non-standard doses) (contains sorbitol).
A suspension can be made by Pharmacy in some centres (see Appendix 1).[370]

Administration – enteral tubes
The capsules have been opened and the contents dispersed in water for administration via enteral feeding tube.[438] Follow the directions in section 3.7. Although this is an unlicensed practice it is believed to have been used widely during the UK swine flu outbreak in 2009, and no problems have been reported.

There is a formula available for preparing a suspension.[434] No information on specific instances of administration of the suspension via enteral feeding tubes have been located.

Oseltamivir has been shown to be adequately absorbed following nasogastric administration in severely ill patients.[426]

Administration – swallowing difficulties
1st choice – Use the suspension (if available).
2nd choice – The capsules can be opened and the contents mixed with a small amount (1 teaspoon) of an appropriate sweetened food, e.g. chocolate syrup, honey, sugar-water, dessert-toppings, sweetened condensed milk, apple sauce, or yogurt.[370] The capsule contents have a bitter taste.[370] The whole dose should be given immediately.

Feed guidance
The absorption of oseltamivir appears to be unaffected by co-administration with food.[370] Taking oseltamivir with food may help to reduce the gastric side effects which tend to occur in the first two days of treatment.

Oxazepam

Presentation
Tablets.

Clinical guidance
Consider changing to another benzodiazepine available as a liquid, e.g. diazepam. The tablets will disperse easily in water,[358] but the manufacturers do not have any information about using crushed or dispersed tablets.[357]

Oxcarbazepine

Presentation
Film-coated tablets.
Oral suspension (contains ethanol and sorbitol[601]).

Administration – enteral tubes / swallowing difficulties
Use the suspension at the same dose as the tablets.[132,601] It can be diluted with water to aid administration.[601] Follow the directions in section 3.6.

Clinical guidance
Changing formulations / product manufacturer
The MHRA has issued guidance recommending that (where possible) patients on oxcarbazepine (when used for seizures) are maintained on a specific manufacturer's product, due to variability in product characteristics which may lead to a loss of seizure control when switching between brands / manufacturers.[651] When managing patients with enteral tubes or swallowing difficulties it may not be possible to maintain the patient on their previous preparation due to the need to change to an appropriate formulation. However all product switches should be carried out with care and close monitoring, and where possible patients should be maintained from then onwards on a single manufacturer's product.

Oxprenolol

Presentation
Coated tablets.
Modified-release tablets.

Administration – enteral tubes / swallowing difficulties
The tablets can be crushed and mixed with water for administration.[105] The crushed tablets taste very bitter.[105] Follow the directions in section 3.5.

Do not crush the modified-release tablets.

Oxprenolol is absorbed from both the small and the large intestine, so it is predicted that administration directly into the jejunum should produce a similar effect to oral administration.[6,401]

Oxprenolol and cyclopenthiazide (Trasidrex®)

Presentation
Sugar-coated tablets (no longer available in the UK).

Clinical guidance
Trasidrex® tablets contain oxprenolol 160mg as a modified-release preparation and cyclopenthiazide 250micrograms.[272] A dose alteration will be required to move to a standard-release formulation. Consider switching to an alternative beta-blocker available as a liquid, e.g. atenolol, and giving cyclopenthiazide as a separate component. Contact Pharmacy for advice if necessary.

Oxybutynin

Presentation
Tablets.
Modified-release tablets.
Elixir (contains sorbitol).
Oral solution (special).[542]
Transdermal patch.

Administration – enteral tubes
1st choice – Use the patches if appropriate.
2nd choice – Use the elixir.[104] Follow the directions in section 3.6.
3rd choice – The tablets have been crushed and mixed with water for administration.[138] Follow the directions in section 3.5.
4th choice – Use the oral solution (if available). Follow the directions in section 3.6.

Do not crush the modified-release tablets.

Administration – swallowing difficulties
1st choice – Use the patches if appropriate.
2nd choice – Use the elixir.[104]
3rd choice – Use the oral solution (if available).
4th choice – The tablets have been crushed and mixed with water for administration.[138] Follow the directions in section 3.5.

Do not crush the modified-release tablets.

Oxycodone

Presentation
Capsules.
Liquid, concentrate.
Injection.
Modified-release tablets.

Administration – enteral tubes
Contact Pharmacy for advice on appropriate management. Consider giving by parenteral injection (if available), or switching to an alternative opioid available via a non-enteral route.

The manufacturers of oxycodone liquid know of no theoretical reason why the liquid couldn't be administered through enteral feeding tubes, but they have no data or anecdotal evidence to support such use.[344]

Administration – swallowing difficulties
1st choice – Use the liquid. OxyNorm® Concentrate liquid can be diluted with a soft drink to aid administration and improve palatability if desired.[328]
2nd choice – Contact Pharmacy for advice on appropriate management. Consider giving by parenteral injection (if available), or switching to an alternative opioid available via a non-enteral route.

Oxytetracycline

Presentation
Tablets.
Capsule.

Administration – enteral tubes
1st choice – Consider switching to doxycycline dispersible tablets due to the lack of a liquid formulation and the need for feed breaks with oxytetracycline.
2nd choice – The tablets have been crushed and mixed with water for administration down enteral feeding tubes.[105] Follow the directions in section 3.5.

(monograph continues on next page)

Administration – swallowing difficulties

The tablets should not be crushed for administration to patients with swallowing difficulties due to the risk of oesophageal ulceration and oesophagitis.[105]   Consider switching to doxycycline dispersible tablets.

Feed guidance

Oxytetracycline absorption can be decreased by milk and dairy products as the drug chelates calcium, iron, magnesium, and zinc. It is recommended that the drug is taken two to three hours apart from milk and dairy products.[2,266] In one study oxytetracycline absorption was decreased by 64% when it was taken with milk.[572]

Oxytetracycline interacts with enteral feeds. Withhold feeds for two hours before and one hour after administration of each dose.[138,225,572,624]

Summary:-	Stop feed 2 hours before dose
	Restart feed 1 hour after dose

Withholding enteral feeds can compromise nutrition and interfere with blood glucose management. If the patient does not have a break in their feeding regimen during which oxytetracycline can be given, the Nutrition Team should be contacted to advise on management.

Pancreatin

Presentation

Tablets, capsules.
Granules, powder.

Administration – NG / PEG tubes

Pancreatic enzymes are often formulated with an enteric coating to protect the pH-sensitive enzymes from being degraded in the acidic environment of the stomach. When the medicine reaches the alkaline environment of the duodenum, the enteric coating breaks down and releases the enzymes.

(monograph continues on next page)

When giving pancreatic enzymes through an enteral feeding tube which terminates in the stomach, formulations which have an enteric coating are best left whole to protect the enzymes from degradation. However when mixed in water for administration, the enteric coating can be come "sticky" causing the granules to clump together, which may lead to tube blockage. To try to reduce this, enteric-coated granules should be administered in a slightly thickened fluid to help separate the granules whilst maintaining their protective coating.[665,666] This is probably only suitable for enteral tubes of size 10Fr and above.[666]

Recommended method – NG / PEG tubes size 10Fr and above

Creon® capsules – open the capsules and disperse the enteric-coated granules inside in slightly thickened water for administration through the enteral feeding tube.

Pancrex® V powder has been used, mixed with water and flushed down the enteral feeding tube.[380,381] See clinical guidance for information on measuring doses.

The frequency of dosing may have to be altered according to the feed type and duration. One recommendation is that if giving with an enteral feed, half the dose should be given before the feed, and half after.[105] Another option is to divide the total daily dose required into doses to be given every 2-3 hours during feeding.[666] Contact Dieticians for advice.

(monograph continues on next page)

Alternative method – tube sizes below 10Fr

Enteric-coated preparations are highly likely to block small-lumen enteral feeding tubes unless the enteric coating is broken down before administration.

1st choice – Switch to a formulation which is not enteric-coated, e.g. Pancrex® V powder, which can be mixed with water and flushed down the enteral feeding tube. See clinical guidance for information on measuring doses.

2nd choice – Neutralise the stomach acid with a proton-pump inhibitor (e.g. lansoprazole) and/or pre-treatment with sodium bicarbonate (these would have to be prescribed), then crush and dissolve the enteric-coated preparation in sodium bicarbonate before administration through the feeding tube.[665,666] One reference recommends 10ml of sodium bicarbonate 8.4% for each 10,000 units of lipase.[666] Contact Pharmacy or the prescriber for advice.

The frequency of dosing may have to be altered according to the feed type and duration. One recommendation is that if giving with an enteral feed, half the dose should be given before the feed, and half after.[105] Another option is to divide the total daily dose required into doses to be given every 2-3 hours during feeding.[666] Contact Dieticians for advice.

Pancreatin products unsuitable for use via NG / PEG tubes

Pancrease HL® capsules (no longer available in the UK) contain enteric-coated minitablets approximately 2mm x 3mm in size, and are therefore unlikely to be suitable for most enteral feeding tubes. Discuss with Pharmacy before administration.[363]

Nutrizym® may block enteral feeding tubes, so its use is not recommended.[138]

(monograph continues on next page)

Administration – NJ / PEJ / PEGJ tubes

When administering pancreatic enzymes through enteral feeding tubes terminating in the jejunum, the acidic environment of the stomach is bypassed, and the protective enteric coating is not required. As the coating can contribute to feeding tube blockage, it should be disrupted and dissolved before administration by crushing the medicine and then dissolving it in sodium bicarbonate. One reference recommends using 10ml of sodium bicarbonate 8.4% for each 10,000 units of lipase.[665,666]

Creon® capsules can be opened, and the enteric-coated granules inside crushed and dissolved in sodium bicarbonate (this must be prescribed) for administration.[105,138]

There is an anecdotal report of Creon® granules being dissolved in 30mL of sodium bicarbonate 8.4% in order to unblock an enteral feeding tube.[439] In order to minimise acid-base disturbance, for ongoing therapy it would seem advisable to use smaller volumes of sodium bicarbonate if these are sufficient to dissolve the Creon®.

Pancrex® V powder has been used, mixed with water and flushed down the enteral feeding tube.[380,381] See clinical guidance for information on measuring doses.

Pancrease HL® capsules (no longer available in the UK) contain enteric-coated minitablets approximately 2mm x 3mm in size. The manufacturers have reports of some hospitals dissolving the tablets in sodium bicarbonate in order to administer directly into the jejunum, but they do not have any outcome data on this.[363]

Nutrizym® may block enteral feeding tubes, so its use is not recommended.[138]

The frequency of dosing may have to be altered according to the feed type and duration. One recommendation is that if giving with an enteral feed, half the dose should be given before the feed, and half after.[105] Another option is to divide the total daily dose required into doses to be given every 2-3 hours during feeding.[666] Contact Dieticians for advice.

(monograph continues on next page)

Administration – swallowing difficulties

Creon® capsules can be opened and the contents mixed with soft food (the granules should not be chewed, therefore this may not be suitable for patients with limited understanding or impaired ability to follow instructions).[104]

Nutrizym® capsules contain enteric-coated minitablets. When swallowing the capsules is a problem, the capsules can be opened and the minitablets taken with water or with soft food, swallowed immediately.[309] They should not be chewed,[309] therefore this may not be suitable for patients with limited understanding or impaired ability to follow instructions.

Pancrease® HL capsules (no longer available in the UK) contain enteric-coated minitablets. When swallowing the capsules is a problem, the capsules can be opened and the minitablets taken with water or with soft food, swallowed immediately.[310] They should not be chewed,[310] therefore this may not be suitable for patients with limited understanding or impaired ability to follow instructions.

Pancrex® granules can be swallowed dry or mixed with water or milk for administration.[311]

Pancrex® V capsules and Pancrex® V 125 can be opened and the contents mixed with liquids or soft food.[312] Such mixtures should be consumed within one hour.[329]

Pancrex® V powder should be mixed with water or milk for administration.[314] See clinical guidance for information on measuring doses.

Pancrex® V tablets and Forte tablets must not be crushed. They should be swallowed whole.[313]

Clinical guidance

Pancrex® V powder 1g equivalent to a level 2.5mL spoonful[586]

Pantoprazole

Presentation
Enteric-coated tablets.
A suspension can be made by Pharmacy in some centres (see Appendix 1).[522]
Injection.

Administration – enteral tubes
1st choice – Use the parenteral injection (for short-term use).
2nd choice – Consider switching to lansoprazole or esomeprazole which are licensed for enteral tube administration.[156,267]

Alternatively, methods for preparing pantoprazole suspensions with expiries of up to 62 days have been described, although bioavailability may be up to 25% lower when the drug is given in this way.[155,203,221,522]

Administration – swallowing difficulties
Consider switching to a medication which is available in a suspension or dispersible form, e.g. esomeprazole tablets, lansoprazole suspension or Fastab®, or omeprazole MUPS®.

Para-aminosalicylic acid (PASA)

Presentation
Tablets (not licensed in the UK).
Granules (not licensed in the UK).

Administration – enteral tubes
There is a case report of para-aminosalicylic acid tablets being crushed and successfully administered via a jejunostomy tube. Peak drug concentrations were slightly higher and earlier than with oral dosing, and levels declined earlier.[197, 423]

Administration of the granules via enteral feeding tube has led to tube blockage, and is not recommended.[424]

(monograph continues on next page)

Administration – swallowing difficulties

Use the granules. They can be sprinkled on apple sauce, yogurt, or suspended in tomato juice, orange juice, cranberry juice or apple juice.[425]

Paracetamol

Presentation
Tablets.
Soluble tablets.
Suspension (some preparations contain sorbitol).
Oral suspension (special).[542,582]
Suppositories.
Infusion.

Administration – enteral tubes
1st choice – Use the suppositories or the infusion if possible.
2nd choice – Use the soluble tablets or the suspension.[104] Follow the directions in sections 3.5 and 3.6. The soluble tablets are preferable to the suspension which is hyperosmolar and may cause diarrhoea when administered via enteral tubes terminating in the jejunum. However the soluble tablets contain a lot of sodium which may be a problem in some patients.[104]

Paracetamol appears to have a similar absorption profile when administered directly into the jejunum as when given orally.[6,404,405,406]

Administration – swallowing difficulties
1st choice – Use the soluble tablets or the suspension.[104] The soluble tablets contain a lot of sodium which may be a problem in some patients.[104]
2nd choice – Use the suppositories or the infusion if possible.

Paroxetine

Presentation
Film-coated tablets.
Liquid.

Administration – enteral tubes
1st choice – Use the liquid, and dilute with an equal volume of water before administration as it is quite viscous.[104,155] Follow the directions in section 3.6.
2nd choice – The tablets can be crushed and mixed with water for administration. They must be crushed well and the tube flushed well as the tablets are film-coated.[105] Follow the directions in section 3.5.

Administration – swallowing difficulties
1st choice – Use the liquid.[104,155] Follow the directions in section 3.6.
2nd choice – The tablets can be crushed and mixed with water for administration. The crushed tablets are bitter and have a slight local anaesthetic effect.[105] Follow the directions in section 3.5.

Penicillamine

Presentation
Tablets.

Administration – enteral tubes / swallowing difficulties
The tablets can be crushed and mixed with water for administration.[133] Give immediately.[155] Follow the directions in section 3.5.

Feed guidance
Withhold enteral feeds for at least half an hour before and half an hour after each dose.[155,225,624]

Summary:-	Stop feed 30 minutes before dose
	Restart feed 30 minutes after dose

(monograph continues on next page)

Withholding enteral feeds can compromise nutrition and interfere with blood glucose management. If the patient does not have a break in their feeding regimen during which penicillamine can be given, the Nutrition Team should be contacted to advise on management.

Penicillin V

See entry under 'Phenoxymethylpenicillin'.

Pentazocine

Presentation
Tablets, capsules.
Suppositories.
Injection.

Administration – enteral tubes / swallowing difficulties
1st choice – Use the suppositories or give by parenteral injection if possible.
2nd choice – The injection has been given enterally, mixed with orange juice immediately before administration.[40] Follow the directions in section 3.6.

Pentoxifylline (Oxpentifylline)

Presentation
Modified-release tablets.
A suspension can be made by Pharmacy in some centres (see Appendix 1).[487]

Administration – enteral tubes / swallowing difficulties
This drug is formulated as a modified-release tablet to reduce the risk of it causing dyspepsia. Crushing the tablets causes a more rapid rise in drug concentration, and a higher peak drug concentration than taking the tablets whole.[602] This has been shown to lead to increased side effects such as nausea, dizziness, excess sweating and headache.[602]

(monograph continues on next page)

If it is clinically important for the patient to receive this medication, then the tablet may be crushed and dispersed in water for administration.[138] Consideration should be given to using a lower dose more frequently in order to reduce side effects.[602] Otherwise it is not advisable to crush the tablets. Contact Pharmacy for advice. Follow the directions in section 3.5.

No information on administering the suspension via enteral feeding tubes has been located.

Feed guidance
Pentoxifylline should be taken with food.[603]

Peppermint oil

Presentation
Enteric-coated capsules.

Clinical guidance
Peppermint water may be an alternative.[138]

Peppermint oil capsules should not be broken open as the contents are irritant.[136]

Perampanel

Presentation
Film-coated tablets.

Clinical guidance
No information on administering perampanel to patients with enteral feeding tubes or swallowing difficulties has been located.

(monograph continues on next page)

<u>Changing formulations / product manufacturer</u>
The MHRA has issued guidance recommending that (where possible) patients on perampanel (when used for seizures) are maintained on a specific manufacturer's product, due to variability in product characteristics which may lead to a loss of seizure control when switching between brands / manufacturers.[651] When managing patients with enteral tubes or swallowing difficulties it may not be possible to maintain the patient on their previous preparation due to the need to change to an appropriate formulation. However all product switches should be carried out with care and close monitoring, and where possible patients should be maintained from then onwards on a single manufacturer's product.

Pergolide

Presentation
Tablets.

Administration – enteral tubes
The tablets will disperse in water.[75] They disperse in one to five minutes.[154] Be sure to flush well to ensure the whole dose is given.[138] Follow the directions in section 3.5.

Administration – swallowing difficulties
The tablets can be crushed and administered in jam or yogurt.[105]

Pericyazine

Presentation
Tablets.
Syrup.

Administration – enteral tubes / swallowing difficulties
1st choice – Use the syrup.[41] Follow the directions in section 3.6.
2nd choice – The tablets will disperse in water for administration.[8,132] They disperse in less than a minute.[8] Follow the directions in section 3.5.

Perindopril arginine

Presentation
Film-coated tablets.

Clinical guidance
No information has been located on giving perindopril arginine to patients with enteral feeding tubes or swallowing difficulties. The manufacturers do not believe that crushing the tablets would be a problem, but can't recommend it.[352] Switch to perindopril erbumine.

2.5mg perindopril arginine equivalent to 2mg perindopril erbumine[273]

Perindopril arginine and indapamide (Coversyl® Arginine Plus)

Presentation
Tablets.

Clinical guidance
Coversyl® Arginine Plus tablets contain perindopril arginine 5mg and indapamide 1.25mg.[272] The manufacturers do not believe that crushing the tablets would be a problem, but can't recommend it.[352] Switch to perindopril erbumine 4mg and either indapamide or an appropriate alternative thiazide diuretic. See individual monographs for details.

Perindopril erbumine

Presentation
Tablets.
Oral solution (special).[542,582]
A suspension can be made by Pharmacy in some centres.

Administration – enteral tubes
Take care! – There are now two salts of perindopril available – perindopril arginine and perindopril erbumine. The information below relates to perindopril erbumine.

1st choice – The tablets can be crushed and mixed with water for administration.[45] Follow the directions in section 3.5.
2nd choice – A suspension can be made by Pharmacy in some centres (3 day expiry).[95] Follow the directions in section 3.6.
3rd choice – Use the oral solution (if available). Follow the directions in section 3.6.

Perindopril erbumine may not be effective when administered through enteral tubes terminating in the jejunum due to decreased absorption.[155]

Administration – swallowing difficulties
Take care! – There are now two salts of perindopril available – perindopril arginine and perindopril erbumine. The information below relates to perindopril erbumine.

1st choice – A suspension can be made by Pharmacy in some centres (3 day expiry).[95]
2nd choice – Use the oral solution (if available).
3rd choice – The tablets can be crushed and mixed with water for administration.[45] Follow the directions in section 3.5.

Feed guidance
Perindopril erbumine should be taken before food, so withhold enteral feeds for at least half an hour before and half an hour after each dose.[76,225,624]

(monograph continues on next page)

Summary:-	Stop feed 30 minutes before dose
	Restart feed 30 minutes after dose

Withholding enteral feeds can compromise nutrition and interfere with blood glucose management. If the patient does not have a break in their feeding regimen during which perindopril erbumine can be given, the Nutrition Team should be contacted to advise on management.

Perphenazine

Presentation
Sugar-coated tablets.
Sugar-free oral solution (special).

Clinical guidance
No information on the use of perphenazine via enteral feeding tubes has been obtained.

Pethidine

Presentation
Tablets.
Injection.

Administration – enteral tubes / swallowing difficulties
1st choice – Give by parenteral injection if possible, or switch to an alternative opoid available via a non-enteral route.
2nd choice – A liquid may be available in some centres.[140] Follow the directions in section 3.6.
3rd choice – The injection can be given enterally.[152] Follow the directions in section 3.6.

Phenelzine

Presentation
Film-coated tablets.

Administration – enteral tubes / swallowing difficulties
The tablets can be crushed and mixed with water for administration.[104,105] The drug is unstable in water, so give immediately.[41] Follow the directions in section 3.5.

Phenobarbital (Phenobarbitone)

Presentation
Tablets.
Elixir.
Oral solution (special).[542,582]
A suspension can be made by Pharmacy in some centres (see Appendix 1).[488,573]
Injection.

Administration – enteral tubes
1st choice – Give by parenteral injection, if appropriate.
2nd choice – Use the elixir. The elixir contains alcohol 38%.[106,461] Follow the directions in section 3.6.
3rd choice – The tablets may be crushed and mixed with water for administration.[152] Follow the directions in section 3.5.
4th choice – A suspension can be made by Pharmacy in some centres (alcohol-free).[488] Follow the directions in section 3.6.
5th choice – Use the special oral solution (if available). Follow the directions in section 3.6.

Administration – swallowing difficulties
1st choice – Use the elixir. The elixir contains alcohol 38%.[106,461]
2nd choice – Give by parenteral injection, if appropriate.
3rd choice – A suspension can be made by Pharmacy in some centres (alcohol-free).[488]
4th choice – Use the special oral solution (if available).
5th choice – The tablets may be crushed and mixed with water for administration.[152] Follow the directions in section 3.5.

(monograph continues on next page)

Clinical guidance

Changing formulations / product manufacturer

The MHRA has issued guidance recommending that patients on phenobarbital (when used for seizures) are maintained on a specific manufacturer's product, due to variability in product characteristics which may lead to a loss of seizure control when switching between brands / manufacturers.[651] When managing patients with enteral tubes or swallowing difficulties it may not be possible to maintain the patient on their previous preparation due to the need to change to an appropriate formulation. However all product switches should be carried out with care and close monitoring, and where possible patients should be maintained from then onwards on a single manufacturer's product.

Phenoxybenzamine

Presentation

Capsules.

A suspension can be made by Pharmacy in some centres (see Appendix 1).[489,573]

Injection.

Administration – enteral tubes

The powder in the capsules is poorly soluble and may block enteral feeding tubes.[109] Therefore administration via enteral feeding tubes is not recommended.

No information on administering the suspension via enteral feeding tubes has been located.

Administration – swallowing difficulties

1st choice – Use the suspension (if available).

2nd choice – The powder has been removed from the capsules for oral administration in patients with swallowing difficulties.[152]

Phenoxymethylpenicillin

Presentation
Tablets.
Suspension.

Administration – enteral tubes
1st choice – Use an intravenous antibiotic if possible.
2nd choice – Use the suspension. Follow the directions in section 3.6.

Administration – swallowing difficulties
1st choice – Use the suspension.
2nd choice – Use an intravenous antibiotic if possible.

Feed guidance
Phenoxymethylpenicillin interacts with enteral feeds leading to unpredictable absorption (30-80%). Consider using doses at the upper end of the normal range. Withhold the feed for two hours before and one hour after each dose.[87,90,225,624] This may not be practical due to the frequency of dosing. Contact Pharmacy for advice.

Summary:-	Stop feed 2 hours before dose
	Restart feed 1 hour after dose

Withholding enteral feeds can compromise nutrition and interfere with blood glucose management. If the patient does not have a break in their feeding regimen during which phenoxymethylpenicillin can be given, the Nutrition Team should be contacted to advise on management.

Phenytoin

Presentation
Tablets, capsules, chewable tablets.
Suspension.
Oral suspension (special).[542,582,658]
Injection.

WARNING!

Numerous papers are available describing the problems of administering phenytoin via enteral feeding tubes. The use of feeding breaks has been shown **NOT** to improve drug absorption.[250] It is recommended that phenytoin should **NEVER** be administered via enteral feeding tube. If parenteral therapy is not possible, alternative treatments should be considered.

Administration – NG / PEG tubes
1st choice – Give by parenteral injection if possible as enteral absorption is extremely unpredictable.[90]

See "Clinical guidance" below before considering the 2nd option.

2nd choice – Convert to phenytoin suspension, preferably as a single daily dose. The suspension should be shaken well before use to ensure dispersion. Mix the phenytoin suspension with the same volume of distilled water to a minimise adsorption to tubing[24,247] and to improve tolerance to the suspension.[37] Flush the enteral tube with 30-60mL of distilled water before and after administration.[2]

Administration – NJ / PEJ / PEGJ tubes
Administering phenytoin directly into the jejunum is not recommended as the drug will be less effective.[37]

(monograph continues on next page)

It has been suggested that insufficient residence time for dissolution of phenytoin suspension coupled with irreversible binding of phenytoin to the enteral feeding tube leads to poor drug absorption when it is administered into the duodenum and jejunum.[243] The suspension is also hyperosmolar and may cause diarrhoea if given directly into the jejunum.[26,104]

If jejunal administration cannot be avoided, particular care must be taken to observe patients closely, monitor plasma levels and adjust dose where appropiate.[11] **See "Clinical guidance" below before considering administering phenytoin through enteral tubes terminating in the jejunum.**

Administration – swallowing difficulties
1st choice – Use the suspension or the chewable tablets.
2nd choice – Give by parenteral injection.

Clinical guidance
Phenytoin administration via enteral feeding tubes is notoriously problematic. Numerous studies have shown that recovery and gastrointestinal absorption of administered doses is unpredictable, interaction with enteral feeds can affect bioavailability, and therapeutic levels achieved with treatment are frequently much lower than expected.[2]

Increasing the dose to achieve desired serum concentrations may expose the patient to prolonged periods of subtherapeutic levels whilst dose adjustment is being carried out, and has the potential for serious phenytoin toxicity if the feed is discontinued or the increased dose is converted to the intravenous route.

Phenytoin administration through enteral feeding tubes should only be carried out if there is no suitable alternative route, and no suitable alternative drug available for patient management, and then only with clear communication between all members of the team caring for the patient so that doses are adjusted appropriately if the patient's circumstances change.

(monograph continues on next page)

Phenytoin has a narrow therapeutic range and therefore the exact dose of phenytoin which the patient receives may be critical. Patient response and levels should be monitored carefully, especially after any changes in the feeding regimen, as the dosage may require adjustment. Phenytoin is highly affected by albumin levels, and doses may require adjustment in patients with low albumin. Contact Pharmacy for advice.

Therapeutic plasma levels are 10-20mg/litre[35] (in patients with a normal albumin level).

There is an increase in time to maximum serum concentration following increasing oral doses of phenytoin – i.e. maximum concentration is reached 8.4 hours after a 400mg oral dose, but takes 31.5 hours after a 1600mg oral dose.[392,393]

Changing formulations / product manufacturer
The MHRA has issued guidance recommending that patients on phenytoin (when used for seizures) are maintained on a specific manufacturer's product, due to variability in product characteristics which may lead to a loss of seizure control when switching between brands / manufacturers.[651] When managing patients with enteral tubes or swallowing difficulties it may not be possible to maintain the patient on their previous preparation due to the need to change to an appropriate formulation. However all product switches should be carried out with care and close monitoring, and where possible patients should be maintained from then onwards on a single manufacturer's product.

Dose equivalence.
When changing from solid dosage forms to the liquid preparation, a dose conversion must occur, as there is a different salt of phenytoin in the liquid than in the tablet / capsule.[35]

Phenytoin suspension 90mg (Phenytoin base)	equivalent to	Phenytoin tablets / capsules 100mg (Phenytoin sodium)[90]

(monograph continues on next page)

If the volumes of phenytoin suspension to be administered are not practical the capsule may be opened and administered according to the general guidelines.[37]

> **Caution – Phenytoin suspension is available in two strengths (30mg/5mL and 90mg/5mL) and this has led to errors. It is recommended to maintain patients on a single preparation (i.e. always on the same strength) and to use only the 30mg/5mL for patients with enteral feeding tubes.**

Feed guidance

Phenytoin exhibits a particularly strong interaction with enteral feeds (especially Osmolite®, Isocal®, Ensure®, and Jevity®[105,225]). It is necessary to stop enteral feeds for two hours before and two hours after giving phenytoin suspension to enhance absorption, otherwise reduced serum levels can occur with loss of seizure control.[2,4,6,11,26] Despite these measures, unexpectedly low phenytoin levels can be observed in patients receiving phenytoin through enteral feeding tubes, and therefore administration of phenytoin through enteral feeding tubes is only recommended when there is no other alternative.

One study of phenytoin administration to healthy subjects showed an absorption time of up to 60 hours when given with enteral feeds. As enteral feeding can be associated with a reduced gastro-intestinal transit time, incomplete absorption could be a factor.[250]

Withholding enteral feeds can compromise nutrition and interfere with blood glucose management. If the patient does not have a break in their feeding regimen during which phenytoin can be given, the Nutrition Team should be contacted to advise on management.

Phosphate

Presentation
Effervescent tablets.
Joulies phosphate solution.
Injection, infusion.

Clinical guidance
Contact Dieticians for advice. Give a high-phosphate enteral / parenteral feed if possible. Correct severe phosphate deficiency by infusion with close monitoring of phosphate, potassium, and calcium.

Phytomenadione

Presentation
Sugar-coated tablets (no longer available in the UK).
'MM' injection.
'MM Paediatric' injection.

Administration – enteral tubes / swallowing difficulties
Use the 'MM Paediatric' injection, which is licensed for oral use (although not for enteral tube administration). If giving via enteral feeding tube, flush well after each dose.[40,104,533]

Pimozide

Presentation
Tablets.

Administration – enteral tubes / swallowing difficulties
The tablets can be crushed and mixed with water for administration.[41] Follow the directions in section 3.5.

Pindolol

Presentation
Tablets.

Administration – enteral tubes / swallowing difficulties
The tablets will disperse in water for administration.[8] They disperse in less than a minute.[8] Follow the directions in section 3.5.

Pindolol and clopamide (Viskaldix®)

Presentation
Tablets.

Administration – enteral tubes / swallowing difficulties
Viskaldix® tablets contain pindolol 10mg and clopamide 5mg.[272] The tablets will disperse in water for administration.[8] They disperse in less than a minute.[8] Follow the directions in section 3.5.

Pioglitazone

Presentation
Tablets.
Oral suspension (special).[580]

Administration – enteral tubes
1st choice – Consider whether switching to insulin would be appropriate.
2nd choice – The tablets can be crushed and mixed with water for administration.[138] Give immediately.[138] Follow the directions in section 3.5.

No information on administering the oral suspension via enteral feeding tubes has been located.

(monograph continues on next page)

Administration – swallowing difficulties
1st choice – Consider whether switching to insulin would be appropriate.
2nd choice – Use the oral suspension (if available).
3rd choice – The tablets can be crushed and mixed with water for administration.[138]   Give immediately.[138]   Follow the directions in section 3.5.

Piracetam

Presentation
Film-coated tablets.
Solution.

Administration – enteral tubes / swallowing difficulties
Use the solution.[41] Follow the directions in section 3.6.

Piroxicam

Presentation
Capsules.
Dispersible tablets.
'Melt' tablets.
Suppositories.
Injection (no longer available in the UK).

Administration – enteral tubes
1st choice – Give by parenteral injection (if available) or use the suppositories.
2nd choice – Use the dispersible tablets and dissolve in at least 50mL of water as they are very irritant.[41,133,560]   Follow the directions in section 3.5.

Administration – swallowing difficulties
1st choice – Use the dispersible tablets and dissolve in at least 50mL of water as they are very irritant.[41,133,560]
2nd choice – Give by parenteral injection (if available) or use the suppositories.

(monograph continues on next page)

Clinical guidance
The CHMP has recommended that piroxicam be restricted to certain patient groups due to the increased risk of gastro-intestinal side effects and serious skin reactions.[605] Consider using an alternative drug available in a suitable formulation, e.g. ibuprofen, diclofenac.

Pizotifen

Presentation
Tablets.
Elixir.

Administration – enteral tubes / swallowing difficulties
1st choice – Use the elixir.[41,104] Follow the directions in section 3.6.
2nd choice – The tablets have been crushed and mixed with water for administration.[133] Follow the directions in section 3.5.

Polysaccharide-Iron Complex

Clinical guidance
See entry under 'Iron preparations'.

Potassium chloride

Presentation
Effervescent tablets.
Modified-release tablets.
Liquid (contains sorbitol).

Administration – enteral tubes
1st choice – Give potassium-containing intravenous fluids if possible (contact Pharmacy for advice), or contact the Nutrition team for advice about increasing dietary intake of potassium (e.g. in Total Parenteral Nutrition).
2nd choice – Use Sando K® effervescent tablets, or Kay-Cee-L® liquid. Kay-Cee-L® liquid is highly concentrated and contains sorbitol so dilute each dose with 60-90mL of water before administration.[9,155,249] Follow the directions in sections 3.5 and 3.6.
(monograph continues on next page)

Do not crush Slow K®, which are modified-release tablets.

Administration – swallowing difficulties
Use Sando K® effervescent tablets, or Kay-Cee-L® liquid (contains sorbitol). Follow the directions in sections 3.5 and 3.6.

Do not crush Slow K®, which are modified-release tablets.

Pramipexole

Presentation
Tablets.

Administration – enteral tubes / swallowing difficulties
The tablets can be crushed and mixed with water for administration.[104,105] Follow the directions in section 3.5.

Pravastatin

Presentation
Tablets.

Administration – enteral tubes / swallowing difficulties
The tablets can be crushed and mixed with water for administration.[77] The drug is very soluble.[253] Use immediately.[77] Follow the directions in section 3.5.

Prazosin

Presentation
Tablets.

Administration – enteral tubes / swallowing difficulties
The tablets can be dispersed in water for administration.[8,104,105,152] The 500mcg tablet disperses immediately.[8,154] The 1mg tablet disperses within one minute.[8,154] The drug is very insoluble, so if giving via enteral feeding tube, flush well after each dose.[105] Follow the directions in section 3.5.

Prednisolone

Presentation
Tablets.
Enteric-coated tablets.
Soluble tablets.
Rectal foam, retention enema.
Suppositories.

Administration – enteral tubes / swallowing difficulties
Use the soluble tablets where possible. The standard 1mg tablets can be crushed and mixed with water for administration when necessary.[8] Without crushing they disperse in two to five minutes.[8] Follow the instructions in section 3.5.

For proctitis, ulcerative colitis and Crohn's disease, consider using the rectal preparations if appropriate to the location of the condition.

The enteric-coated tablets should not be crushed due to the risk of enteral tube blockage (see section 3.3).

Pregabalin

Presentation
Capsules.
Oral solution.
Oral solution (special).[582]

Administration – enteral tubes
Open the capsules and dissolve the contents in water for administration.[125] Follow the directions in section 3.7.

No information on administering the oral solution via enteral feeding tubes has been located.

Administration – swallowing difficulties
1st choice – Use the oral solution.
2nd choice – Use the special oral solution (if available).
3rd choice – Open the capsules and dissolve the contents in water for administration. The capsule contents may have an unpleasant taste.[125] Follow the directions in section 3.7.

Pregaday®

Clinical guidance
Contains ferrous fumarate (100mg iron) and folic acid 350mcg. Use the separate components.[272] See the "Iron Preparations" and "Folic acid" monographs for details.

Prestim®

Presentation
Tablets.

Clinical guidance
Prestim® tablets contain timolol 10mg and bendroflumethiazide 2.5mg.[272] Use the separate components – see individual monographs for details.

Primaquine

Presentation
Tablets.

Administration – enteral tubes / swallowing difficulties
The tablets can be crushed and mixed with water for administration.[133] Follow the directions in section 3.5.

Primidone

Presentation
Tablets.
Liquid (special).[580,582]
A suspension can be made by Pharmacy in some centres.[573]

Administration – enteral tubes
1st choice – The tablets can be crushed and dispersed in water for administration.[8,132] Without crushing they will disperse in two to five minutes.[8] The drug is poorly soluble.[253] Follow the directions in section 3.5.
2nd choice – A suspension can be made by Pharmacy in some centres. Follow the directions in section 3.6.
3rd choice – Use the liquid.[41,104] Follow the directions in section 3.6.

Administration – swallowing difficulties
1st choice – A suspension can be made by Pharmacy in some centres.
2nd choice – Use the liquid.[41,104]
3rd choice – The tablets can be crushed and dispersed in water for administration.[8,132] Without crushing they will disperse in two to five minutes.[8] The drug is poorly soluble.[253] Follow the directions in section 3.5.

Clinical guidance
Changing formulations / product manufacturer
The MHRA has issued guidance recommending that patients on primidone (when used for seizures) are maintained on a specific manufacturer's product, due to variability in product characteristics which may lead to a loss of seizure control when switching between brands / manufacturers.[651] When managing patients with enteral tubes or swallowing difficulties it may not be possible to maintain the patient on their previous preparation due to the need to change to an appropriate formulation. However all product switches should be carried out with care and close monitoring, and where possible patients should be maintained from then onwards on a single manufacturer's product.

Probenecid

Presentation
Tablets.

Administration – enteral tubes / swallowing difficulties
The tablets can be crushed and mixed with water for administration.[133] Without crushing they will disperse in two to five minutes.[8] Follow the directions in section 3.5.

Procainamide

Presentation
Tablets, capsules (no longer available in the UK).
A suspension can be made by Pharmacy in some centres (see Appendix 1).[209,473]
Injection (no longer available in the UK).

Administration – enteral tubes
1st choice – The tablets (if available) can be crushed and mixed with water for administration.[87] Follow the directions in section 3.5.
2nd choice – A suspension can be made at some centres.[173,208,209,473] Follow the directions in section 3.6.

The injection has been diluted 1:1 with syrup and given enterally in some centres, however there is little information available on this, so it is not recommended.[40]

Administration – swallowing difficulties
1st choice – A suspension can be made at some centres.[173,208,209,473]
2nd choice – The tablets (if available) can be crushed and mixed with water for administration.[87] Follow the directions in section 3.5.

The injection has been diluted 1:1 with syrup and given enterally in some centres, however there is little information available on this, so it is not recommended.[40]

Procarbazine

Presentation
Capsules.
A suspension can be made by Pharmacy in some centres.

Administration – enteral tubes / swallowing difficulties
Caution – cytotoxic. Contact Pharmacy for advice before giving.

1st choice – A suspension can be made by Pharmacy in some centres.[138] Follow the directions in section 3.6.
2nd choice – Contact Pharmacy for further advice on how to give (Pharmacists – see Appendix 2).

Prochlorperazine

Presentation
Tablets.
Buccal tablets.
Syrup.
Suppositories (no longer available in the UK).
Injection.

Administration – NG / PEG tubes
1st choice – Give by parenteral injection, or use the buccal tablets or the suppositories (if available) if possible.
2nd choice – Use the syrup.[138] Follow the directions in section 3.6.

The tablets will disperse easily in water,[358] but no information on using dispersed tablets has been located.

Administration – NJ / PEJ / PEGJ tubes
1st choice – Give by parenteral injection, or use the buccal tablets or the suppositories (if available) if possible.
2nd choice – Use the syrup, diluted with an equal amount of water before administration to reduce the osmolality.[22,26,138] Follow the directions in section 3.6.

The tablets will disperse easily in water,[358] but no information on using dispersed tablets has been located.

(monograph continues on next page)

328

Administration – swallowing difficulties
1st choice – Use the buccal tablets.
2nd choice – Use the syrup.[138]
3rd choice – Give by parenteral injection, or use the suppositories (if available) if possible.

The tablets will disperse easily in water,[358] but no information on using dispersed tablets has been located.

Procyclidine

Presentation
Tablets.
Syrup, oral solution.
A suspension can be made by Pharmacy in some centres.
Injection.

Administration – enteral tubes
1st choice – Give by parenteral injection if possible.
2nd choice – Use the syrup or the oral solution. Follow the directions in section 3.6.
3rd choice – A suspension can be made by Pharmacy in some centres.[152] Follow the directions in section 3.6.

The injection has been used enterally at some centres, but there is very little information available on this, so it is not recommended.[40]

Administration – swallowing difficulties
1st choice – Use the syrup or the oral solution.
2nd choice – Give by parenteral injection if possible.
3rd choice – A suspension can be made by Pharmacy in some centres.[152]

The injection has been used enterally at some centres, but there is very little information available on this, so it is not recommended.[40]

Proguanil

Presentation
Tablets.

Administration – enteral tubes
The tablets can be crushed and mixed with water for administration.[104,105,132,152] Follow the directions in section 3.5.

Administration – swallowing difficulties
The tablets can be crushed and mixed with water, milk, or jam.[104,105,132,152] Follow the directions in section 3.5.

Promazine

Presentation
Coated tablets.
Solution.
Injection.

Administration – enteral tubes / swallowing difficulties
Use the solution.[104] Follow the directions in section 3.6.

Promethazine hydrochloride

Presentation
Film-coated tablets.
Elixir.
Injection.

Administration – enteral tubes / swallowing difficulties
Use the elixir.[94,104] Follow the directions in section 3.6.

Propafenone

Presentation
Film-coated tablets.

Administration – enteral tubes / swallowing difficulties
The tablets can be crushed and mixed in 5% glucose for administration.[104,152] The crushed tablets may have a local anaesthetic effect. If given orally, the mouth should be rinsed afterwards to reduce this.[152]

Propantheline

Presentation
Sugar-coated tablets.
A suspension can be made by Pharmacy in some centres.

Administration – enteral tubes
1st choice – The tablets can be crushed and mixed with water for administration.[105] Follow the directions in section 3.5.
2nd choice – A suspension can be made by Pharmacy in some centres.[95,138] Follow the directions in section 3.6.

Administration – swallowing difficulties
1st choice – A suspension can be made by Pharmacy in some centres.[95,138]
2nd choice – The tablets can be crushed and mixed with water for administration.[105] The crushed tablets may have a bitter taste.[132] Follow the directions in section 3.5.

Clinical guidance
Propantheline can decrease gastric emptying.[2]

Feed guidance
Withhold feed for two hours before and one hour after administration.[624]

Summary:-	Stop feed 2 hours before dose
	Restart feed 1 hour after dose

(monograph continues on next page)

Withholding enteral feeds can compromise nutrition and interfere with blood glucose management. If the patient does not have a break in their feeding regimen during which propantheline can be given, the Nutrition Team should be contacted to advise on management.

Propiverine

Presentation
Sugar-coated tablets.
Modified-release capsules.

Administration – enteral tubes / swallowing difficulties
The manufacturers are aware of instances of propiverine being crushed and given via enteral feeding tubes. They do not foresee any problems with doing this, although it is outside the product licence.[374] Follow the directions in section 3.5.

Do not open the modified-release capsules.

Propranolol

Presentation
Tablets.
Modified-release capsules.
Oral solution.
Oral solution (special).[582]
Injection.

Administration – enteral tubes / swallowing difficulties
1st choice – Use the licensed oral solution. Follow the directions in section 3.6.

The oral solution can be diluted with water to reduce the osmolality if desired when giving into the jejunum, however this is outside the product licence.[360]

(monograph continues on next page)

The injection has been given enterally at some centres, mixed in raspberry syrup if given orally.[40] However there is little information available on this, so it is not recommended.[175]

Do not crush / open modified-release preparations. Seek advice from Pharmacy when converting from modified-release preparations.

Clinical guidance
Propranolol is better absorbed from the large than the small intestine,[400] so administration through enteral feeding tubes terminating in the jejunum is not anticipated to cause any absorption problems.

Feed guidance
Absorption of enteral propranolol can be increased by concomitant food or milk.[2] It is therefore advisable to ensure that doses of propranolol are given at the same time of day each day in relation to feeds.[2]

Propylthiouracil

Presentation
Tablets.
A suspension can be made by Pharmacy in some centres (see Appendix 1).[490]

Administration – enteral tubes
The tablets will disperse in water for administration.[8,104,105] They disperse in less than a minute.[8] Follow the directions in section 3.5.

No information on administering the suspension via enteral feeding tubes has been located.

Administration – swallowing difficulties
1st choice – Use the suspension (if available).
2nd choice – The tablets will disperse in water for administration.[8,104,105] They disperse in less than a minute.[8] Follow the directions in section 3.5.

Pseudoephedrine

Presentation
Tablets.
Elixir.

Administration – enteral tubes / swallowing difficulties
Use the elixir.[104] Follow the directions in section 3.6.

Pseudoephedrine tastes unpleasant.[558]

Feed guidance
Pseudoephedrine is incompatible with enteral feeds. Withhold feeds
for one hour before and two hours after each dose.[41]

Summary:-	Stop feed 1 hour before dose
	Restart feed 2 hours after dose

Withholding enteral feeds can compromise nutrition and interfere
with blood glucose management. If the patient does not have a
break in their feeding regimen during which pseudoephedrine can be
given, the Nutrition Team should be contacted to advise on
management.

Pyrazinamide

Presentation
Tablets.
A suspension can be made by Pharmacy in some centres (see
Appendix 1).[454,491,494,573]

Administration – enteral tubes
1st choice – The tablets can be dispersed in water immediately
before administration.[8,95] They disperse in one to five minutes.[8,154]
Follow the directions in section 3.5.
2nd choice – A suspension can be made by Pharmacy in some
centres.[454,491,494] Dilute with the same volume of distilled water
before administration. Follow the directions in section 3.6.

(monograph continues on next page)

Administration – swallowing difficulties
1st choice – A suspension can be made by Pharmacy in some centres.[454,491,494]
2nd choice – The tablets can be dispersed in water immediately before administration.[8,95] They disperse in one to five minutes.[8,154] Follow the directions in section 3.5.

Feed guidance
Withhold enteral feeds for half an hour before and half an hour after each dose.[95,133,225,625]

Summary:-	Stop feed 30 minutes before dose
	Restart feed 30 minutes after dose

Withholding enteral feeds can compromise nutrition and interfere with blood glucose management. If the patient does not have a break in their feeding regimen during which pyrazinamide can be given, the Nutrition Team should be contacted to advise on management.

Pyridostigmine

Presentation
Tablets.

Administration – enteral tubes
1st choice – The tablets can be crushed and mixed with water for administration.[7,40,95] Flush well after administering. Follow the directions in section 3.5.
2nd choice – A liquid can be made by Pharmacy in some centres.[95] Follow the directions in section 3.6.

Administration – swallowing difficulties
1st choice – A liquid can be made by Pharmacy in some centres.[95]
2nd choice – The tablets can be crushed and mixed with water for administration.[7,40,95] Follow the directions in section 3.5.

Pyridoxine

Presentation
Tablets.

Administration – enteral tubes
1st choice – The tablets can be crushed and mixed with water for administration.[8,104,105] The 50mg tablets disperse in one to five minutes.[8,154] Follow the directions in section 3.5.
2nd choice – A liquid can be made by Pharmacy in some centres.[95,573] Follow the directions in section 3.6.

Administration – swallowing difficulties
1st choice – A liquid can be made by Pharmacy in some centres.[95,573]
2nd choice – The tablets can be crushed and mixed with water for administration.[8,104,105] The 50mg tablets disperse in one to five minutes.[8,154] Follow the directions in section 3.5.

Pyrimethamine

Presentation
Tablets.
A suspension can be made by Pharmacy in some centres (see Appendix 1).[492]

Administration – enteral tubes
The tablets can be crushed and mixed with water or juice for administration.[40,152] Follow the directions in section 3.5.

No information on administering the suspension via enteral feeding tubes has been located.

Administration – swallowing difficulties
1st choice – Use the suspension (if available).
2nd choice – The tablets can be crushed and mixed with water or juice for administration.[40,152] Follow the directions in section 3.5.

Quetiapine

Presentation
Tablets.
Oral solution (special), oral suspension (special).[582,585]

Administration – enteral tubes
Quetiapine tablets are not soluble.[46] The tablets can be crushed and mixed with water for administration. Flush well after administration.[105,134] Follow the directions in section 3.5.

No information on administering the oral solution or suspension via enteral feeding tubes has been located.

Administration – swallowing difficulties
1st choice – Use the oral solution or suspension (if available).
2nd choice – The crushed tablets have been added to soft food (e.g. yogurt).[105,134] They taste bitter.[134]

Quinapril

Presentation
Tablets, film-coated tablets.

Clinical guidance
No information has been located about administering quinapril to patients with enteral feeding tubes or swallowing difficulties. Consider switching to an alternative angiotensin converting enzyme inhibitor with which there is more experience, e.g. lisinopril.

Quinapril and hydrochlorothiazide (Accuretic®)

Presentation
Film-coated tablets.

Clinical guidance
Accuretic® tablets contain quinapril 10mg and hydrochlorothiazide 12.5mg.[272] No information has been located on the use of Accuretic® tablets in patients with enteral feeding tubes or swallowing difficulties. Switch to an alternative ACE inhibitor, e.g. lisinopril, and an alternative thiazide diuretic, e.g. bendroflumethiazide.

Quinidine

Presentation
Tablets (no longer available in the UK).
Modified-release tablets (no longer available in the UK).

Administration – enteral tubes / swallowing difficulties
The standard tablets can be crushed and mixed with water for administration.[8,87] Without crushing they disperse in two to five minutes.[8] Follow the directions in section 3.5.

Do not crush the modified-release tablets. Contact Pharmacy for advice on altering the dosage.

Quinine sulphate

Presentation
Tablets.
Oral suspension (special).[580,582]
A suspension can be made by Pharmacy in some centres.[573]

Administration – enteral tubes
Crush the tablets well, and disperse in a large volume (e.g. 200mL) of water. Flush well to minimise blockage and irritancy, as the coating is likely to block narrow-bore enteral feeding tubes.[78] Only use if absolutely necessary and swallowing problems are likely to be long-term. Follow the directions in section 3.5.
(monograph continues on next page)

No information on giving the suspension via enteral feeding tubes has been located.

Administration – swallowing difficulties

1st choice – A suspension can be made by Pharmacy in some centres.

2nd choice – Use the special suspension (if available).

3rd choice – Crush the tablets well, and disperse in a large volume (e.g. 200mL) of water.[78] The crushed tablets have a bitter taste which may be masked by mixing with syrup.[105] Only use if absolutely necessary and swallowing problems are likely to be long-term. Follow the directions in section 3.5.

Rabeprazole

Presentation
Enteric-coated tablets.

Clinical guidance
Crushing is not recommended as stomach acid can destroy the active drug.[105] Consider switching to lansoprazole Fastabs® or esomeprazole which are licensed for enteral tube administration.[156,267]

Raloxifene

Presentation
Tablets

Clinical guidance
The tablets should be discontinued if the patient is immobile, and are therefore probably unsuitable for use in most enteral tube fed patients.[75] Contact Pharmacy for advice on alternatives.

Ramipril

Presentation
Tablets, capsules.
Oral solution.[579]
Oral solution (special).[582]

Administration – enteral tubes
The capsules can be opened, and the contents dispersed in water for enteral tube administration.[62,445] The drug is poorly soluble.[253] Follow the directions in section 3.7.

The tablets can be crushed and dispersed in water for administration.[107] The drug is poorly soluble.[253] Follow the directions in section 3.5.

No information on administering the oral solution via enteral feeding tubes has been located.

Administration – swallowing difficulties
1st choice – Use the licensed oral solution (if available).
2nd choice – Use the special oral solution (if available).
3rd choice – The capsule contents can be placed directly into the mouth, or onto bread if the patient has swallowing difficulties.[62] Stability studies have shown that ramipril can be mixed with apple juice or apple sauce,[445] and this may be helpful for patients with swallowing difficulties.

The capsule contents taste unpleasant.[62]

Clinical guidance
Monitor blood pressure.[558]

Ramipril and felodipine (Triapin®)

Presentation
Film-coated tablets.

Clinical guidance
Triapin® tablets contain ramipril and felodipine in various dosages.[272] They are not suitable for administration via enteral feeding tubes because the ingredients are light sensitive, and the formulation is modified-release.[79] Use the separate components – see individual monographs for details.

Ranitidine

Presentation
Tablets.
Effervescent tablets (some brands contain a significant quantity of sodium).
Syrup, oral solution (some preparations contain alcohol and / or sorbitol).
Injection.

Administration – enteral tubes
1st choice – Give by parenteral injection, if appropriate. A dose alteration is required.
2nd choice – Use the effervescent tablets, dissolved in at least 75mL of water. Follow the directions in section 3.5.
3rd choice – Use the syrup or the oral solution. Follow the directions in section 3.6.
4th choice – The injection can be administered through enteral feeding tubes to achieve therapeutic levels.[6,31] Follow the directions in section 3.6.

Administration – swallowing difficulties
1st choice – Use the effervescent tablets, dissolved in at least 75mL of water.
2nd choice – Use the syrup or the oral solution.
3rd choice – Give by parenteral injection, if appropriate. A dose alteration is required.

(monograph continues on next page)

Clinical guidance
A negligible amount of drug is absorbed from the stomach.[28] Most absorption occurs in the small bowel, with rates being highest in the duodenum.[28,29] Thus, ranitidine will be suitable for administration through enteral tubes terminating in the jejunum.[6] Absorption is not affected by the presence of food.[30]

The syrup is an alternative to the effervescent tablets. It is however more viscous and may block the enteral feeding tube. It also contains alcohol and sorbitol.

Reboxetine

Presentation
Tablets.

Administration – enteral tubes / swallowing difficulties
The tablets can be crushed and mixed with water for administration.[104,105] Follow the directions in section 3.5.

Repaglinide

Presentation
Tablets.

Administration – enteral tubes / swallowing difficulties
1st choice – Consider whether switching to insulin would be appropriate.
2nd choice – The tablets can be crushed and mixed with water for administration.[105] Follow the directions in section 3.5.

Monitor the patient's blood glucose. Repaglinide is absorbed faster in the duodenum than the stomach.[105]

Retigabine

Presentation
Film-coated tablets.

Clinical guidance
No information on administering retigabine to patients with enteral feeding tubes or swallowing difficulties has been located.

Changing formulations / product manufacturer
The MHRA has issued guidance recommending that (where possible) patients on retigabine (when used for seizures) are maintained on a specific manufacturer's product, due to variability in product characteristics which may lead to a loss of seizure control when switching between brands / manufacturers.[651] When managing patients with enteral tubes or swallowing difficulties it may not be possible to maintain the patient on their previous preparation due to the need to change to an appropriate formulation. However all product switches should be carried out with care and close monitoring, and where possible patients should be maintained from then onwards on a single manufacturer's product.

Rifabutin

Presentation
Capsules.
A suspension can be made by Pharmacy in some centres (see Appendix 1).[493]

Administration – enteral tubes
No information on administering rifabutin via enteral feeding tubes has been located.

Administration – swallowing difficulties
Use the suspension (if available).

Rifampicin

Presentation
Capsules.
Syrup.
A suspension can be made by Pharmacy in some centres (see Appendix 1).[454]
Infusion.

Administration – enteral tubes
1st choice – Give by parenteral infusion if appropriate.
2nd choice – Use the syrup, and dilute with an equal volume of water before administration.[132] Follow the directions in section 3.6.
3rd choice – A suspension can be made by Pharmacy in some centres. Follow the directions in section 3.6.

Administration – swallowing difficulties
1st choice – Use the syrup.
2nd choice – Give by parenteral infusion if appropriate.
3rd choice – A suspension can be made by Pharmacy in some centres.

Clinical guidance
Rifampicin is absorbed from the stomach and duodenum.[408,409,410] There is therefore a risk of poor absorption if the drug is given through an enteral feeding tube terminating in the jejunum.

Feed guidance
Absorption of enteral rifampicin can be decreased by concomitant food or milk.[2,410] It should therefore be given on an empty stomach. Enteral feeds should be withheld for two hours before and one hour after administration.[35,117,225,315]

Summary:-	Stop feed 2 hours before dose
	Restart feed 1 hour after dose

Withholding enteral feeds can compromise nutrition and interfere with blood glucose management. If the patient does not have a break in their feeding regimen during which rifampicin can be given, the Nutrition Team should be contacted to advise on management.

(monograph continues on next page)

Combination Products

Use the separate components if possible. If the components are not available, Rifater® and Rimactazid® brands (NB Rimactazid® no longer available in the UK) have been crushed and mixed with water for administration.[105,133] See Rifater® (rifampicin with isoniazid and pyrazinamide) monograph for further information.

Rifampicin and isoniazid (Rifinah®)

Presentation
Sugar-coated tablets.

Clinical guidance
Rifinah® tablets contain rifampicin and isoniazid at various dosages.[272] No information on whether they can be crushed has been located. Use the separate components – see individual monographs for details.

Rifampicin with isoniazid and pyrazinamide (Rifater®)

Presentation
Sugar-coated tablets.

Clinical guidance
Rifater® tablets contain rifampicin 120mg, isoniazid 50mg, and pyrazinamide 300mg.[272] Use the separate components if possible – see individual monographs for details. If the components are not available, Rifater® tablets have been crushed and mixed with water for administration.[105,133]

Feed guidance
Rifater® should be given on an empty stomach. Withhold enteral feeds for half an hour before and half an hour after each dose.[225,429]

Summary:-	Stop feed 30 minutes before dose
	Restart feed 30 minutes after dose

(monograph continues on next page)

Withholding enteral feeds can compromise nutrition and interfere with blood glucose management. If the patient does not have a break in their feeding regimen during which Rifater® can be given, the Nutrition Team should be contacted to advise on management.

Rifater®

See entry under "Rifampicin with isoniazid and pyrazinamide".

Rifaximin

Presentation
Film-coated tablets.
A suspension can be made by Pharmacy in some centres (see Appendix 1).[530]

Administration – enteral tubes
No information on administering rifaximin via enteral feeding tubes has been located.

Administration – swallowing difficulties
Use the suspension (if available).

Rifinah®

Presentation
Sugar-coated tablets.

Clinical guidance
Rifinah® tablets contain rifampicin and isoniazid at various dosages.[272] No information on whether they can be crushed has been located. Use the separate components – see individual monographs for details.

Riluzole

Presentation
Film-coated tablets.

Administration – enteral tubes
The tablets can be crushed and dispersed in water for enteral tube administration.[79,181] Give immediately. Follow the directions in section 3.5. There have been reports of crushed riluzole tablets blocking enteral feeding tubes, so ensure that the tube is flushed well after each dose.[373]

Administration – swallowing difficulties
The tablets can be crushed and mixed with soft food e.g. yogurt or puree, to aid swallowing.[79,181] Tablets crushed onto food should be eaten within fifteen minutes as there is no stability data available for this method of administration.[79,181] Use crushed tablets with care as they may have a local anaesthetic effect in the mouth.[79,181]

Absorption may be affected by fatty food.[150]

Risedronate

Presentation
Tablets.

Clinical guidance
Risedronate is generally not considered suitable for crushing due to gastrointestinal side effects.[80] Administration also requires the patient to be able to sit or stand upright for a period of at least 30 minutes following dosing.

There is a form of zoledronic acid licensed for once-yearly intravenous administration.[544] This is probably the most appropriate form of bisphosphonate for most patients with swallowing problems – contact Pharmacy for advice.

(monograph continues on next page)

A very small study (four patients) of patients receiving risedronate via percutaneous feeding tube found administration to be generally well tolerated.[246] If swallowing problems are likely to be long-term, and bisphosphonate therapy is considered essential, administration of risedronate might be possible, but should only be carried out in the clear understanding of the risks involved. In such cases, the once-weekly preparation should be used, to reduce the risk of adverse effects.

Review whether the medication is still needed. Consider switching to yearly zoledronic acid. Contact Pharmacy for advice. If risedronate is given, enteral feeds should be withheld for two hours before and two hours after each dose.[225,272,624]

Risperidone

Presentation
Film-coated tablets.
Orodispersible tablets.
Liquid.
Depot injection.

Administration – enteral tubes / swallowing difficulties
Use the liquid or the orodispersible tablet.[104,132] Follow the directions in sections 3.5 and 3.6.

Ritonavir

Presentation
Film-coated tablets.
Capsules (no longer available in the UK).
Solution.

Administration – enteral tubes
1st choice – Use the solution.[40] Follow the directions in section 3.6.
2nd choice – The capsules (if available) can be opened and the contents mixed with water for administration.[40,132] Follow the directions in section 3.7.

The tablets should not be chewed, broken, or crushed.[578] See clinical guidance below.

Administration – swallowing difficulties
1st choice – Use the solution.[40] Follow the directions in section 3.6.
2nd choice – The capsules (if available) can be opened and the contents mixed with water for administration. This has an extremely unpleasant taste, which may be masked by chocolate milk.[40,132] Follow the directions in section 3.7.

The tablets should not be chewed, broken, or crushed.[578] See clinical guidance below.

Clinical guidance
The tablets should not be chewed, broken, or crushed.[578] Two human studies and one animal study of a combination (lopinavir/ritonavir) tablet showed a substantial (39-61%) reduction in ritonavir exposure when the tablets were crushed. The reduction was highly variable between individuals, and is therefore unpredictable. It is likely that this may also be the case if the single-component tablet is crushed, although it is not possible to say by how much the absorption will be reduced.[581,652,653,655]

Rivaroxaban

Presentation
Film-coated tablets

Administration – NG / PEG tubes
The tablets can be crushed and mixed with water for administration.[598,599] Follow the directions in section 3.5. A small study of healthy volunteers suggests that rivaroxaban is absorbed when administered via nasogastric tube, but that the C_{max} (peak concentration) and possibly the AUC may be slightly reduced when the drug is given in this manner.[598,599]

Administration – NJ / PEJ / PEGJ tubes
Rivaroxaban is not suitable for administration via enteral feeding tubes terminating beyond the stomach (i.e. in the duodenum or jejunum) due to decreased absorption of the drug when given in this manner.[598]

Administration – swallowing difficulties
The tablets can be crushed and mixed with apple sauce for administration to patients with swallowing difficulties.[598,599]

Rivastigmine

Presentation
Capsules.
Solution.
Patches.

Administration – enteral tubes / swallowing difficulties
1st choice – For patients with long-term swallowing problems, consider switching to the patches.
2nd choice – Use the solution (if available). Follow the directions in section 3.6.
3rd choice – The capsules can be opened, and the contents dispersed in water for administration.[104,138] Follow the directions in section 3.7.

Ropinirole

Presentation
Film-coated tablets.
Oral solution (special).[542]

Administration – enteral tubes
The tablets can be crushed and mixed with water for administration via enteral feeding tubes.[81] Follow the directions in section 3.5. There is no information available to indicate whether ropinirole tablets are likely to block enteral feeding tubes.[81]

No information on administering the oral solution via enteral feeding tubes has been located.

Administration – swallowing difficulties
1st choice – Use the oral solution (if available).
2nd choice – The tablets can be crushed and mixed with soft food for patients with swallowing difficulties.[105]

Rosiglitazone

Presentation
Tablets (no longer licensed in the UK).

Administration – enteral tubes / swallowing difficulties
1st choice – Consider whether switching to insulin would be appropriate.
2nd choice – The tablets can be crushed and dispersed in water for administration.[67] Follow the directions in section 3.5. No information has been located on whether rosiglitazone is likely to block enteral feeding tubes.[67]

Rosuvastatin

Presentation
Film-coated tablets.

Administration – enteral tubes / swallowing difficulties
The tablets can be crushed and mixed with water for administration.[150] Follow the directions in section 3.5.

Rufinamide

Presentation
Film-coated tablets.
Suspension.

Administration – enteral tubes
No information on administering rufinamide to patients with enteral feeding tubes has been located.

Administration – swallowing difficulties
Use the suspension.

Clinical guidance
Changing formulations / product manufacturer
The MHRA has issued guidance recommending that (where possible) patients on rufinamide (when used for seizures) are maintained on a specific manufacturer's product, due to variability in product characteristics which may lead to a loss of seizure control when switching between brands / manufacturers.[651] When managing patients with enteral tubes or swallowing difficulties it may not be possible to maintain the patient on their previous preparation due to the need to change to an appropriate formulation. However all product switches should be carried out with care and close monitoring, and where possible patients should be maintained from then onwards on a single manufacturer's product.

Salbutamol

Presentation
Various preparations for inhalation.
Oral solution.
Tablets.
Modified-release tablets.
Injection.

Administration – enteral tubes / swallowing difficulties
1st choice – Use the oral solution. Follow the directions in section 3.6.
2nd choice – The standard tablets have been crushed and mixed with water for administration.[8,138,152] Without crushing they disperse in two to five minutes.[8] Follow the directions in section 3.5.

Do not crush the modified-release tablets.

Clinical guidance
If changing from modified-release tablets to the oral solution, a change in dose and frequency will be required. The oral solution should be given in three to four divided doses. Do not crush the modified-release tablets. Consider managing the patient with inhaled therapy (e.g. nebules).

Saquinavir

Presentation
Gel-filled capsules.
Capsules.

Administration – enteral tubes / swallowing difficulties
1st choice – Consider using a protease inhibitor which is available as a liquid, e.g. amprenavir, Kaletra®. Contact disease specialist for advice.
2nd choice – The capsules can be opened, and the gel contents dispersed in water for administration. The drug has a very bitter taste.[40] Follow the directions in section 3.7.

Feed guidance
Saquinavir should be taken with food.[176,316]

Secobarbital

Presentation
Capsules (no longer available in the UK).
Powder (no longer available in the UK).

Administration – enteral tubes
No information about the use of this medication via enteral feeding tubes has been located.

Administration – swallowing difficulties
The powder can be administered in neat blackcurrant juice to disguise the very bitter taste.[152]

Selegiline

Presentation
Tablets.
Liquid.
Lyophilisates.

Administration – enteral tubes / swallowing difficulties
1st choice – Use the liquid,[41,104,105] or the lyophilisate if the patient has a moist mouth and is able to safely use the tablet buccally (note – a dose change is necessary when converting to the lyophilisate – see below).[132] Follow the directions in section 3.6.
2nd choice – The tablets can be dispersed in water for administration.[7,353] They disperse within one minute.[154] Follow the directions in section 3.5.

10mg selegiline tablet equivalent to 1.25mg selegiline lyophilisate[272]

Senna

Presentation
Tablets.
Syrup.

Administration – enteral tubes / swallowing difficulties
Use the syrup and flush post-dose with 15-30mL of distilled water.
Follow the directions in section 3.6.

Sertraline

Presentation
Tablets.
Oral suspension (special).[542,582]

Administration – enteral tubes
The tablets can be dispersed in water for administration. They disperse in one to five minutes.[154] Follow the directions in section 3.5.

No information on administered the oral suspension via enteral feeding tubes has been located.

Administration – swallowing difficulties
1st choice – Use the oral suspension (if available).
2nd choice – The tablets can be crushed and mixed with food for patients with swallowing difficulties.[37,152] Crushed tablets have a bitter taste, and an anaesthetic effect on the tongue, so use with caution and take care with hot foods after administration.[37]

Clinical guidance
Consider changing to an alternative drug available as a licensed syrup (e.g. fluoxetine, paroxetine) if swallowing problem is likely to be long-term. Contact Pharmacy for advice.

Sevikar®

Presentation
Film-coated tablets.

Clinical guidance
Sevikar® tablets contain olmesartan and amlodipine at various dosages.[577] Due to lack of information consider switching to an alternative angiotensin-II receptor inhibitor, e.g. losartan, and amlodipine. See individual monographs for details.

Sildenafil

Presentation
Film-coated tablets.
Chewable tablets.
Oral solution (special).[582]
A suspension can be made by Pharmacy in some centres (see Appendix 1).[271]

Administration – enteral tubes
The tablets can be crushed and dispersed in water for administration.[155] Follow the directions in section 3.5.

No information on administering the chewable tablets, the suspension or the oral solution via enteral feeding tubes has been located.

Administration – swallowing difficulties
1st choice – Use the chewable tablets.
2nd choice – A suspension can be made by Pharmacy in some centres.
3rd choice – Use the special oral solution (if available).
4th choice – The tablets can be crushed and dispersed in water for administration.[155] Follow the directions in section 3.5.

Clinical guidance
Sildenafil is mostly absorbed in the jejunum and ileum, with some absorption in the duodenum and colon.[411] Administration through enteral tubes terminating in the jejunum is not anticipated to cause any absorption problems.

Simeticone

Presentation
Various combination preparations.

Administration – enteral tubes / swallowing difficulties
The drops can be administered via enteral feeding tubes.[87]

Simvastatin

Presentation
Tablets.
Suspension.

Administration – enteral tubes
The tablets can be crushed and mixed with water for administration.[63] Crush well as the drug is practically insoluble.[253] Use immediately (light sensitive).[63,95] Follow the directions in section 3.5.

No information on administering the suspension via enteral feeding tubes has been located.

Administration – swallowing difficulties
1st choice – Use the suspension.
2nd choice – The tablets can be crushed and mixed with water for administration.[63] Crush well as the drug is practically insoluble.[253] Use immediately (light sensitive).[63,95] Follow the directions in section 3.5.

Sitagliptin

Presentation
Film-coated tablets.

Clinical guidance
No information on administering sitagliptin via enteral feeding tubes or to patients with swallowing difficulties has been located. The tablets will dissolve rapidly in water.[612] They are film-coated, and may taste unpleasant if the coating is removed.

Sodium bicarbonate

Presentation
Tablets, capsules.
Oral solution (special).[582]
Intravenous injection, infusion.

Administration – enteral tubes
1st choice – The capsules can be opened and the contents mixed with water for administration.[144] Follow the directions in section 3.7.
2nd choice – Use the oral solution (if available). Follow the directions in section 3.6.
3rd choice – The injection can be given enterally.[152,573] Follow the directions in section 3.6.

Administration – swallowing difficulties
1st choice – Use the oral solution (if available).
2nd choice – The capsules can be opened and the contents mixed with water for administration.[144] Follow the directions in section 3.7.
3rd choice – The injection can be given enterally.[152,573] Follow the directions in section 3.6.

Sodium chloride

Presentation
Capsules (special).
Modified-release tablets.
Oral solution (special).[582]
A solution can be made by Pharmacy in some centres.[573]
Injection.

Administration – enteral tubes / swallowing difficulties
1st choice – A solution can be made by Pharmacy in some centres. Follow the directions in section 3.6.
2nd choice – Use the special oral solution (if available). Follow the directions in section 3.6.
3rd choice – The injection can be given enterally.[152] Follow the directions in section 3.6.

Sodium clodronate

Presentation
Capsules.
Film-coated tablets.
Infusion.

Administration – enteral tubes / swallowing difficulties
The capsules can be opened and the contents dispersed in water for administration.[95,104,354,359] This may reduce the bioavailability of the drug.[354] Follow the directions in section 3.7. Only mix with water; do not mix with calcium-containing preparations e.g. milk, or other medicines.[95]

Clinical guidance
There is no need to adjust the dose when switching between Bonefos® tablet and capsule formulations.[330]

The tablet formulation of Loron® has a greater bioavailability than the capsule (discontinued).[331] Two Loron® 400mg capsules are approximately equivalent to one Loron® 520 tablet.[331]

Feed guidance
Withhold enteral feeds for two hours before and two hours after each dose.[104,225,624]

Summary:-	Stop feed 2 hours before dose
	Restart feed 2 hours after dose

Withholding enteral feeds can compromise nutrition and interfere with blood glucose management. If the patient does not have a break in their feeding regimen during which sodium clodronate can be given, the Nutrition Team should be contacted to advise on management.

Sodium cromoglicate (Sodium cromoglycate)

Presentation
Capsules.
Inhaler.
Eye drops.
Nasal spray.

Administration – enteral tubes / swallowing difficulties
The capsule contents can be removed, dissolved in about half a cup (4 fluid ounces) of warm water, and then diluted with the same volume of cold water before administration.[138,152,540]

Feed guidance
Sodium cromoglicate capsules should be taken on an empty stomach.[624] Enteral feeds should be withheld for half an hour before and half an hour after each dose.[225]

Summary:-	Stop feed 30 minutes before dose
	Restart feed 30 minutes after dose

Withholding enteral feeds can compromise nutrition and interfere with blood glucose management. If the patient does not have a break in their feeding regimen during which sodium cromoglicate capsules can be given, the Nutrition Team should be contacted to advise on management.

Sodium feredetate

Clinical guidance
See entry under 'Iron preparations'.

Sodium fusidate

Presentation
Film-coated tablets.
Suspension (contains sorbitol).
Intravenous infusion (no longer available in the UK).

Administration – NG / PEG tubes
1st choice – Use the intravenous infusion (if available) if possible.
2nd choice – Use the suspension (NB the suspension has a different dose to the tablets – see below). Follow the directions in section 3.6.

Administration – NJ / PEJ / PEGJ tubes
Use the intravenous infusion (if available) if possible. See "Clinical guidance" below.

Administration – swallowing difficulties
1st choice – Use the suspension (NB the suspension has a different dose to the tablets – see below).
2nd choice – Use the intravenous infusion (if available).
3rd choice – The tablets can be crushed and mixed with a little jam.[418] They have a bitter taste.[418]

750mg suspension	equivalent to	500mg tablet[90]

Clinical guidance
Sodium fusidate tablets are absorbed throughout the whole length of the gastrointestinal tract.[418] The suspension, however, is only absorbed in the stomach and upper gut.[418] There is therefore a risk of subtherapeutic absorption if the suspension is given through enteral tubes terminating in the jejunum. The intravenous infusion should be used if at all possible in such cases.

Sodium phenylbutyrate

Presentation
Tablets.
Suspension, granules.
Powder.
A suspension can be made by Pharmacy in some centres (see Appendix 1).[494]
Injection.

Administration – NG / PEG tubes
Ammonaps® granules are licensed to be administered via enteral feeding tube. The measured dose of granules should be re-constituted in water to produce a milky white suspension which can then be administered via the feeding tube. The granules are soluble 5g in 10ml of water.[661]

Pheburane® granules are <u>not</u> suitable for use via enteral feeding tubes.[660]

Administration – NJ / PEJ / PEGJ tubes
No information about the use of this medication via NJ / PEJ / PEGJ tubes has been located.

Administration – swallowing difficulties
Use the granules or suspension (if available). The granules can be mixed with mashed potato, apple sauce, water, apple juice, orange juice or protein-free infant formulas.[660,661]

Alternatively the injection can be given orally.[152]

Sodium picosulfate (Sodium picosulphate)

Presentation
Capsules.
Elixir, sachets.

Administration – enteral tubes / swallowing difficulties
Use the elixir.[104]   Follow the directions in section 3.6.   Dulcolax®
liquid can be diluted with water if necessary.[317]

Clinical guidance
Dulcolax® liquid contains ethanol.[317]

Sodium valproate

Presentation
Sugar-free oral liquid, syrup (the liquid contains sorbitol).
Tablets.
Crushable tablets.
Modified-release tablets and capsules.
Modified-release granules.
Injection.

Administration – enteral tubes
1st choice – Give by parenteral injection if possible.
2nd choice – Use the liquid (contains sorbitol). Contact Pharmacy for
advice on the appropriate dosage. If necessary the liquid can be
diluted immediately prior to administration.[361] It should not be diluted
in advance as this would dilute the preservative.[361,362] Follow the
directions in section 3.6.
3rd choice – The crushable tablets can be crushed and dispersed in a
small amount of water for administration.[361] Follow the directions in
section 3.5.

(monograph continues on next page)

Administration – swallowing difficulties

1st choice – Use the liquid (contains sorbitol). Contact Pharmacy for advice on the appropriate dosage.

2nd choice – For patients who are stabilised on modified-release formulations, use the modified-release granules. The granules should not be chewed or crushed, and therefore this method may not be appropriate for patients with limited understanding or impaired ability to follow instructions.

3rd choice – The crushable tablets can be crushed and mixed with a small amount of soft food, e.g yogurt or jam. They have an extremely bitter taste.[361]

4th choice – Give by parenteral injection if possible.

Clinical guidance

Contact Pharmacy for advice on dose conversion, and if patient has previously been receiving Epilim Chrono®, Epilim Chronosphere®, Episenta® or Epival®.

Epilim Chronosphere® and Episenta® granules can be mixed with soft food or a cold drink, and should be swallowed whole without chewing.[607] This method may not be appropriate for patients with limited understanding or impaired ability to follow instructions.

500mg Epilim Chronosphere® granules	equivalent to	500mg Epilim Chrono® tablet[608]

Changing formulations / product manufacturer

The MHRA has issued guidance recommending that (where possible) patients on sodium valproate (when used for seizures) are maintained on a specific manufacturer's product, due to variability in product characteristics which may lead to a loss of seizure control when switching between brands / manufacturers.[651] When managing patients with enteral tubes or swallowing difficulties it may not be possible to maintain the patient on their previous preparation due to the need to change to an appropriate formulation. However all product switches should be carried out with care and close monitoring, and where possible patients should be maintained from then onwards on a single manufacturer's product.

Solifenacin

Presentation
Film-coated tablets.

Clinical guidance
Crushing the tablets is not recommended as the powder released is irritant to the eyes.[265] Consider switching to an alternative treatment available as a liquid, e.g. oxybutynin.

Sotalol

Presentation
Tablets.
A suspension can be made by Pharmacy in some centres (see Appendix 1).[521]
Injection.

Administration – enteral tubes
1st choice – Consider switching to an alternative beta-blocker available as a liquid.
2nd choice – The tablet can be crushed and mixed with water for administration.[68,152] The drug is very soluble.[253] Follow the directions in section 3.5.
3rd choice – A suspension can be made by Pharmacy in some centres.[155] Follow the directions in section 3.6.

Administration – swallowing difficulties
1st choice – Consider switching to an alternative beta-blocker available as a liquid.
2nd choice – A suspension can be made by Pharmacy in some centres.[155]
3rd choice – The tablet can be crushed and mixed with water for administration.[68,152] The drug is very soluble.[253] Follow the directions in section 3.5.

Clinical guidance
Sotalol penetrates all sections of the intestine well,[400] so administration through enteral tubes terminating in the jejunum is not anticipated to cause any absorption problems.

Spironolactone

Presentation
Tablets.
Sugar-free oral suspension (special).[582]
A suspension can be made by Pharmacy in some centres (see Appendix 1).[473,495]
Potassium canrenoate injection (imported special).

Administration – enteral tubes
1st choice – The tablets can be crushed and mixed with water for administration.[138,152,225] Follow the directions in section 3.5.
2nd choice – Use the suspension.[104] Follow the directions in section 3.6. Rosemont do not recommend diluting the suspension with water before administration as this may destabilise the suspension.[360]
3rd choice – Convert to potassium canrenoate injection if appropriate.

Administration – swallowing difficulties
1st choice – Use the suspension.[104]
2nd choice – The tablets can be crushed and mixed with water for administration.[138,152,225] Follow the directions in section 3.5.
3rd choice – Convert to potassium canrenoate injection if appropriate.

Spironolactone and hydrochlorothiazide

Presentation
Tablets (may not be available in the UK).
A suspension can be made by Pharmacy in some centres (see Appendix 1).[206]

Administration – enteral tubes
No information on administering spironolactone and hydrochlorothiazide tablets via enteral feeding tubes has been located.

Administration – swallowing difficulties
Use the suspension (if available).

Stalevo®

See entry under "Co-careldopa and entacapone".

Stanozolol

Presentation
Tablets.

Administration – enteral tubes / swallowing difficulties
The tablet can be crushed and mixed with water for administration.[133]
Follow the directions in section 3.5.

Stavudine

Presentation
Capsules.
Oral solution.

Administration – enteral tubes
Use the oral solution.[138] Follow the directions in section 3.6.

Administration – swallowing difficulties
1st choice – Use the oral solution.[138] Follow the directions in section 3.6.
2nd choice – The capsules can be opened and the contents mixed with food for administration.[318]

Feed guidance
Withhold feed for two hours before and one hour after administration.[624]

Summary:-	Stop feed 2 hours before dose
	Restart feed 1 hour after dose

Withholding enteral feeds can compromise nutrition and interfere with blood glucose management. If the patient does not have a break in their feeding regimen during which stavudine can be given, the Nutrition Team should be contacted to advise on management.

367

Sucralfate

Presentation
Tablets.
Suspension.

Administration – NG / PEG tubes
Review the choice of drug as large breaks in feeding are required for the administration of sucralfate. If treatment is essential, use the suspension and dilute well.[41]

Administration – NJ / PEJ / PEGJ tubes
Do not give. Sucralfrate is ineffective by this route. For treatment of duodenal and gastric ulcers and chronic gastritis, it is recommended to use ranitidine effervescent tablets as an alternative.

Administration – swallowing difficulties
Use the suspension.

Clinical guidance
Sucralfate may affect the absorption of other drugs, so administration of other medications should be separated from the sucralfate dosage by at least two hours.[155]

Feed guidance
Sucralfrate has been reported as the most frequent cause of obstruction of enteral feeding tubes[20] therefore it must be administered with particular care. The aluminium in sucralfate interacts with proteins in enteral feeds to form an insoluble precipitate (bezoar formation).[32] The Committee on the Safety of Medicines (CSM) has advised caution using sucralfate in seriously ill patients, particularly those receiving concomitant enteral feeds, or with predisposing conditions such as delayed gastric emptying.[226]

There have been cases of sucralfate and enteral feed complexes solidifiying around enteral tubes and causing oesophageal blockages.[199]

(monograph continues on next page)

An enteral feeding break of at least one hour before and one hour after administration of sucralfate is recommended.[624] However it is strongly recommended that sucralfate is not administered via enteral feeding tubes if the patient is receiving enteral nutrition.

Withholding enteral feeds can compromise nutrition and interfere with blood glucose management. If the patient does not have a break in their feeding regimen during which sucralfate can be given, the Nutrition Team should be contacted to advise on management. It is seldom practical to administer sucralfate to patients receiving enteral feeds due to the frequency of dosing (four times daily) and the number of feed breaks this would require.

Sulfasalazine (Sulphasalazine)

Presentation
Tablets.
Enteric-coated tablets.
Suspension.
Oral solution (special).[582]
A suspension can be made by Pharmacy in some centres (see Appendix 1).[528]
Suppositories.
Retention enema (no longer available in the UK).

Administration – enteral tubes
1st choice – Consider using the suppositories or the enema (if available) for lower-bowel disease.
2nd choice – Use the suspension.[104,105] Follow the directions in section 3.6.

Administration – swallowing difficulties
1st choice – Use the suspension.[104,105]
2nd choice – Consider using the suppositories or the enema (if available) for lower-bowel disease.

Sulindac

Presentation
Tablets.

Administration – enteral tubes / swallowing difficulties
The tablets will disperse in water for administration.[8,133] They disperse in less than two minutes.[8] Follow the directions in section 3.5.

Sulpiride

Presentation
Tablets.
Solution.

Administration – enteral tubes / swallowing difficulties
1st choice – Use the solution.[104,105] Follow the directions in section 3.6.
2nd choice – The tablets can be dispersed in water for administration.[41] They disperse in one to five minutes.[154] Follow the directions in section 3.5.

The oral solution can be diluted with water to reduce the osmolality if desired when giving into the jejunum, however this is outside the product licence.[360]

Tacrolimus

Presentation
Capsules.
Modified-release capsules.
Granules for oral suspension.
Oral suspension (special).[542,582]
A suspension can be made by Pharmacy in some centres (see Appendix 1).[497,573]
Concentrate for infusion.

Administration – enteral tubes
1st choice – Consider switching to the infusion.
2nd choice – Convert to the granules for oral suspension, which are licensed for nasogastric administration.[604] See "Clinical guidance" below. Contact Pharmacy for advice.
3rd choice – The capsules can be opened and the contents dispersed in water for administration.[111] The carer should wear a mask and gloves when doing this to reduce exposure to the powder. Follow the directions in section 3.7.
4th choice – A suspension can be made by Pharmacy in some centres. Follow the directions in section 3.6.
5th choice – Use the oral suspension (if available). Follow the directions in section 3.6.

Do not open the modified-release capsules.

Administration – swallowing difficulties
1st choice – Convert to the granules for oral suspension. See "Clinical guidance" below. Contact Pharmacy for advice.
2nd choice – Consider switching to the infusion.
3rd choice – A suspension can be made by Pharmacy in some centres.
4th choice – Use the oral suspension (if available).
5th choice – The capsules can be opened and the contents dispersed in water for administration.[111] The carer should wear a mask and gloves when doing this to reduce exposure to the powder. Follow the directions in section 3.7.

Do not open the modified-release capsules.

(monograph continues on next page)

Clinical guidance
To convert a patient from the standard capsules (Prograf®) to the granules for oral suspension (Modigraf®), the total daily dose of granules should be equal to the total daily dose of the capsules.[510] If a directly equal conversion is not possible, the total daily dose of the granules should be rounded down to the nearest total daily dose possible with sachets (do not use part sachets). The granules should be given as two equally-divided doses. If equal doses are not possible, the larger dose should be given in the morning.[510]

For example:-

1.5mg total daily dose of capsules (1mg mane, 0.5mg nocte)	equivalent to	1.4mg total daily dose of granules[510] (0.8mg mane, 0.6mg nocte)

Tacrolimus granules should be added to water to make a suspension. <u>The suspension should not come into contact with PVC-containing equipment.</u>[510]

Feed guidance
Enteral tacrolimus should be given on an empty stomach, at least one hour before or two-three hours after food, to improve absorption.[225,510,624]

Summary:-	Stop feed 2 hours before dose
	Restart feed 1 hour after dose

Withholding enteral feeds can compromise nutrition and interfere with blood glucose management. If the patient does not have a break in their feeding regimen during which tacrolimus can be given, the Nutrition Team should be contacted to advise on management.

Tamoxifen

Presentation
Tablets.
Solution (some preparations contain alcohol and / or sorbitol).

Administration – enteral tubes
Caution – carcinogenic. Care should be taken when handling crushed or broken tablets. See "Clinical guidance" below.
1st choice – Use the solution.[104,105] Follow the directions in section 3.6.
2nd choice – The tablets can be crushed and mixed with water for administration.[94,105] Without crushing they disperse in two to five minutes.[8] Handle with care (see "Clinical guidance" below). Follow the directions in section 3.5.

Administration – swallowing difficulties
Caution – carcinogenic. Care should be taken when handling crushed or broken tablets. See "Clinical guidance" below.
1st choice – Use the solution.
2nd choice – The crushed tablets can be mixed with jam or yogurt for patients with swallowing difficulties.[105] Handle with care (see "Clinical guidance" below).

Clinical guidance
Handle the crushed tablets with care. Avoid the dust being inhaled, coming into contact with the skin, etc.[105,251] The carer should wear gloves, mask, and eye protection when crushing tablets.

Tamsulosin

Presentation
Capsules.
Film-coated modified-release tablets.

Clinical guidance
The tablet is modified-release and should not be crushed. The capsule is modified-release and is not suitable for opening for tube administration,[82] although there are reports of this having been done. Contact Pharmacy for advice.

(monograph continues on next page)

The capsules contain granules which should not be crushed. If no alternative is suitable, they may be mixed with cold water and swallowed whole (only suitable for patients able to follow the instruction not to chew) or given down an enteral feeding tube with good post-dose flushing.[105]

Tarka®

Presentation
Capsules.

Clinical guidance
Tarka® capsules contain trandolapril 2mg and verapamil 180mg as a modified-release preparation.[272] Use trandolapril as a separate component and convert to an appropriate dosage of verapamil as a standard-release preparation. This will require splitting the dose to give it two-three times a day. See individual monographs for details. Contact Pharmacy for advice if necessary.

Telmisartan

Presentation
Tablets.

Administration – enteral tubes / swallowing difficulties
The tablets are only sparingly soluble but there are anecdotal reports of them being crushed and mixed with water for administration. If giving via enteral feeding tube, flush well after administration.[110] Follow the directions in section 3.5.

Telmisartan and hydrochlorothiazide (Micardis Plus®)

Presentation
Tablets.

Clinical guidance
Micardis Plus® tablets contain telmisartan and hydrochlorothiazide at various dosages.[272] Use telmisartan or an alternative angiotensin-II receptor inhibitor such as losartan, and an alternative thiazide diuretic, e.g. bendroflumethiazide.

Temazepam

Presentation
Tablets.
Elixir (some preparations contain alcohol and / or sorbitol).

Administration – enteral tubes / swallowing difficulties
Use the elixir. Do not dilute. Follow the directions in section 3.6.

The tablets should not be used. They are quite insoluble and their use may lead to the blockage of enteral feeding tubes.

Clinical guidance
Temazepam may be less effective when administered through enteral tubes terminating in the jejunum.

Tenif®

Presentation
Capsules.

Clinical guidance
Tenif® capsules contain atenolol 50mg and nifedipine 20mg as a modified-release preparation.[272] Use the individual components – atenolol and an appropriate formulation of nifedipine. This will require splitting the dose and giving it several times a day. See individual monographs for details. Contact Pharmacy for advice if necessary.

Tenofovir

Presentation
Film-coated tablets.

Administration – enteral tubes / swallowing difficulties
The tablets can be dispersed in half a glass of water or orange juice for administration.[132,319] Follow the directions in section 3.5.

Tenofovir with efavirenz and emtricitabine (Atripla®)

Presentation
Film-coated tablets.

Clinical guidance
Atripla® tablets contain efavirenz 600mg, emtricitabine 200mg, and tenofovir 245mg.[272] No information has been located on the use of Atripla® tablets in patients with enteral feeding tubes or swallowing difficulties. Use the individual components. See individual monographs for details.

Tenofovir and emtricitabine (Truvada®)

Presentation
Film-coated tablets.

Administration – enteral tubes
No information has been located about giving Truvada® via enteral feeding tubes.

Administration – swallowing difficulties
The tablets can be dispersed in 100mL of water, orange juice or grape juice for administration to patients unable to swallow them whole.[320] Follow the directions in section 3.5.

Feed guidance
Take with or after food.[429]

Terazosin

Presentation
Tablets.

Administration – enteral tubes / swallowing difficulties
The tablets can be dispersed in water for administration. They disperse in one to five minutes.[154] The excipients may not dissolve so it may be necessary to filter them out to prevent blockage of enteral feeding tubes.[56] Follow the directions in section 3.5.

Terbinafine

Presentation
Tablets.
Oral solution (special).[582]
A suspension can be made by Pharmacy in some centres (see Appendix 1).[499]

Administration – enteral tubes
1st choice – The tablets can be crushed and mixed with water for administration.[41] Follow the directions in section 3.5.
2nd choice – A suspension can be made by Pharmacy in some centres.[155,499] Follow the directions in section 3.6.
3rd choice – Use the oral solution (if available). Follow the directions in section 3.6.

Administration – swallowing difficulties
1st choice – A suspension can be made by Pharmacy in some centres.[155,499]
2nd choice – Use the oral solution (if available).
3rd choice – The tablets can be crushed and mixed with water for administration.[41] Follow the directions in section 3.5.

Tetrabenazine

Presentation
Tablets.
Oral solution (special).[582]

Administration – enteral tubes
The tablets can be crushed and mixed with water for administration.[104] Flush well after administration.[132] Follow the directions in section 3.5.

No information on giving the oral solution via enteral feeding tubes has been located.

Administration – swallowing difficulties
1st choice – Use the oral solution (if available).
2nd choice – The tablets can be crushed and mixed with water for administration.[104] Follow the directions in section 3.5.

Tetracycline

Presentation
Tablets.
A suspension can be made by Pharmacy in some centres (see Appendix 1).[454]

Administration – enteral tubes
No information about giving tetracycline via enteral feeding tubes has been located. Consider switching to doxycycline, which is available as a dispersible tablet.

Administration – swallowing difficulties
1st choice – Consider switching to doxycycline, which is available as a dispersible tablet.
2nd choice – Use the suspension (if available).

(monograph continues on next page)

Feed guidance

Tetracycline absorption can be decreased by milk and dairy products as the drug chelates calcium, iron, magnesium, and zinc. It is recommended that the drug is taken two to three hours apart from milk and dairy products.[225,266,624]

Summary:-	Stop feed 2 hours before dose
	Restart feed 1 hour after dose

Withholding enteral feeds can compromise nutrition and interfere with blood glucose management. If the patient does not have a break in their feeding regimen during which tetracycline can be given, the Nutrition Team should be contacted to advise on management.

Tetrahydrobiopterin

Presentation
Tablets.

Administration – enteral tubes
No information about the use of this medication via enteral feeding tubes has been located.

Administration – swallowing difficulties
The tablets may be dispersed in water or orange juice immediately before administration.[152]

Thalidomide

Presentation
Capsules.

Clinical guidance
The administration of thalidomide via enteral feeding tubes is not recommended due to the nature of the drug.

(monograph continues on next page)

Pharmacy should be contacted for advice prior to considering giving thalidomide to patients with enteral feeding tubes or swallowing difficulties.

Any carer opening thalidomide capsules should wear gloves and a face-mask to prevent inhalation of airbourne particles of the drug, and contact with the skin. It is recommended that women of childbearing potential <u>DO</u> <u>NOT</u> undertake any procedure involving opening the capsules.

There are reports of thalidomide capsules being opened and the contents mixed with water for administration via enteral feeding tube. Thalidomide is not very water-soluble, so enteral tubes should be flushed well post-dose to avoid blockage.[368]

Thalidomide capsules have been opened and their contents mixed with apple-sauce, pudding or ice-cream for administration to patients with swallowing difficulties.[368] If this method is used the carer preparing the medication should also clean the utensils involved after the food has been consumed, to ensure that particles of medication remaining on the utensils do not come into contact with women of child-bearing potential who are unaware of what the food was mixed with.

Theophylline

Presentation
Liquid, sugar-free oral solution (special)[582] (may be hard to obtain).
Tablets (no longer available in the UK).
A suspension can be made by Pharmacy in some centres (see Appendix 1).[500]
Various modified-release preparations.

When an immediate-release preparation is required

Administration – enteral tubes
1st choice – Convert to parenteral aminophylline injection if appropriate. Contact Pharmacy for advice.
2nd choice – Crush Nuelin® tablets (if available) and disperse in water for administration.[152] Follow the directions in section 3.5.
3rd choice – A suspension can be made by Pharmacy in some centres. Follow the directions in section 3.6.
4th choice – Use the special oral liquid (if available), diluted with distilled water before administration. Follow the directions in section 3.6.
5th choice – Give aminophylline injection enterally.[259,260] Follow the directions in section 3.6.

Administration – swallowing difficulties
1st choice – Convert to parenteral aminophylline injection if appropriate. Contact Pharmacy for advice.
2nd choice – A suspension can be made by Pharmacy in some centres.
3rd choice – Use the special oral liquid (if available).
4th choice – Crush Nuelin® tablets (if available) and disperse in water for administration.[152] Follow the directions in section 3.5.
5th choice – Give aminophylline injection enterally.[259,260] Follow the directions in section 3.6.

(monograph continues on next page)

When a modified-release preparation is required

It is recommended to switch to an immediate-release preparation, but if a modified-release preparation is needed, the following method can be used.

Open a Slo-phyllin® capsule and pour the contents, (enteric-coated granules) through the feeding tube, flushing before and after with 15-30mL of distilled water. The granules have also been administered on soft food for patients with swallowing difficulties.[132] The granules should not be chewed or crushed, and therefore this method may not be appropriate for patients with limited understanding or impaired ability to follow instructions.

Do not crush the modified-release tablets.

Clinical guidance
There is a difference in bioavailability between the liquid and the modified-release tablets. The liquid should be given more frequently (usually three times a day). Contact Pharmacy for advice on equivalent doses.

Additional notes
Aminophylline is a salt of theophylline. Switching between the two requires a dosage change. Contact Pharmacy for advice.

250mg oral aminophylline   equivalent to   200mg oral theophylline[176]

Feed guidance
The pharmacokinetics of theophylline can be altered by the nutritional formula of enteral feeds (the half life is decreased by high protein, low carbohydrate diets, and increased by low protein, high carbohydrate diets).[2] Some sources recommend that theophylline is administered on an empty stomach due to a potential interaction with enteral feeds,[11,41] particularly Osmolite®, Ensure® and Ensure Plus®.[105,225] However there are anecdotal reports of patients being successfully managed without withholding the feed.[261,262,263] In either case, the patient should be monitored for loss of efficacy. If the feed is to be withheld, it should be stopped for one hour before and one hour after each dose.[11,87,117]

(monograph continues on next page)

Withholding enteral feeds can compromise nutrition and interfere with blood glucose management. If it is necessary for theophylline to be given during a feeding break, and the patient does not have a break in their feeding regimen, the Nutrition Team should be contacted to advise on management.

Thiamine

Presentation
Tablets.
Oral solution (special).[582]
A suspension can be made by Pharmacy in some centres (see Appendix 1).[512,573]

Administration – enteral tubes
1st choice – The tablets can be crushed and dispersed in water for administration.[94] Follow the directions in section 3.5.
2nd choice – A suspension can be made by Pharmacy in some centres.[155] Follow the directions in section 3.6.
3rd choice – Use the oral solution (if available). Follow the directions in section 3.6.

Administration – swallowing difficulties
1st choice – A suspension can be made by Pharmacy in some centres.[155]
2nd choice – Use the oral solution (if available).
3rd choice – The tablets can be crushed and dispersed in water for administration.[94] Follow the directions in section 3.5.

Thioridazine

Presentation
Film-coated tablets.
Syrup (special), sugar-free oral solution (special).

Clinical guidance
The syrup has been administered via enteral feeding tube in some centres, but there is little information available on this.[133] Follow the directions in section 3.6. Some brands of thioridazine tablets will disperse in water,[8] but others will not,[8] and no reports of thioridazine tablets being dispersed for administration via enteral feeding tubes have been located, so this cannot be advised.

Feed guidance
Thioridazine has been reported as being incompatible with some enteral feeds, so ensure enteral feeding tubes are flushed well before and after each dose.[222]

Tiabendazole

Presentation
Tablets (special).
Syrup, suspension (special).

Administration – enteral tubes
No information about the use of this medication via enteral feeding tubes has been located.

Administration – swallowing difficulties
The tablets may be crushed for administration.[152]

Tiagabine

Presentation
Film-coated tablets.
A suspension can be made by Pharmacy in some centres (see Appendix 1).[501]

Administration – enteral tubes
The tablets can be crushed and mixed with water for administration.[104] Follow the directions in section 3.5.

No information on administering the suspension via enteral feeding tubes has been located.

Administration – swallowing difficulties
1st choice – Use the suspension (if available).
2nd choice – The tablets can be crushed and mixed with water for administration.[104] Follow the directions in section 3.5.

Tiaprofenic acid

Presentation
Tablets.
Modified-release capsules (no longer available in the UK).

Administration – enteral tubes / swallowing difficulties
The tablets can be crushed and mixed with water for administration.[8] Without crushing they disperse in two to five minutes.[8] Follow the directions in section 3.5.

Do not open the modified-release capsules.

Feed guidance
Take with or after food.[429]

Ticagrelor

Presentation
Film-coated tablets.

Administration – enteral tubes
The tablets can be crushed and mixed with water for administration through enteral feeding tubes of size 8 or greater.[657]   Follow the directions in section 3.5. Flush the tube well after administration.

Administration – swallowing difficulties
The tablets can be crushed and mixed with water for administration.[657] Follow the directions in section 3.5.

Timolol

Presentation
Tablets.

Clinical guidance
Consider changing to an alternative beta blocker available as a liquid formulation, e.g. atenolol.

Timolol and bendroflumethiazide (Prestim®)

Presentation
Tablets.

Clinical guidance
Prestim® tablets contain timolol 10mg and bendroflumethiazide 2.5mg.[272]   Use the separate components – see individual monographs for details.

Tinidazole

Presentation
Film-coated tablets.

Administration – enteral tubes / swallowing difficulties
The tablets can be crushed and dispersed in water for administration.[132] They have a very bitter taste which can be disguised with strongly flavoured juice when being administered to patients with swallowing difficulties.[132] Follow the directions in section 3.5.

Tioguanine (Thioguanine)

Presentation
Tablets.
A suspension can be made by Pharmacy in some centres.

Administration – enteral tubes / swallowing difficulties
Caution – cytotoxic. Contact Pharmacy for advice before giving.
A suspension can be made by Pharmacy in some centres.[138] Follow the directions in section 3.6.

Tizanidine

Presentation
Tablets.
Oral suspension (special).[542,582]
A suspension can be made by Pharmacy in some centres.

Administration – enteral tubes
1st choice – The tablets can be crushed and mixed with water for administration.[104] Follow the directions in section 3.5.
2nd choice – A suspension can be made by Pharmacy in some centres.[155] Follow the directions in section 3.6.
3rd choice – Use the oral suspension (if available). Follow the directions in section 3.6.

(monograph continues on next page)

Administration – swallowing difficulties
1st choice – A suspension can be made by Pharmacy in some centres.[155]
2nd choice – Use the oral suspension (if available).
3rd choice – The tablets can be crushed and mixed with water for administration.[104] Follow the directions in section 3.5.

Tolbutamide

Presentation
Tablets.

Administration – enteral tubes / swallowing difficulties
1st choice – Consider whether switching to insulin would be appropriate.
2nd choice – The tablets can be crushed and mixed with water for administration.[104,105] Without crushing they disperse in one to five minutes.[8] Follow the directions in section 3.5.

Monitor the patient's blood glucose.

Tolterodine

Presentation
Film-coated tablets.
Modified-release capsules.
Oral solution (special).[582]

Administration – enteral tubes
The tablets can be dispersed in water for administration.[83] They disperse within one minute.[154] Use immediately. Follow the directions in section 3.5. No information has been located to indicate whether tolterodine is likely to block enteral feeding tubes.[83]

The modified-release capsules are not suitable for use via enteral feeding tubes.

(monograph continues on next page)

Administration – swallowing difficulties
1st choice – Use the oral solution (if available).
2nd choice – The tablets can be dispersed in water for administration.[83] They disperse within one minute.[154] Use immediately. Follow the directions in section 3.5.

The modified-release capsules contain time-release beads which can be removed from the capsule and administered orally whole, to patients with the ability to follow the instruction not to chew,[105] but the preferred form of tolterodine for administration is the standard tablets. Contact Pharmacy for advice if uncertain.

Topiramate

Presentation
Tablets.
Sprinkle capsules.
Oral solution (special).[582]

Administration – enteral tubes
1st choice – The tablets can be crushed and dispersed in water for administration.[95,152,363,366] Follow the directions in section 3.5.

For large-bore tubes the sprinkle capsules have been opened and the contents mixed with water and flushed down the tube. The capsule contents may adhere to the sides of the tube, risking blockage, so this is not recommended.[155,363,366] Flush well to prevent blockage.[101]

No information about administering the oral solution via enteral feeding tubes has been located.

Administration – swallowing difficulties
1st choice – The sprinkle capsules can be opened and the contents sprinkled on food or mixed with water for administration.[101] Follow the directions in section 3.7.
2nd choice – Use the oral solution (if available).
3rd choice – The tablets can be crushed and dispersed in water for administration.[95,152] The crushed tablets have a bitter taste.[95,152] Follow the directions in section 3.5.

(monograph continues on next page)

Clinical guidance
Topiramate is probably absorbed in the upper gastrointestinal tract, therefore absorption and clinical effectiveness may be altered if administered through an enteral tube which terminates in the jejunum.[366] When topiramate is being used for epilepsy, it should only be administered into the jejunum if there is no other option, and the patient should be monitored closely.

Changing formulations / product manufacturer
The MHRA has issued guidance recommending that (where possible) patients on topiramate (when used for seizures) are maintained on a specific manufacturer's product, due to variability in product characteristics which may lead to a loss of seizure control when switching between brands / manufacturers.[651] When managing patients with enteral tubes or swallowing difficulties it may not be possible to maintain the patient on their previous preparation due to the need to change to an appropriate formulation. However all product switches should be carried out with care and close monitoring, and where possible patients should be maintained from then onwards on a single manufacturer's product.

Torasemide

Presentation
Tablets.

Administration – enteral tubes / swallowing difficulties
The tablets can be crushed and dispersed in water for administration. A slurry may be formed, so if giving via enteral feeding tube, flush well after administration.[138] Follow the directions in section 3.5.

Tramadol

Presentation
Capsules.

Soluble tablets, orodispersible tablets, sachets, sugar-free oral solution (special).

A suspension can be made by Pharmacy in some centres (see Appendix 1).[502]

Modified-release tablets, modified-release capsules.

Injection.

Administration – enteral tubes
1st choice – Consider giving by parenteral injection.

2nd choice – Use the soluble tablets, orodispersible tablets, or the oral solution. Follow the directions in sections 3.5 and 3.6.

3rd choice – A suspension can be made by Pharmacy in some centres. Follow the directions in section 3.6.

Administration – swallowing difficulties
1st choice – Use the soluble tablets, orodispersible tablets, or the oral solution.

2nd choice – Consider giving by parenteral injection.

3rd choice – A suspension can be made by Pharmacy in some centres.

Trandolapril

Presentation
Capsules.

Administration – enteral tubes
The capsules can be opened, and the contents dispersed in water for administration.[105] Follow the directions in section 3.7.

Administration – swallowing difficulties
The capsule contents have a bitter taste which can be masked by fruit squash for patients with swallowing difficulties.[155]

Trandolapril and verapamil (Tarka®)

Presentation
Capsules.

Clinical guidance
Tarka® capsules contain trandolapril 2mg and verapamil 180mg as a modified-release preparation.[272] Use trandolapril as a separate component and convert to an appropriate dosage of verapamil as a standard-release preparation. This will require splitting the dose to give it two-three times a day. See individual monographs for details. Contact Pharmacy for advice if necessary.

Tranexamic acid

Presentation
Tablets.
Oral solution (special).[582]
Injection.

Administration – enteral tubes
1st choice – The tablets can be crushed and mixed with water for administration. Without crushing they disperse in two to five minutes.[8,66] Follow the directions in section 3.5.
2nd choice – Use the oral solution (if available). Follow the directions in section 3.6.
3rd choice – The injection can also be used enterally after dilution.[66,104] Use immediately.[66] Follow the directions in section 3.6.

Administration – swallowing difficulties
1st choice – Use the oral solution (if available).
2nd choice – The tablets can be crushed and mixed with water for administration. Without crushing they disperse in two to five minutes.[8,66] Follow the directions in section 3.5.
2nd choice – The injection can also be used enterally after dilution.[66,104] Use immediately.[66] Follow the directions in section 3.6.

Trasidrex®

Presentation
Sugar-coated tablets.

Clinical guidance
Trasidrex® tablets contain oxprenolol 160mg as a modified-release preparation and cyclopenthiazide 250micrograms.[272] A dose alteration will be required to move to a standard-release formulation. Consider switching to an alternative beta-blocker available as a liquid, e.g. atenolol, and giving cyclopenthiazide as a separate component. Contact Pharmacy for advice if necessary.

Trazodone

Presentation
Tablets, capsules.
Liquid.

Administration – enteral tubes / swallowing difficulties
1st choice – Use the liquid. Follow the directions in section 3.6.

Opening the capsules is not recommended but there are reports of this being done.[84] The content of the capsules tastes unpleasant.[84] Follow the directions in section 3.7. There is no information available about crushing the tablets, so this is not recommended.

Triapin®

Presentation
Film-coated tablets.

Clinical guidance
Triapin® tablets contain ramipril and felodipine in various dosages.[272] They are not suitable for administration via enteral feeding tubes because the ingredients are light sensitive, and the formulation is modified-release.[79] Use the separate components – see individual monographs for details.

Trifluoperazine

Presentation
Coated tablets.
Solution (some preparations contain sorbitol).
Modified-release capsules (no longer available in the UK).

Administration – enteral tubes / swallowing difficulties
Use the solution.[94,104,105] Follow the directions in section 3.6.

The oral solution can be diluted with water to reduce the osmolality if desired when giving into the jejunum, however this is outside the product licence.[360]

Trihexyphenidyl (Benzhexol)

Presentation
Tablets.
Syrup.
Oral solution (special).[542]

Administration – enteral tubes
1st choice – Use the syrup.[41] Follow the directions in section 3.6.
2nd choice – The tablets will disperse in water for administration.[8,133]
Follow the directions in section 3.5.
3rd choice – Use the oral solution (if available). Follow the directions in section 3.6.

Administration – swallowing difficulties
1st choice – Use the syrup.[41]
2nd choice – Use the oral solution (if available).
3rd choice – The tablets will disperse in water for administration.[8,133]
Follow the directions in section 3.5.

Trimethoprim

Presentation
Tablets.
Suspension.
Injection (may be difficult to obtain).

Administration – enteral tubes
1st choice – Give by parenteral injection if appropriate.
2nd choice – Use the suspension.[104] Follow the directions in section 3.6.

Administration – swallowing difficulties
1st choice – Use the suspension.[104]
2nd choice – Give by parenteral injection if appropriate.

Feed guidance
Enteral trimethoprim absorption can be reduced when it is taken with food.[155,617] If possible, withhold enteral feeds for half an hour before and half an hour after each enteral dose.[155,225]

Summary:-	Stop feed 30 minutes before dose
	Restart feed 30 minutes after dose

Withholding enteral feeds can compromise nutrition and interfere with blood glucose management. If the patient does not have a break in their feeding regimen during which enteral trimethoprim can be given, the Nutrition Team should be contacted to advise on management.

Trimipramine

Presentation
Tablets, capsules.

Administration – enteral tubes / swallowing difficulties
For long-term therapy, consider switching to an alternative tricyclic antidepressant available as a liquid.

For short-term use, the capsules can be opened and the contents dispersed in water for administration.[92] Follow the directions in section 3.7. Alternatively the tablets can be crushed.[92] Follow the directions in section 3.5. Both have a local anaesthetic action, so take care if used orally in patients with swallowing difficulties.[92]

Clinical guidance
Tricyclic antidepressants can decrease gastric emptying.[2]

Trizivir®

Presentation
Film-coated tablets.

Clinical guidance
Trizivir® tablets contain abacavir 300mg, lamivudine 150mg, and zidovudine 300mg.[272] No information has been located on the use of Trizivir® tablets in patients with enteral feeding tubes or swallowing difficulties. Use the individual components – see individual monographs for details.

Trospium

Presentation
Film-coated tablets.

Administration – enteral tubes / swallowing difficulties
The tablets can be crushed and dispersed in water for administration.[255] Follow the directions in section 3.5. Crushed tablets should be given immediately as there is no stability data available. They may have a bitter taste.[255]

Feed guidance
Withhold feed for two hours before and one hour after administration.[624]

Summary:-	Stop feed 2 hours before dose
	Restart feed 1 hour after dose

Withholding enteral feeds can compromise nutrition and interfere with blood glucose management. If the patient does not have a break in their feeding regimen during which trospium can be given, the Nutrition Team should be contacted to advise on management.

Truvada®

See entry under "Tenofovir and emtricitabine".

Ursodeoxycholic acid

Presentation
Tablets, capsules.
Suspension.
A suspension can be made by Pharmacy in some centres (see Appendix 1).[503,528]

Administration – enteral tubes
1st choice – Use the suspension.[104] Follow the directions in section 3.6. The suspension can be diluted with water before administration if necessary to reduce its viscosity.[345] This should only be done immediately before administration.
2nd choice – The tablets have been crushed and mixed with water for administration.[133] The powder resulting from crushing the tablets has limited solubility and may stick to the inside of enteral feeding tubes; flush well after administration.[138] Follow the directions in section 3.5.
3rd choice – A suspension can be made by Pharmacy in some centres. Follow the directions in section 3.6.

There is no information about opening the capsules, and therefore this is not recommended.

Administration – swallowing difficulties
1st choice – Use the suspension.[104]
2nd choice – A suspension can be made by Pharmacy in some centres.
3rd choice – The tablets have been crushed and mixed with water for administration.[133] Follow the directions in section 3.5.

There is no information about opening the capsules, and therefore this is not recommended.

Valaciclovir

Presentation
Film-coated tablets.

Administration – enteral tubes
No information on giving valaciclovir via enteral feeding tubes has been located.   *(monograph continues on next page)*

Administration – swallowing difficulties
A suspension can be made by Pharmacy in some centres.[346,504]

Valganciclovir

Presentation
Film-coated tablets.
Powder for oral solution.
A suspension can be made by Pharmacy in some centres (see Appendix 1).[505,506]

Administration – enteral tubes
Caution – teratogenic. Care should be taken when handling crushed or broken tablets. See "Clinical guidance" below.
1st choice – Use an alternative treatment available in intravenous form, e.g. ganciclovir.
2nd choice – The tablets can be crushed and mixed with distilled water for administration. Crush well as the tablets are film-coated.[131] Follow the directions in section 3.5.

No information on administering the oral solution or the suspension via enteral feeding tubes has been located.

Administration – swallowing difficulties
1st choice – Use the oral solution. The dose of oral solution is the same as that of the tablets.[343]
2nd choice – Use an alternative treatment available in intravenous form, e.g. ganciclovir.
3rd choice – A suspension can be made by Pharmacy in some centres.
4th choice – The tablets can be crushed and mixed with distilled water or chocolate syrup for administration.[131] Follow the directions in section 3.5.

(monograph continues on next page)

Clinical guidance
Valganciclovir is teratogenic, and should be handled with caution. Inhalation should be avoided. Gloves should be worn when preparing doses. If the medication comes into contact with the skin, the area should be washed thoroughly with soap and water. If it comes into contact with the eye, the eye should be thoroughly washed with water immediately.[343]

Valproic acid (Depakote®)

Presentation
Enteric-coated tablets.

Clinical guidance
Please be aware that valproic acid and sodium valproate are not directly interchangeable.

No information on administration of valproic acid to patients with enteral feeding tubes or swallowing difficulties has been located.

The manufacturers of Depakote® do not recommend crushing the tablets due to the increased risk of gastrointestinal disturbance.[382] There are pharmacokinetic differences between Depakote® and sodium valproate (Epilim®) – Depakote® produces higher peak levels than similar doses of Epilim®, but has a shorter half-life.[382] There is no commercially available liquid formulation of Depakote®, and the manufacturers believe that most clinicians manage their patients with Epilim® liquid when necessary.[382] They also note that in some countries only one of the two products is available, and in those places the same drug is used for both indications.[382]

There is no officially recommended dose conversion between the two products, due to their differing pharmacokinetics. However it would seem sensible to convert patients on Depakote® to the same dose of sodium valproate liquid, and monitor the clinical effect.

Valsartan

Presentation
Capsules.

Administration – enteral tubes / swallowing difficulties
The capsules can be opened, and the contents dispersed in water for administration.[85,104] Use immediately as the drug is not very stable.[104] If giving via enteral feeding tube, flush well after each dose as the capsule contents are not very soluble.[155] Follow the directions in section 3.7.

The capsule contents taste bitter.[85]

Valsartan and hydrochlorothiazide (Co-Diovan®)

Presentation
Film-coated tablets.

Clinical guidance
Co-Diovan® tablets contain valsartan and hydrochlorothiazide at various dosages.[272] Switch to valsartan or an alternative angiotensin-II receptor antagonist such as losartan, and an alternative thiazide diuretic, e.g. bendroflumethiazide. See individual monographs for details.

Vancomycin

Presentation
Capsules.
Injection.

Administration – enteral tubes / swallowing difficulties
1st choice – An oral solution can be made by Pharmacy in some centres. Follow the directions in section 3.6.
2nd choice – The injection can be diluted with 30mL water for injection and given enterally.[40,163] The expiry of the reconstituted injection depends upon the brand. Follow the directions in section 3.6.

Do not administer vancomycin capsules.

Clinical guidance
The indications for vancomycin injection and enteral vancomycin are different. Do not switch to the alternative route except on specialist advice. Contact Pharmacy for advice if necessary.

Venlafaxine

Presentation
Tablets.
Modified-release capsules.
Oral solution (special).[542,582]

Administration – enteral tubes
The tablets can be crushed and mixed with water for administration.[86] Follow the directions in section 3.5.

The modified-release capsules are not suitable for enteral tube administration.[86] Contact Pharmacy for advice on converting to standard tablets. No information on administering the oral solution via enteral feeding tubes has been located.

(monograph continues on next page)

Administration – swallowing difficulties
1st choice – Use the oral solution (if available).
2nd choice – Crushed tablets can be administered in jam for patients with swallowing difficulties.[105]

The modified-release capsules contain modified-release beads which can be emptied out and given in smooth food, e.g. yogurt, for patients with swallowing difficulties. The beads must be swallowed whole, therefore this method may not be appropriate for patients with limited understanding / impaired ability to follow instructions.[105]

Verapamil

Presentation
Tablets.
Sugar-free oral solution.
A suspension can be made by Pharmacy in some centres (see Appendix 1).[206]
Modified-release tablets, modified-release capsules.
Injection.

Administration – enteral tubes
1st choice – Use the oral solution. Follow the directions in section 3.6.
2nd choice – The standard tablets have been crushed and mixed with water for administration.[105,152] Follow the directions in section 3.5.
3rd choice – A suspension can be made by Pharmacy in some centres.[206] Follow the directions in section 3.6.
4th choice – The injection can be given enterally.[40,138,152] Follow the directions in section 3.6.

Do not crush the modified-release tablets or open the capsules.[336]

(monograph continues on next page)

Administration – swallowing difficulties
1st choice – Use the oral solution.
2nd choice – A suspension can be made by Pharmacy in some centres.[206]
3rd choice – The standard tablets have been crushed and mixed with water for administration. They have a bitter taste and a local anaesthetic effect in the mouth.[105,152] Follow the directions in section 3.5.
4th choice – The injection can be given enterally.[40,138,152] Follow the directions in section 3.6.

Do not crush the modified-release tablets or open the capsules.[336]

Clinical guidance
Dose and frequency changes are required if changing from modified-release verapamil to the oral solution. Contact Pharmacy for advice. Zolvera® oral solution contains liquid maltitol, which may cause diarrhoea.[284]

Vigabatrin

Presentation
Film-coated tablets.
Sachets.

Administration – enteral tubes / swallowing difficulties
1st choice – Use the sachets.[104] The manufacturers recommend that the sachets are made up in 100mL of water, fruit juice, or milk.[365] Follow the directions in section 3.6.
2nd choice – The tablets can be crushed and dispersed in water for administration.[138,152] Follow the directions in section 3.5.

Clinical guidance
Where fluid volume is a problem, some centres have dispersed vigabatrin sachets in 10mL of water. The sachets dissolve readily in this smaller volume.[553]

Viskaldix®

See entry under "Pindolol and clopamide".

Vitamin B Co Strong

Presentation
Film-coated tablets.

Clinical guidance
Consider switching to Pabrinex injection or Vigranon B syrup (not available on NHS).[94,136] Contact Pharmacy for advice.

Vitamin E

Presentation
Suspension.

Administration – enteral tubes / swallowing difficulties
Use the suspension.[104] Follow the directions in section 3.6.

Voriconazole

Presentation
Film-coated tablets.
Oral suspension.
Intravenous infusion.

Administration – enteral tubes
1st choice – Give by infusion if possible.
2nd choice – Use the suspension.[132] Follow the directions in section 3.6.
3rd choice – The tablets can be crushed and mixed with water for administration.[132,282] Follow the directions in section 3.5.

Administration – swallowing difficulties
1st choice – Use the suspension.[132]
2nd choice – Give by infusion if possible.
3rd choice – The tablets can be crushed and mixed with water for administration.[132,282] Follow the directions in section 3.5.

(monograph continues on next page)

Clinical guidance

A case report of voriconazole being given via a jejunostomy tube showed levels similar to those after oral administration.[282]

Feed guidance

Withhold feed for two hours before and one hour after administration of enteral doses.[225,283,624]

Summary:-	Stop feed 2 hours before dose
	Restart feed 1 hour after dose

Withholding enteral feeds can compromise nutrition and interfere with blood glucose management. If the patient does not have a break in their feeding regimen during which enteral voriconazole can be given, the Nutrition Team should be contacted to advise on management.

Warfarin

Presentation

Tablets.
Oral suspension.[579]
A suspension can be made by Pharmacy in some centres.[573]

Administration – enteral tubes

1st choice – Use the oral suspension (if available). Follow the directions in section 3.6.

2nd choice – The tablets can be crushed and mixed with water for administration.[38,41] Without crushing they disperse in two to five minutes.[8] Follow the directions in section 3.5.

3rd choice – A suspension can be made by Pharmacy in some centres.[155] Dilute the suspension with the same volume of distilled water before administration. Follow the directions in section 3.6.

(monograph continues on next page)

Administration – swallowing difficulties

1st choice – Use the oral suspension (if available).

2nd choice – A suspension can be made by Pharmacy in some centres.[155]

3rd choice – The tablets can be crushed and mixed with water for administration.[38,41] Without crushing they disperse in two to five minutes.[8] Follow the directions in section 3.5.

Clinical guidance

Warfarin is available as a racemate of two enantiomers. One is much more potent than the other. As putting the tablets into solution will lead to an alteration in the proportions of the two enantiomers, care should be taken.[142] It is advisable to keep patients on a consistent formulation, and monitor the INR closely following any necessary changes. Warfarin has a low solubility at pH levels below 8, and precipitation may occur.[142]

Feed guidance

Withhold enteral feeds for one to two hours before and one to two hours after each dose.

Summary:-	Stop feed 1-2 hours before dose
	Restart feed 1-2 hours after dose

Care is necessary when patients are also receiving enteral feeds with a high vitamin K content. Vitamin K in as little as 50mcg doses has been reported to antagonise the effects of warfarin, i.e. decrease prothrombin time,[33,242] though it generally requires a dose of 140-500mcg.[4] It is particularly important to keep vitamin K intake consistent from day to day. Therefore if dietary or feed intake changes significantly, INR should be monitored closely over the next few days.[574]

Enteral feeds containing sufficient amounts of vitamin K for this interaction to occur include Ensure® (100mcg/100mL),[34] Isocal® (13mcg/100mL[34]), Nutrilite 330®, Osmolite®[225], and Ensure Plus® (21.3mcg/100mL[34]).[11,242] The INR should be monitored closely and the warfarin dose adjusted as necessary.

Avoid feeds containing soya protein.[87]

(monograph continues on next page)

Warfarin resistance may occur in patients receiving enteral feeds, resulting in a need for higher doses. Care should be taken to review and adjust doses down again when the enteral feed is stopped.[2,26]

Withholding enteral feeds can compromise nutrition and interfere with blood glucose management. If the patient does not have a break in their feeding regimen during which warfarin can be given, the Nutrition Team should be contacted to advise on management.

Zafirlukast

Presentation
Film-coated tablets.

Administration – enteral tubes
No information is available on the administration of zafirlukast via enteral feeding tubes.

Administration – swallowing difficulties
The tablets can be halved to make them smaller without altering their release characteristics.[257]

Clinical guidance
Crushing the tablets may result in an increase in peak levels with no change in the AUC. The tablets are very hard and may be difficult to crush.[257]

Feed guidance
Food may decrease bioavailability of the drug, so the tablets should not be taken with meals.[257,624] Withhold enteral feeds for two hours before and one hour after each dose.[225,429]

Summary:-	Stop feed 2 hours before dose
	Restart feed 1 hour after dose

Withholding enteral feeds can compromise nutrition and interfere with blood glucose management. If the patient does not have a break in their feeding regimen during which zafirlukast can be given, the Nutrition Team should be contacted to advise on management.

Zaleplon

Presentation
Capsules.

Clinical guidance
Administration via enteral feeding tube is not recommended as the capsule contents are practically insoluble and would stain the tube.[138]

Zestoretic®

Presentation
Tablets.

Clinical guidance
Zestoretic® tablets contain lisinopril and hydrochlorothiazide in various dosages.[272] Use lisinopril as a separate component, and an appropriate thiazide diuretic, e.g. bendroflumethiazide. See individual monographs for details.

Zidovudine

Presentation
Capsules.
Film-coated tablets.
Syrup.
Injection.

Administration – enteral tubes
1st choice – Give by parenteral injection if possible.
2nd choice – Use the syrup.[41] Follow the directions in section 3.6.

Administration – swallowing difficulties
1st choice – Use the syrup.[41]
2nd choice – Give by parenteral injection if possible.

Zidovudine and lamivudine (Combivir®)

Presentation
Film-coated tablets.

Administration – enteral tubes / swallowing difficulties
1st choice – Change to the separate components (zidovudine and lamivudine).
2nd choice – Place Combivir® tablets in 50mL tepid (not hot) water and allow to dissolve. It has a bitter taste which can be disguised with juice for patients with swallowing difficulties.[132]

Zinc sulphate

Presentation
Effervescent tablets.
Oral solution (special).[582]
Injection.

Administration – enteral tubes
1st choice – Give by parenteral injection if appropriate.
2nd choice - Use the effervescent tablets.[94] Follow the directions in section 3.5.
3rd choice – Use the oral solution (if available). Follow the directions in section 3.6.

Administration – swallowing difficulties
1st choice – Use the effervescent tablets.[94]
2nd choice – Give by parenteral injection if appropriate.
3rd choice – Use the oral solution (if available).

Feed guidance
Enteral zinc sulphate has been reported as being incompatible with some enteral feeds, so ensure enteral feeding tubes are flushed well before and after each dose.[222]

Zolpidem

Presentation
Tablets.

Administration – enteral tubes / swallowing difficulties
The tablets can be crushed and mixed with water for administration.[104] Follow the directions in section 3.5.

Zonisamide

Presentation
Capsules.

Administration – enteral tubes
The capsules can be opened and their contents dispersed in water or apple juice for administration via enteral feeding tubes.[258,367] Follow the directions in section 3.7.

Administration – swallowing difficulties
The capsules can be opened and their contents sprinkled onto apple sauce or chocolate pudding, or mixed with water or apple juice.[367]

Clinical guidance
Due to the indication of this treatment, the medical team should consider the risks and benefits carefully before agreeing to administer the medication in an unlicensed manner.

Changing formulations / product manufacturer
The MHRA has issued guidance recommending that (where possible) patients on zonisamide (when used for seizures) are maintained on a specific manufacturer's product, due to variability in product characteristics which may lead to a loss of seizure control when switching between brands / manufacturers.[651] When managing patients with enteral tubes or swallowing difficulties it may not be possible to maintain the patient on their previous preparation due to the need to change to an appropriate formulation. However all product switches should be carried out with care and close monitoring, and where possible patients should be maintained from then onwards on a single manufacturer's product.

Zopiclone

Presentation
Film-coated tablets.
Oral solution (special).[580,582]

Administration – enteral tubes
The tablets are not suitable for crushing or dissolving, and should not be used, as the powder will thicken quickly and may block enteral feeding tubes. Contact Pharmacy for advice on alternatives.[62]

No information about giving the oral solution via enteral feeding tubes has been located.

Administration – swallowing difficulties
Use the oral solution (if available).

Zotepine

Presentation
Sugar-coated tablets (no longer available in the UK).

Clinical guidance
The tablets are small, sugar-coated and difficult to crush. Administration via enteral feeding tube is not recommended.[138]

Zuclopenthixol

Presentation
Film-coated tablets.
A suspension can be made by Pharmacy in some centres.
Depot injections.

Administration – enteral tubes
1st choice – The tablets can be crushed and mixed with water for administration.[104,105] They are film-coated and may block enteral feeding tubes; flush well after administration. Follow the directions in section 3.5.
2nd choice – A suspension can be made by Pharmacy in some centres.[138] Follow the directions in section 3.6.

Administration – swallowing difficulties
1st choice – A suspension can be made by Pharmacy in some centres.[138]
2nd choice – The tablets can be crushed and mixed with water for administration.[104,105] Follow the directions in section 3.5.

5. Appendix 1 – Extemporaneous formulations

5. Extemporaneous formulations

All products should be made to contemporary standards of extemporaneous preparation. It has been assumed that the products in the following section will be prepared under Section 10 of the Medicines Act 1968, and therefore the expiry dates have been limited to 28 days where appropriate. Units which have a Manufacturing Authorisation – Specials (MS) may be able to prepare these products with longer expiries after consideration of the original papers.

Mark Oldcorne
Quality Assurance Pharmacist

Acetazolamide 125mg/5mL suspension[451]

Acetazolamide 250mg tablets   10 tablets
Vehicle*   to 100mL

*Vehicle =   a 1:1 mixture of Ora-Plus® and Ora-Sweet®
                        or a 1:1 mixture of Ora-Plus® and Ora-Sweet® S.F.
                        or cherry syrup

Method
1, Grind the tablets to a fine powder in a mortar.
2, Add a small quantity of the vehicle, a little at a time, and mix thoroughly to a smooth paste.
3, Add more portions of the vehicle, stirring well, and transfer to a measure.
4, Rinse the mortar with the vehicle, adding the washings to the measure, and make up to volume.
5, Stir well and transfer to an oral medicine bottle.
6, Label the bottle appropriately.

Storage
The suspension can be stored below 25°C. Do not refrigerate.

Expiry
28 days.

Notes
Shake before use.
Protect from light.

Allopurinol 100mg/5mL suspension[451]

Allopurinol 300mg tablets   6 tablets
Vehicle*   to 90mL

*Vehicle =   a 1:1 mixture of Ora-Plus® and Ora-Sweet®
                  or a 1:1 mixture of Ora-Plus® and Ora-Sweet® S.F.
                  or cherry syrup

Method
1, Grind the tablets to a fine powder in a mortar.
2, Add a small quantity of the vehicle, a little at a time, and mix thoroughly to a smooth paste.
3, Add more portions of the vehicle, stirring well, and transfer to a measure.
4, Rinse the mortar with the vehicle, adding the washings to the measure, and make up to volume.
5, Stir well and transfer to an oral medicine bottle.
6, Label the bottle appropriately.

Storage
Store in a refrigerator.

Expiry
28 days.

Notes
Shake before use.
Protect from light.

Alprazolam 5mg/5mL suspension[452]

Alprazolam 2mg tablets*   60 tablets
Vehicle**   to 120mL

**Vehicle =   a 1:1 mixture of Ora-Plus® and Ora-Sweet®
                 or a 1:1 mixture of Ora-Plus® and Ora-Sweet® S.F.
                 or cherry syrup

Method
1, Grind the tablets to a fine powder in a mortar.
2, Add a small quantity of the vehicle, a little at a time, and mix thoroughly to a smooth paste.
3, Add more portions of the vehicle, stirring well, and transfer to a measure.
4, Rinse the mortar with the vehicle, adding the washings to the measure, and make up to volume.
5, Stir well and transfer to an oral medicine bottle.
6, Label the bottle appropriately.

Storage
Store in a refrigerator.

Expiry
28 days.

Notes
Shake before use.
Protect from light.

*Alprazolam tablets may not be available in the UK.

Amiodarone 25mg/5mL suspension[520]

This is the first of two amiodarone suspension formulae (see below).

Amiodarone 100mg tablets   5 tablets
Vehicle*   to 100mL

*Vehicle =   a 1:1 mixture of methylcellulose 1% and Syrup B.P.

Method
1, Grind the tablets to a fine powder in a mortar.
2, Add a small quantity of the vehicle, a little at a time, and mix thoroughly to a smooth paste.
3, Add more portions of the vehicle, stirring well, and transfer to a measure.
4, Rinse the mortar with the vehicle, adding the washings to the measure, and make up to volume.
5, Stir well and transfer to an oral medicine bottle.
6, Label the bottle appropriately.

Storage
Store in a refrigerator.

Expiry
28 days.

Notes
Shake before use.

Amiodarone 200mg/5mL suspension[512]

This is the second of two amiodarone suspension formulae (see above).

Amiodarone 200mg tablets	20 tablets
Methylcellulose suspending agent 2%	to 100mL

Method
1, Grind the tablets to a fine powder in a mortar.
2, Add the methylcellulose 2% suspending agent, a little at a time, and mix thoroughly to a smooth paste.
3, Add more of the methylcellulose 2% suspending agent, stir well, and transfer to a measure.
4, Make up to volume, stir well and transfer to an oral medicine bottle.
5, Label the bottle appropriately.

Storage
Store in a refrigerator.

Expiry
28 days.

Notes
Shake before use.

Amlodipine 5mg/5mL suspension[453]

Amlodipine 5mg tablets   20 tablets
Vehicle*   to 100mL

*Vehicle =   a 1:1 mixture of Ora-Plus® and Ora-Sweet®
                or a 1:1 mixture of 1% methylcellulose and Syrup
                B.P.

Method
1, Grind the tablets to a fine powder in a mortar.
2, Add a small volume of the vehicle, a little at a time, to form a suspension, and transfer to a measure.
3, Rinse the mortar with the vehicle, two or three times, adding the washings to the measure.
4, Make up to volume.
5, Stir well and transfer to an oral medicine bottle.
6, Label the bottle appropriately.

Storage
The suspension can be stored below 25°C, or in a refrigerator.

Expiry
28 days.

Notes
Shake before use.

Azathioprine 250mg/5mL suspension[451]

This is the first of two azathioprine suspension formulae (see below).

Azathioprine tablets	5g
Vehicle*	to 100mL

*Vehicle =   a 1:1 mixture of Ora-Plus® and Ora-Sweet®
or a 1:1 mixture of Ora-Plus® and Ora-Sweet® S.F.
or cherry syrup

Method
1, Grind the tablets to a fine powder in a mortar.
2, Add a small quantity of the vehicle, a little at a time, and mix thoroughly to a smooth paste.
3, Add more portions of the vehicle, stirring well, and transfer to a measure.
4, Rinse the mortar with the vehicle, adding the washings to the measure, and make up to volume.
5, Stir well and transfer to an oral medicine bottle.
6, Label the bottle appropriately.

Storage
The suspension can be stored below 25°C, or in a refrigerator.

Expiry
28 days.

Notes
Shake before use.
Protect from light.

Azathioprine 25mg/5mL suspension[512]

This is the second of two azathioprine suspension formulae (see above).

Azathioprine 25mg tablets	20 tablets
Xanthan suspending agent 1%	50mL
Distilled water	to 100mL

Method
1, Grind the tablets to a fine powder in a mortar.
2, Add a very small quantity of distilled water, a little at a time (approximately 5mL) and mix thoroughly to a smooth paste.
3, Add Xanthan suspending agent 1% a little at a time, stirring well, and transfer to a measure.
4, Rinse the mortar with distilled water, adding the washings to the measure, and make up to volume.
5, Stir well and transfer to an oral medicine bottle.
6, Label the bottle appropriately.

Storage
Store in a refrigerator.

Expiry
28 days.

Notes
Shake before use.
Azathioprine is a cytotoxic drug. Suspension preparation should be carried out using appropriate safety equipment according to local policy.

Bethanechol 25mg/5mL suspension[454]

Bethanechol tablets   500mg
Vehicle*   to 100mL

*Vehicle =   a 1:1 mixture of Ora-Plus® and Ora-Sweet®
                  or a 1:1 mixture of Ora-Plus® and Ora-Sweet® S.F.
                  or cherry syrup

Method
1, Grind the tablets to a fine powder in a mortar.
2, Add a small quantity of the vehicle, a little at a time, and mix thoroughly to a smooth paste.
3, Add more portions of the vehicle, stirring well, and transfer to a measure.
4, Rinse the mortar with the vehicle, adding the washings to the measure, and make up to volume.
5, Stir well and transfer to an oral medicine bottle.
6, Label the bottle appropriately.

Storage
Store in a refrigerator.

Expiry
7 days.

Notes
Shake before use.
Protect from light.

Calcium carbonate 250mg/5mL mixture[512]

Calcium carbonate powder	5g
Xanthan suspending agent 1%	50mL
Raspberry syrup	20mL
Distilled water	to 100mL

Method
1, Place the calcium carbonate powder in a mortar and mix to a smooth paste with a small amount of distilled water.
2, Add Xanthan suspending agent 1% a little at a time, stirring well, and transfer to a measure.
3, Rinse the mortar with Xanthan suspending agent 1%, adding the washings to the measure.
4, Add the raspberry syrup and make up to volume with distilled water.
5, Stir well and transfer to an oral medicine bottle.
6, Label the bottle appropriately.

Storage
The suspension can be stored below 25°C. Do not refrigerate.

Expiry
28 days.

Notes
Shake before use.

Captopril 5mg/5mL suspension[456]

Note – captopril suspensions are not very stable, and are susceptible to small variations in temperature, etc.

This is the first of two captopril suspension formulae (see below).

Captopril 50mg tablets	2 tablets
Sodium ascorbate injection	500mg
Distilled water	to 100mL

Method
1, Grind the tablets to a fine powder in a mortar.
2, Add a small amount of distilled water, a little at a time, to form a suspension, and transfer to a measure.
3, Rinse the mortar with distilled water, two or three times, adding the washings to the measure.
4, Add the sodium ascorbate injection.
5, Make up to volume with distilled water.
6, Stir well and transfer to an oral medicine bottle.
7, Label the bottle appropriately.

Storage
Store in a refrigerator.

Expiry
28 days.

Notes
Shake before use.

Captopril 3.75mg/5mL (nominal) suspension[457]

Note – captopril suspensions are not very stable, and are susceptible to small variations in temperature, etc.

This is the second of two captopril suspension formulae (see above).

Captopril tablets	100mg
Vehicle*	to 134mL

*Vehicle =   a 1:1 mixture of Ora-Plus® and Ora-Sweet®

Method
1, Grind the tablets to a fine powder in a mortar.
2, Add a small quantity of the vehicle, a little at a time, and mix thoroughly to a smooth paste.
3, Add more portions of the vehicle, stirring well, and transfer to a measure.
4, Rinse the mortar with the vehicle, adding the washings to the measure, and make up to volume.
5, Stir well and transfer to an oral medicine bottle.
6, Label the bottle appropriately.

Storage
Store in a refrigerator.

Expiry
7 days.

Notes
Shake before use.
Protect from light.

Clonazepam 0.5mg/5mL suspension[451]

Clonazepam 2mg tablets   6 tablets
Vehicle*   to 120mL

*Vehicle =   a 1:1 mixture of Ora-Plus® and Ora-Sweet®
                 or a 1:1 mixture of Ora-Plus® and Ora-Sweet® S.F.
                 or cherry syrup

Method
1, Grind the tablets to a fine powder in a mortar.
2, Add a small quantity of the vehicle, a little at a time, and mix thoroughly to a smooth paste.
3, Add more portions of the vehicle, stirring well, and transfer to a measure.
4, Rinse the mortar with the vehicle, adding the washings to the measure, and make up to volume.
5, Stir well and transfer to an oral medicine bottle.
6, Label the bottle appropriately.

Storage
Store in a refrigerator.

Expiry
28 days.

Notes
Shake before use.
Protect from light.

Clonidine 0.5mg/5mL suspension[459]

Clonidine 0.3mg tablets	30 tablets
Purified water	3mL
Syrup B.P.	to 90mL

Method
1, Grind the tablets to a fine powder in a mortar.
2, Add the water, a little at a time, and mix thoroughly to a smooth paste.
3, Add a small quantity (about 15mL) of Syrup B.P., stirring well, and transfer to a measure.
4, Rinse the mortar with about 15mL of Syrup B.P. twice, adding the washings to the measure, and make up to volume.
5, Stir well and transfer to an oral medicine bottle.
6, Label the bottle appropriately.

Storage
Store in a refrigerator.

Expiry
7 days.

Notes
Shake before use.

Clopidogrel 25mg/5mL suspension[537]

Clopidogrel 75mg tablets   6 tablets
Vehicle*   to 90mL

*Vehicle =   a 1:1 mixture of Ora-Plus® and Ora-Sweet®

Method
1, Grind the tablets to a fine powder in a mortar.
2, Add a small quantity of the vehicle, a little at a time, and mix thoroughly to a smooth paste.
3, Add more portions of the vehicle, stirring well, and transfer to a measure.
4, Rinse the mortar with the vehicle, adding the washings to the measure, and make up to volume.
5, Stir well and transfer to an oral medicine bottle.
6, Label the bottle appropriately.

Storage
Store in a refrigerator.

Expiry
28 days.

Notes
Shake before use.

Clozapine 50-250mg/5mL suspension[512]

Clozapine tablets	qs
Xanthan suspending agent 1%	50mL
Distilled water	to 100mL

Method
1, Grind the tablets to a fine powder in a mortar.
2, Add a very small quantity of distilled water, a little at a time (approximately 5mL) and mix thoroughly to a smooth paste.
3, Add Xanthan suspending agent 1% a little at a time, stirring well, and transfer to a measure.
4, Rinse the mortar with distilled water, adding the washings to the measure, and make up to volume.
5, Stir well and transfer to an oral medicine bottle.
6, Label the bottle appropriately.

Storage
Store in a refrigerator.

Expiry
28 days.

Notes
Shake before use.

Co-careldopa 31.25mg/5mL suspension[528]

Co-careldopa 100/25 tablets	5 tablets
Vehicle*	to 100mL

*Vehicle =   a 1:1 mixture of Ora-Plus® and Ora-Sweet®

Method
1, Grind the tablets to a fine powder in a mortar.
2, Add a small quantity of the vehicle, a little at a time, and mix thoroughly to a smooth paste.
3, Add more portions of the vehicle, stirring well, and transfer to a measure.
4, Rinse the mortar with the vehicle, adding the washings to the measure, and make up to volume.
5, Stir well and transfer to an oral medicine bottle.
6, Label the bottle appropriately.

Storage
Store in a refrigerator.

Expiry
28 days.

Notes
Shake before use.
Protect from light.

Codeine phosphate 15mg/5mL suspension[460,461]

Codeine phosphate powder 300mg
Ora-Sweet®   to 100mL

Method
1, Place the powder in a mortar.
2, Add a small quantity of Ora-Sweet®, a little at a time, and mix thoroughly to a smooth paste.
3, Add more portions of Ora-Sweet®, stirring well, and transfer to a measure.
4, Rinse the mortar with Ora-Sweet®, adding the washings to the measure, and make up to volume.
5, Stir well and transfer to an oral medicine bottle.
6, Label the bottle appropriately.

Storage
The suspension can be stored below 25°C. Do not refrigerate.

Expiry
28 days.

Notes
Shake before use.
Protect from light.

Cyclizine suspension[155,512]

Cyclizine tablets	qs
Methylcellulose 2%	50mL
Distilled water	to 100mL

Method
1, Grind the tablets to a fine powder in a mortar.
2, Add a small quantity of methylcellulose 2%, a little at a time, and mix thoroughly to a smooth paste.
3, Add more portions of methylcellulose 2%, stirring well, and transfer to a measure.
4, Rinse the mortar with methylcellulose 2%, adding the washings to the measure.
5, Make up to volume with distilled water.
6, Stir well and transfer to an oral medicine bottle.
7, Label the bottle appropriately.

Storage
The suspension can be stored below 25°C. Do not refrigerate.

Expiry
7 days.

Notes
Shake before use.

Dapsone 10mg/5mL suspension[527]

Dapsone 25mg tablets   8 tablets
Vehicle*   to 100mL

*Vehicle =   a 1:1 mixture of Ora-Plus® and Ora-Sweet®

Method
1, Grind the tablets to a fine powder in a mortar.
2, Add a small quantity of the vehicle, a little at a time, and mix thoroughly to a smooth paste.
3, Add more portions of the vehicle, stirring well, and transfer to a measure.
4, Rinse the mortar with the vehicle, adding the washings to the measure, and make up to volume.
5, Stir well and transfer to an oral medicine bottle.
6, Label the bottle appropriately.

Storage
The suspension can be stored below 25°C, or in a refrigerator.

Expiry
28 days.

Notes
Shake before use.
Protect from light.

Diazoxide 250mg/5mL suspension[512]

Diazoxide powder   5g
Xanthan suspending agent 1%   50mL
Distilled water   to 100mL

Method
1, Place the diazoxide powder in a mortar.
2, Add a very small quantity of distilled water, a little at a time and mix thoroughly to a smooth paste.
3, Add Xanthan suspending agent 1% a little at a time, stirring well, and transfer to a measure.
4, Rinse the mortar with distilled water, adding the washings to the measure, and make up to volume.
5, Stir well and transfer to an oral medicine bottle.
6, Label the bottle appropriately.

Storage
Store in a refrigerator.

Expiry
14 days.

Notes
Shake before use.
Protect from light.   If the suspension shows any sign of discolouration it should be discarded.

Diazoxide suspension should be prepared in a fume cupboard. Operators should wear a mask and gloves.

Diltiazem 60mg/5mL suspension[457]

Diltiazem 60mg tablets   20 tablets
Vehicle*   to 100mL

*Vehicle =   a 1:1 mixture of Ora-Plus® and Ora-Sweet®
                       or a 1:1 mixture of Ora-Plus® and Ora-Sweet® S.F.

Method
1, Grind the tablets to a fine powder in a mortar.
2, Add a small quantity of the vehicle, a little at a time, and mix thoroughly to a smooth paste.
3, Add more portions of the vehicle, stirring well, and transfer to a measure.
4, Rinse the mortar with the vehicle, adding the washings to the measure, and make up to volume.
5, Stir well and transfer to an oral medicine bottle.
6, Label the bottle appropriately.

Storage
Store in a refrigerator.

Expiry
28 days.

Notes
Shake before use.
Protect from light.

Dolasetron 50mg/5mL suspension[462]

Dolasetron 50mg tablets*   20 tablets
Vehicle**   to 100mL

**Vehicle =   a 1:1 mixture of Ora-Plus® and Ora-Sweet® S.F.

Method
1, Grind the tablets to a fine powder in a mortar.
2, Add a small quantity of the vehicle, a little at a time, and mix thoroughly to a smooth paste.
3, Add more portions of vehicle, stirring well, and transfer to a measure.
4, Rinse the mortar with vehicle, adding the washings to the measure, and make up to volume.
5, Stir well and transfer to an oral medicine bottle.
6, Label the bottle appropriately.

Storage
The suspension can be stored below 25°C, or in a refrigerator.

Expiry
28 days.

Notes
Shake before use.

*Dolasetron tablets are not available in the UK.

Enalapril 10mg/5mL suspension[512]

This is the first of two enalapril suspension formulae (see below).

Enalapril tablets	200mg
Ora-Plus®	50mL
Ora-Sweet® S.F.	to 100mL

Method
1, Grind the tablets to a fine powder in a mortar.
2, Add a small quantity of Ora-Plus® and mix thoroughly to a smooth paste.
3, Add more Ora-Plus® to form a suspension, and transfer to a measure.
4, Rinse the mortar with Ora-Plus® and Ora-Sweet® two or three times, adding the washings to the measure.
5, Make up to volume with Ora-Sweet®.
6, Stir well and transfer to an oral medicine bottle.
7, Label the bottle appropriately.

Storage
Store in a refrigerator.

Expiry
28 days.

Notes
Shake before use.

Enalapril 5mg/5mL suspension[452]

This is the second of two enalapril suspension formulae (see above).

Enalapril 20mg tablets	5 tablets
Vehicle*	to 100mL

*Vehicle =   a 1:1 mixture of Ora-Plus® and Ora-Sweet®
or a 1:1 mixture of Ora-Plus® and Ora-Sweet® S.F.
or cherry syrup

Method
1, Grind the tablets to a fine powder in a mortar.
2, Add a small quantity of the vehicle, a little at a time, and mix thoroughly to a smooth paste.
3, Add more portions of the vehicle, stirring well, and transfer to a measure.
4, Rinse the mortar with the vehicle, adding the washings to the measure, and make up to volume.
5, Stir well and transfer to an oral medicine bottle.
6, Label the bottle appropriately.

Storage
The suspension can be stored below 25°C, or in a refrigerator.

Expiry
28 days.

Notes
Shake before use.
Protect from light.

Etoposide 50mg/5mL solution[464]

Etoposide 20mg/mL injection (VePesid)   50mL
Sodium chloride 0.9% injection   to 100mL

Method
1, Measure the etoposide injection.
2, Make up to volume with sodium chloride injection.
3, Stir well and transfer to an oral medicine bottle.
4, Label the bottle appropriately.

Storage
The solution can be stored below 25°C. Do not refrigerate.

Expiry
22 days.

Notes
Do not refrigerate – risk of precipitation.
Caution – cytotoxic. Follow local guidelines for cytotoxic handling.

Famotidine 40mg/5mL suspension[465]

Famotidine 40mg tablets   20 tablets
Vehicle*   to 100mL

*Vehicle =   a 1:1 mixture of Ora-Plus® and Ora-Sweet®

Method
1, Grind the tablets to a fine powder in a mortar.
2, Add a small quantity of the vehicle, a little at a time, and mix thoroughly to a smooth paste.
3, Add further small portions of the vehicle, stirring well, and transfer to a measure.
4, Rinse the mortar with vehicle, adding the washings to the measure, and make up to volume.
5, Stir well and transfer to an oral medicine bottle.
6, Label the bottle appropriately.

Storage
The suspension can be stored below 25°C. Do not refrigerate.

Expiry
28 days.

Notes
Shake before use.

Flecainide 100mg/5mL suspension[457]

Flecainide 100mg tablets ..... 20 tablets
Vehicle* ..... to 100mL

*Vehicle = a 1:1 mixture of Ora-Plus® and Ora-Sweet®
or a 1:1 mixture of Ora-Plus® and Ora-Sweet® S.F.
or cherry syrup (cherry syrup concentrate diluted 1:4 with Syrup B.P.)

Method
1, Grind the tablets to a fine powder in a mortar.
2, Add a small quantity of the vehicle, a little at a time, and mix thoroughly to a smooth paste.
3, Add more portions of the vehicle, stirring well, and transfer to a measure.
4, Rinse the mortar with the vehicle, adding the washings to the measure, and make up to volume.
5, Stir well and transfer to an oral medicine bottle.
6, Label the bottle appropriately.

Storage
The suspension can be stored below 25°C, or in a refrigerator.

Expiry
28 days.

Notes
Shake before use.
Protect from light.

Flucytosine 50mg/5mL suspension[451]

This is the first of three flucytosine suspension formulae (see below).

Flucytosine tablets / capsules	1g
Vehicle*	to 100mL

*Vehicle =   a 1:1 mixture of Ora-Plus® and Ora-Sweet®
or a 1:1 mixture of Ora-Plus® and Ora-Sweet® S.F.
or cherry syrup

Method
1, Open the capsules and empty the contents into a mortar, or place the tablets in a mortar.
2, Grind the tablets / capsule contents to a fine powder.
3, Add a small quantity of the vehicle, a little at a time, and mix thoroughly to a smooth paste.
4, Add more portions of the vehicle, stirring well, and transfer to a measure.
5, Rinse the mortar with the vehicle, adding the washings to the measure, and make up to volume.
6, Stir well and transfer to an oral medicine bottle.
7, Label the bottle appropriately.

Storage
The suspension can be stored below 25°C, or in a refrigerator.

Expiry
28 days.

Notes
Shake before use.
Protect from light.

Flucytosine 50mg/5mL suspension[466]

This is the second of three flucytosine suspension formulae (see above and below).

Flucytosine tablets / capsules	1g
Distilled water	to 100mL

Method
1, Open the capsules and empty the contents into a mortar, or place the tablets in a mortar.
2, Grind the tablets / capsule contents to a fine powder.
3, Add a small quantity of distilled water and mix thoroughly to a smooth paste.
4, Add more distilled water to form a suspension, and transfer to a measure.
5, Rinse the mortar with distilled water two or three times, adding the washings to the measure.
6, Make up to volume.
7, Stir well and transfer to an oral medicine bottle.
8, Label the bottle appropriately.

Storage
Store in a refrigerator.

Expiry
7 days.

Notes
Shake before use.

Flucytosine 250mg/5mL suspension[467]

This is the third of three flucytosine suspension formulae (see above).

Flucytosine tablets / capsules	5g
Vehicle*	to 100mL

*Vehicle =   a 1:1 mixture of Ora-Plus® and Ora-Sweet® S.F.
             or a 1:1 mixture of Ora-Plus® and strawberry syrup

Method
1, Open the capsules and empty the contents into a mortar, or place the tablets in a mortar.
2, Grind the tablets / capsule contents to a fine powder.
3, Add a small quantity of the vehicle, a little at a time, and mix thoroughly to a smooth paste.
4, Add more portions of vehicle, stirring well, and transfer to a measure.
5, Rinse the mortar with vehicle, adding the washings to the measure, and make up to volume.
6, Stir well and transfer to an oral medicine bottle.
7, Label the bottle appropriately.

Storage
The suspension can be stored below 25°C, or in a refrigerator.

Expiry
28 days.

Notes
Shake before use.

Fludrocortisone suspension[512]

Fludrocortisone 100microgram tablets	qs
Xanthan suspending agent 1%	50mL
Distilled water	to 100mL

Method
1, Grind the tablets to a fine powder in a mortar.
2, Add a small quantity of Xanthan suspending agent 1%, and mix thoroughly to a smooth paste.
3, Add more Xanthan suspending agent 1% a little at a time, stirring well, and transfer to a measure.
4, Rinse the mortar with distilled water, adding the washings to the measure.
5, Make up to volume.
6, Stir well and transfer to an oral medicine bottle.
7, Label the bottle appropriately.

Storage
Store in a refrigerator.

Expiry
7 days.

Notes
Shake before use.

Ganciclovir 500mg/5mL suspension[468]

Ganciclovir 250mg capsules   40 capsules
Vehicle*   to 100mL

*Vehicle =   Ora-Sweet® or Ora-Sweet® S.F.

Method
1, Open the capsules and empty the contents into a mortar.
2, Grind the capsule contents to a fine powder.
3, Add a small quantity of the vehicle, a little at a time, and mix thoroughly to a smooth paste.
4, Add more portions of vehicle, stirring well, and transfer to a measure.
5, Rinse the mortar with vehicle two or three times, adding the washings to the measure.
6, Make up to volume.
7, Stir well and transfer to an oral medicine bottle.
8, Label the bottle appropriately.

Storage
The suspension can be stored below 25°C. Do not refrigerate.

Expiry
28 days.

Notes
Avoid inhalation of ganciclovir or contact with the skin.
Shake before use.

Granisetron 0.25mg/5mL suspension[469]

This is the first of two granisetron suspension formulae (see below).

Granisetron 1mg tablets   5 tablets
Vehicle*   to 100mL

*Vehicle =   a 1:1 mixture of Ora-Plus® and Ora-Sweet®

<u>Method</u>
1, Grind the tablets to a fine powder in a mortar.
2, Add a small quantity of the vehicle and mix thoroughly to a smooth paste.
3, Add more vehicle to form a suspension, and transfer to a measure.
4, Rinse the mortar with vehicle two or three times, adding the washings to the measure.
5, Make up to volume.
6, Stir well and transfer to an oral medicine bottle.
7, Label the bottle appropriately.

<u>Storage</u>
The suspension can be stored below 25°C, or in a refrigerator.

<u>Expiry</u>
28 days.

<u>Notes</u>
Shake before use.

Granisetron 1mg/5mL suspension[470]

This is the second of two granisetron suspension formulae (see above).

Granisetron 1mg tablets	20 tablets
Distilled water	50mL
Cherry syrup	to 100mL

Method
1, Grind the tablets to a fine powder in a mortar.
2, Add a small quantity of distilled water and mix thoroughly to a smooth paste.
3, Add more distilled water to form a suspension, and transfer to a measure.
4, Rinse the mortar with cherry syrup two or three times, adding the washings to the measure.
5, Make up to volume with cherry syrup.
6, Stir well and transfer to an oral medicine bottle.
7, Label the bottle appropriately.

Storage
The suspension can be stored below 25°C, or in a refrigerator.

Expiry
14 days.

Notes
Shake before use.

Hydroxycarbamide 500mg/5mL suspension[471]

Hydroxycarbamide 500mg capsules   20 capsules
Xanthan suspending agent 1%   50mL
Distilled water   to 100mL

Method
1, Open the capsules and empty the contents into a mortar.
2, Add a small quantity of Xanthan suspending agent 1% and mix thoroughly to a smooth paste.
3, Add more Xanthan suspending agent 1%, stirring well, and transfer to a measure.
4, Rinse the mortar with distilled water, adding the washings to the measure.
5, Make up to volume.
6, Stir well and transfer to an oral medicine bottle.
7, Label the bottle appropriately.

Storage
The suspension can be stored below 25°C. Do not refrigerate.

Expiry
7 days.

Notes
Follow local procedures for handling cytotoxic medications.
Shake before use.

Isoniazid 50mg/5mL suspension[461]

Isoniazid	1g
Citric acid monohydrate	250mg
Sodium citrate	1.2g
Concentrated anise water	1mL
Compound tartrazine solution	1mL
Glycerol	20mL
Chloroform water, double strength	40mL
Water for preparations	to 100mL

Method
1, Dissolve the isoniazid, the citric acid, and the sodium citrate in 30mL water.
2, Add the concentrated anise water, the compound tartrazine solution, the glycerol, and the double strength chloroform water, and mix thoroughly.
3, Make up to volume with water.
4, Stir well and transfer to an oral medicine bottle.
5, Label the bottle appropriately.

Storage
The suspension can be stored below 25°C. Do not refrigerate.

Expiry
28 days.

Notes
Store in filled containers.

Itraconazole 200mg/5mL suspension[472]

Itraconazole 100mg capsules	40 capsules
Ethanol 95%	7-8mL
Syrup B.P.	to 100mL

Method

1, Open the itraconazole capsules and empty the contents into a mortar.

2, Add the ethanol and leave to stand for 3-4 minutes to soften the beads.

3, Grind to a heavy paste. Continue to grind until a fine powder is achieved and the ethanol has evaporated.

4, Add a small quantity of Syrup B.P. and mix thoroughly to a smooth paste.

5, Add more syrup to form a suspension, and transfer to a measure.

6, Rinse the mortar with Syrup B.P. two or three times, adding the washings to the measure.

7, Make up to volume with Syrup B.P.

8, Stir well and transfer to an oral medicine bottle.

9, Label the bottle appropriately.

Storage
Store in a refrigerator.

Expiry
14 days.

Notes
Shake before use.

Ketoconazole 100mg/5mL suspension[473]

Ketoconazole 200mg tablets   10 tablets
Vehicle*   to 100mL

*Vehicle =   a 1:1 mixture of Ora-Plus® and Ora-Sweet®
                  or a 1:1 mixture of Ora-Plus® and Ora-Sweet® S.F.
                  or cherry syrup

Method
1, Grind the tablets to a fine powder in a mortar.
2, Add a small quantity of the vehicle, a little at a time, and mix thoroughly to a smooth paste.
3, Add more portions of the vehicle, stirring well, and transfer to a measure.
4, Rinse the mortar with the vehicle, adding the washings to the measure, and make up to volume.
5, Stir well and transfer to an oral medicine bottle.
6, Label the bottle appropriately.

Storage
Store in a refrigerator.

Expiry
28 days.

Notes
Shake before use.
Protect from light.

Labetalol 200mg/5mL suspension[206]

Labetalol 200mg tablets   20 tablets
Vehicle*   to 100mL

*Vehicle =   a 1:1 mixture of Ora-Plus® and Ora-Sweet®
                  or a 1:1 mixture of Ora-Plus® and Ora-Sweet® S.F.
                  or cherry syrup (cherry syrup concentrate diluted 1:4
                  with Syrup B.P.)

Method
1, Grind the tablets to a fine powder in a mortar.
2, Add a small quantity of the vehicle, a little at a time, and mix thoroughly to a smooth paste.
3, Add more portions of the vehicle, stirring well, and transfer to a measure.
4, Rinse the mortar with the vehicle, adding the washings to the measure, and make up to volume.
5, Stir well and transfer to an oral medicine bottle.
6, Label the bottle appropriately.

Storage
The suspension can be stored below 25°C, or in a refrigerator.

Expiry
28 days.

Notes
Shake before use.
Protect from light.

Lamotrigine 5mg/5mL suspension[527]

Lamotrigine tablets   100mg
Vehicle*   to 100mL

*Vehicle =   a 1:1 mixture of Ora-Plus® and Ora-Sweet®
          or a 1:1 mixture of Ora-Plus® and Ora-Sweet® S.F.

Method
1, Grind the tablets to a fine powder in a mortar.
2, Add a small quantity of the vehicle, a little at a time, and mix thoroughly to a smooth paste.
3, Add more portions of the vehicle, stirring well, and transfer to a measure.
4, Rinse the mortar with the vehicle, adding the washings to the measure, and make up to volume.
5, Stir well and transfer to an oral medicine bottle.
6, Label the bottle appropriately.

Storage
The suspension can be stored below 25°C, or in a refrigerator.

Expiry
28 days.

Notes
Shake before use.
Protect from light.

Lansoprazole 3.3mg/mL suspension[202]

Lansoprazole 30mg capsules   11 capsules
Sodium bicarbonate 8.4% solution   to 100mL

Method
1, Open the capsules and empty the capsule contents into a measure.
2, Add sodium bicarbonate 8.4%, and make up to volume.
3, Stir well and transfer to an oral medicine bottle.
4, Label the bottle appropriately.

Storage
Store in a refrigerator.

Expiry
14 days.

Notes
Shake before use.

Levofloxacin 250mg/5mL suspension[475]

Levofloxacin 500mg tablets   10 tablets
Vehicle*   to 100mL

*Vehicle = a 1:1 mixture of Ora-Plus® and strawberry syrup

Method
1, Grind the tablets to a fine powder in a mortar.
2, Add a small quantity of the vehicle, a little at a time, and mix thoroughly to a smooth paste.
3, Add more portions of vehicle, stirring well, and transfer to a measure.
4, Rinse the mortar with vehicle, adding the washings to the measure, and make up to volume.
5, Stir well and transfer to an oral medicine bottle.
6, Label the bottle appropriately.

Storage
The suspension can be stored below 25°C, or in a refrigerator.

Expiry
28 days.

Notes
Shake before use.

Levothyroxine sodium suspension[512,514]

Levothyroxine sodium tablets	qs
Xanthan suspending agent 1%	50mL
Distilled water	to 100mL

<u>Method</u>
1, Grind the tablets to a fine powder in a mortar.
2, Add a very small quantity of distilled water (approximately 5mL) and mix thoroughly to a smooth paste.
3, Add Xanthan suspending agent 1% a little at a time, stirring well, and transfer to a measure.
4, Rinse the mortar with distilled water, adding the washings to the measure, and make up to volume.
5, Stir well and transfer to an oral medicine bottle.
6, Label the bottle appropriately.

<u>Storage</u>
The suspension can be stored below 25°C. Do not refrigerate.

<u>Expiry</u>
7 days.

<u>Notes</u>
Shake before use.

Lisinopril 5mg/5mL suspension[515]

This is the first of two lisinopril suspension formulae (see below).

Lisinopril 10mg tablets	10 tablets
Methylcellulose 1% with parabens	7.7mL
Syrup B.P.	to 100mL

Method
1, Grind the tablets to a fine powder in a mortar.
2, Add a small quantity of methylcellulose 1%, a little at a time, and mix thoroughly to a smooth paste.
3, Add the rest of the methylcellulose, followed by portions of Syrup B.P., stirring well, and transfer to a measure.
4, Rinse the mortar with the Syrup B.P., adding the washings to the measure.
5, Make up to volume.
6, Stir well and transfer to an oral medicine bottle.
7, Label the bottle appropriately.

Storage
The suspension can be stored below 25°C, or in a refrigerator.

Expiry
28 days.

Notes
Shake before use.
Protect from light.

Lisinopril 5mg/5mL suspension[515]

This is the second of two lisinopril suspension formulae (see above).

Lisinopril 10mg tablets   10 tablets
Vehicle*   to 100mL

*Vehicle =   a 1:1 mixture of Ora-Plus® and Ora-Sweet®

<u>Method</u>
1, Grind the tablets to a fine powder in a mortar.
2, Add a small quantity of the vehicle, a little at a time, and mix thoroughly to a smooth paste.
3, Add more portions of the vehicle, stirring well, and transfer to a measure.
4, Rinse the mortar with the vehicle, adding the washings to the measure, and make up to volume.
5, Stir well and transfer to an oral medicine bottle.
6, Label the bottle appropriately.

<u>Storage</u>
The suspension can be stored below 25°C, or in a refrigerator.

<u>Expiry</u>
28 days.

<u>Notes</u>
Shake before use.
Protect from light.

Mercaptopurine 250mg/5mL suspension[479]

Mercaptopurine 50mg tablets	100 tablets
Ascorbic acid	100mg
Sterile water for irrigation	17mL
Syrup B.P.	33mL
Cherry syrup	to 100mL

Method
1, Place the tablets and ascorbic acid in a mortar and add the sterile water to wet the tablets.
2, Grind the tablets to a smooth paste.
3, Add the Syrup B.P., a little at a time, and mix thoroughly to a smooth paste.
4, Transfer to a measure.
5, Rinse the mortar with cherry syrup, adding the washings to the measure, and make up to volume.
6, Stir well and transfer to an oral medicine bottle.
7, Label the bottle appropriately.

Storage
The suspension can be stored below 25°C. Do not refrigerate.

Expiry
28 days.

Notes
Shake before use.
Mercaptopurine is a cytotoxic drug. Suspension preparation should be carried out using appropriate safety equipment according to local policy.

Methyldopa suspension[512]

Methyldopa tablets	qs
Xanthan suspending agent 1%	50mL
Distilled water	to 100mL

Method
1, Grind the tablets to a fine powder in a mortar.
2, Add a small quantity of Xanthan suspending agent 1% and mix thoroughly to a smooth paste.
3, Add more Xanthan suspending agent 1% a little at a time, stirring well, and transfer to a measure.
4, Rinse the mortar with distilled water, adding the washings to the measure.
5, Make up to volume.
6, Stir well and transfer to an oral medicine bottle.
7, Label the bottle appropriately.

Storage
The suspension can be stored below 25°C. Do not refrigerate.

Expiry
14 days.

Notes
Shake before use.

Metolazone 5mg/5mL suspension[473]

Metolazone tablets	100mg
Vehicle*	to 100mL

*Vehicle =   a 1:1 mixture of Ora-Plus® and Ora-Sweet®
             or a 1:1 mixture of Ora-Plus® and Ora-Sweet® S.F.
             or cherry syrup

Method
1, Grind the tablets to a fine powder in a mortar.
2, Add a small quantity of the vehicle, a little at a time, and mix thoroughly to a smooth paste.
3, Add more portions of the vehicle, stirring well, and transfer to a measure.
4, Rinse the mortar with the vehicle, adding the washings to the measure, and make up to volume.
5, Stir well and transfer to an oral medicine bottle.
6, Label the bottle appropriately.

Storage
The suspension can be stored below 25°C, or in a refrigerator.

Expiry
28 days.

Notes
Shake before use.
Protect from light.

Metoprolol 50mg/5mL suspension[206]

Metoprolol 100mg tablets   10 tablets
Vehicle*   to 100mL

*Vehicle =   a 1:1 mixture of Ora-Plus® and Ora-Sweet®
                or a 1:1 mixture of Ora-Plus® and Ora-Sweet® S.F.
                or cherry syrup (cherry syrup concentrate diluted 1:4
                with Syrup B.P.)

Method
1, Grind the tablets to a fine powder in a mortar.
2, Add a small quantity of the vehicle, a little at a time, and mix thoroughly to a smooth paste.
3, Add more portions of the vehicle, stirring well, and transfer to a measure.
4, Rinse the mortar with the vehicle, adding the washings to the measure, and make up to volume.
5, Stir well and transfer to an oral medicine bottle.
6, Label the bottle appropriately.

Storage
The suspension can be stored below 25°C, or in a refrigerator.

Expiry
28 days.

Notes
Shake before use.
Protect from light.

Mexiletine 50mg/5mL suspension[480]

Mexiletine 150mg capsules   6 capsules
Distilled water   to 90mL

Method
1, Open the capsules and empty the contents into a mortar.
2, Grind the capsule contents to a fine powder.
3, Add a small quantity of vehicle and mix thoroughly to a smooth paste.
4, Add more vehicle to form a suspension, and transfer to a measure.
5, Rinse the mortar with vehicle two or three times, adding the washings to the measure.
6, Make up to volume.
7, Stir well and transfer to an oral medicine bottle.
8, Label the bottle appropriately.

Storage
The suspension can be stored below 25°C, or in a refrigerator.

Expiry
28 days.

Notes
Shake before use.

Midazolam 5mg/5mL suspension[512]

Midazolam 10mg/2mL injection	20mL
Raspberry Syrup B.P.	to 100mL

Method
1, Draw up 22mL of midazolam injection into a syringe (include overage to prime filter).
2, Attach a 0.2 micron filter to the syringe.
3, Prime the filter with midazolam, and continue to expel until only 20mL is left in the syringe.
4, Filter the midazolam into a measure, and make up to volume with raspberry syrup.
5, Stir well and transfer to an oral medicine bottle.
6, Label the bottle appropriately.

Storage
Store in a refrigerator.

Expiry
28 days.

Notes
Shake before use.

Moxifloxacin 100mg/5mL suspension[539]

Moxifloxacin 400mg tablets	5 tablets
Vehicle*	to 100mL

*Vehicle =   a 1:1 mixture of Ora-Plus® and Ora-Sweet®
                or a 1:1 mixture of Ora-Plus® and Ora-Sweet® S.F.

Method
1, Grind the tablets to a fine powder in a mortar.
2, Add a small quantity of the vehicle, a little at a time, and mix thoroughly to a smooth paste.
3, Add more portions of the vehicle, stirring well, and transfer to a measure.
4, Rinse the mortar with the vehicle, adding the washings to the measure, and make up to volume.
5, Stir well and transfer to an oral medicine bottle.
6, Label the bottle appropriately.

Storage
The suspension can be stored below 25°C. Do not refrigerate.

Expiry
28 days.

Notes
Shake before use.

Mycophenolate mofetil 500mg/5mL suspension[481]

This is the first of two mycophenolate suspension formulae (see below).

Mycophenolate mofetil 250mg capsules	40 capsules
Sterile water for irrigation	to wet the powder
Cherry syrup	to 100mL

<u>Method</u>
1, Open the capsules and empty the contents into a mortar.
2, Add sufficient sterile water for irrigation to wet the powder, and mix to a smooth paste.
3, Add a small amount of cherry syrup to form a suspension, and transfer to a measure.
4, Rinse the mortar with cherry syrup two or three times, adding the washings to the measure.
5, Make up to volume with cherry syrup.
6, Stir well and transfer to an oral medicine bottle.
7, Label the bottle appropriately.

<u>Storage</u>
The suspension can be stored below 25°C, or in a refrigerator.

<u>Expiry</u>
28 days.

<u>Notes</u>
Shake before use.
Use cytotoxic drug precautions.

Mycophenolate mofetil 500mg/5mL suspension[482]

This is the second of two mycophenolate suspension formulae (see above).

Vehicle
Ora-Plus®   100mL
Cherry flavouring   0.4mL
Aspartame   300mg

Mycophenolate suspension
Mycophenolate mofetil 250mg capsules   40 capsules
Vehicle (see above)   to 100mL

Method
1, Prepare the vehicle by adding the cherry flavouring and aspartame to the Ora-Plus®. Set aside.
2, Open the mycophenolate capsules and empty the contents into a mortar.
3, Add a small quantity of the vehicle, and mix thoroughly to a smooth paste.
4, Add more vehicle to form a suspension, and transfer to a measure.
5, Rinse the mortar with vehicle two or three times, adding the washings to the measure.
6, Make up to volume.
7, Stir well and transfer to an oral medicine bottle.
8, Label the bottle appropriately.

Storage
Store in a refrigerator.

Expiry
28 days.

Notes
Shake before use.
Use cytotoxic drug precautions.

Naratriptan 2.5mg/5mL suspension[529]

Naratriptan 2.5mg tablets   20 tablets
Vehicle*   to 100mL

*Vehicle =   a 1:1 mixture of Ora-Plus® and Ora-Sweet®
             or a 1:1 mixture of Ora-Plus® and Ora-Sweet® S.F.

Method
1, Grind the tablets to a fine powder in a mortar.
2, Add a small quantity of the vehicle, a little at a time, and mix thoroughly to a smooth paste.
3, Add more portions of the vehicle, stirring well, and transfer to a measure.
4, Rinse the mortar with the vehicle, adding the washings to the measure, and make up to volume.
5, Stir well and transfer to an oral medicine bottle.
6, Label the bottle appropriately.

Storage
Store in a refrigerator.

Expiry
28 days.

Notes
Shake before use.
Protect from light.

Nifedipine 50mg/5mL solution[483]

This is the first of two nifedipine suspension formulae (see below).

Polyethylene glycol 400	47.5mL
Nifedipine powder	800mg
Glycerin	31.75mL
Peppermint oil	0.8mL

Method
1, Add polyethylene glycol 400 to a Teflon beaker containing a Teflon-coated stir bar.
2, Add nifedipine powder to the beaker while stirring.
3, Add glycerin to the beaker while stirring.
4, Heat the cloudy yellow liquid to approximately 95°C while stirring and maintain that temperature until the nifedipine dissolves.
5, Filter the hot clear solution through a 1.2micron glass microfibre filter and stir until the liquid returns to room temperature.
6, Add peppermint oil.
7, Stir well and transfer to a glass oral medicine bottle.
8, Label the bottle appropriately.

Storage
The solution can be stored below 25°C. Do not refrigerate.

Expiry
14 days.

Notes
Protect from light.

Nifedipine 20mg/5mL suspension[527]

This is the second of two nifedipine suspension formulae (see above).

Nifedipine capsules	400mg
Vehicle*	to 100mL

*Vehicle =   a 1:1 mixture of Ora-Plus® and Ora-Sweet®
               or a 1:1 mixture of 1% methylcellulose and Syrup
               B.P.

Method
1, Remove the nifedipine from the capsules by puncturing the top of the capsule with a needle to make a vent, and drawing the solution out using another needle and a syringe. Transfer to a measure.
2, Add the vehicle, a little at a time, and mix thoroughly.
3, Make up to volume with the vehicle.
4, Stir well and transfer to an oral medicine bottle.
5, Label the bottle appropriately.

Storage
The suspension can be stored below 25°C, or in a refrigerator.

Expiry
28 days.

Notes
Check the liquid volume of the capsule prior to preparing the suspension in order to ensure that all of the liquid is obtained with the needle and syringe.
Shake before use.
Protect from light.

Norfloxacin 100mg/5mL suspension[484]

Strawberry syrup
Syrup B.P.   48mL
Strawberry fountain syrup   9mL

Norfloxacin suspension
Norfloxacin 400mg tablets   5 tablets
Vehicle*   to 100mL

*Vehicle =   a 1:1 mixture of Ora-Plus® and strawberry syrup
              (see above)

Method
1, Prepare the strawberry syrup by mixing the Syrup B.P. in small portions into the strawberry fountain syrup.
2, Use the strawberry syrup to prepare the vehicle.
3, Grind the tablets to a fine powder in a mortar.
4, Add a small quantity of the vehicle, a little at a time, and mix thoroughly to a smooth paste.
5, Add more portions of vehicle, stirring well, and transfer to a measure.
6, Rinse the mortar with vehicle, adding the washings to the measure, and make up to volume.
7, Stir well and transfer to an oral medicine bottle.
8, Label the bottle appropriately.

Storage
The suspension can be stored below 25°C. Do not refrigerate.

Expiry
28 days.

Notes
Shake before use.

Omeprazole 10mg/5mL suspension[215]

Omeprazole 20mg capsules
Sodium bicarbonate 8.4% injection

5 capsules
50mL

Method
1, Remove the plunger from a 60mL Luer-Lok syringe, and attach a needle.
2, Empty the contents of the omeprazole capsules into the syringe, and replace the plunger.
3, Draw up 50mL of sodium bicarbonate injection.
4, Remove the needle from the syringe, and replace with a fluid-dispensing connector.
5, Attach a second 60mL syringe to the other end of the fluid-dispensing connector.
6, Gently transfer the syringe contents back and forth until the granules completely dissolve.
7, Transfer the solution to one of the syringes, disconnect the empty syringe, and replace the fluid-dispensing connector with a needle.
8, Transfer to a glass oral medicine bottle.
9, Label the bottle appropriately.

Storage
Store in a refrigerator.

Expiry
14 days.

Oseltamivir 50mg/5mL suspension[370]

This is the first of two oseltamivir suspension formulae (see below).

Oseltamivir 75mg capsules	4 capsules
Vehicle*	to 30mL

*Vehicle =   water containing 0.1% w/v sodium benzoate

Method
1, Open the capsules and empty the capsule contents into a mortar.
2, Grind the capsule contents to a fine powder.
3, Add a small quantity of the vehicle, a little at a time, and mix thoroughly to a smooth paste.
4, Add more portions of vehicle, stirring well, and transfer to a measure.
5, Rinse the mortar with vehicle, adding the washings to the measure, and make up to volume.
6, Stir well and transfer to an oral medicine bottle. Shake well to completely dissolve the active drug.
7, Label the bottle appropriately.

Storage
The suspension can be stored below 25°C, or in a refrigerator.

Expiry
21 days.

Notes
Shake gently before use.
There may be some undissolved residue visible, but this is comprised of inert ingredients which are insoluble. The active drug readily dissolves in the vehicle.

See the Summary of Product Characteristics for Tamiflu® for further information on expiry.

Oseltamivir 75mg/5mL suspension[370]

This is the second of two oseltamivir suspension formulae (see above).

Oseltamivir 75mg capsules	20 capsules
Vehicle*	to 100mL

*Vehicle =   water containing 0.1% w/v sodium benzoate

Method
1, Open the capsules and empty the capsule contents into a mortar.
2, Grind the capsule contents to a fine powder.
3, Add a small quantity of the vehicle, a little at a time, and mix thoroughly to a smooth paste.
4, Add more portions of vehicle, stirring well, and transfer to a measure.
5, Rinse the mortar with vehicle, adding the washings to the measure, and make up to volume.
6, Stir well and transfer to an oral medicine bottle. Shake well to completely dissolve the active drug.
7, Label the bottle appropriately.

Storage
The suspension can be stored below 25°C, or in a refrigerator.

Expiry
21 days.

Notes
Shake gently before use.
There may be some undissolved residue visible, but this is comprised of inert ingredients which are insoluble. The active drug readily dissolves in the vehicle.

See the Summary of Product Characteristics for Tamiflu® for further information on expiry.

Pantoprazole 10mg/5mL suspension[522]

Pantoprazole 40mg tablets   5 tablets
Sodium bicarbonate 4.2% solution   to 100mL

Method
1, Grind the tablets to a fine powder in a mortar.
2, Transfer the powder to glass measure.
3, Rinse the mortar with sodium bicarbonate solution, adding the washings to the measure.
4, Make up to volume with sodium bicarbonate solution.
5, Stir well and transfer to an oral medicine bottle.
6, Label the bottle appropriately.

Storage
Store in a refrigerator.

Expiry
14 days.

Notes
Shake before use.

Pentoxifylline 100mg/5mL suspension[487]

Pentoxifylline 400mg tablets   5 tablets
Distilled water   to 100mL

Method
1, Grind the tablets to a fine powder in a mortar.
2, Add a small quantity of water, a little at a time, and mix thoroughly to a smooth paste.
3, Add more portions of water, stirring well, and transfer to a measure.
4, Rinse the mortar with water, adding the washings to the measure, and make up to volume.
5, Stir well and transfer to an oral medicine bottle.
6, Label the bottle appropriately.

Storage
The suspension can be stored below 25°C, or in a refrigerator.

Expiry
28 days.

Notes
Shake before use.

Phenobarbital 50mg/5mL suspension[488]

Phenobarbital 60mg tablets   15 tablets
Vehicle*   to 90mL

*Vehicle =   a 1:1 mixture of Ora-Plus® and Ora-Sweet®
                       or a 1:1 mixture of Ora-Plus® and Ora-Sweet® S.F.

Method
1, Grind the tablets to a fine powder in a mortar.
2, Add a small quantity of the vehicle, a little at a time, and mix thoroughly to a smooth paste.
3, Add more portions of vehicle, stirring well, and transfer to a measure.
4, Rinse the mortar with vehicle, adding the washings to the measure, and make up to volume.
5, Stir well and transfer to an oral medicine bottle.
6, Label the bottle appropriately.

Storage
The suspension can be stored below 25°C. Do not refrigerate.

Expiry
28 days.

Notes
Shake before use.

Phenoxybenzamine 10mg/5mL suspension[489]

Vehicle.

Citric acid	150mg
Propylene glycol	1mL
Distilled water	to 100mL

Suspension.

Phenoxybenzamine 10mg capsules	20 capsules
Vehicle	to 100mL

Method
1, Prepare the vehicle by dissolving the citric acid in a minimal volume of distilled water in a measure.
2, Add the propylene glycol, and mix well.
3, Make up to volume with distilled water, and set aside.
4, Open the capsules and empty their contents into a mortar.
5, Add a small quantity of the vehicle, a little at a time, and mix thoroughly to a smooth paste.
6, Add more portions of the vehicle, stirring well, and transfer to a measure.
7, Rinse the mortar with the vehicle, adding the washings to the measure, and make up to volume.
8, Stir well and transfer to an oral medicine bottle.
9, Label the bottle appropriately.

Storage
Store in a refrigerator.

Expiry
3 days.

Notes
Shake before use.

Procainamide 250mg/5mL suspension[473]

This is the first of two procainamide suspension formulae (see below).

Procainamide 250mg capsules	20 capsules
Vehicle*	to 100mL

*Vehicle = a 1:1 mixture of Ora-Plus® and Ora-Sweet®
or a 1:1 mixture of Ora-Plus® and Ora-Sweet® S.F.
or cherry syrup

Method
1, Open the capsules and empty the contents into a mortar.
2, Grind the capsule contents to a fine powder.
3, Add a small quantity of the vehicle, a little at a time, and mix thoroughly to a smooth paste.
4, Add more portions of the vehicle, stirring well, and transfer to a measure.
5, Rinse the mortar with the vehicle, adding the washings to the measure, and make up to volume.
6, Stir well and transfer to an oral medicine bottle.
7, Label the bottle appropriately.

Storage
Store in a refrigerator.

Expiry
28 days.

Notes
Shake before use.
Protect from light.

Procainamide 250mg/5mL suspension[209]

This is the second of two procainamide suspension formulae (see above).

Procainamide hydrochloride 500mg capsules	10 capsules
Distilled water	5mL
Cherry syrup	to 100mL

Method
1, Open the capsules and empty the contents into a mortar.
2, Add the distilled water, and mix thoroughly to a smooth paste.
3, Add about 20mL of the cherry syrup, stirring well, and transfer to a measure.
4, Rinse the mortar with cherry syrup, adding the washings to the measure, and make up to volume.
5, Stir well and transfer to an oral medicine bottle.
6, Label the bottle appropriately.

Storage
Store in a refrigerator.

Expiry
28 days.

Notes
Shake before use.

Propylthiouracil 25mg/5mL suspension[490]

Propylthiouracil 50mg tablets	10 tablets
Vehicle*	to 100mL

*Vehicle =   a 1:1 mixture of Ora-Plus® and Ora-Sweet®
or a 1:1 mixture of 1% methylcellulose and Syrup
B.P.

Method
1, Grind the tablets to a fine powder in a mortar.
2, Add a small quantity of the vehicle, a little at a time, and mix thoroughly to a smooth paste.
3, Add more portions of vehicle, stirring well, and transfer to a measure.
4, Rinse the mortar with vehicle, adding the washings to the measure, and make up to volume.
5, Stir well and transfer to an oral medicine bottle.
6, Label the bottle appropriately.

Storage
The suspension can be stored below 25°C, or in a refrigerator.

Expiry
28 days.

Notes
Shake before use.

Pyrazinamide 50mg/5mL suspension[454]

This is the first of three pyrazinamide suspension formulae (see below).

Pyrazinamide 500mg tablets   2 tablets
Vehicle*   to 100mL

*Vehicle =   a 1:1 mixture of Ora-Plus® and Ora-Sweet®
              or a 1:1 mixture of Ora-Plus® and Ora-Sweet® S.F.
              or cherry syrup

Method
1, Grind the tablets to a fine powder in a mortar.
2, Add a small quantity of the vehicle, a little at a time, and mix thoroughly to a smooth paste.
3, Add more portions of the vehicle, stirring well, and transfer to a measure.
4, Rinse the mortar with the vehicle, adding the washings to the measure, and make up to volume.
5, Stir well and transfer to an oral medicine bottle.
6, Label the bottle appropriately.

Storage
The suspension can be stored below 25°C, or in a refrigerator.

Expiry
28 days.

Notes
Shake before use.
Protect from light.

Pyrazinamide 500mg/5mL suspension[491]

This is the second of three pyrazinamide suspension formulae (see above and below).

Pyrazinamide 500mg tablets   20 tablets
Syrup B.P.   to 100mL

Method
1, Grind the tablets to a fine powder in a mortar.
2, Add a small quantity of Syrup B.P., a little at a time, and mix thoroughly to a smooth paste.
3, Add more portions of syrup, stirring well, and transfer to a measure.
4, Rinse the mortar with syrup, adding the washings to the measure, and make up to volume.
5, Stir well and transfer to an oral medicine bottle.
6, Label the bottle appropriately.

Storage
Store in a refrigerator.

Expiry
14 days.

Notes
Shake before use.
Protect from light.

Pyrazinamide 500mg/5mL suspension[491]

This is the third of three pyrazinamide suspension formulae (see above).

Pyrazinamide 500mg tablets   20 tablets
Vehicle*   to 100mL

*Vehicle =   a 1:1 mixture of methylcellulose 1% and Syrup B.P.

Method
1, Grind the tablets to a fine powder in a mortar.
2, Add a small quantity of the vehicle, a little at a time, and mix thoroughly to a smooth paste.
3, Add more portions of the vehicle, stirring well, and transfer to a measure.
4, Rinse the mortar with vehicle, adding the washings to the measure, and make up to volume.
5, Stir well and transfer to an oral medicine bottle.
6, Label the bottle appropriately.

Storage
The suspension can be stored below 25°C. Do not refrigerate.

Expiry
14 days.

Notes
Shake before use.

Pyrimethamine 10mg/5mL suspension[492]

Pyrimethamine 25mg tablets   8 tablets
Vehicle*   to 100mL

*Vehicle =   a 1:1 mixture of Syrup B.P. and 1% methylcellulose

Method
1, Grind the tablets to a fine powder in a mortar.
2, Add a small quantity of the vehicle, a little at a time, and mix thoroughly to a smooth paste.
3, Add more portions of vehicle, stirring well, and transfer to a measure.
4, Rinse the mortar with vehicle, adding the washings to the measure, and make up to volume.
5, Stir well and transfer to an oral medicine bottle.
6, Label the bottle appropriately.

Storage
The suspension can be stored below 25°C, or in a refrigerator.

Expiry
28 days.

Notes
Shake before use.

Rifabutin 100mg/5mL suspension[493]

Rifabutin 150mg capsules   12 capsules
Vehicle*   to 90mL

*Vehicle =   a 1:1 mixture of Ora-Plus® and Ora-Sweet®

Method
1, Open the capsules and empty the contents into a mortar.
2, Add a small quantity of the vehicle, a little at a time, and mix thoroughly to a smooth paste.
3, Add more portions of the vehicle, stirring well, and transfer to a measure.
4, Rinse the mortar with vehicle, adding the washings to the measure, and make up to volume.
5, Stir well and transfer to an oral medicine bottle.
6, Label the bottle appropriately.

Storage
The suspension can be stored below 25°C, or in a refrigerator.

Expiry
28 days.

Notes
Shake before use.

Rifampicin 125mg/5mL suspension[454]

Rifampicin 300mg capsules	10 capsules
Vehicle*	to 120mL

*Vehicle =   a 1:1 mixture of Ora-Plus® and Ora-Sweet®
             or a 1:1 mixture of Ora-Plus® and Ora-Sweet® S.F.

Method
1, Open the capsules and empty the contents into a mortar.
2, Add a small quantity of the vehicle, a little at a time, and mix thoroughly to a smooth paste.
3, Add more portions of the vehicle, stirring well, and transfer to a measure.
4, Rinse the mortar with the vehicle, adding the washings to the measure, and make up to volume.
5, Stir well and transfer to an oral medicine bottle.
6, Label the bottle appropriately.

Storage
The suspension can be stored below 25°C, or in a refrigerator.

Expiry
7 days.

Notes
Shake before use.
Protect from light.

Rifaximin 100mg/5mL suspension[530]

Rifaximin 200mg tablets   10 tablets
Vehicle*   to 100mL

*Vehicle =   a 1:1 mixture of Ora-Plus® and Ora-Sweet®
                 or a 1:1 mixture of Ora-Plus® and Ora-Sweet® S.F.

Method
1, Grind the tablets to a fine powder in a mortar.
2, Add a small quantity of the vehicle, a little at a time, and mix thoroughly to a smooth paste.
3, Add more portions of the vehicle, stirring well, and transfer to a measure.
4, Rinse the mortar with the vehicle, adding the washings to the measure, and make up to volume.
5, Stir well and transfer to an oral medicine bottle.
6, Label the bottle appropriately.

Storage
The suspension can be stored below 25°C. Do not refrigerate.

Expiry
28 days.

Notes
Shake before use.

Sildenafil 12.5mg/5mL suspension[271]

Sildenafil citrate 25mg tablets   10 tablets
Vehicle*   to 100mL

*Vehicle =   a 1:1 mixture of Ora-Plus® and Ora-Sweet®
                        or a 1:1 mixture of 1% methylcellulose and Syrup
                        B.P.

Method
1, Grind the tablets to a fine powder in a mortar.
2, Add a small quantity of the vehicle, a little at a time, and mix
thoroughly to a smooth paste.
3, Add more portions of the vehicle, stirring well, and transfer to a
measure.
4, Rinse the mortar with the vehicle, adding the washings to the
measure, and make up to volume.
5, Stir well and transfer to an oral medicine bottle.
6, Label the bottle appropriately.

Storage
The suspension can be stored below 25°C, or in a refrigerator.

Expiry
28 days.

Sodium phenylbutyrate 1g/5mL suspension[494]

Sodium phenylbutyrate powder   20g
Vehicle*   to 100mL

*Vehicle =   a 1:1 mixture of Ora-Plus® and Ora-Sweet®
               or a 1:1 mixture of Ora-Plus® and Ora-Sweet® S.F.

Method
1, Grind the sodium phenylbutyrate to a fine powder in a mortar.
2, Add a small quantity of the vehicle, a little at a time, and mix thoroughly to a smooth paste.
3, Add more portions of vehicle, stirring well, and transfer to a measure.
4, Rinse the mortar with vehicle, adding the washings to the measure, and make up to volume.
5, Stir well and transfer to an oral medicine bottle.
6, Label the bottle appropriately.

Storage
The suspension can be stored below 25°C. Do not refrigerate.

Expiry
28 days.

Notes
Shake before use.

Sotalol 25mg/5mL suspension[521]

Sotalol 40mg tablets   10 tablets
Vehicle*   to 80mL

*Vehicle =   a 1:1 mixture of Ora-Plus® and Ora-Sweet®
                  or a 1:9 mixture of 1% methylcellulose and Syrup
                  B.P.

Method
1, Grind the tablets to a fine powder in a mortar.
2, Add a small quantity of the vehicle, a little at a time, and mix
thoroughly to a smooth paste.
3, Add more portions of the vehicle, stirring well, and transfer to a
measure.
4, Rinse the mortar with the vehicle, adding the washings to the
measure, and make up to volume.
5, Stir well and transfer to an oral medicine bottle.
6, Label the bottle appropriately.

Storage
The suspension can be stored below 25°C, or in a refrigerator.

Expiry
28 days.

Notes
Shake before use.

Spironolactone 125mg/5mL suspension[473]

This is the first of four spironolactone suspension formulae (see below).

Spironolactone tablets   2.5g
Vehicle*   to 100mL

*Vehicle =   a 1:1 mixture of Ora-Plus® and Ora-Sweet®
                or a 1:1 mixture of Ora-Plus® and Ora-Sweet® S.F.

Method
1, Grind the tablets to a fine powder in a mortar.
2, Add a small quantity of the vehicle, a little at a time, and mix thoroughly to a smooth paste.
3, Add more portions of the vehicle, stirring well, and transfer to a measure.
4, Rinse the mortar with the vehicle, adding the washings to the measure, and make up to volume.
5, Stir well and transfer to an oral medicine bottle.
6, Label the bottle appropriately.

Storage
Store in a refrigerator.

Expiry
28 days.

Notes
Shake before use.
Protect from light.

Spironolactone 12.5mg/5mL suspension[495]

This is the second of four spironolactone suspension formulae (see above and below).

Spironolactone 25mg tablets	10 tablets
Distilled water	5mL
Cherry syrup	to 100mL

Method
1, Grind the tablets to a fine powder in a mortar.
2, Add the distilled water, a little at a time, and mix thoroughly to a smooth paste.
3, Add 30mL cherry syrup, stirring well, and transfer to a measure.
4, Rinse the mortar with cherry syrup, adding the washings to the measure, and make up to volume.
5, Stir well and transfer to an oral medicine bottle.
6, Label the bottle appropriately.

Storage
Store in a refrigerator.

Expiry
28 days.

Notes
Shake before use.

Spironolactone 25mg/5mL suspension[495]

This is the third of four spironolactone suspension formulae (see above and below).

Spironolactone 50mg tablets	10 tablets
Distilled water	5mL
Cherry syrup	to 100mL

Method
1, Grind the tablets to a fine powder in a mortar.
2, Add the distilled water, a little at a time, and mix thoroughly to a smooth paste.
3, Add 30mL cherry syrup, stirring well, and transfer to a measure.
4, Rinse the mortar with cherry syrup, adding the washings to the measure, and make up to volume.
5, Stir well and transfer to an oral medicine bottle.
6, Label the bottle appropriately.

Storage
Store in a refrigerator.

Expiry
28 days.

Notes
Shake before use.

Spironolactone 50mg/5mL suspension[495]

This is the fourth of four spironolactone suspension formulae (see above).

Spironolactone 100mg tablets	10 tablets
Distilled water	5mL
Cherry syrup	to 100mL

Method
1, Grind the tablets to a fine powder in a mortar.
2, Add the distilled water, a little at a time, and mix thoroughly to a smooth paste.
3, Add 30mL cherry syrup, stirring well, and transfer to a measure.
4, Rinse the mortar with cherry syrup, adding the washings to the measure, and make up to volume.
5, Stir well and transfer to an oral medicine bottle.
6, Label the bottle appropriately.

Storage
Store in a refrigerator.

Expiry
28 days.

Notes
Shake before use.

Spironolactone 25mg/5mL plus hydrochlorothiazide 25mg/5mL suspension[206]

Spironolactone-hydrochlorothiazide 25mg/25mg tablets   20 tablets
Vehicle*   to 100mL

*Vehicle =   a 1:1 mixture of Ora-Plus® and Ora-Sweet®
                or a 1:1 mixture of Ora-Plus® and Ora-Sweet® S.F.
                or cherry syrup (cherry syrup concentrate diluted 1:4
                with Syrup B.P.)

Method
1, Grind the tablets to a fine powder in a mortar.
2, Add a small quantity of the vehicle, a little at a time, and mix thoroughly to a smooth paste.
3, Add more portions of the vehicle, stirring well, and transfer to a measure.
4, Rinse the mortar with the vehicle, adding the washings to the measure, and make up to volume.
5, Stir well and transfer to an oral medicine bottle.
6, Label the bottle appropriately.

Storage
Store in a refrigerator.

Expiry
28 days.

Notes
Shake before use.
Protect from light.

These tablets are not available in the UK.

Sulfasalazine 500mg/5mL suspension[528]

Sulfasalazine 500mg tablets	20 tablets
Vehicle*	to 100mL

*Vehicle =   a 1:1 mixture of Ora-Plus® and Ora-Sweet®

Method
1, Place the tablets in a mortar and pour a small amount of the vehicle over them.
2, Allow to settle for 20-30 minutes.
3, Levigate the tablets to a smooth paste.
4, Add more portions of the vehicle, stirring well, and transfer to a measure.
5, Rinse the mortar with the vehicle, adding the washings to the measure, and make up to volume.
6, Stir well and transfer to an glass oral medicine bottle.
7, Label the bottle appropriately.

Storage
The suspension can be stored below 25°C, or in a refrigerator.

Expiry
28 days.

Notes
Shake before use.
Protect from light.
The suspension should be stored in a glass bottle.
The suspension will be thick, opaque, with a creamy brownish-yellow or light orange colour with brownish-yellow particles.

Tacrolimus 2.5mg/5mL suspension[497]

Tacrolimus 5mg capsules   10 capsules

Vehicle*   to 100mL

*Vehicle =   a 1:1 mixture of Ora-Plus® and Syrup B.P.

Method

1, Open the capsules and empty the contents into a mortar.

2, Add a small quantity of the vehicle, a little at a time, and mix thoroughly to a smooth paste.

3, Add more portions of vehicle, stirring well, and transfer to a measure.

4, Rinse the mortar with vehicle, adding the washings to the measure, and make up to volume.

5, Stir well and transfer to an oral medicine bottle.

6, Label the bottle appropriately.

Storage

The suspension can be stored below 25°C. Do not refrigerate.

Expiry

28 days.

Notes

Shake before use.

Gloves and a mask should be worn whilst preparing this suspension.

Erratic bioavailability and plasma concentrations have been reported in clinical practice. A paper has been published where the suspension described above was further investigated, but no results to suggest any deterioration of the product were found. The authors concluded that other factors e.g. poor dosing were responsible for the failures in clinical practice.[498]

Terbinafine 125mg/5mL suspension[499]

Terbinafine 250mg tablets   10 tablets
Vehicle*   to 100mL

*Vehicle =   a 1:1 mixture of Ora-Plus® and Ora-Sweet®

Method
1, Grind the tablets to a fine powder in a mortar.
2, Add a small quantity of the vehicle, a little at a time, and mix thoroughly to a smooth paste.
3, Add more portions of vehicle, stirring well, and transfer to a measure.
4, Rinse the mortar with vehicle, adding the washings to the measure, and make up to volume.
5, Stir well and transfer to an oral medicine bottle.
6, Label the bottle appropriately.

Storage
Store in a refrigerator.

Expiry
7 days.

Notes
Shake before use.
Protect from light.

Tetracycline hydrochloride 125mg/5mL suspension[454]

| Tetracycline 500mg tablets | 5 tablets |
| Vehicle* | to 100mL |

*Vehicle =   a 1:1 mixture of Ora-Plus® and Ora-Sweet®

Method
1, Grind the tablets to a fine powder in a mortar.
2, Add a small quantity of the vehicle, a little at a time, and mix thoroughly to a smooth paste.
3, Add more portions of the vehicle, stirring well, and transfer to a measure.
4, Rinse the mortar with the vehicle, adding the washings to the measure, and make up to volume.
5, Stir well and transfer to an oral medicine bottle.
6, Label the bottle appropriately.

Storage
The suspension can be stored below 25°C, or in a refrigerator.

Expiry
7 days.

Notes
Shake before use.
Protect from light.

Theophylline 25mg/5mL suspension[500]

Anhydrous theophylline extended release 300mg tablet   1 tablet
Vehicle*   to 60mL

*Vehicle =   a 1:1 mixture of Ora-Plus® and Ora-Sweet®
                        or a 1:1 mixture of Ora-Plus® and Ora-Sweet® S.F.

*(Alternatively, 300mg of anhydrous theophylline powder can be used
in place of the theophylline tablet).*

Method
1, Grind the tablet to a fine powder in a mortar.
2, Add a small quantity of the vehicle, a little at a time, and mix
thoroughly to a smooth paste.
3, Add more portions of the vehicle, stirring well, and transfer to a
measure.
4, Rinse the mortar with the vehicle, adding the washings to the
measure, and make up to volume.
5, Stir well and transfer to an oral medicine bottle.
6, Label the bottle appropriately.

Storage
The suspension should be stored below 25°C. Do not refrigerate.

Expiry
28 days.

Notes
Shake before use.

Thiamine suspension[155,512]

Thiamine tablets	qs
Xanthan suspending agent 1%	50mL
Distilled water	to 100mL

Method
1, Grind the tablets to a fine powder in a mortar.
2, Add a small quantity of Xanthan suspending agent 1%, a little at a time, and mix thoroughly to a smooth paste.
3, Add more portions of Xanthan suspending agent 1%, stirring well, and transfer to a measure.
4, Rinse the mortar with Xanthan suspending agent 1%, adding the washings to the measure.
5, Make up to volume with distilled water.
6, Stir well and transfer to an oral medicine bottle.
7, Label the bottle appropriately.

Storage
The suspension can be stored below 25°C. Do not refrigerate.

Expiry
7 days.

Notes
Shake before use.

Tiagabine 5mg/5mL suspension[501]

This is the first of two tiagabine suspension formulae (see below).

Tiagabine hydrochloride 10mg tablets   14 tablets
Vehicle*   to 140mL

*Vehicle =   120mL Syrup B.P. and 20mL methylcellulose 1%

Method
1, Grind the tablets to a fine powder in a mortar.
2, Add a small quantity of the vehicle, a little at a time, and mix thoroughly to a smooth paste.
3, Add more portions of the vehicle, stirring well, and transfer to a measure.
4, Rinse the mortar with the vehicle, adding the washings to the measure, and make up to volume.
5, Stir well and transfer to an oral medicine bottle.
6, Label the bottle appropriately.

Storage
Store in a refrigerator.

Expiry
28 days.

Notes
Shake before use.

Tiagabine 5mg/5mL suspension[501]

This is the second of two tiagabine suspension formulae (see above).

Tiagabine hydrochloride 10mg tablets   10 tablets
Vehicle*   to 100mL

*Vehicle =   a 1:1 mixture of Ora-Plus® and Ora-Sweet®

Method
1, Grind the tablets to a fine powder in a mortar.
2, Add a small quantity of the vehicle, a little at a time, and mix thoroughly to a smooth paste.
3, Add more portions of the vehicle, stirring well, and transfer to a measure.
4, Rinse the mortar with the vehicle, adding the washings to the measure, and make up to volume.
5, Stir well and transfer to an oral medicine bottle.
6, Label the bottle appropriately.

Storage
Store in a refrigerator.

Expiry
28 days.

Notes
Shake before use.

Tramadol 25mg/5mL suspension[502]

Tramadol capsules / tablets	500mg
Vehicle*	to 100mL

*Vehicle =   a 1:1 mixture of Ora-Plus® and Ora-Sweet® S.F.
                      or a 1:1 mixture of Ora-Plus® and strawberry syrup

Method
1, Open the capsules and empty the contents into a mortar, or place the tablets in a mortar.
2, Grind the tablets / capsule contents to a fine powder.
3, Add a small quantity of vehicle, a little at a time, and mix thoroughly to a smooth paste.
4, Add more portions of vehicle, stirring well, and transfer to a measure.
5, Rinse the mortar with vehicle, adding the washings to the measure, and make up to volume.
6, Stir well and transfer to an oral medicine bottle.
7, Label the bottle appropriately.

Storage
The suspension can be stored below 25°C, or in a refrigerator.

Expiry
28 days.

Notes
Shake before use.

Ursodeoxycholic acid 250mg/5mL suspension[503]

This is the first of two ursodeoxycholic acid suspension formulae (see below).

Ursodeoxycholic acid capsules / tablets	5g
Vehicle*	to 100mL

*Vehicle =   a 1:1 mixture of Ora-Plus® and Ora-Sweet® S.F.
         or a 1:1 mixture of Ora-Plus® and strawberry syrup

Method
1, Open the capsules and empty the contents into a mortar, or place the tablets in a mortar.
2, Grind the tablets / capsule contents to a fine powder.
3, Add a small quantity of the vehicle, a little at a time, and mix thoroughly to a smooth paste.
4, Add more portions of vehicle, stirring well, and transfer to a measure.
5, Rinse the mortar with vehicle, adding the washings to the measure, and make up to volume.
6, Stir well and transfer to an oral medicine bottle.
7, Label the bottle appropriately.

Storage
The suspension can be stored below 25°C, or in a refrigerator.

Expiry
28 days.

Notes
Shake before use.

Ursodeoxycholic acid 125mg/5mL suspension[528]

This is the second of two ursodeoxycholic acid suspension formulae (see above).

Ursodeoxycholic acid capsules / tablets	2.5g
Vehicle*	to 100mL

*Vehicle =   a 1:1 mixture of Ora-Plus® and orange syrup

Method
1, Open the capsules and empty the contents into a mortar, or place the tablets in a mortar.
2, Grind the tablets / capsule contents to a fine powder.
3, Add a small quantity of the vehicle, a little at a time, and mix thoroughly to a smooth paste.
4, Add more portions of the vehicle, stirring well, and transfer to a measure.
5, Rinse the mortar with the vehicle, adding the washings to the measure, and make up to volume.
6, Stir well and transfer to an oral medicine bottle.
7, Label the bottle appropriately.

Storage
Store in a refrigerator.

Expiry
28 days.

Notes
Shake before use.
Protect from light.

Valganciclovir 150mg/5mL suspension[505]

This is the first of two valganciclovir suspension formulae (see below).

Valganciclovir hydrochloride 450mg tablets	10 tablets
Vehicle*	to 150mL

*Vehicle =   a 1:1 mixture of Ora-Plus® and Ora-Sweet®

Method
1, Grind the tablets to a fine powder in a mortar.
2, Add a small quantity of the vehicle, a little at a time, and mix thoroughly to a smooth paste.
3, Add more portions of vehicle, stirring well, and transfer to a measure.
4, Rinse the mortar with vehicle, adding the washings to the measure, and make up to volume.
5, Stir well and transfer to an oral medicine bottle.
6, Label the bottle appropriately.

Storage
Store in a refrigerator.

Expiry
10 days.

Notes
Shake before use.

Valganciclovir 300mg/5mL suspension[505]

This is the second of two valganciclovir suspension formulae (see above).

Valganciclovir hydrochloride 450mg tablets	20 tablets
Vehicle*	to 150mL

*Vehicle =   a 1:1 mixture of Ora-Plus® and Ora-Sweet®

Method
1, Grind the tablets to a fine powder in a mortar.
2, Add a small quantity of the vehicle, a little at a time, and mix thoroughly to a smooth paste.
3, Add more portions of vehicle, stirring well, and transfer to a measure.
4, Rinse the mortar with vehicle, adding the washings to the measure, and make up to volume.
5, Stir well and transfer to an oral medicine bottle.
6, Label the bottle appropriately.

Storage
Store in a refrigerator.

Expiry
20 days.

Notes
Shake before use.

Verapamil hydrochloride 250mg/5mL suspension[206]

Verapamil 80mg tablets   50 tablets
Vehicle*   to 80mL

*Vehicle =   a 1:1 mixture of Ora-Plus® and Ora-Sweet®
                or a 1:1 mixture of Ora-Plus® and Ora-Sweet® S.F.
                or cherry syrup (cherry syrup concentrate diluted 1:4
                with Syrup B.P.)

Method
1, Grind the tablets to a fine powder in a mortar.
2, Add a small quantity of the vehicle, a little at a time, and mix thoroughly to a smooth paste.
3, Add more portions of the vehicle, stirring well, and transfer to a measure.
4, Rinse the mortar with the vehicle, adding the washings to the measure, and make up to volume.
5, Stir well and transfer to an oral medicine bottle.
6, Label the bottle appropriately.

Storage
The suspension can be stored below 25°C, or in a refrigerator.

Expiry
28 days.

Notes
Shake before use.
Protect from light.

6. Appendix 2 – Administration of cytotoxics

6. Monographs for cytotoxic medications

This section is intended for use by Pharmacy staff and people trained in the use of cytotoxic medications ONLY.

It is recommended that cytotoxic medications are only administered following discussion with Pharmacy. These medicines are frequently designed to protect carers from handling toxic products, and altering the formulation for administration (such as by crushing or dissolving tablets) removes these safeguards. Usually it would be preferable for cytotoxic medications to be prepared by Pharmacy in an appropriate environment to protect the handlers.

The information provided below is to aid Pharmacists in determining the most appropriate method of providing such medication.

The monographs shown below are complete versions of monographs which may have been abbreviated in the main text in Section 4. This means that there is no need for users of this section to refer back to Section 4 for additional information when studying monographs in Section 6. In some cases the complete monograph is shown both here and in Section 4. This is in order to include all cytotoxics listed in this book in Section 6, as well as supplying appropriate information to non-Pharmacy users in Section 4. It is indicated in the text below whether the monograph is abbreviated or shown in full in Section 4.

Azathioprine

An abbreviated monograph is shown in Section 4.

Presentation
Tablets, film-coated tablets.
Oral suspension (special).[542]
A suspension can be made by Pharmacy in some centres (see Appendix 1).[451,512]
Special suspension available from NOVA laboratories.[346]
Injection.

Clinical guidance
Caution – cytotoxic. Contact Pharmacy for advice before giving.
1st choice – Give by parenteral injection if appropriate.
2nd choice – A suspension can be made by Pharmacy in some centres. Follow the directions in section 3.6. Carers handling the suspension should wear gloves in case of contact with the medication.
3rd choice – Use the special oral suspension (if available). Follow the directions in section 3.6. Carers handling the suspension should wear gloves in case of contact with the medication.
4th choice – Contact Pharmacy for further advice on how to give.

The tablet has a film-coating which usually protects carers from the cytotoxic medication inside.[295,346] It should not be crushed or dissolved except on Pharmacy advice. If no other method is appropriate, on advice from Pharmacy ONLY the tablet can be dispersed in water for administration.[155] The drug is light sensitive, so give immediately.[155]

Azathioprine is absorbed in the upper gastrointestinal tract. No absorption problems are expected if the medication is delivered directly into the jejunum.[346]

Busulfan (Busulphan)

This monograph is also shown in Section 4.

Presentation
Film-coated tablets.
A suspension can be made by Pharmacy in some centres.
Concentrate for infusion.

Administration – enteral tubes / swallowing difficulties
<u>Caution – cytotoxic.</u> The film-coating on the tablets protects carers from coming into contact with the cytotoxic drug.[297] The tablets should therefore not be crushed or divided. Contact Pharmacy for advice before giving.

A suspension can be made by Pharmacy in some centres.[138,455] Follow the directions in section 3.6.

Chlorambucil

This monograph is also shown in Section 4.

Presentation
Film-coated tablets.
A suspension can be made by Pharmacy in some centres.

Administration – enteral tubes / swallowing difficulties
<u>Caution – cytotoxic.</u> Contact Pharmacy for advice before giving.
A suspension can be made by Pharmacy in some centres.[138] Follow the directions in section 3.6.

Cyclophosphamide

An abbreviated monograph is shown in Section 4.

Presentation
Sugar-coated tablets.
A suspension can be made by Pharmacy in some centres.
Injection.

Administration – enteral tubes / swallowing difficulties
<u>Caution – cytotoxic.</u> Contact Pharmacy for advice before giving.
1st choice – Consider giving by parenteral injection.
2nd choice – A suspension can be made in Pharmacy in some centres.[138,139,172] Follow the directions in section 3.6.
3rd choice – The injection has been used enterally in some centres.[143,172,568] Contact Pharmacy for advice before doing this.

Etoposide

An abbreviated monograph is shown in Section 4.

Presentation
Capsules.
A solution can be made by Pharmacy in some centres (see Appendix 1).[464]
Injection.

Administration – enteral tubes / swallowing difficulties
<u>Caution – cytotoxic.</u> Contact Pharmacy for advice before giving.
1st choice – Use the solution (if available). Follow the directions in section 3.6.
2nd choice – The injection has been diluted to 0.4mg/mL with water for administration via enteral feeding tubes, or in orange juice for oral administration in some centres.[138]

Feed guidance
Withhold feed for two hours before and one hour after administration of enteral doses.[624]

(monograph continues on next page)

Summary:-	Stop feed 2 hours before dose
	Restart feed 1 hour after dose

Withholding enteral feeds can compromise nutrition and interfere with blood glucose management. If the patient does not have a break in their feeding regimen during which etoposide can be given, the Nutrition Team should be contacted to advise on management.

Hydroxycarbamide (Hydroxyurea)

An abbreviated monograph is shown in Section 4.

Presentation
Capsules.
Film-coated tablets.
A suspension can be made by Pharmacy in some centres (see Appendix 1).[471]

Administration – enteral tubes / swallowing difficulties
Caution – cytotoxic. Contact Pharmacy for advice before giving.
The capsules are cytotoxic and should not be opened except on Pharmacy advice.

1st choice – Use the suspension (if available). Follow the directions in section 3.6.
2nd choice – If no other method is appropriate, on advice from Pharmacy the capsules can be opened and the contents dispersed in water for administration.[105,556] The contents of the capsules should not be inhaled or allowed to come into contact with the skin or mucous membranes.[556,558] Follow the directions in section 3.7.

Mercaptopurine

This monograph is also shown in Section 4.

Presentation
Tablets.
A suspension can be made by Pharmacy in some centres (see Appendix 1).[479]

Administration – enteral tubes / swallowing difficulties
<u>Caution – cytotoxic.</u> Contact Pharmacy for advice before giving.
A suspension can be made by Pharmacy in some centres.[138,479]
Follow the directions in section 3.6.

The manufacturers recommend that mercaptopurine is handled in accordance with local guidelines for handling cytotoxic drugs.[346]

Methotrexate

An abbreviated monograph is shown in Section 4.

Presentation
Tablets.
Oral solution (special).[582]
Injection.

Administration – enteral tubes / swallowing difficulties
<u>Caution – cytotoxic.</u> Contact Pharmacy for advice before giving.

1st choice – A 'special' suspension may be available.[132] Follow the directions in section 3.6.
2nd choice – The injection has also been given enterally in some centres, however the manufacturers have no information on this, and cannot recommend it.[40,167] Contact Pharmacy for advice.

Procarbazine

An abbreviated monograph is shown in Section 4.

Presentation
Capsules.
A suspension can be made by Pharmacy in some centres.

Administration – enteral tubes / swallowing difficulties
Caution – cytotoxic. Contact Pharmacy for advice before giving.

1st choice – A suspension can be made by Pharmacy in some centres.[138] Follow the directions in section 3.6.
2nd choice – The capsules are cytotoxic and should not be opened except on Pharmacy advice. If no other method is appropriate, on advice from Pharmacy the capsules can be opened and the contents administered in water or flushed down an enteral feeding tube with water. Give immediately as it is unstable. The powder is very irritant.[138] Follow the directions in section 3.7.

Tioguanine (Thioguanine)

This monograph is also shown in Section 4.

Presentation
Tablets.
A suspension can be made by Pharmacy in some centres.

Administration – enteral tubes / swallowing difficulties
Caution – cytotoxic. Contact Pharmacy for advice before giving.
A suspension can be made by Pharmacy in some centres.[138] Follow the directions in section 3.6.

7. References

Please note that information obtained from pharmaceutical companies does not constitute a recommendation by that company that the drug is suitable for administration via an enteral feeding tube or to patients with swallowing difficulties. Such use is usually outside the drug licence, and most information is anecdotal.

1. Chadwick C. Pharmaceutical problems for the nutrition team pharmacist. Hospital Pharmacist 1996; 3: 139-146.

2. Varella L, Jones E, Meguid MM. Drug-Nutrient Interactions in Enteral Feeding: A primary Care Focus. The Nurse Practitioner 1997; 22 (6): 98-104.

3. Oxford Textbook of Medicine.pp1321. Third Edition. Edited by Weatherall, DJ. Oxford University Press, 1996.

4. Beckwith M. A guide to drug therapy in patients with enteral feeding tubes: Dosage form selection and administration methods. Hospital Pharmacy 1997; 32: 57-64.

5. Cutie A. Compatibility of enteral products with commonly employed drug additives. Parental Enteral Nutrition 1983; 7: 186-191.

6. Adams D. Administration of drugs through a jejunostomy tube. British Journal Intensive Care 1994; 4: 10-17.

7. Mistry B. Simplifying oral drug therapy for patients with swallowing difficulties. Pharmaceutical Journal 1995; 254: 808-809.

8. Martin T. Tablet dispersion as an alternative to formulation of oral liquid dosage form. Aust. J. Hospital Pharmacy 1993; 23: 378-386.

9. Reynolds JEF, editor. Martindale: The Extra Pharmacopoeia. 31st Edition London: Pharmaceutical Press, 1996.

10. Clark-Schmidt AL, Garnett WR, Karnes HT. Loss of carbamazepine suspension through nasogastric feeding tubes. Am..J.Hosp.Pharm. 1990; 47: 2034-2037.

11. Stockley IH. Drug Interactions. Fourth Edition. London: Pharmaceutical Press, 1996.

12. D'arcy P F. Drug interactions with medical plastics. ADR toxicol. review 1996; 15: 207-219.

13. Pharmacy Information Sheet. July 1997. Ciprofloxacin.

14. Hillcross: data on file (communication with Brenda Murphy).

15. Micromedex Healthcare Series, volume 104.

16. Ziagen® 20mg/mL Oral Solution Summary of Product Characteristics. GSK, 17th January 2007.

17. Janssen: Data on file (communication with Brenda Murphy).

18. American Hospital Formulary Service. 1997.

19. Flagyl® Summary of Product Characteristics, 96/97. Hawgreen Ltd.

20. Liefold J. Administration of controlled–release morphine sulphate during artificial feeding. Z. Allg. Med. 1996; 76: 707-709.

21. Battino D, et al. Clinical Pharmacokinetics of anti-epileptic drugs in paediatric patients. CPK 1995; 29: 341-369.

22. Dickerson R, Melnik G. Osmolality of oral drug solutions and suspensions. Am. J. Hosp. Pharm. 1998 (1988); 45: 832-834.

23. Miller SW, Strom JG. Stability of Phenytoin in three enteral nutrients formulas. Am. J. Hosp. Pharm. 1998 (1988?); 45: 2529-2523.

24. Archer A. Guideline for nurses on drug administration through enteral feeding tubes Pharmacy Own Magazine 1996; 10: 2-3.

25. Holtz L. Compatibility of medications with enteral feeds. J. Par. Ent. Nutrition 1987; 11: 183-186.

26. Estoup M. Approaches and limitations of medication delivery in patients with enteral feeding tubes. Critical Care Nurse 1994; 14: 68-81.

27. Glucobay® Summary of Product Characteristics. Bayer HealthCare, October 2006.

28. Halpern NA. Segmental intestinal absorption of ranitidine: investigate and therapeutic implications. Am. J. Gastroenterology 1990; 85: 539-543.

29. Gramatté T, El Desoky E, Klotz U. Site-dependent small intestinal absorption of ranitidine. Eur. J. Clin. Pharmacol. 1994; 46: 253-259.

30. Zantac® Summary of Product Characteristics, 96/97. GlaxoWellcome UK.

31. Williams MF, et al. Influence of gastrointestinal anatomic site of drug delivery on the absorption characteristics of ranitidine. Pharmacotherapy, 1989; 9: 184.

32. Tomlin M, Dixon S. Aluminium and naosgastric feeds. (Letter) Pharmaceutical Journal 1995; 256: 40.

33. Mason P. Diet and drug interactions. Pharmaceutical Journal 1996; 255: 94-95.

34. Watson AJM, Pegg M, Green JRB. Enteral feeds may antagonise warfarin. British Medical Journal Clinical Research Ed 1984; 288: 557.

35. BNF No. 42 (Sept. 2001). London: British Medical Association, Royal Pharmaceutical Society of Great Britain, 2001.

36. Ciproxin® Summary of Product Characteristics, 1999/2000. Bayer plc.

37. Personal communication, Medical information, Pfizer Limited, 10th August 2001.

38. Nova laboratories Keltrol compatability bulletin.

39. Dispersal of non-soluble tabs in water (in-house work, Wrexham Maelor Hospital).

40. Tube Feeding Drug Administration Guide, Forest Healthcare, Whipps Cross Hospital, Leytonstone, London.

41. Derriford Hospital Pharmacy enteral feeding guide.

42. Personal communication, Medical Information, Sanofi-Synthelabo, 6th September 2001.

43. Personal communication, Medical Information, Bayer, 16th August 2001.

44. Personal communication, Medical Information, Boehringer Ingelheim, 14th August 2001.

45. Personal communication, Medical Information, Servier, 6th September 2001.

46. Personal communication, Medical Information, AstraZeneca, 14th August 2001.

47. Printed information from Link Pharmaceuticals on Zomorph capsules.

48. Personal communication, Medical Information, Lilly, 16th August 2001.

49. Personal communication, Medical Information, DuPont, 14th August 2001.

50. Fosamax® Summary of Product Characteristics. MSD, August 1997.

51. Arthrotec® Summary of Product Characteristics. Searle, June 1997.

52. Personal communication, Medical Information, Roche, 6th September 2001.

53. Personal communication, Medical Information, AstraZeneca, 23rd July 2001.

54. Personal communication, Medical Information, Pharmacia, 6th September 2001.

55. Personal communication, Medical Information, Pantheon, 16th August 2001.

56. Personal communication, Medical Information, Abbott Laboratories, 13th August 2001.

57. Personal communication, Medical Information, Pharmacia, 12th December 2001.

58. Personal communication, Medical Information, AstraZeneca, 13th August 2001.

59. Personal communication, Medical Informaton, Schering Health, 6th September 2001.

60. Plendil® Summary of Product Characteristics. AstraZeneca, 1999/2000.

61. Personal communication, Medical Information, Fournier, 13th August 2001.

62. Personal communication, Medical Information, Aventis Pharma, 14th August 2001.

63. Personal communication, Medical Information, MSD, 6th September 2001.

64. Proscar® Summary of Product Characteristics. MSD, October 1998.

65. Personal communication, Medical Information, Novartis, 6th September 2001.

66. Personal communication, Medical Information, Pharmacia, 19th September 2001 (letter).

67. Personal communication, Medical Information, GlaxoSmithkline, 10th October 2001.

68. Personal communication, Medical Information, Bristol-Myers Squibb, 14th August 2001.

69. Personal communication, Medical Information, Napp, 13th August 2001.

70. Tavanic® Summary of Product Characteristics. Aventis Pharma, September 1998.

71. Personal communication, Medical Information, Pharmacia, 16th November 2001.

72. Personal communication, Medical Information, Organon, 6th September 2001.

73. Singulair® Summary of Product Characteristics. MSD, January 1998.

74. Personal communication, Medical Information, Solvay Healthcare, 9th August 2001.

75. Personal communication, Medical Information, Lilly, 16th August 2001.

76. Coversyl® Summary of Product Characteristics. Servier, March 1997.

77. Personal communication, Medical Information, Bristol-Myers Squibb, 6th September 2001.

78. Personal communication, Medical Information, Merck, 16th August 2001, communication with Sioned Rowlands.

79. Personal communication, Medical Information, Aventis Pharma, 23rd July 2001.

80. Personal communication, Medical Information, Procter and Gamble Pharm., 16th August 2001.

81. Personal communication, Medical Information, Smithkline Beecham, 3rd August 2001.

82. Flomax® Summary of Product Characteristics. Yamanouchi, July 1998.

83. Personal communication, Medical Information, Pharmacia, 10th October 2001.

84. Personal communication, Medical Information, Aventis Pharma, 25th October 2001.

85. Personal communication, Medical Information, Novartis, 29th June 2001.

86. Personal communioation, Medical Information, Wyeth, 6th September 2001.

87. Engle K, Hannawa TE, Techniques for administering oral medications to critical care patients receiving continuous enteral nutrition. Am J Health-Syst Pharm. 1999; 56:1441-1444.

88. Tenormin[®] Syrup Summary of Product Characteristics. Zeneca Pharma, February 1998.

89. Personal communication, Medical Information, Celltech, 10th October 2001.

90. Thomson FC, Naysmith MR, Lindsay A. Managing drug therapy in patients receiving enteral and parenteral nutrition. Hospital Pharmacist 2000; 7:155-164.

91. Personal communication, Medical Information, Merck, 10th July 2002.

92. Personal communication, Medical Information, Aventis Pharma, 11th July 2002.

93. BNF No. 43 (March 2002). London: British Medical Association, Royal Pharmaceutical Society of Great Britain, 2002.

94. Queen Victoria Hospital's Drug Adminstration via Enteral Feeding Tubes guide, March 2001.

95. Thomson F. A to Z guide to administration of drugs via nasogastric/PEG tube. Southern General Hospital, Victoria Infirmary, South Glasgow University Hospitals NHS Trust, University of Strathclyde/GGHB Pharmacy Practice Unit, Western General Hospital, Lothian University Hospitals NHS Trust, University of Strathclyde/Lothian Pharmacy Practice Unit. June 2001.

96. Product Information, Catapres[®] Transdermal Plasters, Boehringer Ingelheim.

97. Personal communication, Medical Information, Borg Medicare, 27th September 2002.

98. Personal communication, Medical Information, Waymed Healthcare, 27th September 2002.

99. Personal communication, Medical Information, Celltech, 27th September 2002.

100. Personal communication, Medical Information, Boehringer Ingelheim, 27th September 2002.

101. Topamax[®] Summary of Product Characteristics. Janssen-Cilag, 17th February 1999.

102. Personal communication, Medical Information, Link Pharmaceuticals, 28th February 2003.

103. Personal communication, Medical Information, Roche Consumer Health, 28th February 2003.

104. Guidelines for the administration of Drugs through Enteral Feeding Tubes. County Durham and Darlington Acute Hospitals NHS Trust. 2nd edition. July 2003.

105. Drugs via Enteral Feeding Tubes Guide (draft copy), Stockport NHS Trust, received September 2003.

106. BNF No. 45 (March 2003). London: British Medical Association, Royal Pharmaceutical Society of Great Britain, 2003.

107. Personal communication, Medical Information, Aventis Pharma, 24th December 2003.

108. Personal communication, Medical Information, UCB Pharma, 12th February 2004.

109. Personal communication, Medical Information, Goldshield, 15th January 2004.

110. Personal communication, Medical Information, Boehringer Ingelheim, 15th January 2004.

111. Prograf® Summary of Product Characteristics. Fujisawa Ltd, June 2002.

112. Administering Drugs via Enteral Feeding Tubes: A Practical Guide. Poster produced by the British Association for Parenteral and Enteral Nutrition, and The British Pharmaceutical Nutrition Group, July 2004.

113. Drug Administration via Enteral Feeding Tubes: A Guide for General Practitioners and Community Pharmacists. Leaflet produced by the British Association for Parenteral and Enteral Nutrition, and The British Pharmaceutical Nutrition Group, July 2004.

114. Tube Feeding and Your Medicines: A Guide for Patients and Carers. Leaflet produced by the British Association for Parenteral and Enteral Nutrition, and The British Pharmaceutical Nutrition Group, July 2004.

115. Griffith R. Tablet Crushing and the Law. Pharmaceutical Journal 2003; 271: 90-91.

116. Wright D. Swallowing Difficulties Protocol: Achieving best practice in Medication Administration. 2002.

117. Carrington C, McKay J. Administering Drugs via Enteral Feeding Tubes. Pharmacy Department, Queensland, Australia. November 2000.

118. MDA/2004/026 – Enteral feeding tubes (nasogastric). Safety alert produced by the Medicines and Healthcare products Regulatory Agency, 14th June 2004.

119. Anderson R. Personal correspondance, 10th May 2004.

120. Reducing the harm caused by misplaced nasogastric feeding tubes. National Patient Safety Agency, 21st February 2005.

121. Bird K. Is levothyroxine suspension effective? [letter] Pharmaceutical Journal 2004; 273: 680.

122. Perrin JH. Do not suspend levothyroxine. [letter] Pharmaceutical Journal 2004; 273: 748.

123. Cipramil® Summary of Product Characteristics. Lundbeck Limited, 25th September 2003.

124. Personal communication, Medical Information, MSD. 8th June 2005.

125. Personal communication, Medical Information, Pfizer. 13th June 2005.

126. Personal communication, Medical Information, Roche. 16th August 2005.

127. CellCept® Suspension Summary of Product Characteristics. Roche Products Limited, April 2005.

128. Personal communication, Medical Information, Leo Laboratories Limited. 16th August 2005.

129. Rosemont Pharmaceuticals Specials List. July 2004.

130. Personal communication, Medical Information, Boehringer Ingelheim, 19th August 2005.

131. Medical Information, Roche, via Katy Hand, St. Helier Hospital, Surrey, 26th August 2005.

132. Guide to administration of medicines to patients with swallowing difficulties or feeding tubes (NG/PEG). Gloucestershire Hospitals NHS Foundation Trust. November 2004.

133. Sinden E. Drug Administration Guidelines. Poole Hospital NHS Trust Pharmacy Department, July 2002.

134. Communication from AstraZeneca Medical Information to Julie Davis, University Hospital of North Staffordshire NHS Trust, 3rd July 2003.

135. Martin S, Davidson R, Holland D. Medication and Enteral Feeding. Calderdale and Huddersfield NHS Trust, February 2004.

136. BNF No. 49 (March 2005). London: British Medical Association, Royal Pharmaceutical Society of Great Britain, 2005.

137. Appendix 10. Palliativedrugs.com, 2002.

138. Reeves VJ. The Administration of medication via a Percutaneous Endoscopic Gastrostomy (PEG) tube. Pharmacy Department, Broomfield Hospital, Mid Essex Hospitals Services NHS Trust. March 2002.

139. Burnett L. Personal communication, 6th September 2005.

140. Working party for drug administration. Drug Administration via enteral tubes. University Hospital of North Staffordshire. Draft One, October 2003.

141. Temgesic® Summary of Product Characteristics. Schering-Plough Ltd, April 2004.

142. Information from Colin Ranshaw, Principal Pharmacist, Quality Assurance and Control, Cardiff.

143. Information from Mark Craig, Senior Clinical Pharmacist, Mayday University Hospital.

144. Information from Rachel Harries, Nevill Hall Hospital, Abergavenny, 4th February 2005.

145. Information from Christopher Livsey, Clinical Pharmacist, Royal Lancaster Infirmary, 26th April 2005.

146. Letter on file. Napp Pharmaceuticals.

147. Information on file, Wrexham Maelor Hospital Pharmacy Department.

148. Letter from Medical Information, AstraZeneca, 12th April 2000.

149. Communication with Elayne Harris, Area Pharmacy Specialist (Palliative Care), Glasgow, 4th February 2005.

150. Communication with Christopher Livsey, Clinical Pharmacist, Royal Lancaster Infirmary.

151. Communication with Jennifer Smith, Medicines Information Manager, North Staffordshire University Hospitals.

152. Medicines for Children, 2003. Royal College of Paediatrics and Child Health, Neonatal and Paediatric Pharmacists Group.

153. Losec MUPS® Patient Information Leaflet. AstraZeneca, March 2005.

154. In house data, July-August 2005.

155. Fair R, Proctor B. Administering Medicines Through Enteral Feeding Tubes. The Royal Hospitals, Belfast. 2nd edition.

156. Nexium® Summary of Product Characteristics. AstraZeneca UK Limited, October 2004.

157. Furazolidone Drug Evaluation. Micromedex Healthcare Series, Volume 126, 2005.

158. Adams D. Administration of drugs through a jejunostomy tube. British Journal of Intensive Care 1994: 10-17.

159. Personal communication, Medical Information, Roche, 11th October 2005.

160. BNF for children, 2005. London: BMJ Publishing Group Ltd, Royal Pharmaceutical Society of Great Britain, RCPCH Publications Ltd, 2005.

161. Personal communication, Medical Information, MSD, 25th November 2005.

162. Acitretin Safety Data Sheet. Roche, 2nd September 2003.

163. Vancocin® CP Injection Summary of Product Characteristics. Flynn Pharma Ltd, 17th August 2001.

164. Personal communication, Medical Information, Link Pharmaceuticals, 4th January 2006.

165. Personal communication, Medical Information, Amdipharm, 4th January 2006.

166. Personal communication, Medical Information, Procter and Gamble, 4th January 2006.

167. Personal communication, Medical Information, Wockhardt UK, 4th January 2006.

168. Personal communication, Medical Information, 3M Healthcare, 4th January 2006.

169. Personal communication, Medical Information, Shire, 4th January 2006.

170. Personal communication, Medical Information, Boehringer Ingelheim, 4th January 2006.

171. Personal communication, Medical Information, GlaxoSmithkline, 4th January 2006.

172. Cyclophosphamide monograph. Lexi-Drugs. On-palm database, Lexi-Comp, 2005.

173. Procainamide monograph. Lexi-Drugs. On-palm databse, Lexi-Comp, 2005.

174. Metoprolol monograph. Lexi-Drugs. On-palm databse, Lexi-Comp, 2005.

175. Personal communication, Medical Information, AstraZeneca, 5th January 2006.

176. McEvoy GK (editor). AHFS Drug Information, 2001. American Society of Health-System Pharmacists. Bethesda, MD, 2001.

177. Nasogastric Administration of Omeprazole. Pharmacy Drug Advisory Newsletter, Oct. 1994; 10 (2). Women's and Children's Hospital.

178. Recommendations for administration of omeprazole via NG tube. Alder Hey Drug Information Advisory Line (DIAL), communication with Suzanne Cotter, 23rd December 1997.

179. Kaper R. Zispin SolTab (letter). Organon Laboratories Ltd, April 2004.

180. Lanoxin (letter), reference TARHE/200697/2452/hc. Communication from GlaxoWellcome UK Ltd Medical Information to L Bellis, 20th June 1997.

181. Rilutek, reference Q000696. Communication from Aventis Medical Information, 11th January 2000.

182. Newton DW, Rogers AG, Becker CH, Toroslan G. Extemporaneous preparation of methyldopa in two syrup vehicles. Am. J. Hosp. Pharm 1975; 32: 817-821.

183. Sharma VK, Ugheoke AE, Vasudeva R, Howden CW. Lansoprazole effectively suppresses intragastric acidity when administered *via* gastrostomy as intact granules in orange juice. Gastroenterology 1998; 114: 4 (2) A283.

184. Chun AHC, Shi HH, Achari MSR, Dennis S, Cavanaugh JH. Lansoprazole: Administration of the Contents of a Capsule Dosage Formulation Through a Nasogastric Tube. Clinical Therapeutics 1996; 18 (5): 833-842.

185. McAndrews KL, Eastham JH. Omeprazole and lansoprazole suspensions for nasogastric administration. Am. J. Health-Syst. Pharm. 1999; 56: 81.

186. Peckman HJ. Alternative method for administering proton pump inhibitors through nasogastric tubes. Am J. Health-Syst. Pharm. 1999, 56: 1020.

187. Zoton, reference AP/000225/3234 10G (letter). Communication from Wyeth Medical Information to Elaine Sturman, 29th February 2000.

188. Neoral, reference DR/010810/23921 (letter). Communication from Novartis Medical Information to Jen Smyth, 10th August 2001.

189. Jamieson NV. De novo use of Neoral in liver transplant recipients. In: Neoral: the new microemulsion formulation of cyclosporine, Cedar Knolls (NJ): World Medical Press, (Special Report), May 1995; 34-39.

190. van Mourik IDM, *et al.* Efficacy of Neoral in the immediate postoperative period in children post-liver transplantation. Liver Transplant Surg. 1998; 4: 491-498.

191. Fish DN, Abraham E. Pharmacokinetics of a Clarithromycin Suspension Administered via Nasogastric Tube to Seriously Ill Patients. Antimicrobial Agents and Chemotherapy 1999; 43 (5): 1277-1280.

192. van der Bemt PMLA, *et al.* Quality improvement of oral medication administration in patients with enteral feeding tubes. Qual. Saf. Health Care 2006; 15: 44-47.

193. Healy DP. Ciprofloxacin absorption is impaired in patients given enteral feedings orally and via gastrostomy and jejunostomy tubes. Antimicrobial agents and Chemotherapy 1996; 40 (1): 6-10.

194. Mueller BA. Effect of enteral feeding with Ensure on oral bioavailabilities of ofloxacin and ciprofloxacin. Antimicrobial Agents and Chemotherapy 1994; 38 (9): 2101-2105.

195. Wright DH. Decreased *in vitro* fluoroquinolone concentrations after admixture with an enteral feeding formulation. JPEN 2000; 24 (1): 42-48.

196. Bauer LA. Interference of oral phenytoin absorption by continuous nasogastric feedings. Neurology 1982; 32 (5): 570-572.

197. Reid J. Marciniuk D, Peloquin CA, Hoeppner V. Pharmacokinetics of antituberculosis medications delivered via percutaneous gastrojejunostomy tube. Chest 2002; 121: 281-284.

198. Mimoz O, *et al*. Pharmacokinetics and absolute bioavailability of ciprofloxacin administered through a nasogastric tube with continuous enteral feeding to critically ill patients. Intensive Care Medicine 1998; 24: 1047-1051.

199. Garcia-Luna PP, *et al*. Esophageal obstruction by solidification of the enteral feed: a complication to be prevented. Intensive Care Medicine 1997; 23: 790-792.

200. Rosemurgy AS, *et al*. Bioavailability of fluconazole in surgical intensive care unit patients: a study comparing routes of administration. J Trauma 1995; 39 (3): 445-447.

201. Buijk SLC, *et al*. Pharmacokinetics of sequential intravenous and enteral fluconazole in critically ill surgical patients with invasive mycoses and compromised gastro-intestinal function. Intensive Care Medicine 2001; 27: 115-121.

202. Phillips JO, Metzler MH, Olsen K. The stability of simplified lansoprazole suspension. Gastroenterology 1999; 116 (4 part 2): A89.

203. Detinger P, Swenson CF, Anaizi NH. Stability of pantoprazole in an extemporaneously compounded oral liquid. Am. J. Health-Syst. Pharm. 2002; 59: 953-956.

204. White CM, *et al*. Delivery of esomeprazole magnesium enteric-coated pellets through small caliber and standard nasogastric tubes and gastrostomy tubes in vitro. Am. J. Health-Syst. Pharm. 2002; 59: 2085-2088.

205. Swenson CF. Importance of Following Instructions when Compounding. Am. J. Hosp. Pharm. 1993; 50 (2): 261.

206. Allen LV, Erickson III MA. Stability of labetalol hydrochloride, metoprolol tartrate, verapamil hydrochloride, and spironolactone with hydrochlorothiazide in extemporaneously compounded oral liquids. Am. J. Health-Syst. Pharm. 1996; 53: 2304-2309.

207. Omeprazole Drug Evaluation. Micromedex Healthcare Series, accessed 4th July 2006.

208. Alexander KS, Pudipeddi M, Parker GA. Stability of procainamide hydrochloride syrups compounded from capsules. Am. J. Hosp. Pharm. 1993; 50: 693-698.

209. Metras JI, Swenson CF, McDermott MP. Stability of procainamide hydrochloride in an extemporaneously compounded oral liquid. Am. J. Hosp. Pharm. 1992; 49: 1720-1724.

210. Zoton, reference Zoton*\1-6185948 (letter). Communication from Wyeth Medical Information to Jen Smyth, 12th September 2005.

211. Hsyu PH, et al. Comparison of the pharmacokinetics of an ondansetron solution (8mg) when administered intravenously, orally, to the colon, and to the rectum. Pharmaceutical Research 1994; 11 (1): 156-159 (abstract).

212. Seifert CF, Johnston BA. A nationwide survey of long-term care facilities to determine the characteristics of medication administration through enteral feeding catheters. Nutrition in Clinical Practice 2005; 20 (3): 354-362 (abstract).

213. Church C, Smith J. How stable are medicines moved from original packs into compliance aids? Pharmaceutical Journal 2006; 276: 75-81.

214. Belknap DC. Administration of medications through enteral feeding catheters. Am. J. Crit. Care 1997; 6: 382-392.

215. Quercia RA. Stability of omeprazole in an extemporaneously prepared oral liquid. AJHP 1997; 54: 1833-1836.

216. Anderson W. Esophageal medication bezoar in a patient receiving enteral feedings and sucralfate. Am. J. Gastroenterol. 1989: 205-206.

217. Sharma VK. Simplified lansoprazole suspension – a liquid formulation of lansoprazole effectively suppresses intragastric acidity when administered through a gastrostomy. The American Journal of Gastroenterology, 94(7): 1813-1817.

218. Balaban DH. Nasogastric omeprazole: effects on gastric pH in critically ill patients. The American Journal of Gastroenterology, 1997, 92 (1), 79-83.

219. Phillips JO. A randomised , pharmacokinetic and pharmacodynamic, cross-over study of duodenal or jejunal administration compared to nasogastric administration of omprazole suspension in patients at risk for stress ulcers. Am. J. Gastroenterol. 2001, 96: 367-372.

220. Song JS. Pharmacokinetic comparison of omeprazole capsules and a simplified omeprazole suspension. AJHP, 2001, 58: 689-694.

221. Ferron G. Oral bioavailability of pantoprazole suspended in sodium bicarbonate solution. AJHP, 2003, 60, 1324-1329.

222. Burns PE, Physical compataibility of enteral formulas with various common medications, J Am Dietetic Assoc, 1998, 88: 1094-1096.

223. Nicolau D, Bioavailability of fluconazole administered via a feeding tube in intensive care unit patients, Journal of Antimicrobial Chemotherapy, 1995, 36:395-401.

224. Udeani GO, Compatability of oral morphine sulphate solution with enteral feeding products. The Annals of Pharmacotherapy, 1994, 28: 451-455.

225. Gilbar PJ, A guide to enteral drug administration in palliative care, Journal of Pain and Symptom Management, 1999, 17 (3): 197-207.

226. BNF No. 52 (September 2006). London: BMJ Publishing Group Ltd, RPS Publishing, 2006.

227. Ehrenpreis E, et al. Malabsorption of digoxin tablets, gel caps, and elixir in a patient with an end jejunostomy. The Annals of Pharmacotherapy, 1994, 28:1239-1240.

228. Davis G, et al. Pharmacokinetics of fluconazole in trauma patients with postpyloric feeding tubes. The Annals of Pharmacotherapy, 2001, 35: 1492-1494.

229. Crowther RS. In vitro stability of ranitidine hydrochloride in enteral nutrient formulas, The Annals of Pharmacotherapy. 1995, 29: 859-862.

230. Cousins DH, Upton DR (editors). Inappropriate syringe use leads to fatalities. Pharmacy in Practice, 1998, (May): 209-210.

231. Naysmith MR, Nicholson J. Nasogastric drug administration. Professional Nurse, 1998, 13 (7): 424-427.

232. Woolfrey S, Geddes A, Hussain A, Cox J. Nutrition: Percutaneous Endoscopic Gastrostomy. Pharmaceutical Journal, 1996; 257: 181-184.

233. Creamer M, Wood S. Artificial feeding: The delivery routes for artificial feeding. Hospital Pharmacist, 1996; 3: 133-135.

234. Monk JS. Products for enteral nutrition. Hospital Pharmacist, 1996; 3: 136-138.

235. Neoral® Soft Gelatin Capsules, Neoral® Oral Solution. Summary of Product Characteristics. Novartis. 18th December 2004.

236. Personal communication, Medical Information, AstraZeneca, 12th September 2006.

237. Acetylcysteine drug evaluation. Micromedex Healthcare Series, accessed 25th April 2007.

238. Zovirax® 400mg tablets Summary of Product Characteristics. GlaxoSmithKline, 9th January 2007.

239. Zovirax® Suspension Summary of Product Characteristics. GlaxoSmithKline, 29th November 2004.

240. Zovirax® Double-Strength Suspension Summary of Product Characteristics. GlaxoSmithKline, 29th November 2004.

241. Agenerase® 15mg/mL Oral Solution Summary of Product Characteristics. GlaxoSmithKline, 28th February 2007.

242. Martin JE, Lutomski DM. Warfarin resistance and enteral feedings. JPEN, 1989; 13 (2): 206-208.

243. Fleisher D, Sheth N, Kou JH. Phenytoin interaction with enteral feedings administered through nasogastric tubes. JPEN, 1990; 14 (5): 513-516.

244. Randall C, Tett S, Lauchlan R. Effect of enteral feeds on anticonvulsant concentrations. Clin. Exp. Pharmacol. Physiol. 1991. Suppl. 18: 50.

245. Guenter P, Jones S, Ericson M. Enteral nutrition therapy. Nursing Clinics of North America, 1997. 32; 4: 651-668.

246. Bobo Tanner S, Taylor HM. Feeding tube administration of bisphosphonates for treating osteoporosis in institutionalised patients with developmental disabilities. Bone 2004; 34 (Suppl. 1): S97-S98.

247. Cacek AT, DeVito JM, Koonce JR. In vitro evaluation of nasogastric administration methods for phenytoin. Am. J. Hosp. Pharm. 1986; 43: 689-692.

248. Rajagopalan P, *et al.* Enteral fluconazole population pharmacokinetics in patients in the surgical intensive care unit. Pharmacotherapy, 2003; 23(5): 592-602.

249. Gora ML, Tschampel MM, Visconti JA. Considerations of drug therapy in patients receiving enteral nutrition. Nutr. Clin. Pract. 1989; 4: 105-110.

250. Doak KK. Bioavailability of phenytoin acid and phenytoin sodium with enteral feedings. Pharmacotherapy, 1998; 18(3): 637-645.

251. Griffith R, Hebdon R. Liquid medicines can be the key that enables patients with swallowing difficulties to take their medicines. Pharmacy in Practice, 2007; 17(4): 135-139.

252. Gibberd FB, Webley M. Studies in man of phenytoin absorption and its implications. Journal of Neurology, Neurosurgery, and Psychiatry, 1975; 38: 219-224.

253. Sweetman SC, editor. Martindale: The Extra Pharmacopoeia. 35th Edition, London: Pharmaceutical Press, 2007.

254. Personal communication, Medical Information, Lundbeck, 18th April 2006.

255. Personal communication, Medical Information, Galen, 11th September 2006.

256. Keppra® Summary of Product Characteristics. UCB Pharma Limited, November 2007.

257. Personal communication, Medical Information, AstraZeneca, 2nd January 2007.

258. Personal communication, Sarah Garmory, Medical Information, Sheffield Children's Hospital, 27th November 2006.

259. Personal communication, Hazel King, 11th January 2006.

260. Personal communicaton, Steve Bowden, 11th January 2006.

261. Personal communication, Hazel King, 12th January 2006.

262. Personal communication, John Dade, 13th January 2006.

263. Personal communicaton, Mark Tomlin, 13th January 2006.

264. John Wiley & Sons, Chichester. InfoPOEM: IV metoclopramide reduces nausea/discomfort during NG tube insertion. Ozucelik DN, Karaca MA, Sivri B. Effectiveness of pre-emptive metoclopramide infusion in alleviating pain, discomfort and nausea associated with nasogastric tube insertion: A randomized, double-blind, placebo-controlled trial. Int. J. Clin. Pract. 2005; 59: 1422-1427. Accessed via http://www.essentialevidenceplus.com 9th July 2008.

265. Personal communication, Jackie Williams, 31st July 2006.

266. BNF No. 55 (March 2008). London: BMJ Group, RPS Publishing, 2008.

267. Zoton FasTab® Summary of Product Characteristics, Wyeth Pharmaceuticals, 9th August 2007.

268. Merbentyl® Summary of Product Characteristics, Sanofi Aventis, December 2006.

269. Glivec® Summary of Product Characteristics, Novartis Pharmaceuticals, 20th November 2007.

270. DiGiacinto JL, et al. Stability of suspension formulations of lansoprazole and omeprazole stored in amber coloured plastic oral syringes. Ann Pharmacother. 2000; 34: 600-604.

271. Nahata MC, Morosco RS, Brady MT. Extemporaneous sildenafil citrate oral suspensions for the treatment of pulmonary hypertension in children. Am J Health Syst Pharm. 2006; 63(3): 254-257.

272. BNF No. 56 (September 2008). London: BMJ Group, RPS Publishing, 2008.

273. Anon. New perindopril tablets mean a change in dosage for patients. Pharmaceutical Journal 2008; 280 (7495): 352.

274. Email letter to Jane Walker from Medical Information, Roche Products Ltd, Ref. HS-Nov08-08-3302E-Letter, 20th November 2008.

275. Personnal communication, Alistair Ellis-Jones and Roche Medical Information, 18th November 2008.

276. Xeloda® Summary of Product Characteristics. Roche Products Limited, 31st October 2008.

277. Losec MUPS® Summary of Product Characteristics. AstraZeneca UK Ltd, 19th February 2008.

278. Robbins B, Reiss RA. Amitriptyline absorption in a patient with short bowel syndrome. Am J Gastroenterol. 1999; 94(8):2302-2304.

279. Diflucan® Summary of Product Characteristics. Pfizer Ltd, April 2007.

280. Ridaura® Tiltab Summary of Product Characteristics. Astellas Pharma Ltd, 28th January 2008.

281. Cohn SM, et al. Enteric absorption of ciprofloxacin during tube feeding in the critically ill. J Antimicrob Chemother. 1996; 38: 871-876.

282. Martinez V, et al. Serum voriconazole levels following administration via percutaneous jejunostomy tube. Antimicrob. Agents Chemother. 2003; 47 (10): 3375.

283. Vfend® Summary of Product Characteristics. Pfizer Limited, 14th October 2008.

284. Zolvera® Summary of Product Characteristics. Rosemont Pharmaceuticals Ltd., 23rd February 2007.

285. Maxolon® Syrup Summary of Product Characteristics. Amdipharm PLC, 16th June 1995.

286. Dulphalac® Summary of Product Characteristics. Solvay Healthcare Limited, March 2004.

287. Rothwell J (letter). Lisinopril oral solution 5mg/mL. Rosemont Pharmaceuticals Ltd., 21st March 2005.

288. Button L (letter). Tegretol suppositories. Novartis Pharmaceuticals UK Ltd., 17th September 2008.

289. Lioresal® Liquid Summary of Product Characteristics. Novartis Pharmaceuticals UK Ltd., 12th April 2007.

290. Lyflex® Oral Solution Summary of Product Characteristics. Chemidex Pharma Limited, October 2008.

291. Dulcolax® Summary of Product Characteristics. Boehringer Ingelheim Limited, August 2008.

292. Keflex® Summary of Product Characteristics. Flynn Pharma Limited, September 2005.

293. Anastrozole Drug Evaluation. Micromedex Healthcare Series, accessed 27th November 2008.

294. Atorvastatin Drug Evaluation. Micromedex Healthcare Series, accessed 27th November 2008.

295. Imuran® Tablets 50mg Summary of Product Characteristics. The Wellcome Foundation, 12th September 2008.

296. Tagretin® capsules Summary of Product Characteristics. Eisai Ltd., 30th April 2007.

297. Myleran® Summary of Product Characteristics. The Wellcome Foundation Ltd, 23rd October 2006.

298. Suprax® Powder for Paediatric Oral Suspension Summary of Product Characteristics. Sanofi-Aventis, 4th July 2008.

299. Fish DN, Abraham E. Pharmacokinetics of a clarithromycin suspension administered via nasogastric tube to seriously ill patients. Antimicrob Agents Chemother. 1999; 43(5):1277-1280.

300. Argenti D, Ireland D, Heald DL. A pharmacokinetic and pharmacodynamic comparison of desmopressin administered whole, chewed and crushed tablets, and as an oral solution. J Urol. 2001; 165(5): 1446-1451.

301. Cardura® XL Summary of Product Characteristics. Pfizer Limited, September 2007.

302. Cipralex® Summary of Product Characteristics. H. Lundbeck A/S, 16th October 2008.

303. Diamicron® MR Summary of Product Characteristics. Les Laboratoires Servier, May 2005.

304. Sporanox® Oral Solution Summary of Product Characteristics. Janssen-Cilag Ltd, September 2008.

305. Nizoral® Tablets Summary of Product Characteristics. Janssen-Cilag Ltd, October 2008.

306. Orudis® Suppositories Summary of Product Characteristics. Sanofi-aventis, 24th September 2007.

307. Oruvail® IM Injection Summary of Product Characteristics. Sanofi-aventis, 9th March 2007.

308. Oruvail® Gel Summary of Product Characteristics. Sanofi-aventis, November 2006.

309. Nutrizym® 10 Summary of Product Characteristics. E Merck Ltd, 22nd October 2007.

310. Pancrease® HL Capsules Summary of Product Characteristics. Janssen-Cilag Ltd, April 2008.

311. Pancrex® Granules Summary of Product Characteristics. Paines and Byrne Limited, 25th October 2007.

312. Pancrex® V Capsules Summary of Product Characteristics. Paines and Byrne Limited, 25th October 2007.

313. Pancrex® V Tablets Summary of Product Characteristics. Paines and Byrne Limited, 25th October 2007.

314. Pancrex® V Powder Summary of Product Characteristics. Paines and Byrne Limited, 25th October 2007.

315. Rifadin® Capsules Summary of Product Characteristics. Sanofi-aventis, July 2007.

316. Invirase® Film-coated Tablets Summary of Product Characteristics. Roche Registration Limited, 31st October 2008.

317. Dulcolax® Liquid Summary of Product Characteristics. Boehringer Ingelheim Limited, November 2008.

318. Zerit® Hard Capsules Summary of Product Characteristics. Bristol-Myers Squibb Pharma EEIG, 19th January 2007.

319. Viread® film-coated tablets Summary of Product Characteristics. Gilead Sciences International Limited, September 2008.

320. Truvada® film-coated tablets Summary of Product Characteristics. Gilead Sciences International Limited, August 2008.

321. Dollery C, editor. Therapeutic Drugs, 2nd edition. Churchill Livingstone, Edinburgh, 1999.

322. Reminyl® tablets Summary of Product Characteristics. Shire Pharmaceuticals Limited, September 2007.

323. Reminyl® oral solution Summary of Product Characteristics. Shire Pharmaceuticals Limited, September 2007.

324. Mebeverine Drug Evaluation. Micromedex Healthcare Series, accessed 27th January 2009.

325. Glucophage® Summary of Product Characteristics. Lipha Pharmaceuticals Limited, 18th October 2004.

326. Zomorph® Summary of Product Characteristics. Laboratoires Ethypharm, 15th September 2005.

327. Bass J, Miles MV, Tennison MB, Holcombe BJ, Thorn MD. Effects of enteral tube feeding on the absorption and pharmacokinetic profile of carbamazepine suspension. Epilepsia. 1989; 30(3):364-369.

328. OxyNorm® liquid and concentrate Summary of Product Characteristics. Napp Pharmaceuticals Ltd, July 2008.

329. Pancrex® V capsules Patient Information Leaflet. Paines and Byrne Limited.

330. Bonefos® Summary of Product Characteristics. Bayer plc, 1st May 2008.

331. Loron® 520 Summary of Product Characteristics. Roche Products Limited, October 2006.

332. Personal communication, Medical Information, Alliance Pharmaceuticals, 3rd February 2009.

333. Personal communication, Medical Information, Boehringer Ingelheim, 9th March 2009.

334. NICE Technology Appraisal TA90: Vascular disease – clopidogrel and dipyridamole: guidance. 25th May 2005.

335. Losec MUPS® Summary of Product Characteristics. AstraZeneca UK Ltd, 19th February 2008.

336. Personal communication, Medical Information, Cephalon, 10th March 2009.

337. Pentasa® Slow Release Tablets Summary of Product Characteristics. Ferring Pharmaceuticals Ltd, February 2005.

338. Personal communication, Medical Information, Goldshield Pharmaceuticals Ltd, 10th March 2009.

339. Email communication, Medical Information, Bayer plc, 31st March 2009.

340. Email communication, Medical Information, Ferring, 10th March 2009.

341. Personal communication, Medical Information, Chemidex, 23rd April 2009.

342. Personal communication, Medical Information, Amdipharm, 23rd April 2009.

343. Valcyte® Powder for Oral Solution Summary of Product Characteristics, Roche Products Limited, 9th September 2008.

344. Personal communication, Medical Information, Napp Pharmaceuticals Limited, 23rd April 2009.

345. Personal communication, Medical Information, Dr Falk Pharma, 27th April 2009.

346. Personal communication, Medical Information, GlaxoSmithKline, 28th April 2009.

347. Personal communication, Medical Information, MSD, 28th April 2009.

348. Personal communication, Medical Information, Merck, 28th April 2009.

349. Email communication, Medical Information, MSD, 28th April 2009.

350. Personal communication, Medical Information, BristolMyers Squibb, 28th May 2009.

351. Sustiva® Oral Solution Summary of Product Characteristics, BristolMyers Squibb Pharma EEIG, 29th April 2004.

352. Personal communication, Medical Information, Servier, 28th April 2009.

353. Personal communication, Medical Information, Orion Pharma, 28th May 2009.

354. Personal communication, Medical Information, Roche, 28th May 2009.

355. Letter from Medical Information, Pfizer, ref. KM/090612/09/2727L, 12th June 2009.

356. Email letter from Medical Information, Roche Products Ltd, 11th June 2009.

357. Personal communication, Medical Information, Actavis, 24th June 2009.

358. In-house data, April-June 2009.

359. Personal communication, Medical Information, Bayer, 25th June 2009.

360. Personal communication, Medical Informaton, Rosemont Pharmaceuticals, 25th June 2009.

361. Personal communication, Medical Information, Sanofi-Aventis, 25th June 2009.

362. Epilim® Summary of Product Characteristics. Sanofi-Aventis Limited, 14th June 2009.

363. Personal communication, Medical Information, Janssen-Cilag, 25th June 2009.

364. Personal communication, Medical Information, UCB Pharma, 26th June 2009.

365. Personal communication, Medical Information, Sanofi Aventis, 26th June 2009.

366. Email communication, Medical Information, Janssen-Cilag, 26th June 2009.

367. Royal Bournemouth and Christchurch Hospitals Drug Administration website, http://www.rbch.nhs.uk/pharmacy/Home/home.html, accessed 16th January 2009.

368. Royal Bournemouth and Christchurch Hospitals Drug Administration website, http://www.rbch.nhs.uk/pharmacy/Home/home.html, accessed 2nd February 2009.

369. Royal Bournemouth and Christchurch Hospitals Drug Administration website, http://www.rbch.nhs.uk/pharmacy/Home/home.html, accessed 20th July 2009.

370. Tamiflu® Summary of Product Characteristics, Roche Registration Ltd., 11th May 2009.

371. Tamiflu® NHS Direct Medicines Fact Sheet, 10th June 2009.

372. Information from Maya, Birmingham Childrens' Hospital, 15th June 2009.

373. Information from Fatemeh Leedham, Basildon and Thurrock University Hospitals, 11th October 2007.

374. Information from Julian D'Enrico, 13th August 2007.

375. Glucophage® powder for oral solution in sachets Summary of Product Characteristics, Lipha Pharmaceuticals Limited, 19th November 2008.

376. Email communication from Merck Serono Medical Information to Liz Davies, Practice Pharmacist, Wrexham LHB, 28th May 2009.

377. Information from David Anderton, Medicines Information, Derby Hospitals NHS Foundation Trust, 20th May 2009.

378. Information from Ruth, St Georges, London, 11th June 2007.

379. Information from Hazel King, 22nd May 2006.

380. Information from Hazel King, 5th May 2008.

381. Information from Kirsty Warren, West Herts Hospitals NHS Trust, 28th September 2009.

382. Personal communication, Medical Information, Sanofi, recorded in an email to UKCPA, 4th April 2008.

383. Azithromycin Drug Evaluation, Micromedex Healthcare Series, accessed 19th October 2007.

384. Zithromax® Capsules and Suspension Summary of Product Characteristics, Pfizer Limited, July 2006.

385. Zithromax® (letter), reference JE/071022/07/7639E-Letter. Communication from Pfizer Pharmaceuticals Ltd, 22nd October 2007.

386. Luke DR, Foulds G, Cohen SF, Levy B. Safety, toleration, and pharmacokinetics of intravenous azithromycin. Antimicrobial Agents and Chemotherapy, 1996; 40 (11): 2577-2581.

387. Simicevic VN, et al. Lack of effect of food on the bioavailability of oral azithromycin tablets. Clin Drug Invest, 1998; 16 (5): 405-410.

388. Hopkins S. Clinical toleration and safety of azithromycin. The American Journal of Medicine, 1991; 91 (suppl. 3A): 40S-45S.

389. Thakker KM, et al. Pharmacokinetics of azithromycin oral suspension following 12mg/kg/day (maximum 500mg/day) for 5 days in fed pediatric patients. Abstract presented at 38th Interscience conference on Antimicrobial Agents and Chemotherapy; September 24-27th 1998; San Diego, CA; and American Society for Microbiology, 1998; Washinton, DC.

390. Drew RH, Gallis HA. Azithromycin – Spectrum of activity, pharmacokinetics, and clinical applications. Pharmacotherapy, 1992; 12 (3): 161-173.

391. Pelz RK, Lipsett PA, Swoboda SM, Merz W, Rinaldi MG, Hendrix CW. Enteral fluconazole is well absorbed in critically ill surgical patients. Surgery, 2002; 131 (5):534-540.

392. McCauley DL, Tozer TN, Winter ME. Time for phenytoin concentration to peak: consequences of first-order and zero-order absorption. Therapeutic Drug Monitoring, 1989; 11: 540-542.

393. Jung D, Powell JR, Walson P, Perrier D. Effect of dose on phenytoin absorption. Clin. Pharmacol. Ther., 1980; 28(4): 479-485.

394. Tisdale JE, *et al.* Prospective evaluation of serum amiodarone concentrations when administered via a nasogastric tube into the stomach conduit after transthoracic esophagectomy (abstract only). Clinical Therapeutics, 2007; 29 (10): 2226-2234.

395. Dhaliwal S, Jain S, Singh HP, Tiwary AK. Mucoadhesive microspheres for gastroretentive delivery of acyclovir: In vitro and in vivo evaluation (abstract only). AAPS Journal, 2008; 10 (2): 322-330.

396. Digenis GA, *et al.* Gastrointestinal behaviour of orally administered radiolabelled erythromycin pellets in man as determined by gamma scintigraphy (abstract only). Journal of Clinical Pharmacology, 1990; 30 (7): 621-631.

397. Diamond JM, Ehrlich BE, Morawski SG, Santa Ana CA, Fordtran JS. Lithium absorption in tight and leaky segments of intestine (abstract only). Journal of Membrane Biology, 1983; 72 (1-2): 153-159.

398. Nyberg L, Mansson W, Abrahamsson B, Seidegard J, Borga O. A convenient method for local drug administration at predefined sites in the entire gastrointestinal tract: Experiences from 13 phase 1 studies (abstract only). European Journal of Pharmaceutical Sciences, 2007; 30 (5): 432-440.

399. Masaoka Y, Tanaka Y, Kataoka M, Sakuma S, Yamashita S. Site of drug absorption after oral administration: Assessment of membrane permeability and luminal concentration of drugs in each segment of gastrointestinal tract (abstract only). European Journal of Pharmaceutical Sciences, 2006; 29 (3-4 Spec. Iss.): 240-250.

400. Narawane M, Podder SK, Bundgaard H, Lee VH. Segmental differences in drug permeability, esterase activity and ketone reductase activity in the albino rabbit intestine (abstract only). Journal of Drug Targeting, 1993; 1 (1): 29-39.

401. Fara JW, Myrback RE, Swanson DR. Evaluation of oxprenolol and metoprolol Oros systems in the dog: comparison of in vivo and in vitro drug release, and of drug absorption from duodenal and colonic infusion sites (abstract only). British Journal of Clinical Pharmacology, 1985; 19 (Suppl. 2): 91S-95S.

402. Vidon N, *et al.* Investigation of drug absorption from the gastrointestinal tract of man. II. Metoprolol in the jejunum and ileum (abstract only). British Journal of Clinical Pharmacology, 1985; 19 (Suppl. 2): 107S-112S.

403. Taylor DC, Pownall R, Burke W. The absorption of beta-receptor antagonists in rat in-situ small intestine; the effect of lipophilicity (abstract only). Journal of Pharmacy & Pharmacology, 1985; 37 (4): 280-283.

404. Ueno T, Tanaka A, Hamanaka Y, Suzuki T. Serum drug concentrations after oral administration of paracetamol to patients with surgical resection of the gastrointestinal tract (abstract only). British Journal of Clinical Pharmacology, 1995; 39 (3): 330-332.

405. Saano V, Elo HA, Paronen P. Effect of central muscle relaxants on single-dose pharmacokinetics of peroral paracetamol in man (abstract only). International Journal of Clinical Pharmacology Therapy and Toxicology, 1990; 28 (1): 39-45.

406. Nelson EB, Abernethy DR, Greenblatt DJ, Ameer B. Paracetamol absorption from a feeding jejunostomy (abstract only). British Journal of Clinical Pharmacology, 1986; 22 (1): 111-113.

407. Bagnall WE, Kelleher J, Walker BE, Losowsky MS. The gastrointestinal absorption of paracetamol in the rat (abstract only). Journal of Pharmacy & Pharmacology, 1979; 31 (3): 157-160.

408. Mariappan TT, Singh S. Gastrointestinal permeability studies using combinations of rifampicin and nucleoside analogue reverse transcriptase inhibitors in rats (abstract only). Indian Journal of Pharmacology, 2007; 39 (6): 284-290.

409. Mariappan TT, Singh S. Regional gastrointestinal permeability of rifampicin and isoniazid (alone and their combination) in the rat (abstract only). International Journal of Tuberculosis and Lung Disease, 2003; 7 (8): 797-803.

410. Kenny MT, Strates B. Metabolism and pharmacokinetics of the antibiotic rifampin (abstract only). Drug Metabolism Reviews, 1981; 12 (1): 159-218.

411. Osman MA, El Maghraby GM, Hedaya MA. Intestinal absorption and presystemic disposition of sildenafil citrate in the rabbit: Evidence for site-dependent absorptive clearance (abstract only). Biopharmaceutics and Drug Disposition, 2006; 27 (2): 93-102.

412. Nimodipine Drug Evaluation. Micromedex Healthcare Series, accessed 14th October 2009.

413. Personal communication, Medical Information, Sanofi-Aventis, 14th October 2009.

414. Personal communication, Medical Information, Pfizer, 14th October 2009.

415. Personal communication, Medical Information, Abbott, 14th October 2009.

416. Personal communication, Medical Information (Karen Warrillow), Lundbeck, 16th October 2009.

417. Personal communication, Medical Information, Organon, 16th October 2009.

418. Personal communication, Medical Information, Leo, 16th October 2009.

419. Personal communication, Medical Information, Actavis, 16th October 2009.

420. Bothwell TH, MacPhail AP. The potential role of NaFeEDTA as an iron fortificant (abstract). International Journal for Vitamin & Nutrition Research, 2004; 74 (6): 421-434.

421. Personal communication, Medical Information, Link Pharmaceuticals, 16th October 2009.

422. Email communication, Medical Information (Lauren Turner), Merck Serono Limited, 23rd April 2009.

423. Para-aminosalicylic acid Drug Evaluation. Micromedex Healthcare Series, accessed 21st October 2008.

424. Email communication, Maja Balic, St Mary's Hospital, Imperial College NHS Trust, London, 21st October 2008.

425. Para-aminosalicylic acid Drugpoint Summary. Micromedex Healthcare Series, accessed 28th October 2009.

426. Oseltamivir is adequately absorbed following nasogastric administration to adult patients with severe H5N1 influenza (abstract). PLoS ONE, 2008; 3 (10): e3410.

427. Personal communication, Medical Information, GlaxoSmithkline, 22nd October 2009.

428. Personal communication, Medical Information, UCB Pharma, 26th June 2009.

429. BNF No. 57 (March 2009). London: BMJ Group, RPS Publishing, 2009.

430. Sandimmun® Concentrate for Solution for Infusion 50mg/mL Summary of Product Characteristics. Novartis Pharmaceuticals UK Limited. 21st May 2009.

431. BNF No. 58 (September 2009). London: BMJ Group, RPS Publishing, 2009.

432. Lanoxin® Injection Summary of Product Characteristics. The Wellcome Foundation Limited, 14th May 2009.

433. Nexium® granules for oral suspension, sachet, Summary of Product Characteristics. AstraZeneca UK Limited, 21st September 2009.

434. Tamiflu® 75mg hard capsule Summary of Product Characteristics. Roche Registration Limited, 23rd October 2009.

435. Vimpat® Summary of Product Characteristics. UCB Pharma SA, July 2009.

436. Rosemont Specials Product List, April 2009.

437. Rosemont Licensed Product List, April 2009.

438. Local experience, Wrexham Maelor Hospital Intensive Care Unit, November 2009.

439. Email communication from Helen Laing, Stirling Royal Infirmary, with information from Solvay Healthcare, 27th November 2009.

440. Kruger KA, Garnett WR, Comstock TJ, Fitzsimmons WE, Karnes HT, Pellock JM. Effect of two administration schedules of an enteral nutrient formula on phenytoin bioavailability. Epilepsia, 1987; 28 (6): 706-712.

441. Mitchell J. Oral dosage forms that should not be crushed or chewed. Hospital Pharmacy, 2002; 37 (2): 213-214.

442. Scanlan M, Frisch S. Nasoduodenal feeding tubes: prevention of occlusion. J Neurosci. Nurs. 1992; 24 (5): 256-259.

443. Maynard GA, Jones KM, Guidry JR. Phenytoin absorption from tube feedings. Arch. Intern. Med. 1987; 147: 1821.

444. Yamreudeewong W, Danthi SN, Hill RA, Fox JL. Stability of ondansetron hydrochloride injection in various beverages. Am. J. Health-Syst. Pharm. 1995; 52: 2011-2014.

445. Allen LV, Stiles ML, Prince SJ, McLaury H, Sylvestri MF. Stability of ramipril in water, apple juice, and applesauce. Am J Health-Syst Pharm 1995; 52: 2433-2436.

446. Email communication from Lauren Turner, Merck Serono, 4th December 2009.

447. Ozuna J, Friel P. Effect of enteral tube feeding on serum phenytoin levels. J. Neurosurg. Nurs. 1984; 16 (6): 289-291.

448. Murray, L. Administration of essential drugs in patients who are "nil by mouth". Southern General Hospital, Glasgow, April 2003.

449. Lepage R, Walker S, Paradiso-Hardy F, Myers M. Pharmacokinetics and pharmacodynamics of intact and crushed nifedipine prolonged action (PA) tablets. Can. J. Cardiol. 2000; 16 (Suppl F): 106F [Abstract 56].

450. Persiani S, et al. Pharmacodynamics and relative bioavailability of cabergoline tablets vs solution in healthy volunteers. J. Pharm. Sci. 1994; 83(10): 1421-1424.

451. Allen LV, Erickson MA. Stability of acetazolamide, allopurinol, azathioprine, clonazepam, and flucytosine in extemporaneously compounded oral liquids. Am. J. Health-Syst. Pharm. 1996; 53: 1944-1949.

452. Allen LV, Erickson MA. Stability of alprazolam, chloroquine phosphate, cisapride, enalapril maleate, and hydralazine hydrochloride in extemporaneously compounded oral liquids. Am. J. Health-Syst. Pharm. 1998; 55: 1915-1920.

453. Nahata MC, Morosco RS, Hipple TF. Stability of amlodipine besylate in two liquid dosage forms. J. Am. Pharm. Assoc. 1999; 39 (3): 375-377.

454. Allen LV, Erickson MA. Stability of bethanechol chloride, pyrazinamide, quinidine sulphate, rifampin, and tetracycline hydrochloride in extemporaneously compounded oral liquids. Am. J. Health-Syst. Pharm. 1998; 55: 1804-1809.

455. Allen LV. Busulfan oral suspension. US Pharmacist, 1990; 15: 94-95.

456. Nahata M, Morosco R, Hipple T. Stability of captopril in three liquid dosage forms. Am. J. Hosp. Pharm. 1994, 51: 95-96.

457. Allen LV, Erickson MA. Stability of baclofen, captopril, diltiazem hydrochloride, dipyridamole, and flecainide acetate in extemporaneously compounded oral liquids. Am. J. Health-Syst. Pharm. 1996; 53: 2179-2184.

458. Lye MYF, Yow KL, Lim LY, Chan SY, Chan E, Ho PC. Effects of ingredients on stability of captopril in extemporaneously prepared oral liquids. Am. J. Health-Syst. Pharm. 1997; 54: 2483-2487.

459. Levinson ML, Johnson CE. Stability of an extemporaneously compounded clonidine hydrochloride oral liquid. Am. J. Hosp. Pharm. 1992; 49: 122-125.

460. Dentinger PJ, Swenson CF. Stability of codeine phosphate in an extemporaneously compounded syrup. Am. J. Health-Syst. Pharm. 2007; 64: 2569-2573.

461. The Pharmaceutical Codex, 11th edition. Pharmaceutical Press, London, 1979.

462. Johnson CE, Wagner DS, Bussard WE. Stability of dolasetron in two oral liquid vehicles. Am. J. Health-Syst. Pharm. 2003; 60: 2242-2244.

463. Nahata M, Morosco R, Hipple T. Stability of enalapril maleate in three extemporaneously prepared oral liquids. Am. J. Health-Syst. Pharm. 1998; 55: 1155-1157.

464. McLeod HL, Relling MV. Stability of etoposide solution for oral use. Am. J. Hosp. Pharm. 1992; 49: 2784-2785.

465. Dentinger PJ, Swenson CF, Anaizi NH. Stability of famotidine in an extemporaneously compounded oral liquid. Am. J. Health-Syst. Pharm. 2000; 57: 1340-1342.

466. Wintermeyer SM, Nahata MC. Stability of flucytosine in an extemporaneously compounded oral liquid. Am. J. Health-Syst. Pharm. 1996; 53: 407-409.

467. VandenBussche HL, Johnson CE, Yun J, Patel SA. Stability of flucytosine 50mg/mL in extemporaneous oral liquid formulations. Am. J. Health-Syst. Pharm. 2002; 59: 1853-1855.

468. Anaizi NH, Swenson CF, Dentinger PJ. Stability of ganciclovir in extemporaneously compounded oral liquids. Am. J. Health-Syst. Pharm. 1999; 56: 1738-1741.

469. Nahata MC, Morosco RS, Hipple TF. Stability of granisetron hydrochloride in two oral suspensions. Am. J. Health-Syst. Pharm. 1998; 55: 2511-2513.

470. Quercia RA, Zhang J, Fan C, Chow MSS. Stability of granisetron hydrochloride in an extemporaneously prepared oral liquid. Am. J. Health-Syst. Pharm. 1997; 54: 1404-1406.

471. Hydroxycarbamade (hydroxyurea) 100mg/mL suspension formula. Received by facsimile from Alder Hey Hospital, 18th November 2008.

472. Jacobson PA, Johnson CE, Walters JR. Stability of itraconazole in an extemporaneously compounded oral liquid. Am. J. Health-Syst. Pharm. 1995; 52: 189-191.

473. Allen LV, Erickson MA. Stability of ketoconazole, metolazone, metronidazole, procainamide hydrochloride, and spironolactone in extemporaneously compounded oral liquids. Am. J. Health-Syst. Pharm. 1996; 53: 2073-2078.

474. Nahata MC. Stability of labetalol hydrochloride in distilled water, simple syrup, and three fruit juices. DICP 1991; 25: 465-469.

475. VandenBussche HL, Johnson CE, Fontana EM, Meram JM. Stability of levofloxacin in an extemporaneously compounded oral liquid. Am. J. Health-Syst. Pharm. 1999; 56: 2316-2318.

476. Taubel JJ, Sharma VK, Chiu YL, Lukasik NL, Pilmer BL, Pan WJ. A comparison of simplified lansoprazole suspension administered nasogastrically and pantoprazole administered intravenously: effects on 24-h intragastric pH. Aliment. Pharmacol. Ther. 2001; 15 (11): 1807-1817.

477. Boulton DW, Fawcett P, Woods DJ. Stability of an extemporaneously compounded levothyroxine sodium oral liquid. Am. J. Health-Syst. Pharm. 1996; 52: 1157-1161.

478. Thompson KC, Zhao Z, Mazakas JM, Beasley CA, Reed RA, Moser CL. Characterization of an extemporaneous liquid formulation of lisinopril. Am. J. Health-Syst. Pharm. 2003; 60: 69-74.

479. Alibadi HM, Romanick M, Desai S, Lavasanifar A. Effect of buffer and antioxidant on stability of a mercaptopurine suspension. Am. J. Health-Syst. Pharm. 2008; 65: 441-447.

480. Nahata MC, Morosco RS, Hipple TF. Stability of mexiletine in two extemporaneous liquid formulations stored under refrigeration and at room temperature. J. Am. Pharm. Assoc. 2000; 40: 257-259.

481. Anaizi NH, Swenson CF, Dentinger PJ. Stability of mycophenolate mofetil in an extemporaneously compounded oral liquid. Am. J. Health-Syst. Pharm. 1998; 55: 926-929.

482. Swenson CF, Dentinger PJ, Anaizi NH. Stability of mycophenolate mofetil in an extemporaneously compounded sugar-free oral liquid. Am. J. Health-Syst. Pharm. 1999; 56: 2224-2226.

483. Dentinger PJ, Swenson CF, Anaizi NH. Stability of nifedipine in an extemporaneously compounded oral solution. Am. J. Health-Syst. Pharm. 2003; 60: 1019-1022.

484. Johnson CE, Price J, Hession JM. Stability of norfloxacin in an extemporaneously prepared oral liquid. Am. J. Health-Syst. Pharm. 2001; 58: 577-579.

485. Burnett JE, Balkin ER. Stability and viscosity of a flavored omeprazole oral suspension for pediatric use. Am. J. Health-Syst. Pharm. 2006; 63: 2240-2247.

486. Phillips JP, Metzler MH, Palmieri TL Huckfeldt RE, Dahl NG. A prospective study of simplified omeprazole suspension for the prophylaxis of stress-related mucosal damage. Crit. Care Med. 1996; 24(11): 1793-1800.

487. Abdel-Rahman SM, Nahata MC. Stability of pentoxifylline in an extemporaneously prepared oral suspension. Am. J. Health-Syst. Pharm. 1997; 54: 1301-1303.

488. Cober MP, Johnson CE. Stability of an extemporaneously prepared alcohol-free phenobarbital suspension. Am. J. Health-Syst. Pharm. 2007; 64: 644-646.

489. Lim L, Tan L, Chan EWY, Yow K, Chan S, Ho PCL. Stability of phenoxybenzamine hydrochloride in various vehicles. Am. J. Health-Syst. Pharm. 1997; 54: 2073-2078.

490. Nahata MC, Morosco RS, Trowbridge JM. Stability of propylthiouracil in extemporaneously prepared oral suspensions at 4 and 25°C. Am. J. Health-Syst. Pharm. 2000; 57: 1141-1143.

491. Nahata MC, Morosco RS, Peritore SP. Stability of pyrazinamide in two suspensions. Am. J. Health-Syst. Pharm. 1995; 52: 1558-1560.

492. Nahata MC, Morosco RS, Hipple TF. Stability of pyrimethamine in a liquid dosage formulation sotred for three months. Am. J. Health-Syst. Pharm. 1997; 54: 2714-2716.

493. Haslam JL, Egodage KL, Chen Y, Rajewski RA, Stella V. Stability of rifabutin in two extemporaneously compounded oral liquids. Am. J. Health-Syst. Pharm. 1999; 56: 333-336.

494. Caruthers RL, Johnson CE. Stability of extemporaneously sodium phenylbutyrate oral suspensions. Am. J. Health-Syst. Pharm. 2007; 64: 1513-1515.

495. Mathur LK, Wickman A. Stability of extemporaneously compounded spironolactone suspensions. Am. J. Hosp. Pharm. 1989; 46: 2040-2042.

496. Fish DN, Beall HD, Goodwin SD, Fox JL. Stability of sumatriptan succinate in extemporaneously prepared oral liquids. Am. J. Health-Syst. Pharm. 1997; 54: 1619-1622.

497. Jacobson PA, Johnson CE, West NJ, Foster JA. Stability of tacrolimus in an extemporaneously compounded oral liquid. Am. J. Health-Syst. Pharm. 1997; 54: 178-180.

498. Han J, Beeton A, Long PF, Wong I, Tuleu C. Physical and microbiological stability of an extemporaneous tacrolimus suspension for paediatric use. Journal of Clinical Pharmacy and Therapeutics, 2006; 31: 167-172.

499. Abdel-Rahman SM, Nahata MC. Stability of terbinafine hydrochloride in an extemporaneously prepared oral suspension at 25 and 4°C. Am. J. Health-Syst. Pharm. 1999; 56: 243-245.

500. Johnson CE, VanDeKoppel S, Myers E. Stability of anhydrous theophylline in extemporaneously prepared alcohol-free oral suspensions. Am. J. Health-Syst. Pharm. 2005; 62: 2518-2520.

501. Nahata MC, Morosco RS. Stability of tiagabine in two oral liquid vehicles. Am. J. Health-Syst. Pharm. 2003; 60: 75-77.

502. Wagner DS, Johnson CE, Cichon-Hensley BK, DeLoach SL. Stability of oral liquid preparations of tramadol in strawberry syrup and a sugar-free vehicle. Am. J. Health-Syst. Pharm. 2003; 60: 1268-1270.

503. Johnson CF, Streetman DD. Stability of oral suspensions of ursodiol made from tablets. Am. J. Health-Syst. Pharm. 2002; 59: 361-363.

504. Fish DN, Vidaurri VA, Deeter RG. Stability of valaciclovir hydrochloride in extemporaneously prepared oral liquids. Am. J. Health-Syst. Pharm. 1999; 56: 1957-1960.

505. Henkin CC, Griener JC, Ten Eick AP. Stability of valganciclovir in extemporaneously compounded liquid formulations. Am. J. Health-Syst. Pharm. 2003; 60: 687-690.

506. Anaizi NH, Dentinger PJ, Swenson CF. Stability of valganciclovir in an extemporaneously compounded oral liquid. Am. J. Health-Syst. Pharm. 2002; 59: 1267-1270.

507. UKMi Medicines Q&A 307.1. Academic detail aid for prescribers – choosing medicines for patients unable to take solid oral dosage forms. January 2010, www.nelm.nhs.uk.

508. UKMi Medicines Q&A 294.1. Therapeutic options for patients unable to take solid oral dosage forms. December 2009, www.nelm.nhs.uk.

509. Neoral® Summary of Product Characteristics. Novartis Pharmaceuticals UK Ltd. 17th November 2009.

510. Modigraf® Summary of Product Characteristics. Astellas Pharma Europe BV. 15th May 2009.

511. Drug Safety Update 2010; 3 (7). Medicines and Healthcare products Regulatory Agency & Commission on Human Medicines.

512. Data on file, Pharmacy Department, Wrexham Maelor Hospital, February 2010.

513. Email communication from Una Convery, Northern Ireland Regional Medicines and Poisons Information Centre, 19th February 2010.

514. St Marys Pharmaceutical Unit, Cardiff.

515. Nahata MC, Morosco RS. Stability of lisinopril in two liquid dosage forms. Annals of Pharmacotherapy 2004; 38: 396-399.

516. Justice J, Kupiec TC, Matthews P, Cardona P. Stability of Adderall in extemporaneously compounded oral liquids. Am. J. Health-Syst. Pharm. 2001; 58: 1418-1421.

517. Carrier MN, Garinot O, Vitzling C. Stability and compatability of tegaserod from crushed tablets mixed in beverages and foods. Am. J. Health-Syst. Pharm. 2004; 61: 1135-1142.

518. Siden R, Johnson CE. Stability of a flavoured formulation of acetylcysteine for oral administration. Am. J. Health-Syst. Pharm. 2008; 65: 558-561.

519. Dentinger PJ, Swenson CF, Anaizi NH. Stability of amphotericin B in an extemporaneously compounded oral suspension. Am. J. Health-Syst. Pharm. 2001; 58: 1021-1024.

520. Nahata MC. Stability of amiodarone in an oral suspension stored under refrigeration and at room temperature. Annals of Pharmacotherapy 1997; 31: 851-852.

521. Nahata MC, Morosco RS. Stability of sotalol in two liquid formulations at two temperatures. Annals of Pharmacotherapy 2003; 37: 506-509.

522. Ferron GM, Ku S, Abell M, et al. Oral bioavailability of pantoprazole suspended in sodium bicarbonate solution. Am. J. Health-Syst. Pharm. 2003; 60: 1324-1329.

523. Okeke CC, Medwick T, Nairn G, Khuspe S, Grady LT. Stability of hydralazine hydrochloride in both flavoured and nonflavoured extemporaneous preparations. International Journal of Pharmaceutical Compounding 2003; 7 (4): 313-319.

524. Allen LV, Erickson MA. Stability of extemporaneously prepared pediatric formulations using Ora-Plus with Ora-Sweet and Ora-Sweet SF – Part 1. Secundum Artem; 5 (4).

525. Allen LV, Erickson MA. Stability of extemporaneously prepared pediatric formulations using Ora-Plus with Ora-Sweet and Ora-Sweet SF – Part 2. Secundum Artem; 6 (1).

526. Allen LV, Erickson MA. Stability of extemporaneously prepared pediatric formulations using Ora-Plus with Ora-Sweet and Ora-Sweet SF – Part 3. Secundum Artem; 6 (2).

527. Allen LV, Erickson MA. Stability of extemporaneously prepared oral liquid formulations – Part 4. Secundum Artem; 14 (1).

528. Allen LV, Erickson MA. Stability of extemporaneously prepared oral liquid formulations – Part 5. Secundum Artem; 14 (3).

529. Allen LV, Erickson MA. Stability of extemporaneously prepared oral liquid formulations – Part 6. Secundum Artem; 15 (1).

530. Cober MP, Johnson CE, Lee J, Currie K.   Stability of extemporaneously prepared rifamixin suspensions. Am. J. Health-Syst. Pharm. 2010; 67: 287-289.

531. Personal communication from Medical Information, Merck Sharpe and Dohme Limited, to Medicines Information, University Hospital of North Staffordshire NHS Trust, recorded in an email from Jen Smith to UKMi discussion group, 11th November 2010.

532. Dupuis LL, Lingertat-Walsh K, Walker SE.   Stability of an extemporaneous oral liquid aprepitant formulation. Support Care Cancer 2009; 17: 701-706.

533. Email communication from Laura Millward, Senior Medicines Information Pharmacist, Glan Clwyd Hospital, 2nd August 2010.

534. Email communication from Sue Brown, Senior Technician, Medicines Information, Darent Valley Hospital, 19th August 2010.

535. Email communication from Catherine Horne, Medicines Information Pharmacist, Newcastle upon Tyne Hospitals NHS Foundation Trust, to UKMi discussion group, 13th September 2010.

536. Email communication from Matthew Jones, Senior Pharmacist, Medicines Information, Royal United Hospital, to UKMi discussion group, 5th November 2010.

537. Skillman KL, Caruthers RL, Johnson CE.   Stability of an extemporaneously prepared clopidogrel oral suspension. Am. J. Health-Syst. Pharm. 2010; 67: 559-561.

538. Abobo CV, Wei B, Liang D.   Stability of zonisamide in extemporaneously compounded oral suspensions. Am. J. Health-Syst. Pharm. 2009; 66: 1105-1109.

539. Hutchinson DJ, Johnson CE, Klein KC. Stability of extemporaneously prepared moxifloxacin oral suspensions. Am. J. Health-Syst. Pharm. 2009; 66: 665-667.

540. Sodium cromoglicate Drug Evaluation.   Micromedex Healthcare Series, accessed 7th December 2010.

541. Rosemont Pharmaceuticals Ltd. Licensed Product List, June 2010.

542. Rosemont Pharmaceuticals Ltd. Specials Product List, June 2010.

543. Wright D, Tomlin S. How to help if a patient can't swallow. Pharmaceutical Journal 2011; 286: 271-274.

544. Aclasta[®] Summary of Product Characteristics. Novartis Pharmaceuticals UK, 12th May 2010.

545. Vallergan[®] Syrup Summary of Product Characteristics.   Winthrop Pharmaceuticals UK Ltd, 13th November 2008.

546. Denzapine[®] Oral Suspension Summary of Product Characteristics.   Merz Pharma UK Ltd, 8th June 2010.

547. Questran® Patient Information Leaflet. Bristol-Myers Squibb Holdings Ltd, May 2010.

548. Exjade® Summary of Product Characteristics. Novartis Europharm Limited, 20th December 2010.

549. BNF No. 61 (March 2011). London: BMJ Group, Pharmaceutical Press, 2011.

550. Ferriprox® Oral Solution Summary of Product Characteristics. Apotex Europe B.V., 23rd September 2009.

551. Lanoxin PG® Elixir Summary of Product Characteristics. Aspen Europe GmbH, 4th November 2009.

552. Personal communication, Medical Information, Pfizer. 7th April 2011.

553. Email communication from Suzanne Cotter, Paediatric Pharmacist, 18th May 2011.

554. Personal experience on Critical Care Unit, Wrexham Maelor Hospital.

555. Elfant AB *et al.* Bioavailability of medication delivered via nasogastric tube is decreased in the immediate postoperative period. Am. J. Surg. 1995; 169 (4); 430-432.

556. Hydrea® Summary of Product Characteristics. E.R. Squibb & Sons Limited, 2nd July 2010.

557. Astbury, M. Pharmacists must be empowered to supply out-of-the-ordinary medicines. Pharmaceutical Journal 2011; 287: 212.

558. Pharmaceutical issues when Crushing, Opening or Splitting Oral Dosage Forms. Royal Pharmaceutical Society, June 2011.

559. Personal communication, Medical Information, AstraZeneca, 6th September 2011.

560. Murhammer J, Ross M, Bebout K. Medications that should not be crushed. Rx Update; March 2004. www.healthcare.uiowa.edu/pharmacy/rxupdate/2004/04rxu.html accessed 7th September 2011.

561. Gowan J. Crushing tablets – issues to consider. Autumn 2010. www.ndgp.org.au/secure/downloadfile.asp?fileid=1002259 accessed 7th September 2011.

562. Good Practice Guidance on: The procurement and supply of pharmaceutical specials. Update June 2011. Royal Pharmaceutical Society of Great Britain.

563. Good Practice Guidance on: The procurement and supply of pharmaceutical specials. Pharmacy Professional 2010; June: 28-32.

564. Clifton M. NEEMMC Guidelines for tablet crushing and administration via enteral feeding tubes. Colchester Hospital University NHS Foundation Trust. April 2010.

565. Medicines, Ethics and Practice. Edition 35; July 2011. Royal Pharmaceutical Society, London.

566. Rosenbloom K, Wakeman R, Scrimshaw P. The Disability Discrimination Act. Pharmaceutical Journal 2005; 275: 747-750.

567. The supply of unlicensed relevant medicinal products for individual patients. MHRA Guidance Note No. 14, revised January 2008.

568. Ashley C, Currie A. The Renal Drug Handbook, 3rd edition. Radcliffe Medical Press Ltd, Oxfordshire, 2009.

569. Guidelines for the administration of drugs via enteral feeding tubes. Enteral Parenteral Nutrition Support Committee, Midlands Regional Hospital, Tullamore, 2009.

570. Clipper® Summary of Product Characteristics. Chiesi Limited, 22nd December 2008.

571. Cystadane® Summary of Product Characteristics. Orphan Europe SARL, 15th February 2007.

572. Baxter K. Stockley's Drug Interactions. 7th edition. Pharmaceutical Press, London.

573. Jackson M, Lowey A. Handbook of Extemporaneous Preparation. Pharmaceutical Press, London, 2010.

574. Email communication from Sarah Gooda, Dietician, Wrexham Maelor Hospital, 19th September 2011.

575. Vimpat® Summary of Product Characteristics. UCB Pharma SA, May 2011.

576. Personal communication, Medical Information, Janssen-Cilag, 11th November 2011.

577. BNF No. 62 (September 2011). London: BMJ Group, Pharmaceutical Press, 2011.

578. Norvir® Summary of Product Characteristics. Abbott Laboratories Limited, 16th April 2010.

579. Rosemont Pharmaceuticals Ltd. Licensed Product List, January 2012.

580. Rosemont Pharmaceuticals Ltd. Hospital Specials Price List, January 2012.

581. Personal communication, Medical Information, Abbott Laboratories Limited, 22nd November 2011.

582. Martindale Pharma Specials Price List, Martindale Pharma, received 19th January 2012.

583. Rosemont Pharmaceuticals Ltd. Licensed Product List, March 2012.

584. Rosemont Pharmaceuticals Ltd. Specials Product List, March 2012.

585. Email communication from Rosemont Pharmaceuticals Ltd. 2nd May 2012.

586. Personal communication, Medical Information, Paines & Byrne Limited, 4th May 2012.

587. Personal communication to Laura Whitney, Pharmacy Department, St George's Hospital, London, from Medical Information, Astellas Pharma Ltd, 11th May 2012.

588. Budenofalk® granules Summary of Product Characteristics. Dr Falk Pharma GmbH, December 2010.

589. Email communication from Rosemont Pharmaceuticals Ltd. 22nd November 2012.

590. Letter from Chiara Facco, Medical Information Department, Bayer HealthCare, to Saghir Hussain, Medical Information, Heart of England NHS Trust, 13th December 2012, provided by Amanda Berry, Medical Information Pharmacist, Heart of England NHS Trust, 17th December 2012.

591. Personal communication, Elaine Roberts, Antimicrobial Pharmacist, Wrexham Maelor Hospital, Betsi Cadwaladr University Health Board, 4th January 2013.

592. Radia H. MHRA publishes a report on levothyroxine tablet products: A review of the clinical and quality considerations. NeLM news service, 8th January 2013. www.nelm.nhs.uk, accessed 10th January 2013.

593. Toedter Williams N. Medication administration through enteral feeding tubes. Am. J. Health-Syst. Pharm. 2008; 65: 2347-2357.

594. Boullata JI. Drug administration through an enteral feeding tube. American Journal of Nursing 2009; 109 (10): 34-42.

595. Guidelines for confirming correct positioning of nasogastric feeding tubes. National Nurses Nutrition Group. June 2004.

596. NPSA Patient Safety Alert 19: Promoting safer measurement and administration of liquid medicines via oral and other enteral routes. National Patient Safety Agency. 28th March 2007.

597. NPSA Patient Safety Alert NPSA/2011/PSA002: Reducing the harm caused by misplaced nasogastric feeding tubes in adults, children and infants. National Patient Safety Agency. 10th March 2011.

598. Personal communication from Laura Kearney, Senior Medicines Information Pharmacist, Leicester Royal Infirmary. Letter from Jana Little, Medical Services Executive, Bayer Healthcare dated 19th November 2012, received 10th December 2012.

599. Moore et al. The relative bioavailability of single-dose rivaroxaban, a novel oral anticoagulant and a selective direct factor Xa inhibitor, administered orally (as a whole or crushed tablet) and via nasogastric tube (as a crushed tablet suspension). Abstract presented at American College of Clinical Pharmacy (ACCP) 2012. Received from Bayer Healthcare via Laura Kearney, Senior Medicines Information Pharmacist, Leicester Royal Infirmary, 10th December 2012.

600. Personal communication from Laura Kearney, Senior Medicines Information Pharmacist, Leicester Royal Infirmary. Letter from Adele Herbst, Medical Information Officer, Boehringer Ingelheim, dated 14th November 2012, received 10th December 2012.

601. Trileptal® Oral Suspension Summary of Product Characteristics. Novartis Pharmaceuticals UK Limited. 15th October 2009.

602. Cleary JD, Evans PC, Hikal AH, Chapman SW. Administration of crushed extended-release pentoxifylline tablets: bioavailability and adverse effects (abstract only). Am. J. Health-Syst. Pharm. 1999; 56 (15): 1529-1534.

603. Trental® tablets Summary of Product Characteristics. Sanofi-aventis, 20th July 2012.

604. Modigraf® granules for oral suspension Summary of Product Characteristics. Astellas Pharma Europe BV, 18th February 2013.

605. BNF No. 64 (September 2012). London: BMJ Group, Pharmaceutical Press, 2012.

606. Back IN. Palliative Medicine Handbook, 3rd edition. BPM Books, Cardiff, 2001.

607. BNF No. 65 (March 2013). London: BMJ Group, Pharmaceutical Press, 2013.

608. Epilim Chronosphere® Summary of Product Characteristics. Sanofi-aventis, 28th November 2012.

609. Personal communication (exemestane) to Julian D'Enrico, Pharmacist, Wrexham Maelor Hospital, from Eros Biasiolo, Medical Information Associate, Pfizer European Medical Information, 10th June 2011.

610. Tapclob oral suspension Summary of Product Characteristics. Martindale Pharmaceuticals Ltd, 11th February 2013.

611. Capecitabine Drugdex Drug Evaluation. Micromedex Healthcare Series, accessed 12th August 2013.

612. Personal communication to Jane Walker, Clinical Pharmacist, Wrexham Maelor Hospital, from MSD Medical Information, 13th May 2013.

613. Hopkins R, Goundrey-Smith S. Specials are important and here to stay. Pharmaceutical Journal 2011; 287: 287.

614. Dodou K, Nazar H. Oral formulations adapted for the old and the young and to prevent misuse. Pharmaceutical Journal 2012; 288: 683-684.

615. Glipizide Drugdex Drug Evaluation. Micromedex Healthcare Series, accessed 6th September 2013.

616. Distigmine Drugdex Drug Evaluation. Micromedex Healthcare Series, accessed 6th September 2013.

617. Trimethoprim Drugdex Drug Evaluation. Micromedex Healthcare Series, accessed 6th September 2013.

618. Pyrazinamide Drugdex Drug Evaluation. Micromedex Healthcare Series, accessed 6th September 2013.

619. Calcium Drugdex Drug Evaluation. Micromedex Healthcare Series, accessed 6th September 2013.

620. Levofloxacin Drugdex Drug Evaluation. Micromedex Healthcare Series, accessed 6th September 2013.

621. Norfloxacin Drugdex Drug Evaluation. Micromedex Healthcare Series, accessed 6th September 2013.

622. Ofloxacin Drugdex Drug Evaluation. Micromedex Healthcare Series, accessed 6th September 2013.

623. Hydralazine Drugdex Drug Evaluation. Micromedex Healthcare Series, accessed 6th September 2013.

624. BNF No. 65 (March – September 2013). London: BMJ Group, Pharmaceutical Press, 2013.

625. Peloquin CA, Bulpitt AE, Jaresko GS, Jelliffe RW, James GT, Nix DE. Pharmacokinetics of pyrazinamide under fasting conditions, with food, and with antacids (abstract only). Pharmacotherapy 1998; 18 (61): 1205-1211.

626. Wohlt PD, Zheng L, Gunderson S, Balzar SA, Johnson BD, Fish JT. Recommendations for the use of medications with continuous enteral nutrition. Am. J. Health-Syst. Pharm. 2009; 66: 1458-1466.

627. Chui D, Cheng L, Tejani AM. Clinical equivalency of ciprofloxacin 750mg enterally and 400mg intravenously for patients receiving enteral feeding: Systematic review (abstract only). Canadian Journal of Hospital Pharmacy 2009; 62 (2): 127-134.

628. Deppermann KM, Lode H. Fluoroquinolones: interaction profile during enteral absorption (abstract only). Drugs 1993; 45 (Suppl. 3): 65-72.

629. Wright DH, Pietz SL, Konstantinides FN, Rotschafer JS. Decreased In Vitro Fluoroquinolone Concentrations After Admixture With an Enteral Feeding Formulation (abstract only). Journal of Parenteral & Enteral Nutrition 2000; 24 (1): 42-48.

630. Lee LJ, Hafkin B, Lee ID, Hoh J, Dix R. Effects of food and sucralfate on a single oral dose of 500 milligrams of levofloxacin in healthy subjects. Antimicrob. Agents Chemother. 1997; 41 (10): 2196-2200.

631. Ciprofloxacin Drugdex Drug Evaluation. Micromedex Healthcare Series, accessed 23rd September 2013.

632. Spenard J, Aumais C, Massicotte J *et al.* Effects of food and formulation on the relative bioavailability of bismuth biskalcitrate, metronidazole, and tetracycline given for *Helicobacter pylori* eradication. British Journal of Clinical Pharmacology 2005; 60 (4): 374-377.

633. Turner J, Dobbs SM, Nicholson PW, Rodgers EM. Influence of diet on digoxin dose requirements. British Journal of Pharmacology 1977; 4: 489-491.

634. Johnson BF, O'Grady J, Sabey GA, Bye C. Effect of a standard breakfast on digoxin absorption in normal subjects (abstract only). Clinical Pharmacology and Therapeutics 1978; 23 (3): 315-319.

635. Lanoxin PG Elixir Summary of Product Characteristics. Aspen Pharma Trading Limited, 9th March 2012.

636. Waldman SA, Morganroth J. Effects of food on the bioequivalence of different verapamil sustained-release formulations (abstract only). Journal of Clinical Pharmacology 1995; 35 (2): 163-169.

637. Hoon TJ, McCollam PL, Beckman KJ, Hariman RJ, Bauman JL. Impact of food on the pharmacokinetics and electrocardiographic effects of sustained-release verapamil in normal subjects (abstract only). American Journal of Cardiology 1992; 70 (11): 1072-1076.

638. Kozlowski GD, DeVito JM, Johnson JB, Holmes GB, Adams MA, Hunt TL. Bioequivalence of verapamil hydrochloride extended-release pellet-filled capsules when opened and sprinkled on food and when swallowed intact (abstract only). Clinical Pharmacy 1992; 11 (6): 539-542.

639. Woodcock BG, Kraemer N, Rietbrock N. Effect of a high protein meal on the bioavailability of verapamil. British Journal of Pharmacology 1986; 21: 337-338.

640. Verapamil Drugdex Drug Evaluation. Micromedex Healthcare Series, accessed 24th September 2013.

641. Semple HA, Koo W, Tam YK, Ngo L-Y, Coutts RT. Interactions between hydralazine and oral nutrients in humans (abstract only). Therapeutic Drug Monitoring 1991; 13 (4): 304-308.

642. Jackson SHD, Shepherd AMM, Ludden TM et al. Effect of food on oral availability of apresoline and controlled release hydralazine in hypertensive patients (abstract only). Journal of Cardiovascular Pharmacology 1990; 16 (4): 624-628.

643. Walden RJ, Hernandez R, Witts D. Effect of food on absorption of hydralazine in man (abstract only). European Journal of Clinical Pharmacology 1981; 20 (1): 53-58.

644. Shepherd AMM, Irvine NA, Ludden TM. Effect of food on blood hydralazine levels and response in hypertension (abstract only). Clinical Pharmacology and Therapeutics 1984; 36 (1): 14-18.

645. Desmond PV, Harman PJ, Gannoulis N, Kamm M, Mashford ML. The effect of an antacid and food on the absorption of cimetidine and ranitidine (abstract only). Journal of Pharmacy and Pharmacology 1990; 42 (5): 352-354.

646. Vincon G, Fleury B, Demotes-Mainard F. Influence of food on bioavailability of cimetidine (abstract only). Therapie 1983; 38 (6): 607-612.

647. Bodemar G, Norlander B, Fransson L, Walan A. The absorption of cimetidine before and during maintenance treatment with cimetidine and the influence of a meal on the absorption of cimetidine: Studies in patients with peptic ulcer disease (abstract only). British Journal of Clinical Pharmacology 1979; 7 (1): 23-31.

648. Zimmerman T, Yeates RA, Laufen H, Pfaff G, Wildfeuer A. Influence of concomitant food intake on the oral absorption of two triazole antifungal agents, itraconazole and fluconazole (abstract only). European Journal of Clinical Phamacology 1994; 46 (2): 147-150.

649. Bhandal S, Pattinson J. How to support patients taking new oral anticoagulant medicines. Clinical Pharmacist 2013; 5: 268-270.

650. Personal communication Idoya Pezonaga. Letter to Dr. Satinder Bhandal from Bristol-Myers Squibb Pharmaceuticals, dated 6th August 2013.

651. Antiepileptic drugs: new advice on switching between different manufacturers' products for a particular drug. Drug Safety Update 2013; 7 (4): 2-3.

652. Email communication with Alex Weston, Senior Medicines Information Pharmacist, Wessex Drug & Medicines Information Centre, Southampton General Hospital, 12th May 2014.

653. Personal communication with Shazad Jafri, Medical Information, AbbVie Ltd, 28th May 2014.

654. Personal communication between Graham Holland, Clinical pharmacist specialising in palliative care and medicines information, Liverpool Heart and Chest Hospital, and Kamini Pindoria, Medical Information and Patient Safety Specialist, AstraZeneca UK Limited, 4th June 2014.

655. Best BM et al. Pharmacokinetics of Lopinavir/Ritonavir Crushed Versus Whole Tablets in Children. J Acquir. Immune Defic. Syndr. 2011; 58 (4): 385-391.

656. Personal communication, Medical Information, AbbVie Ltd, 28th May, 18th June, 24th June 2014.

657. Ticagrelor® Summary of Product Characteristics, AstraZeneca AB, 24th July 2014.

658. Liquid medicines product list, Palliative Solutions Ltd, provided to Elaine Sturman, Pharmacist, Wrexham Maelor Hospital, 4th July 2014.

659. Email communication from Rosemont Pharmaceuticals Ltd, 29th April 2014.

660. Pheburane® Summary of Product Characteristics, Lucane Pharma, accessed on 27th August 2014, www.ema.europa.eu/docs/en_GB/document_library/EPAR_-_Product_Information/human/002500/WC500147373.pdf

661. Ammonaps® Summary of Product Characteristics, Swedish Orphan Biovitrum International AB, March 2014.

662. Sancuso® Summary of Product Characteristics, ProStraken Limited, 14th May 2014.

663. Personal communication, Medical Information, Amdipharm Mercury Company Limited, 27th August 2014.

664. Forceval Soluble FAQs, accessed on 28th August 2014, www.forceval.co.uk/hcp/faq/forceval_soluble

665. Nicolo M, Stratton KW, Rooney W, Boullata J. Pancreatic enzyme replacement therapy for enterally fed patients with cystic fibrosis. Nutrition in Clinical Practice 2013; 28 (4): 485-489.

666. Ferrie S, Graham C, Hoyle M. Pancreatic enzyme supplementation for patients receiving enteral feeds. Nutrition in Clinical Practice 2011; 26 (3): 349-351.

667. Personal communication to Janet Sear, Medicines Information, Royal Berkshire Hospital, from Medical Information, Abbott Healthcare Products Ltd, 26th June 2014.

8. Monograph index

Monograph index

A

Abacavir	45
Abacavir and lamivudine	45
Abacavir with lamivudine and zidovudine	45
Acamprosate	46
Acarbose	46
Accuretic®	47
Acebutolol	47
Aceclofenac	47
Acenocoumarol	48
Acetazolamide	48, 416
Acetylcysteine	49
Aciclovir	50
Acipimox	50
Acitretin	51
Albendazole	51
Alendronic acid	52
Alfacalcidol	53
Alfuzosin	54
Alimemazine	54
Allopurinol	55, 417
Alprazolam	56, 418
Aluminium hydroxide	56
Alverine citrate	57
Amantadine	57
Amiloride	57
Amiloride and cyclopenthiazide	58
Aminophylline	58
Amiodarone	59, 419, 420
Amisulpride	60
Amitriptyline	61
Amlodipine	61, 421
Amlodipine and valsartan	62
Amoxapine	62
Amoxicillin	63
Amphotericin	64
Ampicillin	64
Amprenavir	64

Anastrazole	65
Antacids	65
Apixaban	65
Aprepitant	66
Arginine	66
Arthrotec®	67
Asasantin®	153
Ascorbic acid	67
Aspirin	68
Atazanavir	68
Atenolol	69
Atenolol and co-amilozide	69
Atenolol and nifedipine	70
Atorvastatin	70
Atripla®	71
Atropine sulphate	71
Auranofin	72
Avandamet®	72
Azathioprine	73, 422, 423
Azithromycin	73

B

Baclofen	75
Balsalazide	75
Beclometasone	76
Bendroflumethiazide	76
Bendroflumethiazide and potassium	77
Benperidol	77
Benzatropine	78
Beta-Adalat®	78
Betahistine	78
Betaine	79
Betamethasone	79
Bethanechol	79, 424
Bexarotene	80
Bezafibrate	81
Bicalutamide	81
Biotin	82